THE DEBATABASE BOOK

THE DEBATABASE BOOK

A Must-Have Guide for Successful Debate

▪ SIXTH EDITION ▪

THE EDITORS OF IDEA

Introduction by Robert Trapp

International Debate Education Association

New York, London & Amsterdam

Published by:
International Debate Education Association
105 East 22nd Street
New York, NY 10010

Library of Congress Cataloging-in-Publication Data

The debatabase book : a must-have guide for successful debate / the
editors of IDEA ; introduction by Robert Trapp. -- Sixth edition.
   pages cm
 ISBN 978-1-61770-077-4
1. Debates and debating. I. International Debate Education
Association.
 PN4181.D3945 2013
 808.53--dc23

                            2013033050

Design by Kathleen Hayes

Printed in the USA

CONTENTS

INTRODUCTION

Debatabase is a starting point on the road to participating in debates. The volume provides a beginning for those debaters who would like to learn about important topics being argued in the public sphere. Debaters can use this volume as a method of discovering the basic issues relevant to some of the more important topics being discussed in various public forums. It will provide debaters a brief look at some of the claims that can be used to support or to oppose many of the issues argued about by persons in democratic societies; it will also provide some sketches of evidence that can be used to support these claims. This volume is, however, only a starting point. Debaters interested in becoming very good debaters or excellent debaters will need to go beyond this volume if they intend to be able to intelligently discuss these issues in depth.

This introduction is intended to provide a theoretical framework within which information about argumentation and debate can be viewed; no attempt has been made to provide a general theory of argumentation. I begin with some basic distinctions among the terms communication, rhetoric, argumentation, and debate, progress to a description of the elements of argument that are most central to debate, and then to a discussion of how these elements can be structured into claims to support debate propositions. Following the discussion of argument structures, I move to a more detailed discussion of claims and propositions and finally discuss the kinds of evidence needed to support claims and propositions.

A caveat is needed before proceeding to the theoretical portion of this introduction. This introduction does not intend to be a practical, how-to guide to the creation of arguments. It does intend to provide the conceptual groundwork needed for debaters to learn how to create arguments according to a variety of methods.

Communication, rhetoric, argumentation, and debate

Communication, rhetoric, argumentation, and debate are related concepts. Starting with communication and proceeding to debate, the concepts become progressively narrowed. By beginning with the broadest concept, communication, and ending at the narrowest, debate, I intend to show how all these terms are interrelated.

Communication may be defined as the process whereby signs are used to convey information. Following this definition, communication is a very broad concept ranging from human, symbolic processes to the means that animals use to relate to one another. Some of these means are a part of the complex biology of both human and nonhuman animals. For instance, the behaviors of certain species of birds when strangers approach a nest of their young are a part of the biology of those species. The reason we know these are biological traits is that all members of the species use the same signs to indicate intrusion. Although all of our communication abilities—including rhetorical communication—are somehow built into our species biologically, not all communication is rhetorical.

The feature that most clearly distinguishes rhetoric from other forms of communication is the symbol. Although the ability to use symbolic forms of communication is certainly a biological trait of human beings, our ability to use symbols also allows us to use culturally and individually specific types of symbols. The clearest evidence that different cultures developed different symbols is the presence of different languages among human beings separated geographically. Even though all humans are born with the ability to use language, some of us learn Russian, others French, and others English. The clearest example of symbolic communication is language. Language is an abstract method of using signs to refer to objects. The concept of a symbol differentiates rhetoric from other forms of communication. Symbols, hence rhetoric, are abstract methods of communication.

Still, not all rhetoric is argumentation. Rhetorical communication can be divided into various categories, two of which are narrative and metaphor.[1] Just to give a couple of examples, the narrative mode of rhetoric focuses on sequential time, the metaphoric mode of rhetoric focuses on comparing one thing to another, and the argumentative mode of rhetoric focuses on giving reasons. All of these modes of rhetoric are useful in debate, but the mode of rhetoric that is most central to debate is argumentation.

Argumentation is the process whereby humans use reason to communicate claims to one another. According to this definition, the focus on reason becomes the feature that distinguishes argumentation from other modes of rhetoric.[2] When people argue with one another, not only do they assert claims but they also assert reasons they believe the claims to be plausible or probable. Argumentation is a primary tool of debate, but it serves other activities as well. Argumentation is, for instance, an important tool in negotiation, conflict resolution, and persuasion. Debate is an activity that could hardly exist without argumentation.

Argumentation is useful in activities like negotiation and conflict resolution because it can be used to help people find ways to resolve their differences. But in some of these situations, differences cannot be resolved internally and an outside adjudicator must be called. These are the situations that we call debate. Thus, according to this view, debate is defined as the process of arguing about claims in situations where the outcome must be decided by an adjudicator. The focus of this introduction is on those elements of argumentation that are most often used in debate.

In some regards this focus is incomplete because some nonargumentative elements of communication and rhetoric often are used in debate even though they are not the most central features of debate. Some elements of rhetoric, namely metaphor and narrative, are very useful to debaters, but they are not included in this introduction because they are less central to debate than is argumentation. Beyond not including several rhetorical elements that sometimes are useful in debate, this introduction also excludes many elements of argumentation, choosing just the ones that are most central. Those central elements are evidence, reasoning, claims, and reservations. These elements are those that philosopher Stephen Toulmin introduced in 1958[3] and revised 30 years later.[4]

The Elements of Argument

Although in this introduction some of Toulmin's terminology has been modified, because of its popular usage the model will still be referred to as the Toulmin model. Because it is only a model, the Toulmin model is only a rough approximation of the elements and their relationships to one another. The model is not intended as a descriptive diagram of actual arguments for a variety of reasons. First, it describes only those elements of an argument related to reasoning. It does not describe other important elements such as expressions of feelings or emotions unless those expressions are directly related to reasoning. Second, the model describes only the linguistic elements of reasoning. To the extent that an argument includes significant nonverbal elements, they are not covered by the model.[5] Third, the model applies only to the simplest of arguments. If an argument is composed of a variety of warrants or a cluster of evidence related to the claim in different ways, the model may not apply well, if at all. Despite these shortcomings, this model has proven itself useful for describing some of the key elements of arguments and how they function together. The diagrams shown on the following pages illustrate the Toulmin model.

The basic Toulmin model identifies four basic elements of argument: claim, data (which we call evidence), warrant, and reservation. The model of argument is most easily explained by a travel analogy. The evidence is the argument's starting point. The claim is the arguer's

---

1. As far as I know, no one has successfully organized modes of rhetoric into a coherent taxonomy because the various modes overlap so much with one another. For instance, narratives and metaphors are used in arguments as metaphors and arguments are frequently found in narratives.
2. This is not to say that other forms of rhetoric do not involve the use of reason, just that the form of rhetoric where the focus on reason is most clearly in the foreground is argumentation.
3. *The Uses of Argument* (Cambridge: Cambridge University Press, 1958).
4. Albert R. Jonsen and Stephen Toulmin, *The Abuse of Casuistry: A History of Moral Reasoning* (Berkeley: University of California Press, 1988).
5. Charles Arthur Willard, "On the Utility of Descriptive Diagrams for the Analysis and Criticism of Arguments," *Communication Monographs* 43 (November, 1976), 308–319.

destination. The warrant is the means of travel, and the reservation involves questions or concerns the arguer may have about arrival at the destination. Toulmin's model can be used to diagram the structure of relatively simple arguments.

Structure of an Argument

A simple argument, for instance, consists of a single claim supported by a piece of evidence, a single warrant, and perhaps (but not always) a single reservation. The following diagram illustrates Toulmin's diagram of a simple argument:

Simple Argument

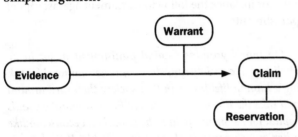

Toulmin illustrates this diagram using a simple argument claim that Harry is a British citizen because he was born in Bermuda. Here is how the structure of that argument was diagramed by Toulmin:

Simple Argument

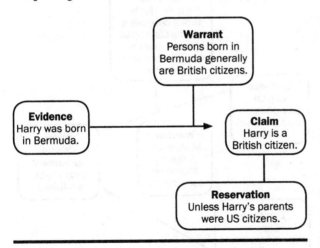

Although this diagram of an argument clearly illustrates how an argument moves from evidence to a claim via a warrant, very few arguments are ever quite as simple. For this reason, I have adapted Toulmin and Jonsen's model to illustrate a few different argument structures.

In addition to the simple argument suggested above, other argument structures include convergent and independent arguments. Although these do not even begin to exhaust all potential argument structures, they are some of the more common ones encountered in debate.

Convergent Arguments

A convergent argument is one wherein two or more bits of evidence converge with one another to support a claim. In other words, when a single piece of evidence is not sufficient, it must be combined with another piece of evidence in the effort to support the claim.

Convergent Argument

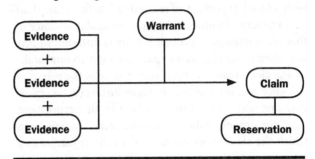

Consider as an illustration, the following convergent argument:

Lying is generally considered an immoral act. The use of placebos in drug testing research involves lying because some of the subjects are led falsely to believe they are being given real drugs. Therefore, placebos should not be used in drug testing unless they are the only method available to test potentially life-saving drugs.

Convergent Argument

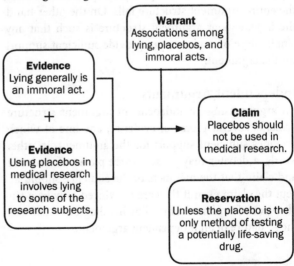

This particular argument begins with two pieces of evidence. The first piece involves the value statement that "lying generally is considered an immoral act." This piece of evidence is a statement that is consistent with the audience's values regarding lying. The second piece of evidence is the factual statement that "the use of placebos in medical research involves a form of lying." The second piece of evidence involves the fact that when a researcher gives a placebo (e.g., a sugar pill) to a portion of the subjects in a study of a potentially life-saving drug, that researcher is lying to those subjects as they are led to believe that they are receiving a drug that may save their lives. The warrant then combines the evidence with a familiar pattern of reasoning—in this case, if an act in general is immoral then any particular instance of that act is likewise immoral. If lying is immoral in general, then using placebos in particular is also immoral.

The claim results from a convergence of the pieces of evidence and the warrant. In some instances, an arguer may not wish to hold to this claim in all circumstances. If the arguer wishes to define specific situations in which the claim does not hold, then the arguer adds a reservation to the argument. In this case, a reservation seems perfectly appropriate. Even though the arguer may generally object to lying and to the use of placebos, the arguer may wish to exempt situations where the use of a placebo is the "only method of testing a potentially life-saving drug."

The unique feature of the convergent structure of argument is that the arguer produces a collection of evidence that, if taken together, supports the claim. The structure of the argument is such that all of the evidence must be believed for the argument to be supported. If the audience does not accept any one piece of evidence, the entire argument structure falls. On the other hand, the independent argument structure is such that any single piece of evidence can provide sufficient support for the argument.

Independent Arguments

An arguer using an independent argument structure presents several pieces of evidence, any one of which provides sufficient support for the argument. In other words, a debater may present three pieces of evidence and claim that the members of the audience should accept the claim even if they are convinced only by a single piece of evidence. The following diagram illustrates the structure of an independent argument:

Independent Arguments

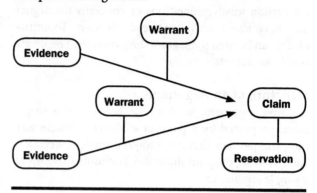

Take for instance the following argument against capital punishment:

On moral grounds, capital punishment ought to be abolished. If a society considers a murder immoral for taking a human life, how can that society then turn around and take the life of the murderer? Beyond moral grounds, capital punishment ought to be abolished because, unlike other punishments, it alone is irreversible. If evidence is discovered after the execution, there is no way to bring the unjustly executed person back to life.

This argument about capital punishment can be represented in the following diagram:

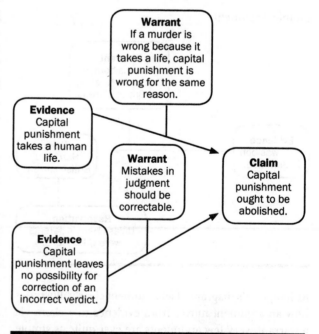

This example of an independent argument structure is based on two pieces of evidence, either of which is strong enough to support the claim that capital punishment ought to be abolished. The first piece of evidence involves the value of taking a human life, while the second involves the value of being able to correct a mistake. According to this argument, capital punishment ought to be abolished even if only one of the items of evidence is believed by the audience. The moral stricture against taking a life is, by itself, a sufficient reason to oppose capital punishment as is the danger of making an uncorrectable mistake. The strategic advantage of this form of argument structure is obvious. Whereas with convergent structures, the loss of one part of the argument endangers the entire argument, in the independent structure, the argument can prevail even if only a part of it survives.

The Toulmin diagram of an argument is useful because it illustrates the various parts of an argument and shows how they function together as a whole. The modifications with regard to argument structure make it even more useful. Still, the model has its shortcomings. One difficulty with the Toulmin diagram is that it does not provide any details regarding some of the elements. Some questions that the diagram leaves unanswered include:

- What are the different kinds of claims?
- How can different claims be combined to support various propositions?
- What are the different forms of evidence?
- What are the different kinds of argumentative warrants?
- What distinguishes good arguments from bad ones?

Claims and Propositions

Conceptually claims and propositions are the same kind of argumentative elements. Both are controversial statements that need reason for support. Both claims and propositions are created by a relationship between evidence and a warrant. Frequently, debaters combine several of these statements to support another statement. Each of the initial statements is a claim and the concluding statement is called a proposition.

Types of Claims and Propositions

Most authors divide claims and propositions into the traditional categories of fact, value, and policy. I have chosen not to use these traditional categories for two reasons. First, the traditional categories have no place for some important kinds of propositions that are not facts, or values, or policy. More specifically, the traditional categories have no place for propositions that seek to define concepts nor for propositions that seek to establish relationships between or among concepts. Second, the traditional categories separate evaluative and policy propositions while the system used here will consider propositions of policy as a specific kind of evaluative proposition. I use four main categories of propositions: definition, description, relationship, and evaluation. These categories, while they may not be exhaustive or mutually exclusive, provide a coherent system for the discussion of claims.

Definitions

Definitions answer the question, "Does it serve our purposes to say that Z is the proper definition of X?"[6] Arguing for a claim of definition involves two steps: positing the definition and making an argument for that definition. In carrying out the first step, one simply states that "X" is defined in this way. "Rhetoric is an action humans perform when they use symbols for the purpose of communicating with one another."[7] This sentence posits a definition of rhetoric.

Much of the time arguers perform the first step of positing a definition without constructing an argument to support it. They may do this because their audience does not require them to make an explicit argument in favor of the definition. The definition may, by itself, create a frame of mind in the audience that does not lead the audience to demand an argument in support of the definition. For instance, anti-abortion forces in the United States succeeded in defining a procedure physicians called "intact dilation and extraction" as "partial-birth abortion."[8] Their definition was successful because it dominated the discourse on abortion and turned the controversy away from the issue of choice and toward a particular medical procedure that anti-abortion forces could use more successfully. On the surface, the definition of "intact dilation and extraction" as "partial-birth abortion" may have seemed so sensible that no further argument was required.

An argument to support a claim of definition becomes necessary when the audience refuses to accept

6. Perhaps a more accurate way of stating the question is "Does it best serve our purposes to say that Z is the proper definition of X?" This way of phrasing the question more clearly identifies the value dimensions of definitions—dimensions that will be discussed more fully later.
7. Sonja K. Foss, Karen A. Foss, and Robert Trapp, *Contemporary Perspectives on Rhetoric* (Prospect Heights, IL: Waveland, 1991), 14.
8. David Zarefsky, "Definitions" (keynote address, Tenth NCA/AFA Summer Argumentation Conference, Alta, Utah, August 1997).

the definition that was posited without a supporting argument. An arguer's opponent will frequently encourage the audience to demand support for a definition. When anti-abortion advocates defined their position as "pro-life," some in the "pro-choice" movement objected, claiming that "pro-choice" is also "pro-life." In cases like this one, the entire argument can turn on whether or not the arguer is able to successfully support a claim of definition.

In those instances when an arguer chooses to construct an argument to support a definition, the argument frequently revolves around the reasonableness of the scope and breadth of the definition. Is the definition so narrow that it excludes instances of the concept that ought to be included? Is the definition so broad that it fails to exclude instances that do not properly belong to the concept? Thus, in constructing an argument for a definition, an arguer might posit a definition, then argue that the definition is reasonable in terms of its scope and breadth. In fact, this is the criterion implicit in the objection to defining "anti-abortion" as "pro-life." Choice advocates claimed that the definition of "pro-life" was so narrow in scope that it excluded pro-choice advocates. So, in some cases, the arguments supporting a claim of definition are important. In other cases, the definition becomes evidence (sometimes implicit) for further arguments about whether a claim of definition was actually made.

Definitions themselves frequently are important, but they are also important to subsequent argumentative moves. Definitions are important because they often do the work of argument without opening the arguer's position to as much controversy as would otherwise be expected. Definitions may avoid controversy in two ways: by implying descriptions and by implying values.

Definitions imply descriptions by including elements in the definition that properly require evidentiary support. For instance, an arguer might claim that affirmative action is unfair and might define affirmative action as "racial preference quotas." Whether affirmative action programs require racial preference quotas is a matter of much controversy. But if the definition is not contested by an audience member or by an adversary, the definition shortcuts the argumentative process by avoiding controversy.

Definitions imply values by including terms that are value laden. For instance, when anti-abortion advocates define the medical procedure of intact dilation and extraction as "partial-birth abortion" or even as "partial-birth infanticide," the values associated with birth and with infanticide are likely to be transferred to the medical procedure as well. In this case, anti-abortion forces succeeded in shortcutting the argumentative process by avoiding the value controversy that is inherent in their definition.

So claims of definition are important. Ironically, they probably are less important when they are actually completed with supporting evidence than when they are implicitly used as descriptive and value evidence for further arguments.

Descriptions

Descriptions may characterize some feature of an object, concept, or event or may describe the object, concept, or event itself. Examples of descriptive claims include:

- The rifle purported to have killed President Kennedy requires a minimum of 2.3 seconds between shots.
- Affirmative action programs must, by their nature, include hiring quotas.
- Jack Ruby was spotted in Parkland Hospital thirty minutes after President Kennedy was murdered.

Each of these statements is descriptive because they provide a verbal account or characterization of something. They are claims in the argumentative sense because they are controversial[9] and because they require reasons for support. Because some descriptions are not controversial, all descriptions are not descriptive arguments. Many or even most descriptions are not argumentative because they are not controversial. For instance, if a person simply describes observations of the colors of flowers—roses are red; violets blue—that person would not ordinarily give reasons to support these descriptions.

One kind of descriptive claim is a claim of historical fact. All statements about history are not historical claims. To be a historical claim a statement must be controversial and must require reason for its support. The statement, "O. J. Simpson won the Heisman Trophy," is not controversial and therefore not an argumentative claim. On the other hand, the statement, "O. J. Simpson killed Nicole Brown Simpson," not only is controversial, but also requires an arguer to present reasons supporting or denying it.

9. With regard to the first example, some people claim that this action requires closer to four seconds when one takes into account the fact that a shooter must reacquire the subject in the scope. Regarding the second example, some supporters of affirmative action argue that hiring quotas are required only for a company with a past record of discrimination. In the third example, the primary source of the claim regarding Jack Ruby was AP reporter Seth Kantor; the Warren Commission claimed that Kantor was mistaken in his report.

Another kind of description is a claim of scientific fact. Scientific facts are statements that command the belief of the scientific community: "The Earth is the third planet from the sun." A claim of scientific fact is a controversial scientific statement believed by a scientist or a group of scientists, but not yet accepted by the entire scientific community: "Cold fusion can be produced in the laboratory." Like other factual statements, all scientific statements are not claims of scientific fact either because they are not controversial or because they do not require reasons to be given in their support. To say, "The Earth is the third planet from the sun," is not a claim because it is not controversial and because a person making that statement would not be expected to give reasons to support it. But the statement, "Cold fusion can be produced in a laboratory," is a controversial statement, and the scientific community would challenge anyone making that statement to support it with reason and evidence.

Illustrating different examples of descriptive claims is important in and of itself because people frequently argue about descriptive claims with no goal other than to try to settle a controversy regarding an account of science or history. As just one example, several hundred books and articles have been written presenting many different accounts of the assassinations of John Kennedy, Robert Kennedy, and Martin Luther King. But beyond being important for their own sake, descriptive claims also are important because they are needed when arguing about subsequent kinds of claims as well.

Descriptive claims frequently are used as evidence in relational and evaluative arguments. A claim describing the nature of an object frequently is needed before arguing that one object is related to another object. People might need to argue, for instance, that hiring quotas are essential features of affirmative action (a descriptive claim) before they can argue that affirmative action leads to differential treatment of persons in hiring pools (relational claim). Similarly, people may need to describe an object or phenomenon prior to evaluating that object. In this example, they would need to describe affirmative action before they argue that it is either good or bad.

A scientific description can be the final product of an argument or can be used as evidence for the further development of another kind of argument. Whether the primary determinant of homosexuality is genetic or cultural is an interesting claim from a purely scientific perspective. People can argue the facts that support the genetic explanation or the cultural one. However, this claim frequently has been used in the debate about the morality of homosexuality.[10] So in the case of the determinants of homosexuality, the descriptive claim is both important for its own sake and for the sake of other potential claims as well.

Descriptive historical claims are interesting both because they make statements about whether or not an event occurred as asserted and because they can be used as evidence in making further arguments.

- Lee Harvey Oswald killed President John Kennedy.
- O. J. Simpson murdered Nicole Brown Simpson and Ronald Goldman.
- US ships *Maddox* and *Turner Joy* were attacked by the North Vietnamese in the Gulf of Tonkin.

Each of these is an interesting and controversial claim of historical fact. These and other claims of historical fact also can be used as evidence for relational and evaluative arguments. For instance, the argument that the *Maddox* and *Turner Joy* were attacked by the North Vietnamese was used by President Johnson to persuade the Senate and the House of Representatives to pass the Gulf of Tonkin Resolution giving Johnson a blank check to pursue the war in Vietnam. Subsequently arguments that the attack was, at best, provoked and, at worse, faked were used by opponents of the Vietnam War to show that Johnson's actions were improper and even immoral.

Relationship Statements

Descriptive claims are about the nature of reality—what is the essence of X or Y. Claims of relationship depend on, but go beyond, the essence of X or Y to the relationship between X and Y. Claims of relationship assert a connection between two or more objects, events, or phenomena. Like descriptive claims, claims of relationship can be important in their own right or they can serve as evidence for the development of evaluative claims. Consider these claims:

- Secondhand smoke contributes significantly to health problems.
- The scandals of the Clinton administration are like those of the Nixon administration.
- Advertising has changed the role of women in the United States.

All of these are claims of relationship because they assert a relationship between two objects or concepts (secondhand smoke and health, Clinton and Nixon,

10. Some argue, for instance, that because the tendency for homosexuality is genetic, it is not a "choice" and therefore cannot be considered moral or immoral.

advertising and women). The relationships asserted in these examples are of two kinds: of contingency and of similarity.

Contingency

Some claims of relationship assert a relationship of contingency. The secondhand smoking example and the advertising example are of this kind. In each case, these claims assert that one object or phenomenon is dependent on another in one way or another. Sign and cause are two ways objects can be dependent on one another via some form of contingency.

Relationships of sign are one way to show that one thing is dependent on another thing.

Consider these:

- The pain in your child's abdomen probably means she has appendicitis.
- The palm print on the Mannlicher-Carcano rifle proves that Oswald handled the rifle supposedly used to shoot President Kennedy.

Both of the previous statements are claims about relationships of sign. The pain in the abdomen as a sign of appendicitis is dependent on the belief that the child actually has abdominal pain and a belief in the relationship between that pain and her appendix. The belief that Oswald handled the rifle that supposedly was used to shoot President Kennedy is dependent on the belief that he actually left his palm print on the murder weapon.

Arguments of sign played a very important—perhaps crucial—role in the criminal trial of O.J. Simpson for the murders of Ron Goldman and Nicole Brown Simpson. The prosecution claimed that the presence of a bloody glove near Simpson's home was a sign that he was the murderer. In a dramatic turn of events, Simpson tried on the glove in the presence of the jury; it appeared to be too small to fit on his hand. This evidence allowed the defense to support its own claim in quite poetic language: "If the glove doesn't fit, you must acquit." According to the prosecution's claim, the glove was a sign of Simpson's guilt. According to the defense's claim, the glove signaled his innocence. This was a clear case where the argument centered around the relationship between the bloody glove and Simpson's guilt or innocence.

In the Simpson example, the claim of sign is important because if it were believed, the claim alone is sufficient to establish guilt (or innocence, depending on the nature of the argument). But like other claims, a claim of sign also can be used as evidence to establish a different claim. Say, for instance, that a person claims that "Photographs from the yacht, 'Monkey Business,' showed that presidential candidate Gary Hart was an adulterer." The photographs are not direct evidence of adultery, but given their nature, they are strong signs of infidelity. One could then use this claim of sign to support an evaluative argument: "Gary Hart is not worthy of being president since he is an adulterer." In this case, the claim of sign becomes evidence to support an evaluative claim.

Relationships of sign may or may not involve relationships of cause. The relationship between pain and appendicitis is one of both sign and cause. The pain is a sign of the appendicitis and the appendicitis is a cause of the pain. A causal relationship is not directly involved in the example of the double murder of Goldman and Brown Simpson or in the example about Oswald's palm print on the rifle. Although the palm print and the bloody glove were signs of murder, they were not causes of the murder.[11] Thus, relationships of sign are different from relationships of cause at least in terms of their focus.

Causal relationships are important in many forms of argument. The kind of causal claim varies from one instance to the next. A few examples include contributory causes, necessary and sufficient causes, blocking causes, and motive or responsibility.

Contributory causes are special kinds of causal statements. In many or most cases, a single event is not the cause of an effect. Certain conditions predispose certain effects; other conditions influence the occurrence of those effects. Finally, some condition precipitates that effect. For example, consider these three possible claims about the causes of heart attacks:

- Genetics are the cause of heart attacks.
- A high cholesterol diet can cause heart attack.
- Vigorous exercise causes heart attacks.

We know that some people are genetically more predisposed to heart attacks than others. If a person who already is predisposed to heart attacks regularly consumes a diet high in cholesterol, that diet contributes to the likelihood of heart attack. Suppose a person dies of a heart attack while on a morning jog. What was the cause? Genetics? Diet? Exercise? The answer is that all three factors may have been contributory causes. No

---

11. One can make a case for a causal relationship between the murder and the bloody glove in that the act of committing the murder caused blood to get on the glove. The causal relationship between the palm print and the Kennedy murder is less direct, although one could say that the act of murdering President Kennedy caused Oswald's palm print to be on the murder weapon. This last claim is a weak one since the palm print could have been on the rifle long before the assassination.

single cause may have caused the heart attack, but all three conditions in combination may have resulted in a heart attack.

Necessary and sufficient causes frequently deal with singular causes rather than contributory causes. "Money is essential to happiness" is an example of a claim of necessary causation. To say that money is a necessary cause of happiness is not to say that the presence of money automatically leads to happiness. The claim does, however, imply that without money happiness is impossible. If one wanted to make a claim of sufficient causation using the same example, one might claim that "money is the key to happiness." Depending on how one interpreted that claim, it might mean that money brings happiness regardless of other conditions. In that case, one would have made a claim about a sufficient cause.

Necessary and sufficient causes are useful when arguing about relationships between and among various phenomena. They are also useful as evidence from which to construct other kinds of claims, particularly claims that evaluate a course of action. When an arguer proposes a strategy to eliminate an undesirable effect, evidence derived from a claim about a necessary condition of that effect is useful. Having made a claim about a necessary cause, one can forward a proposal to eliminate that necessary cause and thus eliminate the effect. For instance, if people believe that overeating is a necessary condition of obesity, they could use this causal claim as evidence to convince others that they need to quit overeating. Thus, making a claim about a necessary cause is a good way to support a plan for eliminating an effect.

Similarly, evidence derived from a claim about a sufficient cause is a good way to support a plan for producing an effect. If one can present a proposal that adds a sufficient cause, one can then claim that the proposal will produce some good effect. For instance, some diet commercials claim that their products are sufficient to cause one to lose weight. This claim of a sufficient causal condition can then be used as evidence to convince buyers to try their diet programs. Implied in such a claim is that regardless of what else one does, following the proposed diet will lead to weight loss.

Statements about motive are causal claims about the effects of human agents. Many causal claims, like those already discussed, are related to physical or biological phenomena. The relationships among genetics, diet, exercise, and heart disease are biological relationships. Various elements in a biological system affect other elements in that same system. In a similar manner, motives are a kind of causal explanation when human choice is involved in creating effects. Why, for instance, do senators and representatives stall legislation for campaign finance reform? Why do corporations knowingly produce dangerous products? The answers to these questions involve causal claims, but causal claims of a different order from those discussed earlier.

In an earlier example, genetics, diet, and exercise did not "choose" to cause heart disease. But in human systems choice is frequently an important element in determining what actions lead to what effects. One might claim that "representatives' and senators' self-interest motivate them to stall campaign finance reform" or that the "profit motive induces corporations knowingly to produce dangerous products." The kinds of causal questions that deal with motives are very useful when arguing about the effects of human actions.

Like other causal claims, claims about motive are useful as evidence in the construction of evaluative claims. A claim based on a senator's motive for stalling campaign finance reform might, for instance, be used as evidence to construct a further claim relevant to the wisdom of reelecting that senator. A claim that a particular corporation's desire for profits led to the production of unsafe products might be used as further evidence to support a claim asking for a boycott of that corporation.

The claims of relationship that have been discussed so far have involved relationships of contingency. In relationships of contingency, one phenomenon depends on or affects another. These claims of relationships have generally been divided into the categories of signs and cause. However, claims of contingency are not the only kind of claims of relationship. Claims of similarity are equally important kinds of relational claims.

Similarity

In addition to relationships based on contingency, other statements of relationship assert a relationship of similarity. A claim of similarity asserts that two or more objects or concepts are similar in important ways. Claims of similarity are frequently found in what is called argument by analogy or argument by parallel case. Examples of claims of similarity include:

- Abortion is virtually the same as infanticide.
- The Clinton administration is like the Nixon administration.
- Capital punishment is state-sanctioned murder.

Each of these examples shares certain characteristics. First, each example includes two objects or concepts (Clinton and Nixon, abortion and infanticide, and capital punishment and murder). Second, each example states that the two concepts or objects are similar in important regards.

Claims of similarity are useful when an arguer wants to do nothing more than support the idea that two or more objects and concepts are similar. Although the claim focuses on the similarity between the objects, it frequently carries another implied claim of evaluation. The claim that capital punishment is state-sanctioned murder is not a value-neutral statement. When confronted with such a claim, most audiences begin with the assumption that murder is a negatively valued concept. An arguer who succeeds in supporting the claim of similarity also succeeds in transferring the negative value associated with murder to the concept of capital punishment. In all of the above examples of claims of similarity, the arguer has two different purposes: to show that the two concepts or objects have similar characteristics, or to show that the two concepts or objects are evaluated in similar ways.

In some cases, the audience may not have enough familiarity with either of the two objects to understand the values associated with them. In such a case, a claim of similarity is sometimes the first step toward proving a claim of evaluation. Consider a hypothetical claim that states "Senator X's medical care plan is similar to one instituted in Canada." If the audience knew nothing about either Senator X's plan or the Canadian one, the arguer might establish this claim to be used as evidence in a later evaluative claim that "Senator X's plan should be accepted (or rejected)." In this case the arguer might present an evaluative claim regarding the success of the Canadian plan and then combine the two claims—one of similarity and one regarding acceptance or rejection.

Thus, claims of relationship fall into three broad categories: sign, causation, and similarity. In some cases, claims of relationship are supported by evidence built on claims of fact. Likewise, relational claims can be used to establish evaluative claims.

Claims of Evaluation

Evaluative claims go beyond descriptive claims and claims of relationship to the evaluation of an object, event, or concept. Evaluative claims are more complex kinds of claims because they ordinarily require some combination of other definitions, descriptions, and relational statements.

Evaluative claims bear a family resemblance to one another because they attach a value to one or more objects or events. Still, evaluative claims are so vast in number and in characteristics that they can be more easily viewed in these three categories: those that evaluate a single object, those that compare two objects with respect to some value, and those that suggest an action with respect to some object.

Claims That Evaluate a Single Object

Some evaluative claims simply argue that an object is attached in some way (positively or negatively) with some value. These kinds of claims involve both an object of evaluation and some value judgment to be applied to the object:

- Capital punishment is immoral.
- Private property is the root of all evil.
- Capitalism is good.

These examples of claims that attach a value to a single object all contain some object to be evaluated (capital punishment, private property, capitalism) and some value judgment that is applied to the objects (immoral, evil, good).

Some claims, like those mentioned above, imply rather broad value judgments. Others may contain more specific ones:

- Capital punishment is unfair in its application to minorities.
- Private property has led to an uncontrolled and immoral ruling class.
- Capitalism provides incentive for individual enterprise.

These examples contain value judgments that are more specific than the broad ones cited earlier.

Claims That Compare Two Objects

Instead of evaluating a single object, some claims compare two objects with respect to some value to constitute a second category of evaluative claim. Unlike the previous category of evaluative claims, claims in this category include at least two objects of evaluation and at least one value judgment to be applied to those objects. Consider these claims:

- Lying is more proper than hurting someone's feelings.
- Reagan was a better president than Clinton.

Each of these examples contains two objects (lying and hurting someone's feelings; Reagan and Clinton) and one value judgment to be applied to each object (more proper and better president).

Claims of Action

Claims of action, sometimes called claims of policy, are yet another category of evaluative claim:

- Capital punishment should be abolished.
- The United States should adopt a policy of free trade with Cuba.

These claims evaluate a concept by suggesting that action be taken with respect to that concept. Because an action can be evaluated only by comparison or contrast to other possible actions, claims of action by necessity compare at least two objects. The claim that capital punishment should be abolished compares the presence of capital punishment with its absence. The claim regarding free trade with Cuba implies a comparison of a policy of free trade with the present policy of trade embargo. In this regard, claims of action are similar to claims that compare two objects.

In a different regard, claims of action are different from the other categories of evaluative claims in that they rarely state the value judgment used to compare the two objects. The reason the value judgment is not ordinarily stated in the claim is that an action claim is frequently supported by a variety of other claims of evaluation each of which may be relying on a different value judgment. The claim about the abolition of capital punishment, for example, might be supported by other evaluative claims like

- Capital punishment is immoral.
- Capital punishment contributes to the brutalization of society.
- Capital punishment is racist.

To complicate matters even more, evaluative claims of action inherently are comparative claims. To argue in favor of a particular action is possible only in comparison to other actions. For instance, the previous claims imply that capital punishment is less moral, more brutal, and more racist than the alternatives. Because action claims usually require multiple, comparative claims as evidence to support them, action claims generally are more complicated than the other categories of claims.

According to this category system, evaluative claims are generally divided into three types: claims that evaluate a single object, claims that evaluate two or more objects, and action claims. As indicated, one evaluative claim can sometimes be used as support for another evaluative claim, leading eventually to complicated claims built on a web of other claims.

In addition to the fact that evaluative claims are used both as the end product of an argument and as evidence for other evaluative claims, almost all evaluative claims are dependent on earlier descriptive claims and relational claims. Depending on whether or not the audience is familiar with and accepts the arguer's descriptive of the concept to be evaluated, the arguer making an evaluative claim may also want to explicitly make prior descriptive claims as well. In the previous examples, for instance, one can easily see how an arguer

might need to describe certain features of capital punishment, private property, lying, Clinton, Reagan, free trade, or Cuba before launching into an evaluation of those concepts.

In many, but not all instances, an arguer also would need to use a claim of relationship as evidence to support the evaluative claim. To illustrate instances when a relational claim is and is not needed, consider the two examples of claims evaluating a single object. The claim that "capital punishment is immoral" can be supported by describing a feature of capital punishment (that it is the intentional taking of a human life) and evaluating that feature negatively (the intentional taking of a human life is an immoral act). A description and an evaluation are all that are necessary; relational evidence is not needed. The second claim that "private property is the root of all evil" is different. To make this claim, one first might describe the concept of private property, then argue that private property leads to greed and selfishness (a relational claim), then argue that greed and selfishness are evil. A significant difference exists between the first argument and the second one: the first requires relational evidence and the second does not. In the first instance, the argument is evaluating an inherent feature of capital punishment; in the second, the argument evaluates an effect of private property. When arguing an inherent feature of a concept, relational evidence is unnecessary because the evaluation is of the feature rather than of an effect of the feature. But many times, by the nature of the claim, an arguer is forced to evaluate an effect of a concept. In those instances, the arguer is required to establish the effect by means of relational evidence.

In summary, four categories of evidence and claims include definitions, descriptions, relational statements (of contingency and of similarity), and evaluations. Sometimes claims are the end products of arguments; at other times they are used as evidence for the construction of further claims. This introduction has presented a category system and begun to explain how various types of claims are related to one another when one is used as evidence for another. This introduction has done little or nothing toward explaining how one constructs arguments for these various types of claims. The methods and processes of constructing these claims are the topics of later chapters.

Theory and Practice

This essay has provided some theoretical background relevant to argumentation in debating. Specifically, it has provided a discussion of the Toulmin model of argument and a more detailed description of two of Toulmin's elements: claims and evidence. The reason for focusing on these two elements is that the remainder of this volume provides information that can be transformed into evidence and claims to support propositions. Claims and evidence are the foundational elements of supporting propositions. Warrants and reservations, which are more likely to be individual creations than foundations, did not receive the same detailed discussion.

When using this volume, debaters need to remember that it is only a starting point. Good debaters, much less excellent debaters, will need to go beyond this volume. They will need to engage in individual and perhaps collective research into the details of other claims and evidence.

Then, of course, comes the actual practice of debating where debaters will be required to combine the evidence provided in this volume and from their own research with warrants and reservations to support claims and to combine those claims into arguments supporting or refuting propositions.

Robert Trapp
Professor of Rhetoric
Willamette University
Salem, Oregon, USA

■ **DEBATE TOPICS**

ABORTION, FREE ACCESS TO

According to the Guttmacher Institute, the average cost of a first trimester surgical abortion is $451. Estimates for later abortions range from $3,000 to $10,000. For some middle- or low-income women, these costs are prohibitively high. Thus, some argue that the government should provide free access to abortion services for women who cannot afford them. Opponents argue that providing free abortions is outside the government's mandate. This issue is particularly controversial among those who believe that all abortion is immoral.

PROS

Free access to abortion is vital in affirming a woman's right to control her own body. On January 22, 1973, in the case of *Roe v. Wade*, the Supreme Court ruled that abortion is covered by the Due Process Clause of the Fourteenth Amendment; any state interest in restricting abortion must be balanced against a woman's right to control her own body. It was, therefore, ruled that abortion during the first trimester is a constitutional right. If something is a constitutional right, access to it should not be based on an individual's ability to pay. For example, legal representation for defendants facing criminal prosecution is deemed a constitutional right; therefore, those who cannot afford their own attorney are assigned public defenders.

Free access to abortion is better for society as a whole. Limiting access to abortion—and effectively prohibiting it among low-income women and teenagers unable to ask their parents for help—simply increases the number of unwanted pregnancies. Research has consistently shown that unwanted pregnancies have a negative effect on society, producing children who are more likely to be neglected or mistreated, parents who are unable to provide for their children, which forces them onto welfare, and women who suffer health problems due to repeated childbirth. Free access to abortions helps to break cycles of deprivation by allowing low-income women to raise families that they can support both emotionally and financially. This is hugely beneficial to society.

Access to free abortion is not advocating for increased abortion for low-income women: it is advocating for equal abortion access for low-income women. No one is arguing that poor and minority women should be having more abortions, but that if they want or need an abortion, they should not be disqualified for financial reasons. Furthermore, research shows that low-income women are in the greatest need of access to abortion services; a 2011 analysis by the Guttmacher Institute found that poor women were more than five times as likely to have an

CONS

There is no explicit constitutional guarantee of abortion. In *Roe v. Wade*, the Supreme Court found that overbearing and vague restrictions on abortion were unconstitutional, but never ruled that the government had a duty to provide abortion services to women. While the right to privacy, which prohibits government intervention in the first trimester of pregnancy, prevents the government from banning abortion, it does not mandate that the government fund abortion.

Society is damaged by a lack of sexual responsibility. For example, a study by George Mason University showed that abortion access led to increased rates of sexually transmitted disease. Free access to abortion will lead to a decline in personal responsibility over the consequences of unsafe sex, and the government and taxpayers will be responsible for the repercussions. The solution to limiting unwanted pregnancies is contraception or abstinence, not free abortion. It is also morally reprehensible to use abortion to prevent unwanted children from being a drain on society. Those most likely to utilize free abortion services are the poor and minorities, which means that free access to abortion is effectively advocating population control of these demographics.

Research shows that abortion providers such as Planned Parenthood target low-income and minority women by placing clinics in the communities where these groups reside; free abortion access would increase this pressure on low-income women to end their pregnancies. The average cost of an abortion in the United States is less than $500; if a woman is truly committed to aborting a pregnancy, she will find a way to raise these funds. This is demonstrated by the fact that 70% of US women who had an abortion in 2012 described themselves as poor

PROS	CONS
unintended pregnancy than wealthy women. Therefore, free access to abortion will assist those who need it most.	or near poor, yet they were able to obtain an abortion nevertheless. Low-income women already get abortions. Therefore, free abortions do not allow low-income women to get abortions—but actually encourage them to do so.
Providing free access to abortion is well within the government's roles and responsibilities. The government funds many health programs, from free clinics to Medicare and Medicaid. Free access to abortions promotes the general welfare and helps those in areas where access to abortion would otherwise be prohibitively expensive. Private organizations such as Planned Parenthood simply do not have the resources to provide costly abortions and are already facing defunding or restrictions because of their commitments to facilitating women's rights to abortion.	Government-provided abortions would be an overextension of the government's role. The government offers a safety net to help those who cannot help them themselves. Hence, in cases where the mother's life is at risk, abortions can already be performed. In all other cases, the abortion procedure is one of convenience rather than necessity. Privately funded organizations, not government, should fill the gap.

Sample Motions:

This House believes that the state should provide free access to abortion services.

This House believes in a means-tested right to abortion.

Web Links:

- BBC. <http://www.bbc.co.uk/ethics/abortion/mother/for_1.shtml> Arguments in favor of abortion.
- Guttmacher Institute. <http://www.guttmacher.org/media/presskits/abortion-WW/statsandfacts.html> Statistics and facts about abortion..
- United States Supreme Court. <http://caselaw.lp.findlaw.com/scripts/getcase.pl?navby=CASE&court=US&vol=410&page=113> *Roe v. Wade* court opinion.

Further Readings:

Levine, Phillip B. *Sex and Consequences: Abortion, Public Policy, and the Economics of Fertility.* Princeton University Press, 2007.

Rose, Richard. *Safe, Legal, and Unavailable? Abortion Politics in the United States.* CQ Press, 2006.

Solinger, Rickie. *Beggars and Choosers: How the Politics of Choice Shapes Adoption, Abortion, and Welfare in the United States.* Hill and Wang, 2002.

■ ■

ABORTION ON DEMAND

Whether a woman has the right to terminate a pregnancy, and, if so, under what conditions, is one of the most contentious issues facing modern societies. For some, the question is even more fundamental: at what stage is the fetus to be regarded as a child? The battle lines are drawn between "pro-life" supporters, who argue that abortion is never permissible, and "pro-choice" adherents, who emphasize a woman's right to choose. In 1973 the US Supreme Court ruled that abortion was legal in its landmark decision Roe v. Wade. *Since then antiabortion groups have pressed to have the ruling overturned and have succeeded in having several states pass laws limiting the conditions under which abortion is permitted. Both anti-abortion and pro-choice groups have made support of* Roe *the litmus test for political and judicial candidates wanting their backing.*

PROS

Women should have control over their own bodies—they have to carry the child during pregnancy and undergo childbirth. No one else carries the child for her; it will be her responsibility alone, and thus she should have the sole right to decide. If a woman does not want to go through the full nine months and subsequent birth, then she should have the right to choose not to do so. There are few—if any—other cases where something with such profound consequences is forced upon a human being against her or his will. To appeal to the child's right to life is just circular—whether a fetus has rights or not, or can really be called a "child," is exactly what is at issue. Everyone agrees that children have rights and shouldn't be killed. Not everyone agrees that fetuses of two, four, eight, or even twenty weeks are children.

Not only is banning abortion a problem in theory, offending against a woman's right to choose, it is also a practical problem. A ban would not stop abortion but would drive it once again underground and into conditions where the health and safety of the woman are almost certainly at risk. Women would also circumvent the ban by traveling to countries where abortion is legal. Either the state would have to take the draconian measure of restricting freedom of movement, or it would have to admit that its law is unworkable in practice and abolish it.

Are we really talking about a "life"? At what point does a life begin? Is terminating a fetus, which can neither feel nor think and is not conscious of its own "existence," really commensurate with the killing of a person? If you affirm that human life is a quality independent of, and prior to, thought and feeling, you leave yourself the awkward task of explaining what truly "human" life is.

In cases where terminating a pregnancy is necessary to save a mother's life, surely abortion is permissible.

Not only medical emergencies present compelling grounds for termination. Women who have been raped

CONS

Of course, human rights should be respected, but no one has a right to make a decision with no reference to the rights and wishes of others. In this case, does the father have any rights in regard to the fate of the fetus? More important, though, pro-choice groups actively ignore the most important right—the child's right to life. What is more important than life? All other rights, including the mother's right to choice, surely stem from a prior right to life; if you have no right to any life, then how do you have a right to an autonomous one? A woman may ordinarily have a reasonable right to control her own body, but this does not confer on her the entirely separate (and insupportable) right to decide whether another human lives or dies.

Unborn children cannot articulate their right to life; they are vulnerable and must be protected. Many laws are difficult to implement, but degree of difficulty does not diminish the validity and underlying principle. People will kill other people, regardless of the law, but it does not follow that you shouldn't legislate against murder.

Whether the state should restrain women from traveling for abortions is a separate question, but one that can be answered in the affirmative given what is at stake. Restricting someone's freedom is a small price to pay for protecting an innocent life.

The question of what life is can certainly be answered: it is sacred, inviolable, and absolute. The fetus, at whatever stage of development, will inevitably develop the human abilities to think, feel, and be aware of itself. The unborn child will have every ability and every opportunity that you yourself have, given the chance to be born.

While emergencies are tragic, it is by no means obvious that abortion is permissible. The "mother vs. child" dilemma is one that defies solution, and aborting to preserve one of the lives sets a dangerous precedent that killing one person to save another is acceptable. This is a clear, and unpalatable, case of treating a human being as a means to an end.

While rape is an appalling crime, is it the fault of the unborn child? The answer is no. Denying someone life should not have to suffer the additional torment of being pregnant with the product of that ordeal. To force a woman to produce a living, constant reminder of that act is unfair to both mother and child.

Finally, advances in medical technology have enabled us to determine during pregnancy whether the child will be disabled. In cases of severe disability, in which the child would have a very short, very painful and tragic life, it is surely right to allow parents to choose a termination. This avoids both the suffering of the parents and of the child.

because of the circumstances of conception is as unfair as anything else imaginable.

What right does anyone have to deprive another of life on the grounds that he deems that life not worth living? This arrogant and sinister presumption is impossible to justify, given that many people with disabilities lead fulfilling lives. What disabilities would be regarded as the watershed between life and termination? All civilized countries roundly condemn the practice of eugenics.

Sample Motions:

This House would forbid abortion on demand.

This House believes in a woman's right to choose.

Web Links:

- American Civil Liberties Union. <http://www.aclu.org/reproductiverights/index.html> Provides information on the status of reproductive issues and reproductive rights from a pro-choice perspective.
- Gordon, John-Stewart. <http://www.iep.utm.edu/abortion/> Encyclopedia entry discusses philosophical perspectives on abortion.
- Hillar, Marian. <http://www.socinian.org/abortion.html> Discusses philosophical approaches to the debate on abortion; bibliography contains several important articles on the subject.
- The National Right to Life Committee. <http://www.nrlc.org/default.html> Presents information on abortion methodology and alternatives to abortion from a pro-life perspective.
- New York Times. <http://topics.nytimes.com/top/reference/timestopics/subjects/a/abortion/index.html> Links to recent articles on abortion.

Further Reading:

Dombrowski, Daniel A., and Robert Deltete. *A Brief, Liberal, Catholic Defense of Abortion*. University of Illinois Press, 2006.

Kaczor, Christopher. *The Ethics of Abortion: Women's Rights, Human Life, and the Question of Justice*. Routledge, 2010.

Meyers, Chris. *The Fetal Position: A Rational Approach to the Abortion Issue*. Prometheus Books, 2010.

■ ■

ABORTION, PARENTAL NOTIFICATION/CONSENT

Whether a teenager should have to notify or get the permission of her parents before having an abortion is one of the contentious issues surrounding abortion. Parental notification or consent laws exist in 44 US states, although in nine of those states the laws are enjoined or not enforced. Some of the statutes provide for a court-bypass procedure should a teenager be unable to involve her parents. Most include exceptions for medical emergencies. In 2005 the US Supreme Court agreed to hear a challenge to a New Hampshire law requiring parental notification, but the following year avoided a major decision by returning the case to the lower court because the statute did not allow an exemption from notification if the girl's health was in danger. In 2007 New Hampshire became the first state to repeal a parental notification law.

PROS

Children under 16 need parental consent for medical treatment and surgery: abortion should not be an exception. Children need parental consent for many activities—from participating in extracurricular sports or school trips to marrying. Abortion is at least as important a decision as any of these.

Parents have a right to know what their children are doing. They are legally responsible for their care, and, as parents, they have a proper interest. Good parents would want to help their daughter make her decision.

Parental notification helps ensure that pregnant teenagers get support and guidance from their parents in deciding whether to continue the pregnancy. This decision has a major long-term effect on a woman's psychological and emotional well-being, her ability to continue formal education, and her future financial status. She needs the guidance of adults in helping make this decision.

We appreciate that in some exceptional cases notifying parents may be inappropriate—for example, if a daughter is estranged from them, if she has been abused, or if telling her parents would present a serious foreseeable threat to her safety. In such cases, the courts could allow a waiver. In normal circumstances, however, parents should be informed. That unusual circumstances may arise does not affect the principle that this is a sensible law.

Requiring parental consent will lead to a fall in the number of abortions. In Minnesota, for example, the number of legal teenage abortions fell by 25% when this measure was introduced. Both pro-choice advocates and abortion opponents agree that lowering the number of abortions is good.

When the "quick-fix" of abortion is no longer easily available, attitudes change. Teenagers are less likely to have sex or are more likely to use contraception if they do. Abstention and practicing safe sex have positive effects on health by diminishing the risk of unwanted pregnancies and sexually transmitted diseases.

CONS

Parental consent is not legally necessary to have a baby nor should it be. The mother, not the grandparents, should have the ultimate authority over whether to have a baby. To say that someone is old enough to have a baby but not old enough to have an abortion is absurd. In any case, parental consent for surgery is a legal sham because physicians can get a court order to override a parent's refusal. The proposition has not presented a good example.

Children have good reasons for not telling parents of a pregnancy. Parents who are opposed to abortion may force their daughter to continue a pregnancy against her wishes, even at a risk to her health or life. Disclosing that a girl is pregnant confirms that she is sexually active. Some parents may be so opposed to premarital sex that they disown their daughter or physically or mentally abuse her.

This measure is unnecessary for stable and supportive families, in which daughters may well choose to discuss their pregnancy with their parents. It is ineffective and cruel in unstable and troubled families, where telling parents that their daughter is pregnant may make the family situation worse.

Obtaining parental consent necessarily imposes a delay into the abortion process, which increases the likelihood of complications. Judicial waivers introduce even more delays—on average at least 22 days in the US. For the sake of the mother's health, it is better not to require parental consent.

Requiring parental consent does not limit abortions. Teens go to states that do not have such requirements.

We should encourage campaigns for sexual abstinence and contraceptive awareness, but we must remember that they are not alternatives to abortion. No sensible person would choose abortion as an alternative to contraception. Abortion is a last resort. If sexual abstinence is not a sensible reaction to making abortion more inaccessible, then making abortion more inaccessible is not a sensible way of increasing sexual abstinence.

This House would require parental consent for abortion.

This House would look after its children.

This House believes that parental consent is in the best interests of the teen.

Web Links:

- American Civil Liberties Union. <http://www.aclu.org/reproductiverights/youth/16388res20010401.html> Presents arguments against laws that mandate parental involvement in abortion.
- Center for Reproductive Rights. <http://reproductiverights.org/en/project/parental-involvement-laws> Discussion of parental involvement laws from a pro-choice group.
- Yes on Proposition 4. <http://www.yeson4.net/default.aspx> Organization dedicated to passing Proposition 4, a proposed piece of legislation in California that would mandate that doctors notify at least one adult family member before performing abortions on girls under 18.

Further Reading:

Joyce, Ted. *Parental Consent for Abortion and the Judicial Bypass Option in Arkansas: Effects and Correlates.* Guttmacher Institute, 2010.

Macleod, Catriona. *Adolescence, Pregnancy and Abortion: Constructing a Threat of Degeneration.* Taylor and Francis, 2010.

Medoff, Marshall H. "Unintended Pregnancy and Abortion Access in the United States." *International Journal of Population Research,* 2012.

■ ■

ADVERTISING: DIGITALLY ENHANCED IMAGES OF WOMEN

The media's presentation of women has long been criticized for setting an unrealistic standard of beauty, which negatively affects the body image, emotional well-being, and health of women. Though previous debates have centered on the use of underweight models and the narrow definition of beauty, more recently, advertisers have been criticized for their use of digitally altered images of women. Images can be altered in a variety of ways—the most controversial alterations are those that make women appear thinner (although digital alterations that lighten the skin tone of women of color are also the subject of criticism). Several countries have proposed legislation to counter this practice: Israel now requires advertisers to disclose when their models have been digitally thinned, and both French and British politicians have proposed similar laws. However, with numerous studies linking thin images of women to body dissatisfaction and eating disorders, many think that these warnings do not go far enough; instead, they would like to ban advertisers from digitally enhancing models, particularly in order to make them look thinner.

PROS

Digitally enhanced images of models project an unrealistic ideal of the female body, contributing to a social aversion to the normal female body shape. Despite the fact that models already weigh approximately 23% less than the average US woman, digital manipulation is almost exclusively used to make models thinner still. This often achieves completely unattainable proportions. For example, a digitally enhanced Ralph Lauren advertisement, released in 2009, featured a model with hips that

CONS

Advertising allows a form of escapism that many women welcome and, indeed, pursue. As with most artistic media, an implicit understanding exists that what is depicted does not necessarily mirror real life—to many viewers this is the very attraction of the images. Models reflect how many women want to look, which is the purpose of the fashion and cosmetic industries; digital alterations simply enhance this aspirational beauty. Furthermore, women know that photographic techniques are used were far narrower than her head as a result of digital manipulations. Digitally altering the female form in this way creates a distorted and completely unhealthy cultural notion of what women should look like.

to make models look a certain way; just as with special effects in films, people viewing images of models are aware that they have likely been altered to create a specific effect. Photography is a form of creative expression — the government should not be able to put restrictions on creative expression, whether it is produced by advertisers or any other form of media.

Studies have shown that exposure to images of thin models negatively affects women's self-esteem, and makes them more likely to see themselves as fat even if they are of a completely healthy weight. Glamorizing images of artificially thinned women can have severe psychological consequences for the women who view them. Current research estimates that up to 13% of Western women suffer from an eating disorder. Eating disorders also have the highest mortality rate of any mental illness. With images of extreme thinness contributing to ill health and even death in young women, it is time for advertisers to be restricted.

Nobody forces women to look at images of thin models. If women do not like the images, they should not purchase the magazines that contain them or consume the products being advertised — advertisers would quickly change their tactics if this happened. Attempts to ban women from viewing certain images is arguably more sexist than the images themselves; women are fully able to make decisions for themselves regarding the images that they want to view. Furthermore, eating disorders are serious psychological illnesses with complex causes — there is no scientific consensus that images of thin women directly cause eating disorders.

Digital alterations are used to remove any "imperfection" from models, rendering them homogeneous and void of any distinguishing characteristics. This reduces women to a standardized set of features and body parts, rather than fully realized people with unique attributes. Furthermore, since most digital enhancement of women is filtered through a male lens, it can reinforce a chauvinistic view of women as sex objects. We see this in the fact that most alternations are used to make women more sexually appealing, elongating their legs, narrowing their waists, and augmenting their breasts. In doing this, digital enhancement is perpetuating a sexist view of women.

Portraying women as sexually attractive or aesthetically perfect is not sexist — beauty in no way undermines a woman's autonomy. In addition, the vast majority of digital alterations to images do not change the way models look — they are still completely recognizable and retain all of their unique characteristics — but instead make minor adjustments, correcting flaws created during the photography process. Scott Kelby, president of the National Association of Photoshop Professionals, affirms that digital enhancement simply makes the camera as forgiving as the eye; cameras capture flaws that the human eye does not, thus requiring digital modification in order to produce a more natural image.

The unattainable standard of beauty created through digitally altering models is used to manipulate women into purchasing products that they do not need. Advertisers consciously tailor images of women to make them feel badly about themselves, leading them to believe that buying a certain product will make them feel better. A 2008 study conducted at Villanova University and the College of New Jersey found that images of thin models in advertising made women feel insecure, but also made them more likely to purchase the product being advertised. Digitally thinned women take this to a new extreme, creating a thinness that could never naturally be achieved — and psychologically harming women in the process — just to make money. Purposefully harming

All advertising, regardless of whether or not it uses digitally altered images, is used to persuade people to buy products — digitally enhanced images are used to persuade, not "manipulate." In addition, using digitally enhanced images to falsely overstate the effects of a certain product is already restricted; for example, a mascara advertisement cannot digitally enhance the model's eyelashes and claim that the mascara produced that effect. Furthermore, the use of digitally enhanced female models in advertising aimed at women is just the inevitable response to market demand. Through their ongoing consumption of and demand for pictures of "perfect" bodies, women effectively signal a tacit acceptance of such images. If enough women objected, advertisers

PROS	CONS
other people in order to make money is immoral, and the government should regulate advertisers that do this.	would change their approach rather than alienate their target consumers.

Sample Motions:
This House would ban advertisers from using digitally enhanced images of women.
This House believes that the use of digitally enhanced imaging in advertising does more harm than good.

Web Links:
- HuffingtonPost.com. <http://www.huffingtonpost.com/vivian-diller-phd/photoshop-body-image_b_891095.html> Article examining the relationship between digitally enhanced images and body image.
- Jezebel. <http://jezebel.com/tag/photoshop-of-horrors> Feminist blog that showcases images that have undergone extreme photoshopping.
- Los Angeles Times. <http://www.latimes.com/features/image/la-ig-photoshop2-2009aug02,0,4042697.story> Discusses the use of Photoshop by advertisers.
- New York Times. <http://www.nytimes.com/2009/05/28/fashion/28RETOUCH.html?pagewanted=all&_r=0> Argues for restrictions on digitally enhanced images.

Further Reading:
Gill, Rosalind. *Gender and the Media.* Polity, 2007.
Nigam, Divya, and Jyotsna Jha. *Women in Advertising: Changing Perceptions.* DGM Icfai Books, 2007.
Woolf, Emma. *The Ministry of Thin: How the Pursuit of Perfection Got Out of Control.* Summersdale, 2013.
Wykes, Maggie, and Barrie Gunter. *The Media and Body Image: If Looks Could Kill.* Sage, 2005.

AFFIRMATIVE ACTION

Affirmative action in the United States was born of the civil rights and women's movements of the 1960s and 1970s. These programs are designed to provide historically disadvantaged groups—minorities and women—special consideration in education, housing, and employment. Those institutions with affirmative action policies generally set goals for increased diversity, although the courts have ruled that quotas are unconstitutional. By the end of the twentieth century, Supreme Court decisions had limited affirmative action, and a vocal opposition movement was arguing that it was no longer necessary. In June 2003, however, the Supreme Court ruled that universities could use race as one factor in making admission decisions, although the deeply divided court seemed to put limits on the consideration race should receive. The court became more conservative following the appointment of John Roberts and Samuel Alito in 2006. The following year, in Parents Involved in Community Schools v. Seattle School District No. 1, *a sharply divided court ruled unconstitutional the use of race as the primary factor in assigning students to specific elementary or secondary schools. In 2013, a case concerning affirmative action at public universities,* Fisher v. University of Texas, *was heard by the Supreme Court; though the court sent the case back to a lower court, its ruling indicated that increased scrutiny of race-based admissions policies may be necessary.*

PROS

Women and minorities have frequently faced obstacles and difficulties in access to education and employment that white males did not. Affirmative action levels the playing field.

Affirmative action unlocks the unrealized potential of millions. Minority applicants are just as skilled as those from the majority but their talents are untapped because of lack of opportunity. The country gains enormously by using the talents of all its citizens.

Successful minority members are role models who will encourage the development of minority youngsters.

Bringing more minority applicants into the workplace will change racist and sexist attitudes because workers will begin to know each other as individuals rather than stereotypes.

The proportion of minorities in particular jobs should mirror that of the minority in the general population. The underrepresentation of minorities and women in certain fields leads to perceptions of institutional racism and sexism.

Getting minority candidates into top jobs will enable them to change the system "from the inside" to make it fairer for all.

CONS

All discrimination is negative. It is always wrong to select on any basis other than merit and ability. Affirmative action leads to able applicants being unfairly passed over.

Affirmative action results in less able applicants filling positions. Employers must have the flexibility to employ the best candidates to ensure efficiency and productivity.

Affirmative action undermines the achievements of minority members by creating the impression that success was unearned. Some members of minorities see affirmative action as patronizing and as tokenism on the part of the majority.

Affirmative action causes resentment among those who do not benefit from it and creates a backlash against minorities.

Granted, we should aim for improving minority representation in high-profile positions, but we should not sacrifice our emphasis on merit and ability. Instead we should give everyone better access to education so that we can choose on merit and without discrimination.

Educational institutions are becoming more diverse. This diversity ultimately will lead to increasing minority representation in senior positions in business, education, and government. Although the pace of change is not as fast as it might be, we have seen improvement. Continued implementation of affirmative action could lead to a backlash that stops progress.

Sample Motions:

This House believes in affirmative action.

This House believes race does matter.

This House would act affirmatively.

Web Links:

- American Civil Liberties Union. <http://www.aclu.org/racial-justice/affirmative-action> Links to recent cases, articles, and documents relating to affirmative action.
- Fullinwider, Robert. <http://plato.stanford.edu/entries/affirmative-action/> Philosophical analysis of affirmative action.
- PBS. <http://www.pbs.org/now/shows/434/index.html> Provides a brief description of current events relating to affirmative action and provides links to articles.

Further Reading:

Espenshade, Thomas J. *No Longer Separate, Not Yet Equal: Race and Class in Elite College Admission and Campus Life*. Princeton University Press, 2009.

Rosenfeld, Michael. *Affirmative Action and Justice: A Philosophical and Constitutional Inquiry*. Yale University Press, 2009.

Sterba, James P. *Affirmative Action for the Future*. Cornell University Press, 2009.

▪ ▪

AGE DISCRIMINATION

Age discrimination occurs when a decision is made on the basis of a person's age. In the workplace these are most often decisions about recruitment, promotion, and dismissal. Although such discrimination can be seen in a reluctance to hire workers who are perceived to be too young and immature for the job, in practice it refers to a bias against older workers. In societies that celebrate youthfulness above almost all else, it can be very difficult for even highly qualified professionals to find new positions after the age of 50. Nationwide laws against age discrimination are some 30 years old in the US, 20 years old in Canada, and 10 years old in Australia. The European Employment Directive also prohibits age discrimination. But around the world the issue remains controversial, both in general and in particular concerning the practice of setting mandatory retirement ages.

PROS

Older people are just as capable as younger people. Since age is not necessarily an indication of inferior ability or potential, treating people less favorably purely on the basis of their age is just as unreasonable and unfair as doing so on the basis of race or religion. It is also inconsistent with the principles of equal treatment and nondiscrimination at the heart of the notion of individual rights.

For example, if a particular older worker has less concentration or manual strength than a younger worker, and this objectively and reasonably makes someone less qualified for the particular job, employers can still make their decisions based on a worker's relative lack of suitability for the job—not on age. Age by itself is not a determinant.

Discriminatory practices in recruitment and promotion are detrimental to the economy. Age discrimination reduces productivity by inefficiently matching job and advancement opportunities to workers, thus wasting talent. Higher participation rates among older workers lead to better matching of jobs to people, increased employment rates, and enhanced competition among workers, which stimulates the labor market in the long run.

It is a well-known fallacy that the economy has only a limited number of jobs and that when older workers remain in the labor market they deny job opportunities

CONS

In theory, hiring should be based on ability. In reality, certain abilities are hard to test accurately, so employers use age as a proxy—in the same way that they use sports as an indication of one's ability to be a team player, or extracurricular leadership as an indicator of management potential.

Though not foolproof, age is often an indicator of qualities such as concentration, memory, energy, and so on, which may be important in specific cases. For example, a fashion designer justifiably wants salespersons to have a certain level of energy and vitality, and it is crucial for air traffic controllers and surgeons to have high levels of fitness and concentration.

The result of laws against age discrimination may merely be that old people are working more, and not that more old people are working. Research on age discrimination laws in the US shows that increased employment rates among older workers are due mostly to their remaining in jobs longer, and not due to increased hiring rates among older workers.

Worse, the increased supply of older workers, at least in the short term, generates market pressures for wages to fall, such that all existing older workers suffer.

to younger people or push down wages. In fact, wages are especially unlikely to decline in industries with existing or projected shortages, such as teaching and nursing.

Without age discrimination and a mandatory retirement age, employers benefit from lower turnover and thus lower recruitment costs.

By contrast, discrimination discourages potentially talented job seekers from applying. Beginning with the recruitment stage, employers lose by having a smaller pool of workers to draw upon and by failing to make the most of the existing skills potential of the population.

The argument that antidiscrimination laws are good for employers contradicts economics and common sense. If hiring and promoting older workers were in firms' best interests, the firms would do so without the need for such laws.

Furthermore, at any firm there is always a limited number of senior jobs. If older workers staying on indefinitely occupy these jobs, firms may find it difficult to recruit, motivate, and retain younger workers looking to replace them, which leads to high turnover among younger staff. Firms may also find that with no mandatory retirement age they have no idea when people will leave, which creates problems of uncertainty in manpower planning and possible bottlenecks.

Ageism is the most prevalent form of discrimination in the workforce today. Legislation helps to change these prejudiced attitudes if it operates in conjunction with other policies to promote equal rights and educate employers and workers about their obligations and rights.

By protecting a group in society that is often left out and less advantaged, we are also raising the level of equality in society.

In Australia, Canada, and the US, where antidiscrimination laws have long been in place, there is no clear evidence so far of any significant shift in the attitude of employers and society to older workers. In fact, there is some evidence that employers are less likely to hire older workers, and younger coworkers are more resentful because employers are not allowed to set a mandatory retirement age.

Sample Motions:

This House believes that age discrimination should be illegal in the workplace.

This House believes that old is gold.

This House would honor its elders.

Web Links:

- Age Discrimination: How Old Is Too Old? <http://jobsearch.about.com/cs/careerresources/a/agediscriminat.htm> Summary of problems facing older job seekers.
- US Department of Labor: Age Discrimination. <http://www.dol.gov/dol/topic/discrimination/agedisc.htm> Links to anti–age discrimination legislation and regulation.
- US Equal Opportunities Commission: Facts About Age Discrimination. <http://www.eeoc.gov/facts/age.html> Summary of US Age Discrimination in Employment Act.

Further Reading:

Hulett, John K. *Age Discrimination: An Epidemic in America*. AuthorHouse, 2011.

Sargeant, Malcolm. *Age Discrimination: Ageism in Employment and Service Provision*. Gower, 2011.

Sargeant, Malcolm, ed. *Age Discrimination and Diversity: Multiple Discrimination from an Age Perspective*. Cambridge University Press, 2011.

▪ ▪

AIDS DRUGS FOR DEVELOPING COUNTRIES

The vast majority of people infected with HIV/AIDS live in Africa, more specifically, sub-Saharan Africa. These typically poorer and developing countries are confronting the issue of the cost of drugs for treating the disease. Some nations say that they cannot afford the drugs and that drug companies are making an immoral profit; some nations have threatened to ignore the patents of pharmaceutical companies and to manufacture generic forms of HIV/AIDS drugs unless the companies agree to lower their prices for poorer markets. Bending to international pressure, in the opening years of the 21st century, some of the world's largest drug companies announced that they planned to cut the cost of HIV/AIDS drugs in the world's poorest countries.

PROS

Without a doubt many of the world's pharmaceutical companies are making large profits by selling drugs to poor nations that have a great portion of their population infected with HIV/AIDS. This is an immoral exploitation of those AIDS sufferers who can least afford to pay for treatment and who have the least power internationally to negotiate cheaper prices.

The countries with the biggest AIDS problems are a captive market and are forced to pay whatever the drug companies demand for their products. Poor nations are thus justified in using the threat of producing generic drugs to force drug companies to lower prices.

Generic drugs would be far cheaper to produce and would avoid the shipping costs from factories in Europe or America. Generic drugs have no research and development costs to recoup, so they could be sold for a price greatly reduced from current levels. The cost of keeping a person on AZT or other drug cocktails is exorbitant; such cost would be greatly reduced through the use of generic drugs.

Millions of people will continue to suffer while drug companies refuse to make AIDS medication available to poorer nations at an affordable price. Are the drug companies trying to use the millions of HIV sufferers as hostages in their battle to get the prices they want?

CONS

Just like any business, the pharmaceutical companies need to recoup significant financial investment in research and development. The development of AIDS drugs is highly technical, and a measurable return on initial financial investment is needed if companies are to continue drug research and development.

Drug companies are as much subject to the forces of the free market as any other business. The threat of illegally producing generic drugs only further serves to discourage drug companies from creating new and more effective medicines because the developing nations have shown them that patent protections will be ignored.

Because most of the drug companies are based in richer, First World nations, they have both the technology to produce effective medicines and the funding to ensure that no corners are cut in the process. Poorer nations would almost certainly cut chemical corners in manufacturing generic drugs should the technology for large-scale manufacture even be available. In addition, by contravening international treaties covering patents, they would not benefit from the next generation of AIDS drugs because companies would be reluctant to supply the newer drugs to a country that steals a drug formula to manufacture generic drugs.

Is it right that those infected with HIV in the Third World get huge discounts while those in the First World pay full price? Developed nations may even have to pay more if the drug companies decide to subsidize their "charity sales" to poor countries. Are not poor countries themselves using sufferers as hostages? Many developing nations could realize significant long-term savings by buying and using preventive medicines to stop mother-to-child transmission, etc.

PROS

Drug companies will not lose money by reducing prices; their market will expand. If prices are reduced, the drugs will become affordable to millions of sufferers, many of whom will be using products like AZT for the rest of their lives.

HIV/AIDS treatments are as cheap as they can be at present. By buying the medicines now, especially for preventive purposes, developing nations can reduce the chance of future HIV infection in their populations and thus not need to buy the next generation of (inevitably more expensive) drugs.

CONS

The majority of Third World countries would be unable to afford the drugs even at a breakeven price. One-off treatments to prevent mother-to-child transmission, for example, would be expensive enough. The cost for complex drug cocktails would still be completely out of reach of developing nations. Drug companies would have to sell their medications at a loss to make them affordable to most developing nations.

No matter how low the drug companies price HIV/AIDS treatments, they are unlikely to ever be cheap enough: as the number of HIV infected people in Africa grows, the strain on national health budgets will become unbearable. Developing countries are better off pursuing preventative measures and education. Governments will need to use their health care funds carefully; producing generic medicines offers significant savings.

Sample Motions:

This House would insist on cheaper drugs.

This House wants the First World to help.

This House would fight AIDS.

Web Links:

- Avert. <http://www.avert.org/generic.htm> Provides a history of the conflict over AIDS drug pricing and suggests reforms.
- Fisher, William W., and Cyrill P. Rigamonti. <http://cyber.law.harvard.edu/people/tfisher/South%20Africa.pdf> A case study of South Africa's battle against AIDS and the controversy surrounding patent law.
- Khanna, Arun Kumar. "Pharmaceutical Industry's Corporate Social Responsibility Towards HIV/AIDS." <http://www.bioline.org.br/pdf?jp06063> Discusses pharmaceutical companies' responsibility to help fight HIV/AIDS.

Further Reading:

Condon, Bradly J., and Tapen Sinha. *Global Lessons from the AIDS Pandemic: Economic, Financial, Legal and Political Implications.*Springer, 2008.

Coriat, Benjamin. *The Political Economy of HIV/AIDS in Developing Countries: TRIPS, Public Health Systems and Free Access.* Edward Elgar Publishing, 2008.

Lu, Yichen, Max Essex, and Chris Chanyasulkit, eds. *HIV/AIDS Treatment in Resource Poor Countries: Public Health Challenges.* Springer, 2013.

Osewe, Patrick Lumumba et al. *Improving Access to HIV/AIDS Medicines in Africa: Assessment of Trade-Related Aspects of Intellectual Property Rights Flexibilities Utilization.* World Bank Publications, 2008.

■ ■

ALTERNATIVELY FUELED CARS, GOVERNMENT INCENTIVES FOR

As the number of automobiles increases globally, the world is experiencing more airborne pollution despite agreements by many governments to cut such emissions. For years, the auto industry has been researching cars that use alternate fuels, including hydrogen, solar power, battery, or fuel cells. Vehicles that can run on these fuels are beginning to attract political attention. For example, California has long had mandatory targets for sales of alternatively fueled vehicles; in addition, the federal government has introduced tax breaks for certain environmentally friendly cars such as plug-in hybrid electric vehicles.

PROS

Cars that use fuel that is less environmentally damaging than petroleum are good for the protection of the environment. Gasoline and diesel engines produce pollution both locally and globally, contributing to poor health and global warming. They are also a major consumer of nonrenewable energy, depleting global reserves and making us dependent on oil-rich states for our energy security. Therefore, encouraging people to use alternative fuels instead of petroleum will have a positive environmental, economic, and political impact.

An incentive is an effective way to encourage more widespread use of alternatively fueled vehicles. New technologies are expensive to research and are often prohibitively expensive in their early stages, before there is a critical mass of adoption. This vicious cycle means that the dominant fuel, petroleum, has an inbuilt defensive advantage over new, possibly competitive rivals. Incentives negate this disadvantage, even if they are used during the initial phases before the alternatively fueled cars are more widely used.

Operating a centralized transportation policy is appropriate for government. A successful, effective transportation system markedly increases a country's economic success. It also has a widespread and positive social impact. Using incentives to advance a particular form of transportation, for example, alternatively fueled cars, is a perfectly natural fit with such a plan.

Incentives are an effective way to make people act in a certain way. Even if people accept that petroleum-fueled

CONS

The environmental impact of encouraging alternatively fueled cars is mixed. Conventional engines are much more fuel efficient and much less polluting than they were 20 years ago, and further improvements are likely in the future. Alternative fuels may not be less damaging than petroleum: it may just be that they have not been around long enough for their full consequences to be appreciated. For example, the energy to power up batteries or fuel cells, or to produce hydrogen, is often derived from fossil fuels. Even if there is less local pollution, the environmental impact of powering vehicles is simply transferred somewhere else, rather than removed. Whether this is so or not, such a scheme does not encourage people to use public transportation. Indeed, people may interpret the government's inducement to drive certain kinds of cars as support of the use of private cars.

Government incentives are economically inefficient. They are a form of social engineering, since people express their preferences through the market, and incentives are a way of changing the market conditions so people's views change. Incentives amount to using public funds to "bribe" people to make the choices that the government thinks they should.

Such a plan uses government power to disadvantage private choices. People should be allowed to choose the most suitable form of transportation based on their individual circumstances. Taxpayer-funded government incentives interfere with private choice.

Alternatively fueled automobiles are not what the car-driving public wants. If drivers thought the benefits of cars are environmentally damaging and thus ultimately less desirable than alternatives, this may be a "soft" preference. Monetary incentives are often a more effective way of actually persuading people to amend their choices.

This is an effective policy even if only on a small scale. Granted petroleum-fueled cars are only one factor contributing to environmental problems, but adopting a policy such as this one sends out a strong message affirming a positive approach to environmental matters. Such policy could have a "snowball" effect. It can be pursued in tandem with other policies, and so even if it is only a relatively small part of the overall environmental problem, tackling it is worthwhile.

such cars were significant, they would buy them in large enough numbers that subsidies would not be necessary. The fact that they do not is an indication that those drivers are content driving petroleum-fueled cars.

This policy is too small to make any difference. First, petroleum-fueled cars are only one of many factors that contribute to environmental problems. Cars in any one country are an even smaller part of this overall picture, and so this policy is only a drop in the ocean in terms of the net effect. This is especially so as it simply pits one country's regulation against other countries' more deregulatory approach and can thus lead to shifting of the problem rather than its actual resolution.

Sample Motions:

This House supports government subsidies for alternatively fueled cars.

This House would introduce tax breaks for environmentally friendly cars.

This House would increase taxes on petroleum-fueled cars.

This House would adopt quotas for the production of alternatively fueled vehicles.

Web Links:

- Fuel Economy. <http://www.fueleconomy.gov/> US government site reviewing alternatively fueled cars and their advantages and disadvantages. Also gives information on tax incentives.
- Taylor, Jerry, and Peter Van Doren. "The Green Energy Economy Reconsidered." <http://www.cato.org/publications/commentary/green-energy-economy-reconsidered> Argument against government support for alternative energy.
- Yacobucci, Brent D. <http://fpc.state.gov/documents/organization/61498.pdf> 2006 report on Congressional discussions of alternative energy and incentives.

Further Reading:

Anderson, Curtis D., and Judy Anderson. *Electric and Hybrid Cars: A History.* McFarland, 2010.

Rack, Florentin. *Adoption of Alternative Fuel Vehicles: A Consumer Perspective.* GRIN Verlag, 2012.

Sperling, Daniel et al. *Two Billion Cars: Driving Towards Sustainability.* Oxford University Press, 2010.

■ ■

ANIMAL RIGHTS

In the nineteenth century reformers began urging the more humane treatment of animals and founded groups such as the American Society for the Prevention of Cruelty to Animals to improve the conditions first of working animals and then of domestic and farm animals as well. In the 1970s Australian philosopher Peter Singer became one of the first to argue that animals have rights. While most people agree that humans have an obligation to care for animals and treat them humanely, the idea that they have rights remains contentious.

PROS

Human beings are accorded rights because they are able to think and to feel pain. Many other animals are also able to think (to some extent) and are certainly able to feel pain. Therefore nonhuman animals should also be accorded rights, e.g., to a free and healthy life.

Ever since the publication of Charles Darwin's *Origin of Species* in 1859, we have known that human beings are related by common ancestry to all other animals. We owe a duty of care to our animal cousins.

We should err on the side of caution in ascribing rights to human or nonhuman creatures. If we place high standards (such as the ability to think, speak, or even enter into a social contract) on the ascription of rights, there is a danger that not only animals but also human infants and mentally handicapped adults will be considered to have no rights.

Cruelty to animals is the sign of an uncivilized society; it encourages violence and barbarism in society more generally. A society that respects animals and restrains base and violent instincts is a more civilized one.

That a small number of extremists and criminals have attached themselves to the animal rights movement does not invalidate the cause. Why shouldn't animal rights supporters and activists take medicine? They are morally obligated to take care of themselves in the best way they can until more humane research methods are developed and implemented.

CONS

Human beings are infinitely more complex than any other living creatures. Their abilities to think and talk, to form social systems with rights and responsibilities, and to feel emotions are developed well beyond any other animals. Trying to prevent the most obvious cases of unnecessary suffering or torture of animals is reasonable, but beyond that, nonhuman animals do not deserve to be given "rights."

That we are (incredibly distantly) related to other animals does not mean that animals have "rights." This sort of thinking would lead to absurdities. Should we respect the "right" to life of bacteria? We might wish to reduce unnecessary animal suffering, but not because all creatures to which we are distantly related have rights.

Only human beings who are members of society have rights. Rights are privileges that come with certain social duties and moral responsibilities. Animals are not capable of entering into this sort of "social contract"—they are neither moral nor immoral, they are amoral. They do not respect our "rights," and they are irrational and entirely instinctual. Amoral and irrational creatures have neither rights nor duties—they are more like robots than people. All human beings or potential human beings (e.g., unborn children) can potentially be given rights, but nonhuman animals do not fall into that category.

Using animals for our own nutrition and pleasure is completely natural. In the wild animals struggle to survive, are hunted by predators, and compete for food and resources. Human beings have been successful in this struggle for existence and do not need to feel ashamed of exploiting their position as a successful species in the evolutionary process.

Animal rights activists are hypocrites, extremists, and terrorists who don't care about human life. Organizations like the Animal Liberation Front use terrorist tactics and death threats; People for the Ethical Treatment of Animals is also an extremist organization. These extremists still avail themselves of modern medicine, however, which could not have been developed without experiments and tests on animals. Animal welfare is a reasonable concern, but talking of animal "rights" is a sign of extremism and irrationality.

Sample Motions:
This House believes that animals have rights, too.
This House would respect animals' rights.
This House condemns the exploitation of animals.

Web Links:

- Animal Rights FAQ. <http://www.animal-rights.com/arpage.htm> Includes about 100 FAQs that address key arguments in favor of animal rights, biographies of animal rights activists, lists of US and UK organizations, and links to other animal rights groups.
- Ethics Update. <http://ethics.sandiego.edu/Applied/Animals/index.asp> Links to surveys and resources addressing current events pertaining to animal rights and discussing the moral status of animals.
- People for the Ethical Treatment of Animals. <http://www.peta.org> Home page for animal rights organization includes news stories on animals and animal rights.

Further Reading:
Cochrain, Alasdair. *An Introduction to Animals and Political Theory.* Palgrave Macmillan, 2010.
Kazez, Jean. *Animalkind: What We Owe to Animals.* Wiley-Blackwell, 2010.
Singer, Peter. *Animal Liberation.* Harper Perennial Modern Classics, 2009. First published in 1975.

■ ■

ASSISTED SUICIDE

Assisted suicide is currently being discussed and debated in many countries. The central question is: If a terminally ill person decides that he or she wishes to end his or her life, is it acceptable for others, primarily physicians, to assist that person? For many years, assisted suicide was illegal in all US states, but, in the past few decades, organizations such as the Compassion & Choices have campaigned for a change in the law. They argue that terminally ill patients should not be made to suffer needlessly and should be able to die with dignity. In 1997, Oregon became the first state to legalize physician-assisted suicide. Four years later, conservative Attorney General John Ashcroft ordered federal drug agents to punish doctors who used federally controlled drugs to help the terminally ill die. In 2002, a district judge ruled that Ashcroft had overstepped his authority; in 2006, the Supreme Court let the Oregon law stand. In 2010, only four places had authorized active assistance in dying of patients: Oregon, Belgium, the Netherlands, and Switzerland.

PROS

Every human being has a right to life, perhaps the most basic and fundamental of all our rights. However, with every right comes a choice. The right to speech does not remove the option to remain silent; the right to vote brings with it the right to abstain. In the same way, the right to choose to die is implicit in the right to life.

Those in the late stages of a terminal disease have a horrific future: the gradual decline of the body, the failure of organs, and the need for artificial life support. In some cases, the illness will slowly destroy their minds, the essence of themselves. Even when this is not the case, the huge amounts of medication required to "control" pain will often leave them in a delirious and incapable

CONS

There is no comparison between the right to life and other rights. When you choose to remain silent, you may change your mind at a later date; when you choose to die, you have no such second chance. Participating in someone's death is to participate in depriving them of all choices they might make in the future and is therefore immoral.

It is always wrong to give up on life. Modern palliative care is immensely flexible and effective, and helps to preserve quality of life as long as possible. Terminally ill patients need never be in pain, even at the very end. Society's role is to help them live their lives as well as they can. Counseling, which helps patients come to terms with their condition, can help.

state. Faced with this, it is surely more humane that these individuals be allowed to choose the manner of their own end and die with dignity.

Society recognizes that suicide is unfortunate but acceptable in some circumstances. Those who end their own lives are not seen as evil. The illegality of assisted suicide is therefore particularly cruel for those who are disabled and are unable to die without assistance.

Those who commit suicide are not evil, and those who attempt to take their own lives are not prosecuted. However, if someone is threatening to kill himself or herself, your moral duty is to try to stop them. You would not, for example, simply ignore a man standing on a ledge and threatening to jump simply because it is his choice; and you would definitely not assist in his suicide by pushing him. In the same way, you should try to help a person with a terminal illness, not help him to die.

Suicide is a lonely, desperate act, carried out in secrecy and often is a cry for help. The impact on the family can be catastrophic. By legalizing assisted suicide, the process can be brought out into the open. In some cases, families might have been unaware of the true feelings of their loved one. Being forced to confront the issue of a family member's illness may do great good, perhaps even allowing the family to persuade the patient not to end his life. In other cases, it makes the family part of the process. They can understand the reasons behind a patient's decision without feelings of guilt and recrimination, and the terminally ill patient can speak openly to them about her feelings before her death.

Demanding that family members take part in such a decision can be an unbearable burden. Many may resent a loved one's decision to die and would be either emotionally scarred or estranged by the prospect of being in any way involved with the death. Assisted suicide also introduces a new danger, that the terminally ill may be pressured into ending their lives by others who are not prepared to support them through their illness. Even the most well regulated system would have no way to ensure that this did not happen.

At the moment, doctors are often put into an impossible position. A good doctor will form close bonds with patients and will want to give them the best quality of life possible. However, when a patient has lost or is losing his ability to live with dignity and expresses a strong desire to die, doctors are legally unable to help. To say that modern medicine can totally eradicate pain is a tragic oversimplification of suffering. While physical pain may be alleviated, the emotional pain of a slow and lingering death, of the loss of the ability to live a meaningful life, can be horrific. A doctor's duty is to address his or her patient's suffering, be it physical or emotional. As a result, doctors are already helping their patients to die—although it is not legal, assisted suicide does happen. It would be far better to recognize this and bring the process into the open, where it can be regulated. True abuses of the doctor–patient relationship and incidents of involuntary euthanasia would then be far easier to limit.

A doctor's role must remain clear. The guiding principle of medical ethics is to do no harm: a physician must not be involved in deliberately harming her patient. Without this principle, the medical profession would lose a great deal of trust; admitting that killing is an acceptable part of a doctor's role would likely increase the danger of involuntary euthanasia, not reduce it. Legalizing assisted suicide also places an unreasonable burden on doctors. The daily decisions made to preserve life can be difficult enough. To require them to also carry the immense moral responsibility of deciding who can and cannot die, and the further responsibility of actually killing patients, is unacceptable. This is why the vast majority of medical professionals oppose the legalization of assisted suicide: ending the life of a patient goes against all they stand for.

Sample Motions:
This House would legalize assisted suicide.

This House would die with dignity.

Web Links:

- BBC. <http://www.bbc.co.uk/ethics/euthanasia/against/against_1.shtml> Overview of arguments against euthanasia.
- Final Exit. <http://www.finalexit.org> Organization in favor of legalizing euthanasia provides general information and advocacy positions.
- Messerli, Joe. <http://www.balancedpolitics.org/assisted_suicide.htm> Provides an overview of arguments for and against doctor-assisted suicide.

Further Reading:

Gorsuch, Neil M. *The Future of Assisted Suicide and Euthanasia.* Princeton University Press, 2009.

Lewy, Guenter. *Assisted Death in Europe and America: Four Regimes and Their Lessons.* Oxford University Press, 2010.

Warnock, Mary, and Elisabeth Macdonald. *Easeful Death: Is There a Case for Assisted Dying?* Oxford University Press, 2009.

■ ■

BIODIVERSITY AND ENDANGERED SPECIES

"Biodiversity" refers to the variety of bacteria, plants, and animals that live on our planet and the unique behavioral patterns and activities of each species. Scientists believe that biodiversity is essential to human life on Earth. In recent years environmentalists have become concerned about the decline in the number of species. International agreements such as the Convention on International Trade in Endangered Species of Wild Fauna and Flora (CITES) aim to protect biodiversity. Nevertheless, current research suggests that species are disappearing at an alarming rate and that approximately one-quarter of all species will be extinct within the next few decades. Environmentalists are particularly concerned about endangered species in developing nations, where the economic needs of a poor population may threaten the existence of other life.

PROS

The species Homo sapiens is unprecedented and unique among all life on Earth. Human sentience and intelligence far surpass those of other creatures. These gifts have allowed human beings to populate the Earth, construct civilizations and build industry, and affect the environment in a way that no other species can. This great power comes with great responsibility, and we should avoid abusing our planet, lest we cause irreparable damage—damage like the extinction of species and the consequent reduction in biodiversity caused by deforestation, over-fishing, hunting, and the illegal trade in animal products and exotic animals.

Protecting endangered species is an extension of our existing system of ethics. Just as modern civilization protects its weaker and less able members, so humanity safeguard the welfare of other, less-privileged species. Animals are sentient creatures whose welfare we should protect (even if they may not have the same full "rights" that we accord to human beings).

CONS

The idea that extinctions will lead to ecological disaster is an exaggeration. Fossil evidence shows that mass extinctions have occurred many times throughout the history of life on Earth, one of the most recent being the die-out of the dinosaurs. After every collapse of biodiversity, it has rebounded, with Earth coming to no lasting harm. Extinctions are simply part of the natural evolutionary process.

No species on Earth would put the interest of another species above its own, so why should human beings? Furthermore, since the very beginnings of life, nature has operated by the Darwinian principle of "survival of the fittest." Life forms will always risk extinction unless they adapt to new challenges. Humans have no obligation to save the weaker species; if they cannot match our pace, they deserve to die out and be supplanted by others.

PROS

The most successful pharmaceuticals have often used nature as a starting point. Antibiotics were first discovered through the study of fungi, and many anti-cancer drugs are derived from the bark of Amazon trees. Every time a species becomes extinct, scientists forever lose an opportunity to make a new discovery.

As occupants of this planet, we must have respect for other life forms, especially since life on Earth may be the only life in the universe. We can show this respect by making every effort to prevent the extinction of existing species, thereby preserving biodiversity.

Maintaining biodiversity is a global problem and demands a global solution. The developed world should apply pressure on the developing world to adopt more environmentally friendly policies.

CONS

Modern science has advanced to the point where inspiration from nature is no longer required. Today, medicines derived from natural products are in the minority. In any case, the upcoming era of genetic engineering will allow humankind to rid itself of disease without resorting to medicines.

Even if this respect was justified, its expression comes at a significant cost. Biodiversity policies are costly and spend taxpayers' money that could better be used on health care and social services. It does not make sense for us to concentrate on other species when humanity has not yet sorted out its own welfare.

Environmental protection and the protection of biodiversity are very much a luxury of developed nations (First World). Many of these policies are beyond the financial means of developing nations, and implementing them would stunt economic growth and disenfranchise their citizens. It is hypocritical for developed nations to criticize the lack of environmental protection in the developing world, considering that the First World got to its current position through an Industrial Revolution that paid no heed to biodiversity, pollution, and other such concerns.

Sample Motions:

This House believes in biodiversity.

This House fears the way of the dodo.

Web Links:

- Picard, Kathryn. <http://bama.ua.edu/~joshua/archive/aug06/Kathryn%20Picard.pdf> A discussion about whether humans have a responsibility to preserve biodiversity.
- The Natural History Museum, London: Biodiversity and World Map. <http://www.nhm.ac.uk/science/projects/worldmap/> Contains map of global biodiversity as well as information on biogeography and conservation priorities.
- Shah, Anup. <http://www.globalissues.org/issue/169/biodiversity> A collection of articles on the importance of biodiversity.

Further Reading:

Chivian, Eric, and Aaron Bernstein, eds. *Sustaining Life: How Human Health Depends on Biodiversity.* Oxford University Press, 2008.

McManis, Charles R. *Biodiversity and the Law: Intellectual Property, Biotechnology and Traditional Knowledge.* Earthscan Publications, 2009.

Roe, Dilys, and Joanna Elliot, eds. *The Earthscan Reader in Poverty and Biodiversity Conservation.* Earthscan Publications, 2010.

■ ■

BIOFUELS

Biofuels are sources of energy that come from living, renewable sources, such as corn, palm oil, and even animal manure. In recent years biofuels have come to mean fuels such as ethanol and biodiesel, which can be burned in engines to drive vehicles in place of fossil fuels like petroleum and diesel fuel. Biofuels have also been promoted as a way of reducing carbon emissions and thus tackling global climate change. More than 40 countries now offer some sort of subsidy to encourage the production and use of biofuels instead of fossil fuels. This topic looks at whether biofuels really are better than fossil fuels, and whether governments should continue to develop policies to promote biofuel production and use.

PROS

Biofuels are the best way of reducing our emissions of the greenhouse gases that are responsible for global climate change. As with fossil fuels, burning biodiesel or ethanol to drive an engine or generate electricity releases carbon into the atmosphere. Unlike with fossil fuels, however, growing the plants from which biofuels are made takes carbon from the air, making the overall process carbon neutral. This means policies to increase the use of biofuels could greatly reduce overall levels of carbon emissions, and thus make a major contribution to tackling global climate change. They can also help improve local air quality because mixing ethanol with fossil fuels helps meet clean air standards.

Unlike oil, biofuels are renewable and sustainable. At present humankind is using up fossil fuel resources at an alarming rate, and often damaging the environment in order to extract them. If we continue to rely on fossil fuels, they will one day run out, and not only will our descendants no longer have viable energy reserves, but they will also have to cope with the ecological damage that coal, oil, and gas extraction have inflicted on the earth. Making fuel from crops provides a perfect, sustainable solution.

The reliance of America and its Western allies on conventional fossil fuels, chiefly oil, is a major security issue. Much of the world's oil and gas is produced by unstable, unfriendly, or undemocratic regimes, none of whom can be counted on as reliable long-term partners when

CONS

In theory, biofuels appear to reduce overall carbon emissions, but in practice, they are much less environmentally friendly than their proponents claim. Although growing plants absorb carbon from the atmosphere, growing crops for biofuels uses large amounts of fertilizers, as well as fuel for running farm machinery and transporting the crops. The manufacture of biofuels also requires a lot of energy. All of this produces additional carbon emissions and means that biofuels are often not much better for the atmosphere than the fossil fuels they would replace, especially as more fuel needs to be burned to travel the same distance (because biofuels are less efficient than fossil fuels). Some biofuel crops (e.g., sugar cane) do produce much more energy than is needed to grow them, but making ethanol from corn may actually take 30% more energy than what it generates as fuel—and it is corn-based ethanol that US policy is backing so heavily.

The increased production of biofuels presents a growing environmental threat. If biofuels are to meet a significant part of our energy needs, vast areas will need to be devoted to crops such as oilseed rape, corn, sugar cane, and oil palms. These monocultures are very bad for biodiversity, denying wildlife and native plants places to live. And as the crops will not be grown for human consumption, it is likely that there will be greater use of pesticides, herbicides, and genetically modified crops—all very bad for the natural environment. The greatest environmental threat will be in the developing world, where profits from biofuel production provide strong incentives to cut down the remaining rainforest areas to create sugar cane or palm oil plantations, a process that can already be seen in Brazil and Indonesia.

Attempting complete independence from other countries is impossible and undesirable—the world is now too interconnected and interdependent. Our prosperity rests on being able to trade goods and services widely with people in other countries and attempts to retreat from this considering our future energy security. The past actions of OPEC and the recent willingness of Russia to use its supplies of natural gas to threaten European states both point to a need to reduce our dependence on fossil fuels. Some commentators have also argued that the money we pay to conservative Islamic states for oil often ends up funding terrorism and propping up potential enemies. Increasing the use of biofuels can, therefore, contribute to our security by ensuring that more of our energy needs are met from within our own country, reducing our dependence on foreign suppliers.

There is plenty of scope to produce much greater quantities of biofuels without squeezing food production. Many developed countries have been overproducing crops such as wheat in past decades, leading to programs whereby farmers are paid not to grow crops on some of their land. Agricultural productivity continues to rise, especially in the developing world where new techniques and strains of seed, including types that are genetically modified to suit harsh conditions, will have a major impact.

The growth of biofuels will be good for farmers. In recent decades farmers in the developed world have produced more food than the market required, resulting in large surpluses and very low prices. A great many farmers have been driven out of business as a result, and few young people wish to try to make a living from the land. Meanwhile, surplus grain from America and the EU has often been dumped on markets in the developing world, harming local farmers who are unable to compete. Both kinds of farmers stand to benefit from increased demand for biofuels, as farm incomes improve and market-distorting surpluses disappear. Taxpayers may also benefit as there will be less need to subsidize more prosperous farmers.

free market will impoverish us as well as them. Nor are the United States and its Western allies frighteningly dependent on just one source for their fossil fuel needs—new countries such as Angola, Nigeria, and Canada have all become major energy suppliers in the past decade. In any case, America's demand for energy is so great that there is no possibility of achieving energy independence through biofuels. Trying to produce enough ethanol domestically would require replacing food farming with biofuel crops—meaning the US could no longer feed itself, and would thus become heavily dependent on food imports instead.

Using agricultural land to grow biofuel crops means that fewer crops are grown for human consumption (or for feeding livestock). This pushes up the price of food for everyone but especially affects the poor, both in developed countries and in the developing world. Already Mexicans have found the price of their staple tortillas has risen sharply, as American corn is diverted to subsidized biofuel plants in the Midwest. The prices of sugar and palm oil have also experienced steep increases recently. If biofuel production is promoted even more, this trend will continue, contributing to increased poverty, malnutrition, and suffering. Given that our energy needs can be met by fossil fuels, it seems immoral to divert our agricultural resources unnecessarily.

Biofuels will not guarantee a glorious future for farmers. Oil prices have fluctuated widely over the past 20 years, and may well collapse again in the future, especially as high prices have encouraged investment in new production. Thus, more oil is likely to be produced in the next few years. Changes in the international situation could also reduce the "security premium" paid for fossil fuels since 2001. If oil prices sink back even to the (historically high) level of $50 a barrel, then biofuels will look much less economical and farmers will go bust as a result.

And agriculture in the developing world is held back by the web of tariffs and subsidies the rich world uses to support its own farmers, not by market failure. Truly freeing the market in commodities such as cotton, grain, and sugar would do much more to bring prosperity to many desperately poor countries than any promise biofuels may seem to offer. After all, if the US or the EU really wanted to promote biofuels, they would reduce their high tariffs on imports of cheap Brazilian sugar-cane ethanol rather than pay their own farmers to produce biofuel from much less efficient corn or rapeseed.

PROS

Biofuels are now an economic alternative to fossil fuels, and with advances in technology and the scaling up of production, their price per gallon (or liter) will continue to fall. It appears likely that oil will maintain its current high prices well into the future, due to the exhaustion of many existing fields, strong demand from developing economies such as India and China, and security concerns that are unlikely to go away. Given these long-term trends, without investment in biofuel technology we actually run the risk that our economies will be crippled by sky-high fuel costs. Some subsidies to this investment seem highly justified, especially as they can replace existing agricultural support payments, rather than being additional money.

Biofuels are also a sensible bridge to a greener future, allowing us to develop a more sustainable future without unbearable economic or social cost. Unlike alternatives such as hydrogen fuel cells, biofuels do not need a completely different infrastructure to be widely adopted.

Biofuels already have a great deal to offer today, but prospects for the future are even more exciting and deserve our support. Crops like Jatropha, which are hearty succulents, promise to produce much more energy from a given amount of land. They also flourish without annual replanting or chemical inputs on marginal land. In the longer term, bioengineers are working on producing "cellulosic" biofuels—in which the stems and leaves, not just the fruits or seeds, of plants or trees are used to produce ethanol. Cellulosic biofuels would allow much more fuel to be produced from a given amount of land and could also be made from the waste products of food or timber production, such as straw and woodchips.

CONS

Biofuels are only competitive with fossil fuels because they are heavily subsidized, especially in the US, where the farming lobby has promoted ethanol out of pure self-interest. Subsidies on biofuels at the federal or state level cost American taxpayers about $5.5 to $7.5 billion each year. More costs will come if governments force automakers to build engines that can run on higher proportions of biofuel, as these will be passed on to the consumer in the form of more expensive vehicles. All of this subsidy and investment will be useless if the price of oil returns to its long-term average over the past 30 years, which will make biofuels uneconomic and ruin many farmers and industrial investors.

Biofuel technology may improve, but this is not guaranteed, and it may require more use of genetic engineering than the public is willing to tolerate. Even if the industry does live up to its proponents' optimistic promises, biofuels are still not the right focus of our energy policy. They may be a little better than fossil fuels, but they will never realistically replace them entirely, and their promotion takes attention away from more worthwhile approaches. Biofuels not only let the auto industry continue with business much as usual, they also provide a cover for the fossil-fuel industry by prolonging the life of the oil economy. A much better approach would be to concentrate on reducing our use of energy more radically. This could be achieved through conservation measures, improved fuel efficiency standards, new types of engine, replacing much private vehicle use with public transport provision, better town planning, and so on.

Sample Motions:

This House believes that biofuels are the future.

This House calls for more government support for biofuels.

This House believes that the government should act to encourage the production and use of biofuels.

Web Links:

- BBC News. <http://news.bbc.co.uk/2/hi/science/nature/6294133.stm> Overview article on biofuels with good web links.
- Rosenthal, Elisabeth. <http://www.nytimes.com/2008/02/07/health/07iht-biofuel.5.9849073.html> Describes two 2008 studies that concluded that the production of biofuels emits more greenhouse gases than the conventional energy sources biofuels are intended to replace.
- Zubrin, Robert. <http://www.thenewatlantis.com/publications/in-defense-of-biofuels> A comprehensive defense of biofuels.

Further Reading:

Giampietro, Mario, and Kozo Mayumi. *The Biofuel Delusion: The Fallacy of Large Scale Agro-Biofuel Production.* Earthscan Publications, 2009.

Mousdale, David M. *Biofuels: Biotechnology, Chemistry, and Sustainable Development.* CRC, 2008.

Rosillo-Calle, Frank, and Francis X. Johnson, eds. *Food Versus Fuel: An Informed Introduction to Biofuels.* Zed Books, 2010.

■ ■

BIRTH CONTROL, GOVERNMENT COVERAGE OF

Under President Obama's signature health care reform bill, the Patient Protection and Affordable Care Act of 2010 (PPACA, or "Obamacare"), health insurers are required to include contraception in their coverage. This mandate extends to employers that provide health insurance to their employees. Although the government allowed a religious exemption, this applies only to churches themselves, and not to affiliated organizations such as schools and hospitals. A proposed amendment that would have allowed employers to refuse contraception coverage if it "violated their religious or moral beliefs" was voted down in the US Senate. Opponents of the bill argue that, without this amendment, it infringes upon religious liberty and constitutes an overreach of government. Proponents of the bill, however, see access to contraception as essential to women's health. These two opposing views—one that sees contraception as a moral issue, and the other that sees it as a medical issue—are at the center of this debate.

PROS

Employers do not have the right to impose their religious beliefs on those that they employ. If employers are allowed to let their religious beliefs determine the health care options of their employees, a dangerous precedent is set. For example, some Jehovah's Witnesses object to blood transfusions, Scientologists oppose psychiatric treatment, and Christian Scientists tend to eschew all conventional medicine. If we allow some religious organizations to refuse their employees contraceptive coverage, we must then allow other religious organizations to remove any treatments they disapprove of from their health care coverage. To avoid this gross overreach of employers into the lives of their employees, we must completely separate the religious beliefs of the former from the medical decisions of the latter.

Birth control pills are a health care necessity. They have a wide range of medical uses, such as correcting hormonal imbalances, reducing the risk of certain cancers, and controlling or eliminating painful periods. In addition, pregnancy can be life threatening and therefore preventing it is essential to the health of many women. The nonpartisan Institute of Medicine recommended that birth control be covered as it is necessary "to ensure women's health and well-being."

CONS

Religious organizations are not prohibiting their employees from using contraception; they are merely saying that they should not be forced to pay for it through their health coverage. Employees will still be able to access whatever contraception they desire by paying for it privately. Furthermore, it is misguided to equate the issue of contraception with other medical treatments such as blood transfusions. Contraception is a lifestyle decision, not a medical necessity; therefore it should be an out-of-pocket expense, rather than one paid for by the employer. Instead of mandating that employers cover contraception, the government should focus on making contraception widely available for any individuals who wish to purchase it.

Most women use birth control for the purpose its name suggests: to have sexual intercourse without pregnancy. This is not a medical necessity, but a personal lifestyle decision. For those who have purely medical issues, specific medication based on the birth control pill could be made. However, for the vast majority of users, birth control does not align with the purpose of health insurance, which is to protect against illness and injury.

PROS

Opposition to the inclusion of contraception in health coverage is fundamentally sexist and connected to a broader "war on women." There is no drive by politicians or religious organizations to govern or limit the health care decisions of men. In fact, medications that improve male sexual health, such as Viagra, are encouraged by the Catholic Church and included in their health care coverage.

Simply because women work for a religious organization does not mean they lose the rights provided to the employees of nonreligious organizations and companies. If an employer has a religious opposition to contraception, this should influence their own personal decisions regarding birth control – it should not influence the birth control decisions of their employees. Religious freedom does not mean imposing your beliefs on others. Furthermore, the Patient Protection and Affordable Care Act already includes exemptions for most religious organizations, requiring their insurers to provide birth control at no additional cost to the institution.

Birth control is expensive, and expecting all women to purchase it on their own disproportionately affects low-income women. A 2010 survey found that more than a third of female voters have struggled to afford prescription birth control at some point in their lives, and as a result, they have used birth control inconsistently. Providing birth control actually helps insurers because its costs are lower than those for prenatal care or an unwanted child's medical bills.

CONS

Allowing employers and insurers to choose what to cover has nothing to do with sexism; male sterilization is also opposed by many religious organizations. Insurers cover other prescriptions, such as Viagra, because of market demand. No government statute forces them to do so. Creating one in this case sets a terrible precedent, allowing private entities to be forced into providing goods or services in the interest of fairness.

Religious organizations should not have to pay for any services that conflict with their religious beliefs; forcing them to do so infringes on their religious freedom. The current religious exemption is meaningless insofar as religious institutions that provide health care insurance will still be indirectly paying for birth control. A government mandate that they do this is a clear violation of both the free exercise and establishment clauses of the First Amendment.

The cost of birth control is determined by the free market and largely irrelevant given the greater rights debate. Many products of convenience are expensive, yet there is no expectation that anyone must provide them. Politicians should not be the ones determining what is or is not profitable, and have no right to impose their decisions on individuals and businesses in the private market.

Sample Motions:

This House would mandate that insurance companies cover birth control.

This House believes that requiring employers to provide insurance that covers contraception is unjust.

Web Links:

- American Medical Association Journal of Ethics. <http://virtualmentor.ama-assn.org/2012/02/msoc1-1202.html> Argument for the creation of a male birth control pill.
- New York Times. <http://www.nytimes.com/2012/02/17/us/politics/birth-control-coverage-rule-debated-at-house-hearing .html?_r=0> Article about congressional debates on President Obama's birth control plan.
- Planned Parenthood Action. <http://www.plannedparenthoodaction.org/issues/birth-control/facts-birth-control-coverage -women/> Facts on birth control coverage for women.
- Post and Courier. <http://www.postandcourier.com/article/20121005/PC16/121009572> Study shows that free birth control reduces abortions and teen births.

Further Reading:

Engelman, Peter C. *A History of the Birth Control Movement in America*. Praeger, 2011.

Feldt, Gloria. *The War on Choice: The Right-Wing Attack on Women's Rights and How to Fight Back*. Bantam, 2004.

Haussman, Melissa. *Reproductive Rights and the State*. Praeger, 2013.

■ ■

CAMPAIGN FINANCE

For years, we have debated the concept of "corporate personhood": whether or not corporations deserve the same rights and privileges as individuals. The debate is particularly heated in the context of political campaigns, where corporations and unions can exercise a great deal of influence because of their ability to make large monetary contributions to candidates. In 2010, the Supreme Court ruled that, due to free-speech protections, corporations and unions had the constitutional right to spend unlimited amounts in elections. Consequently, during the 2012 elections, outside organizations—primarily corporations and unions—spent approximately $1 billion to influence the race, including $528 million on the presidential race alone. There are two main questions: Should corporations have the right to endorse and campaign for particular candidates; and should corporations be allowed to finance politicians' campaigns? Those in favor of giving corporations these rights claim that political speech should not be suppressed just because it comes from a corporate body; those opposed to giving corporations these rights maintain that profit-making entities should not have the same ability to influence governance as do individual citizens.

PROS

Because corporations have such immense financial resources, they have great potential to swing elections through multimillion dollar contributions or by financing sweeping ad campaigns. Allowing corporate entities to become more politically important than individual citizens is destructive to democracy, overwhelming the voices of individual citizens or candidates and making far less likely the election of candidates opposed to narrow corporate interests. Elections should not be controlled by wealthy, profit-motivated groups.

Corporations are artificial entities that are organized solely for the purpose of making a profit. They are created to serve the economic interests of their managers and shareholders—if they cease to be useful, we can dissolve them. Thus, unlike humans, they possess no inherent worth; accordingly, we have no compelling reason to give them any rights or privileges.

The free marketplace of ideas is predicated on the concept that ideas should be debated and discussed by equals. Because corporations exist for specific purposes and because they have so much economic and political clout, they cannot be considered to have the same influence as an individual—in fact, they have considerably more. However, we do recognize that corporations' agendas should not have the same weight as the opinion of an individual voter—evidenced by the fact that no country allows corporations to vote or run for office.

The more expensive campaigns become, the more likely third or independent party candidates are to be discouraged from running for office. During the 2012 elections, each presidential candidate raised around $1 billion, with

CONS

Some individuals and groups are always going to have more resources than others. Celebrities and the media both have a great deal of influence on elections, but we do not prevent them from endorsing candidates. Indeed, corporations arguably hold a much wider range of views than celebrities and journalists, who are often left-leaning. And, lots of people own stock in corporations or are members of unions, so, if anything, their voices are made stronger when corporations are given more rights.

Corporations should be legally considered as persons. They are made up of groups of individuals, and, like individuals, they wish to have their interests represented in government. A corporation consists entirely of human beings, thus restricting corporate speech restricts individuals' speech—a basic human right.

Restrictions on corporate speech or financing are tantamount to censorship, preventing legitimate ideas or viewpoints to be expressed. To deny corporations the ability to present their positions interferes with the marketplace and free exchange of ideas. All ideas possess inherent value, regardless of their source.

Forbidding corporations to donate to election campaigns harms all candidates, not just those from the major parties. In fact, independent or third-party candidates can benefit immensely from corporate donations, since total spending on all candidates reaching $6 billion; 2012 was the most expensive election ever, by a margin of over $700 million. The more corporations are allowed to contribute, the more running for office will cost, creating a larger barrier to entry for less popular or less well-known candidates.

lesser-known candidates may have a harder time initially getting donations to fund their campaigns.

Sample Motions:

This House would forbid corporations from donating to political campaigns.

This House opposes restrictions on corporate donations to political campaigns.

This House believes in a corporation's right to endorse and campaign for political candidates.

Web Links:

- Campaign Finance Reform. <http://www.pbs.org/now/classroom/ campaignfinance.html> Lesson plan on campaign finance reform; contains a variety of links to useful documents and sources.
- Corporations Aren't People. <http://www.npr.org/templates/ story/story.php?storyId=112714052> Article arguing that corporations are morally distinct from individuals.
- Supreme Court: Campaign-Finance Limits Violate Free Speech. <http://www.csmonitor.com/USA/Justice/2010/0121/Supreme-Court-Campaign-finance-limits-violate-free-speech> Article on the Supreme Court's 2010 decision to allow corporate political speech during and near elections.
- 2012 Election Spending Will Reach $6 billion. <http://www.opensecrets.org/news/2012/10/2012-election-spending-will-reach-6.html> Article on spending during the 2012 elections.

Further Reading:

Clements, Jeffrey D. *Corporations Are Not People.* Berrett-Koehler, 2012.

Kallen, Thomas P. *Campaign Finance: Background, Regulation and Reform.* Nova Science, 2009.

Samples, John. *The Fallacy of Campaign Finance Reform.* University of Chicago Press, 2006.

Smith, Rodney A. *Money, Finance & Elections: How Campaign Finance Reform Subverts American Democracy.* Louisiana State University Press, 2006.

Youn, Monica. *Money, Politics, and the Constitution: Beyond Citizens United.* Century Foundation, 2011.

■ ■

CAPITAL PUNISHMENT

According to Amnesty International, more than two-thirds of the world's nations have abolished the death penalty in law or practice. The United States still has and imposes the death penalty; under the Constitution, each state can formulate its own policy. Thirty-two of the 50 states have laws that allow the imposition of the death penalty. Capital punishment has always been controversial, but it has become more so since advances in forensics have resulted in the release of more than 100 individuals from death row. Moreover, evidence has come to light that some individuals may have been executed for crimes they did not commit.

PROS

The principle of capital punishment is that certain crimes deserve nothing less than death as a just, proportionate,

CONS

Execution is, in simplest terms, state-sanctioned killing. It devalues the respect we place on human life. How can we and effective response. The problems associated with the death penalty are concerned with its implementation rather than its principle. Murderers forgo their rights as humans the moment they take away the rights of another human. By wielding such a powerful punishment as the response to murder, society is affirming the value that is placed on the right to life of the innocent person. Many more innocent people have been killed by released, paroled, or escaped murderers than innocent people executed.

Capital punishment is 100% effective as a deterrent to the criminal being executed; that killer cannot commit any more crimes. As a deterrent to others, it depends on how often the death penalty is applied. In the US, where less than 1% of murderers are executed, it is difficult to assess the true effect of deterrence. But a 1985 study (Stephen K. Layson, University of North Carolina) showed that one execution deterred 18 murders.

If and when discrimination occurs, it should be corrected. Consistent application of the death penalty against murderers of all races would abolish the idea that it can be a racist tool. Make the death penalty mandatory in all capital cases.

Opponents of the death penalty prefer to ignore the fact that they themselves are responsible for its high costs by filing a never-ending succession of appeals. Prisons in many countries are overcrowded and underfunded. This problem is made worse by life sentences or delayed death sentences for murderers. Why should the taxpayer bear the cost of supporting a murderer for an entire lifetime?

Different countries and societies can have different attitudes toward the justifiability of executing mentally incompetent or teenaged murderers. If society opposes such executions, then implementation of the death penalty in these cases is a problem. For opponents to seize on such cases is to cloud the issue; this is not an argument against the principle.

Some criminals are beyond rehabilitation. Perhaps capital punishment should be reserved for serial killers, terrorists, murderers of policemen, and so on.

say that killing is wrong if we sanction killing criminals? More important is the proven risk of executing innocent people. The Death Penalty Information Center reports that since 1973, over 140 individuals sentenced to death were exonerated. They had their conviction overturned *and* were acquitted at retrial or all charges were dropped; or they were given an absolute pardon by the governor based on new evidence of innocence. These people could have been wrongly executed.

High execution rates do not deter crimes. Murder rates have declined in every region in the US except in the South, where executions are most prevalent. According to the 2011 FBI Uniform Crime Report, the South had the highest murder rate in the US, yet accounted for 80% of executions. The Northeast, which has less than 1% of all executions has the lowest murder rate.

Implementation of the death penalty, particularly in the US, may be negatively influenced by racial and gender bias. Studies consistently show that those who kill white victims are more likely to receive the death penalty than those who murder blacks. Nearly 90% of those executed were convicted of killing whites, despite the fact that nonwhites make up more than 50% of all murder victims. There is also overwhelming evidence that the death penalty is used against men and not women.

Capital punishment costs more than life without parole as state studies in the US have shown. For example, a study found that the death penalty costs North Carolina $2.16 million per execution over the costs of a nondeath penalty system imposing a maximum sentence of imprisonment for life. A 2011 study of executions in California revealed that, based on the 13 executions between 1976 and 2011, each execution cost the state more than $300 million.

Defendants who are mentally incompetent will often answer "Yes" to questions in the desire to please others. This can lead to false confessions. Over 30 mentally retarded people have been executed in the US since 1976.

By executing criminals you are ruling out the possibility of rehabilitation. You have to consider that they may repent of their crime, serve a sentence as punishment, and emerge as useful members of society.

Sample Motions:

This House supports the death penalty.

This House would take an eye for an eye, a tooth for a tooth, and a life for a life.

Web Links:

- Amnesty International. <http://www.amnesty.org/en/death-penalty> Takes an anti–death penalty stance and presents facts and figures as well as discusses current developments pertaining to the issue.
- Death Penalty Information Center. <http://www.deathpenaltyinfo.org/documents/FactSheet.pdf> Fact sheet on the death penalty in the US updated annually.
- Derechos Human Rights. <http://www.derechos.org/dp/> Links to hundreds of sites addressing all aspects of the death penalty, both pro and con.
- Pro-Death Penalty. <http://www.prodeathpenalty.com> Offers information from a pro–death penalty point of view; also contains good statistical information.

Further Reading:

Bedaue, Hugo Adam, and Paul G. Cassell, eds. Debating the Death Penalty: Should America Have Capital Punishment? The Experts on Both Sides Make Their Case. Oxford University Press, 2005.

Garland, David. Peculiar Institution: America's Death Penalty in an Age of Abolition. Belknap Press of Harvard University Press, 2010.

Ives, Susan. Capital Ideas: 150 Classic Writers on the Death Penalty, From the Code of Hammurabi to Clarence Darrow. CreateSpace, 2009.

Melusky, Joseph A. and Keith A. Pesto. Capital Punishment. Greenwood, 2011.

■ ■

CENSORSHIP OF THE ARTS

While all modern democracies value free expression, freedom of speech is never absolute. The restrictions a nation puts on speech are a product of its experience and culture. The United States views free speech as the cornerstone of American civil liberties and has few restrictions on expression. Nevertheless, conservatives have called for some type of censorship of art that they find morally offensive. Many people are also disturbed by studies that show a correlation between watching violent films and television shows and violent behavior.

PROS

An individual's rights end when they impinge on the safety and rights of others. By enacting laws against incitement to racial hatred and similar hate speech, we acknowledge that freedom of expression should have limits. Art should be subject to the same restrictions as any other form of expression. By making an exception for art, we would be creating a legal loophole for content such as hate speech, which could seek protection on the grounds that it was a form of art.

Certain types of content (e.g., sexual content) are unsuitable for children despite its artistic merits. We should be able to develop a system of censorship, based on age, that protects our children.

CONS

Civil rights should not be curtailed in the absence of a clear and present danger to the safety of others. Furthermore, as long as no illegal acts were committed in the creative process, the public should have a choice in deciding whether to view the resulting content. Arguments about child pornography displayed as art are irrelevant because child pornography is illegal.

An age-rated system is a very blunt tool. It does not take into account differing levels of education or maturity. Censorship also deprives parents of the right to raise their children as they see fit. Adults have the right to vote, bear arms, and die for their country. Why should they be deprived of the ability to decide what they or their children see? Finally, we have to remember that people are not forced to view art; they don't have to look at something they think is offensive.

Censorship may actually help artists. The general public is far more likely to support erotic art if it knows that children won't see it!

Censorship is far more likely to hurt the arts. If the government labels art as unsuitable for children, the general public is not going to want to fund it.

Many forms of modern art push the boundaries of what is acceptable or aim for the lowest level of taste. This type of content is unacceptable, and governments should have the right to ban it.

Content that we consider acceptable today would have been regarded as taboo 50 years ago. If a novel or controversial piece of art is out of touch with society, society will reject it.

Excessive sex and violence in the media lead to similar behavior in viewers. This alone should justify censorship.

The correlation between watching violence and committing violent crimes is still not established. These studies are not exhaustive, and often are funded by special interest groups. We must also realize that correlation is different from causation. An alternative interpretation is that people with violent tendencies are more likely to be connoisseurs of violent art. Even if we believe that some people are likely to be corrupted, why should all of society be penalized? There are far better ways of reducing the crime rate, with far less cost in civil liberties, than censorship.

Even if some individuals manage to circumvent censorship laws, government has sent an important message about what society considers acceptable. The role of the state in setting social standards should not be underestimated, and censorship (be it through bans or minimum age requirements) is an important tool in this process.

Censorship is ultimately not feasible. Try censoring art on the Internet, for example! In addition, censoring art merely sends it underground and might glamorize the prohibited artwork. It is far better to display it so that people can judge for themselves.

Sample Motions:

This House supports censorship of the arts.

This House believes that you are what you see.

Web Links:

- American Civil Liberties Union. <http://www.aclu.org/free-speech/censorship> A comprehensive overview of censorship in America from an anticensorship perspective.
- Ockerbloom, John Mark. <http://digital.library.upenn.edu/books/banned-books.html> Online exhibit discussing books that have been the object of censorship and censorship attempts.
- PBS. <http://www.pbs.org/wgbh/cultureshock/> A companion site to a PBS series on art, cultural values, and freedom of expression.

Further Reading:

Freedman, Leonard. *The Offensive Art: Political Satire and Its Censorship Around the World from Beerbohm to Borat.* Praeger, 2008.

Howells, Richard, Andrea Deciu Ritivoi, and Judith Schachter, eds. *Outrage: Art, Controversy, and Society.* Palgrave Macmillan, 2012.

Tepper, Steven J. *Not Here, Not Now, Not That!* University of Chicago Press, 2011.

■ ■

CHILD LABOR

In the past, activists have urged consumers to boycott companies that use child labor to produce goods. Is this response enough? Should the international community impose sanctions against governments that permit child labor? Ultimately the issue of using child labor is more a question of solving poverty than a simple moral or emotional issue. Any proposed sanctions would need to address several considerations—both general (Who would impose sanctions? How and to what extent would they be enforced?) and questions particular to this topic (What age is a "child"? Is child labor inherently an issue or is the debate really about minimum labor standards for all employees and employers?).

PROS

Governments have a duty to uphold human dignity. All people have the right to the benefits gained from education, a good quality of life, and independent income. Child labor destroys the future of the young and must be stopped.

Sanctions provide the only means of forcing countries to take action. Consumer pressure is too weak to do so. While people say they are willing to pay more for products manufactured in humane conditions, very few put this into daily practice.

Pressure on transnational companies is not enough. Not all child labor is in sweatshops for multinationals in poor countries. Children also work on family farms and as prostitutes. Some countries also force children into their armies.

Ending child labor will allow the young a greater chance to get an education and to develop fully both physically and socially, thus benefiting a nation's human resources and encouraging economic growth. The large number of underemployed adults in most developing countries can replace children. Often these will be the parents of current child workers, so there will be little or no overall effect on family income.

The international community was able to place human rights over the cause of free trade in the cases of South Africa and Burma—so why not here?

This is an argument for a targeted and more sophisticated use of sanctions, not against them in any form. Sometimes free market economics is simply an excuse for denying responsibility.

CONS

While sanctions are effective for enforcing political and legal standards, they are less effective in dealing with social and economic ones. The world community cannot force an impoverished state to maintain Western standards of education and labor laws, which did not exist when the West industrialized.

Consumer power has proved highly effective in forcing transnational companies to institute ethical practices. Boycotts of one producer have led others to change their practices out of fear of negative publicity and possible boycotts. The market takes care of the problem itself.

Imposing sanctions on states is unfair because they are not wholly responsible for the actions of their citizens. Should we impose sanctions on the United States because it has illegal sweatshops?

The vision of all former child laborers leaving work for school is utopian. Evidence shows that many either cannot afford to pay school tuition or continue to work while attending school. In fact, many transnational companies have now set up after-work schools within the very factories that activists criticize.

Placing sanctions on some companies will merely push child labor underground. Moving poor children who have to work into unregulated and criminal areas of the economy will only worsen the situation.

Sanctions harm the poorest in society. Companies will simply move to areas that do not have restrictions on child labor. Past experience has shown that government interference with the market does more harm than good.

Sample Motions:
> This House believes that children should be free.
> This House would end child labor.
> This House would put sanctions on states using child labor.

Web Links:
- Budhwani, Nadir N. et al. <http://www.tc.umn.edu/~budh0004/childlaborarticle.pdf> A discussion of child labor from the perspective of human resource development; argues that child labor must be addressed differently in different areas and that an outright ban is inappropriate.
- Child Labor Public Education Project. <http://www.continuetolearn.uiowa.edu/laborctr/child_labor/about/what_is_child_labor.html> A history of child labor in the United States and its relation to world issues.
- UNICEF. "Child Labour: The Challenge." <http://www.childinfo.org/labour_challenge.html> Research and analysis on child labor, such as its trade-off with education.
- International Labour Organization. "International Programme on the Elimination of Child Labour (IPEC): What Is Child Labour." <http://www.ilo.org/ipec/facts/lang--en/index.htm> Information on child labor worldwide from the United Nations agency ILO.
- Child Labor Coalition. <http://www.stopchildlabor.org> Information on child labor around the world and campaigns to end it.
- DeGregori, Thomas. <http://www.cato.org/pub_display.php?pub_id=3621> Argues that child labor is sometimes necessary and that we should be more nuanced in our attempts to rid the world of it.
- International Labour Organization. <http://www.ilo.org/ipec/lang--en/index.htm> Statistics and information on the International Programme on the Elimination of Child Labour.

Further Reading:
> Bagchi, Subrata Sankar. *Child Labor and the Urban Third World.* University Press of America, 2010.
> Kaushal, Lata. *Child Labour & Human Rights: A Social Dimension.* MD Publications, 2009.
> Switala, Andre. *Essays in the Economics of Education and Child Labor.* ProQuest, 2011.

..

CHILD SOLDIERS, PROSECUTION OF FOR WAR CRIMES

The United Nations defines child soldiers as any members of a militia under the age of 18. However, questions about child soldiers generally focus on soldiers under the age of 15 and sometimes as young as 7 years. Child soldiers offer advantages to adult military or paramilitary members—they are nimble, easily intimidated into obeying orders, impressionable, and considered more dispensable. And enemy troops are often hesitant to fire at minors. Some child soldiers, most notably Omar Khadr, a Taliban child soldier detained by the US military, have been put on trial for war crimes. The International Criminal Court currently holds 18 as the age of criminal accountability, while tribunals in Sierra Leone have prosecuted children as young as 15. Critics argue that child soldiers are victims who are not responsible for their actions and should be cared for, not prosecuted.

PROS

Children are not the only ones forcibly conscripted, adult soldiers who are drafted or otherwise compelled to serve are still held accountable for their actions. Soldiers may fight against their will, but they are still personally responsible for refusing to commit war crimes.

"Child soldiers" can be as old as 17, and even younger teens are capable of knowing right from wrong. Child

CONS

Child soldiers are the victims, not the criminals. Child soldiers are typically forced into combat. A person should not be held accountable for an action he did not willingly commit. Children are easily manipulated and intimidated and can thus be compelled to commit atrocities they do not wish to.

Children's minds are malleable; the adults surrounding child soldiers tell them or force them to commit atrocities.

PROS

soldiers are typically at least 10, usually 13 or 14, years old; though most adolescents experience some ethical confusion, they know that inflicting unnecessary pain on others is wrong. We cannot excuse everyone who has lived in a hostile environment from prosecution; if we did, then we would have to excuse wifebeaters who came from bad homes or rapists who were molested as children. Poor learning environments are unfortunate, but ultimately all individuals are responsible for their own actions.

Refraining from prosecuting child soldiers only increases the incentive to use them. Warlords will prefer using "soldiers" who cannot be held accountable for their actions over those who can. This increases a warlord's incentive to delegate the most brutal and traumatic tasks to child soldiers.

Child soldiers are victims, but they are still dangerous and must be apprehended. A grenade is no less deadly when thrown by a minor. Child soldiers may be exempt from the harshest punishments, but they cannot simply be released. Omar Khadr, for example, was a teenage child soldier for the Taliban in Afghanistan until he was captured and transferred to Guantanamo Bay by US soldiers. While Khadr has certainly been misused, he is nevertheless dangerous outside prison, as well as useful to the US for his knowledge of the Taliban. The US cannot detain Khadr in rehabilitation indefinitely, and it should not be obligated to release Khadr—which would allow him to continue fighting for the Taliban.

CONS

Certainly the children get no moral guidance. These children cannot be expected to distinguish right from wrong as we could expect an adult to. Children learn morality from their surroundings and from how they are treated and see how others are treated; child soldiers cannot learn compassion or respect for life in the environment of a military camp. In the US legal system, defendants can plead insanity—defined as an inability to distinguish right from wrong as society defines it. Such defendants are placed in mental institutions rather than prison. Child soldiers should be considered legally insane and should be rehabilitated, not punished.

Soldiers are only prosecuted for war crimes after they are captured and incapable of fighting anyway, so warlords are not particularly concerned with what happens to them. Whether a child is being rehabilitated or imprisoned makes no tactical difference to his military superior; thus, how soldiers are treated after capture is unlikely to affect military strategy and the use of child soldiers.

Combatant troops should apprehend child soldiers, but children should not be prosecuted. Just as the mentally ill can be institutionalized indefinitely until they are again able to function in society, child soldiers should be held in rehabilitation programs until they are able to reenter society and not present a threat to others. Prosecuting a child for actions he is not really responsible for merely increases the anger and confusion his ordeal has created, thereby retarding the rehabilitation process.

Sample Motions:

This House holds all people responsible for their actions.

This House demonstrates compassion toward children.

This House will prosecute child soldiers for war crimes.

Web Links:

- Bakker, Christine. "Prosecuting International Crimes Against Children: The Legal Framework." <http://www.unicef-irc.org/publications/pdf/iwp_2010_13.pdf> Explores states' obligations to prosecute international criminals, focusing on children in particular.
- Grossman, Nienke. "Rehabilitation or Revenge: Prosecuting Child Soldiers for Human Rights Violations." <http://papers.ssrn.com/sol3/papers.cfm?abstract_id=1328982> A paper arguing that child soldiers should face rehabilitation as victims rather than prosecuted as perpetrators.
- Human Rights First. "The Case for Omar Ahmed Khadr, Canada." <http://www.humanrightsfirst.org/our-work/law-and-security/military-commissions/cases/omar-ahmed-khadr/> Explains the ordeal of Omar Khadr, a child soldier detained by US forces at Guantanamo Bay.

Further Reading:

Drumbl, Mark A. *Reimagining Child Soldiers in International Law and Policy.* Oxford University Press, 2012.

Rosen, David M. *Child Soldiers.* ABC-CLIO, 2012.

■ ■

CHINA: PARTNER OR ADVERSARY?

As an emerging economic superpower, and the most populous nation on Earth, China is an integral player on the international stage. However, China's communist system of government and record of human rights abuses make diplomatic relations with the country fraught with distrust and uncertainty. Despite these diplomatic tensions, the United States and China are increasingly economically bound to one another: US–China trade rose from $2 billion in 1979 to approximately $459 billion in 2010. This economic relationship is blighted by ongoing allegations of Chinese currency manipulation and impropriety with regard to trade. The question of whether or not China poses a threat to the United States was recurrent during the 2012 US presidential race. Though President Barack Obama remained publicly undecided on the issue, labeling China "an adversary, and also a potential partner," the administration announced that it would expand its missile-defense shield in the Asia Pacific, in part due to concerns over China's growing military capabilities. With China set to overtake the US as the largest economy in the world by approximately 2016 — according to the International Monetary Fund — this is one of the most pressing issues facing US foreign policy experts.

PROS

China does not follow rules when it comes to international trade; this actively hurts the US economy. The Chinese government manipulates its currency by endlessly printing new currency, which it then uses to buy large amounts of US dollars. China hoards these dollars in vast reserves, using them to keep its own currency, the yuan, artificially low. By purposefully weakening the yuan, China cheapens the price of its exports, unfairly undercutting international competitors. This illegal manipulation drives US companies out of business, leading to unemployment and a weaker US economy. Furthermore, China consistently flouts international copyright laws. The International Intellectual Property Alliance conservatively estimates that this costs US businesses $3.7 billion in lost sales. Until China shows that it can respect the international trade laws that other nations obey, the United States cannot trust it as an ally.

Economic engagement with China means directly funding the Chinese military, which poses a growing threat. The People's Liberation Army, the military arm of the Communist Party of China, has approximately three million members, making it the largest military force in the world. China's military spending has risen by approximately

CONS

China is neither the only currency manipulator nor the worst currency manipulator. US allies such as Israel and Denmark also manipulate their currencies, while both Switzerland and Japan are, arguably, worse currency manipulators than China. In addition, the argument that China is a currency manipulator is a dated one; China has made significant improvements and allowed the yuan to rise substantially in recent years. Similarly, China is rapidly improving its copyright laws, having released a range of new proposals in the summer of 2012. It is crucial to understand that the Chinese economy has expanded on an unprecedented scale, which has transformed an undeveloped nation into a global superpower in just a matter of decades. While it has been tough for government legislation to keep pace with this change, China has demonstrated that it is committed to maintaining good trade relations with other countries and making improvements in areas that have been lacking.

Concerns over China's military growth are nothing more than hypocrisy and hysteria. China currently spends less than a quarter of what the US does on military, despite having four times the population. Media coverage of China's military growth is consistently alarmist; a 2011 *New York Times* article reported a "double-digit

10% every year for the past 15 years, with the Chinese government vastly underreporting the actual amount that it spends on its military. In 2012, China launched a new wave of military modernization, updating both the technology and the hardware of its armed forces. A 2011 report by the International Institute for Strategic Studies revealed that, assuming that recent trends in Chinese military spending continue, China will have a military equal to that of the United States within 15 to 20 years. As an authoritarian regime with a bloody history of human rights abuses, this poses a danger to both the region and the world at large.

China's economic hold over the US government constitutes one of the most serious threats to national security. China currently owns almost $1 trillion of US government debt, giving it an enormous amount of leverage over the US — if China were to recall this debt, the US economy would crash. As Hilary Clinton contended, dependence on Chinese investments is leading to "a slow erosion of our own economic sovereignty." Chinese commentators regularly suggest using these debt holdings as a tool to pressure the US on policies regarding Taiwan, an island over which China controversially claims sovereignty. In August 2011, a senior editor at *People's Daily* — the Communist Party of China's daily newspaper — wrote "now is the time for China to use its 'financial weapon' to teach the US a lesson if it moves forward [with arms sales to Taiwan]." With the US government deficit now exceeding $1 trillion, and its credit rating downgraded in 2011, China is in an alarmingly strong position when it comes to using debt to influence US policy.

Recent cyber-attacks by China on the US government confirm that China is not to be trusted. There is overwhelming evidence that a secret Chinese military unit, People's Liberation Army Unit 61398, has undertaken Web-based attacks on US corporations for several years, in addition to stealing vast amounts of data directly from the US government. This unit is under the direct command of the highest levels of the Chinese military; as such, the Chinese government should be held responsible for this systematic espionage against the United States. If the Chinese military were caught infiltrating US territory or airspace in order to carry out espionage, it would be deemed a hostile nation; with the Internet now essential to state functioning, cyber-espionage should be treated as seriously as conventional espionage.

increase" in Chinese military spending to refer to just an 11% increase — not so much more than the rate of inflation or spending increases in other sectors. As the largest country in the world, it is completely reasonable that China would want large and well-equipped armed forces. China is not an aggressive nation and has not been at war since a brief border war fought with Vietnam in 1979, which lasted just 28 days. In contrast, US military forces have been engaged in numerous wars, invading four foreign nations since 1950. It would be far more reasonable for China to worry about the US as posing a military threat, than vice versa.

China holds just a small fraction of the total US government debt; the majority is held by large investment banks such as JP Morgan and Goldman Sachs. With a recent history of gross financial mismanagement, these debt holders pose a much greater threat to US economic security. China's government debt holdings would be a national security risk only if China were able to use them to dictate US policy, which it is not able to do. The United States has numerous other sources of credit; were China to threaten the United States with this debt, money could be borrowed from elsewhere. The reality is that China has never attempted to dictate US policy or harm the US economy. The Chinese economy relies on exporting to the United States, which means that harming the US economy would be self-destructive for China. The two economies are too mutually dependent for China to attempt to harm the United States. A report by the Pentagon agreed, saying: "China attempting to use US Treasury securities as a coercive tool would have a limited effect and likely would do more harm to China than to the US."

The claim that China has engaged in cyber-attacks is based on one report by a private security company — it is a flimsy claim. Cyber-attacks are notoriously difficult to trace, often being carried out internationally and anonymously. Numerous cyber-security experts have come forward to confirm that it is virtually impossible to know for certain where the attacks in question originated. Furthermore, this situation is not unusual — all state governments and large companies fall victim to cyber-attacks. In fact, China is one of the largest targets, with a considerable number of these attacks originating from the US. As a spokesman from the Chinese defense ministry said: "we have never used this as a reason to accuse the United States." The vast majority of cyber-attacks against governments are initiated by individuals and nongovernment groups — these recent attacks seem no different.

Sample Motions:

Sample Motions:

This House would regard China as a global power.

This House thinks that China is merely a regional power.

This House believes that China poses a threat to international stability.

This House welcomes the rise of China.

Web Links:

- BBC News. <http://www.bbc.co.uk/news/world-asia-pacific-13761711> Article about China's military reach.
- Cato Institute. <http://www.cato.org/sites/cato.org/files/articles/dorn_bjwa_142.pdf> Information on the impact of debt on China–US relations.
- Congressional Research Service. <http://fpc.state.gov/documents/organization/155009.pdf> Brief on China–US trade issues.
- Foreign Affairs. <http://digitalcommons.law.umaryland.edu/cgi/viewcontent.cgi?article=2287&context=fac_pubs> Article questioning whether China's rise will lead to conflicts.
- New York Times. <http://topics.nytimes.com/top/reference/timestopics/subjects/c/currency/yuan/index.html> Links to articles about the yuan.
- Peterson Institute for International Economics. <http://www.iie.com/publications/pb/pb12-19.pdf> Policy brief on currency manipulation.
- Yahoo News. <http://news.yahoo.com/us-ready-strike-back-against-china-cyberattacks-225730552--finance.html> Article about possible American retaliation for Chinese cyber-attacks.

Further Reading:

Foot, Rosemary, and Andrew Walter. *China, the United States, and Global Order.* Cambridge University Press, 2010.

Friedberg, Aaron. *A Contest for Supremacy: China, America, and the Struggle for Mastery in Asia.* Norton, 2012.

Shambaugh, David. *Tangled Titans: The United States and China.* Rowman and Littlefield, 2012.

· ·

CIVIL DISOBEDIENCE

Civil disobedience is the deliberate disobeying of a law to advance a moral principle or change government policy. Those who practice civil disobedience are willing to accept the consequences of their lawbreaking as a means of furthering their cause. Henry David Thoreau first articulated the tenets of civil disobedience in an 1849 essay, "On the Duty of Civil Disobedience." He argued that when conscience and law do not coincide, individuals have the obligation to promote justice by disobeying the law. Civil disobedience was a major tactic in the women's suffrage movement, the campaign for the independence of India, the civil rights movement in the United States, and the abolition of apartheid in South Africa.

PROS

Elections do not give the people sufficient opportunity to express their will. In certain circumstances civil disobedience is a powerful method of making the will of the public heard. If a law is oppressive it cannot be opposed in principle by obeying it in practice. It must be broken.

Civil disobedience has a history of overcoming oppression and unpopular policies where all other methods have failed. For example, Mohandas Gandhi's civil

CONS

The "voice of the people" is heard in many ways. Elections take place regularly, and members of the public can write their local, state, or national representatives expressing their opinion. Legislators are there to represent and serve the people. Because citizens have many ways to express their views, civil disobedience is unnecessary. Protests can be made perfectly well without breaking the law.

Peaceful protest is quite possible in any society—to go further into actual lawbreaking is pointless. Civil disobedience can devolve into lawlessness. Indeed, it can disobedience was instrumental in winning liberty for India, and Martin Luther King's tactics won basic rights for African Americans in the United States. In these cases no other avenue was open to express grievances.

be counterproductive by associating a cause with terror and violence.

In actual fact, the conflict with the authority gives any protest its power and urgency and brings an issue to a wider audience. The women's suffrage movement in Britain and the civil rights movement in the United States are both examples of an eventually successful campaign that won by its confrontation with authority, where more sedate methods would simply not have succeeded.

Too often this "productive violence" is directed against innocent members of the public or against the police, often causing serious injuries. No cause is worth the sacrifice of innocent lives; protest must be peaceful or not at all.

Sample Motions:

This House supports civil disobedience.

This House believes the ends justify the means.

This House would break the law in a good cause.

Web Links:

- Brownlee, Kimberley. <http://plato.stanford.edu/entries/civil-disobedience/> Philosophical discussion of the arguments for and against civil disobedience.
- Cohen, Carl. "Seven Arguments Against Civil Disobedience." <http://carl-cohen.org/books/CivilDisobedience/chapter6.pdf> Chapter of a book discussing arguments against civil disobedience.
- Fiedler, Sergio. "The Right to Rebel: Social Movements and Civil Disobedience." <http://epress.lib.uts.edu.au/journals/index.php/mcs/article/view/1205/1309> Essay arguing that civil disobedience is a basic right.
- Suber, Peter. <http://www.earlham.edu/~peters/writing/civ-dis.htm> Responses to common arguments against civil disobedience.
- Thoreau, Henry David. <http://thoreau.eserver.org/civil.html> Annotated version of Thoreau's famous piece, *Resistance to Civil Government*.

Further Reading:

Lovell, Jarret. *Crimes of Dissent: Civil Disobedience, Criminal Justice and the Politics of Conscience.* NYU Press, 2009.

Singer, Peter. *Democracy and Disobedience.* Ashgate Publishing, 1994,

Thoreau, Henry David. *Resistance to Civil Government: On Civil Disobedience and Other Essays Annotated.* Warfield Press, 2010.

■ ■

CLIMATE CHANGE: REGULATIONS VS. MARKET MECHANISM IN DEALING WITH

Over the past 20 years most scientists and many politicians have come to believe that humankind is changing the world's climate. This is often called "global warming," and is blamed on the release of carbon gases into the air. This debate compares the two main ways that have been put forward for cutting carbon emissions: regulations and market mechanisms. Regulations would involve bringing in new government rules that companies and families have to follow. For example, regulations could set new standards for vehicle fuel economy or require companies and families to save energy by putting in green technologies, such as pollution filters, solar panels, more efficient heating systems, and low energy light bulbs. The other proposal is to put a price on carbon, so that it becomes expensive to release it into the air. This approach is called a market mechanism. Pricing carbon would give people and companies a strong reason to find ways of reducing their carbon emissions. There are two ways that a price could be put on carbon—a tax or a cap-and-trade system. A carbon tax would allow the government to charge people a sum of money for every ton of carbon they release into the air. A cap-and-trade system would set an overall limit on the amount of carbon that could be emitted each year. Companies would be given permits allowing them to release a certain amount of carbon into the air, and fined very heavily for exceeding their limit. Companies that could not reduce their emissions to the level allowed in their permit would have to buy permits in a carbon market. They would be buying from other companies that had successfully cut their emissions and so had spare permits to sell.

PROS

Market mechanisms put a cost on carbon emissions so that polluting becomes expensive. They will give a strong push to businesses and families to be more careful in their use of energy. Bringing in new technology to cut the amount of carbon their factories, vehicles, and homes put out will save them money. The more they cut emissions, the more they save (and the more profit companies will make).

The market will work better at a global level. Because each country generally sets its own regulations, pollution limits and vehicle fuel standards differ. This makes it difficult and expensive for international business to follow different regulations. And as increased regulation impacts trade and economic growth, individual countries (especially developing countries) may choose to set weak standards. Market methods are more likely to work across borders, linking every country into the same international system, as is already the case in global trade and finance. Developing states are more likely to accept a market system because they can profit from a carbon tax or from selling carbon permits.

Using the market will persuade people to choose greener ways of living. Regulations force people to do things against their will, which can be unfair and could make green ideas unpopular. Market mechanisms change the prices people pay but still allow them choices about how they live. A carbon tax or cap-and-trade system would raise the cost of electricity and gasoline, thus encouraging (rather than forcing) many people to change their lifestyle. They may choose to live closer to where they work or to their children's schools, take the bus or train rather than drive, vacation at home rather than abroad, or update their home heating system to one that uses less energy. Such changes will come quite quickly with market mechanisms, but regulations often take a long time to be

CONS

We already have regulations to cut carbon emissions, so we do not need market methods. After all, businesses' greed has led them to pour pollution into our air, so they are unlikely to stop unless the government makes them. There are good examples of successful regulation. California as well as some European governments have set standards for fuel efficiency and exhaust levels, successfully reducing the environmental impacts of vehicle fuels. We should aim to expand and tighten these existing regulations rather than take a gamble on something untested.

Using the market sounds good in theory but it will not work in practice. There are many different types of carbon emissions, and some damage the climate much more than others. Allowing for these differences in a market system is hard, but regulations can be more flexible, targeting the worst types of emissions with tougher rules. Moreover, significant polluters such as China and India have less open economies than those of most Western countries. Consequently, a market system would not work equally across the world. Unless we put off dealing with climate change until all economies work the same way, regulation is the only means to make an immediate difference.

Economists love the idea of market mechanisms but they do not understand ordinary people. Consumers are actually not very sensitive to increased energy prices. Even if energy prices go up, they still have to cook and to light and heat their homes. So they will grumble about it but pay more rather than cut the amount of energy they use. Similarly, if they need a car to go to work, they will not drive any less if fuel costs more. Instead they will cut back on other things, like vacations, clothes, or entertainment. Poor people with no spare money will end up suffering more than the rich do, whereas regulations will make everyone contribute to reducing emissions. In the long run, it might make sense to spend money making your house energy efficient or buying a more expensive but implemented and effective. While tough standards generally apply only to new buildings, cars, or products, most people make do with what they already own for many years. This means it might take more than a decade after new rules are adopted for emissions to drop significantly.

Market solutions can take advantage of the fact that the cost of reducing carbon emissions is not the same everywhere. Western cars, homes, and factories are often so efficient that reducing their carbon output by even a tiny amount would cost a huge sum of money. In contrast, the older technology in less developed countries is often much more polluting. Spending a little bit of money to update it would prevent a huge amount of carbon from being pumped out. Putting a price on carbon means that money will be spent where it has the greatest effect. This means we can tackle climate change more quickly and with less damage to the world economy than we can by using regulations. That market mechanisms are likely to move money from the rich world to the poor is a positive side effect of the system.

The European trading system has run into problems, but this is primarily because politicians have interfered to protect industries in their own countries. Such meddling is even more common with government regulations, which often change so quickly that business cannot plan properly for the future. The EU is already improving its carbon trading scheme, and we can learn to design a global system based on their experience. For example, a smaller number of permits can be issued, and auctioned off to the highest bidders rather than given for free to old and inefficient industries. On the other hand, we could choose to implement a carbon tax instead, thus reliably putting a cost on pollution and ensuring that emissions are cut.

We all have some responsibility for climate change. Our lifestyles result in the release of large amounts of carbon into the air. Unless ordinary people can be convinced to change their behavior, we will never be able to tackle climate change. It is thus fair to use market methods that raise the price of energy to achieve this goal. Ways can be found to ensure that no one suffers under this new system. For example, other taxes can be cut to compensate for a carbon tax. Furthermore, using regulations to deal with emissions raises the cost of energy and fuel. Producers pass the increased costs of regulation on to consumers, and we have to pay more one way or another.

Market systems are easy to understand and run efficiently because everyone acts out of self-interest. Regulation means government control, and that means plenty of

greener car, but the up-front cost of doing these things is too high for most people, even if they might recoup their initial investment in lower costs many years later. Governments will have to change the law if they want to make people to change their behavior.

Regulations are the best way to make every country play its part in tackling climate change. While rich countries are the ones that have pumped the most carbon into the atmosphere, market mechanisms will allow them to avoid their moral duty to make the most changes. A carbon market would allow them to buy a permit from a poorer country rather than change their own ways. In exchange, the developing country would not even have to actually reduce its own carbon output—it can merely promise not to increase it as much as it might have. Given the weak government and corruption in some developing countries, many people wonder how much some of these promises would be worth.

Instituting regulations is more reliable than trying to put a price on carbon emissions. The European carbon trading system has not worked well. The price for permits to release carbon into the air was extremely volatile before declining to such a low level that it is unlikely to have any impact on companies' behavior. Regulations better ensure that change takes place because they clearly specify the actions businesses must take. This allows companies to plan properly and encourages research and development of green technologies.

Putting a price on carbon unfairly punishes ordinary families. Making people pay more to heat their homes, cook meals, drive their cars, and so on will push many into poverty. We already pay high taxes, and this is just another way politicians have found to get their hands into our wallets. By contrast, big business makes plenty of profit and can afford to spend some of it on meeting new emissions regulations.

Regulations are the best way to cut carbon emissions because, unlike market methods, they can be introduced with public support. Opinion polls show that people bureaucracy and red tape. A huge, complicated, costly system will be created to manage any new emission rules and standards. This not only raises taxes but also hurts the economy as business struggles to cope with the regulations. And because governments are so bad at regulation, the chances are that the system will fail to cut emissions significantly. Companies may cheat on the rules, realizing correctly that they are unlikely to get caught, and even if they are, any fines will probably be smaller than the cost of obeying the regulations.

understand and back regulations like fuel efficiency rules, home energy standards, and so on. By contrast, carbon taxes are very unpopular because people do not trust the politicians who want to introduce them. Because cap-and-trade systems are so difficult to explain to ordinary consumers, the public will not back them. Moreover, running an international cap-and-trade system would require a big bureaucracy to enforce the emissions limits and prevent cheating. But unlike a system of national regulations, a cap-and-trade bureaucracy would be an international body, and thus be seen as a threat to our national independence.

Sample Motions:

This House believes that market methods are better than regulations in cutting carbon emissions.

This House believes the price is right.

This House believes in market solutions to the problem of climate change.

This House would rather put its faith in the market than in bureaucrats.

Web Links:

- BBC News. <http://news.bbc.co.uk/2/hi/business/4919848.stm> Article explaining the carbon trade.
- Friends of the Earth. <http://www.foe.co.uk/resource/factsheets/energy_climate_change.pdf> Overview of the topic from a broadly pro-regulation perspective.
- Institute for Policy Studies. "After Kyoto: Alternative Mechanisms to Control Global Warming." <http://www.fpif.org/reports/after_kyoto_alternative_mechanisms_to_control_global_warming> Reviews of varying solutions to global warming and other global public goods.

Further Reading:

Bayon, Ricardo, Amanda Hawn, and Katherine Hamilton. *Voluntary Carbon Markets: An International Business Guide to What They Are and How They Work.* Earthscan Publications, 2007.

Houser, Trevor et al. *Leveling the Carbon Playing Field: International Competition and US Climate Policy Design.* Peterson Institute, 2008.

Labatt, Sonia, and Rod R. White. *Carbon Finance: The Financial Implications of Climate Change.* Wiley, 2007.

■ ■

CONDOMS IN SCHOOLS

Should public schools actively promote the use of condoms as a way to prevent pregnancy, the spread of sexually transmitted diseases, and the proliferation of HIV infection? While scientific evidence overwhelmingly supports the contention that condoms, when properly used, reduce the incidence of these problems, numerous critics fear that advocating condom use would encourage children to become sexually active earlier than they otherwise would. In particular, more conservative religious traditions, as well as religious groups that oppose contraception, oppose the distribution of condoms in schools out of fear that such access might undermine basic religious values in their children.

PROS

Providing condoms to students in public schools will reduce the incidence of underage pregnancy and the spread of sexually transmitted diseases.

Providing condoms to students is the pragmatic thing to do. Educators need not endorse sexual activity, but they can encourage students to make wise choices if they decide to have sex. Such an approach is sensible because it accepts the inevitability that some young people, regardless of the strength of an abstinence message, will still have sex.

Providing condoms to students is a wise investment of government funds. World governments spend a fortune annually addressing the public health problems created by risky sexual behavior. The cost of raising the many children created through unintended pregnancies over a lifetime can be astronomical. The cost of treating a patient with HIV can be enormous.

Condom distribution encourages the responsibility of men and increases choices for women. It can also establish condom use as the norm, not something that women continually have to negotiate, often from a position of weakness.

Condoms are one of the most effective and cost-effective means of protecting against sexually transmitted diseases, HIV, and pregnancy.

CONS

Providing students with condoms actually encourages beginning sexual activity earlier.

Presenting condoms to students in public schools is offensive to people from a variety of religions who oppose birth control and sex outside of marriage.

Taxpayers should not have to support programs that they find morally objectionable, even if there seem to be pragmatic justifications for the action. Moreover, if overall sexual activity increases as the result of encouraging "safer sex," the number of people occasionally engaging in risky behavior will increase, and the risk of these problems spreading will increase with it.

Widespread condom distribution will establish sexual activity as the norm among young teens, creating peer pressure to participate in sex. The added temptation to engage in sexual activity that is "protected" will result in more women having sex at a younger age, perhaps contributing to their exploitation.

The effectiveness of condoms is grossly exaggerated. If not used properly, condoms can be highly ineffective. Young people are more likely to use condoms incorrectly, due to lack of experience or because they are drunk. Moreover, the temptation to have sex without a condom may be significant where the supply of condoms is not plentiful.

Sample Motions:

This House would provide free condoms to all high school students.

This House believes abstinence-based sex education is superior to condom distribution in schools.

This House would give students the option of free access to condoms through their schools.

Web Links:

- Dodd, Kerri J. <http://www.advocatesforyouth.org/index.php?option=com_content&task=view&id=449&Itemid=177> Fact sheet on condom availability in high schools written from a pro-availability stance.
- The Kaiser Family Foundation. "Condom Availability in High Schools Does Not Affect Amount of Sexual Activity, Study Says." <http://www.kaiserhealthnews.org/Daily-Reports/2003/May/29/dr00017970.aspx> Report on the effect of condom availability on high schools.
- Reising, Michelle. <http://healthpsych.psy.vanderbilt.edu/condomConumdrum.htm> Brief overview of pro and con arguments as well as empirical evidence and links to information on both sides of the argument.

Further Reading:

Kendall, Nancy. *The Sex Education Debates*. University of Chicago Press, 2012.

Lord, Alexander. *Condom Nation: The U.S. Government's Sex Education Campaign from World War I to the Internet.* Johns Hopkins University Press, 2009.

Luker, Kristin. *When Sex Goes to School: Warring Views on Sex—and Sex Education—Since the Sixties.* Norton, 2007.

Taylor, Neil, Frances Quinn, Michael Littledyke, and Richard K. Coll, eds. *Health Education in Context: An International Perspective on Health Education in Schools and Local Communities.* Springer, 2012.

..

CREATIONISM IN PUBLIC SCHOOLS

In the mid-nineteenth century, Charles Darwin articulated his theory of evolution, which argues that human beings evolved, over the course of millennia, from more primitive animals. This theory conflicts with the account of man's creation in Genesis, wherein Adam is created by God as the first fully formed human, having no predecessors; this belief is termed "creationism." Over the past 150 years, evolution has received widespread empirical support and is considered by biologists as one of the most reliably established theories in science. In the United States, a branch of creationism termed intelligent design responded to the theory of evolution by contending that the process is guided by a supernatural force rather than Darwinian natural selection. The Supreme Court has ruled that teaching creationism, including intelligent design, in public schools is unconstitutional, as it is a religious belief rather than an established theory. Several state legislators have challenged this decision. In 2008, Louisiana Governor Bobby Jindal signed the Louisiana Science Education Act into law. This legislation allows public school teachers to introduce into science lessons supplemental materials that are critical of established scientific theories, such as evolution and global warming. While proponents of the law assert that it is designed to encourage critical thinking among students, critics label it the "creationism law" and allege that it is designed simply to place religious teachings into public school science classes. Several high-profile efforts have been made to repeal this law, with 78 Nobel laureates endorsing the repeal.

PROS

The Constitution forbids the establishment of any one religion, but it also guarantees freedom of religion, which means that the government cannot suppress religion. By teaching that evolution is true, schools are violating the religious beliefs of students.

Evolution has not been proved; it is a theory used to explain observable facts. But those facts can be explained just as well, and in some cases, even better, by intelligent design theory. Moreover, evolutionists do not acknowledge that the evidence essential for proving their ideas—for example, fossil remains of transitional, evolving beings—simply does not exist. Creationism is a theory that is at least as worthy as evolution and should be taught along with it.

CONS

In practice, there is no question that the supporters of creationism depend upon one religious tradition—the Judeo-Christian—and upon the account of creation in its sacred texts. Teaching creationism establishes, in effect, only that specific religious tradition, to the detriment of other religions and of nonbelievers. Teaching creationism in a publicly funded school is clearly a violation of the Constitution.

No scientific theory has ever been "proved"—asserting this as a criticism of evolution misunderstands what science is. Scientific theories are supported by evidence, making them strong scientific theories, but—unlike in mathematics, for example—scientific theories are never definitively proven; when new evidence emerges, scientific theories adapt. Teaching creationism because evolution has not been proven is equivalent to teaching acupuncture as a cure for cancer, because chemotherapy has never been proven—the best current scientific evidence supports evolution and also supports chemotherapy as a cure for cancer, and so this is what students should learn.

PROS

By teaching intelligent design theory, a school is not doing anything to establish any particular religion. Intelligent design is accepted by Christians, Jews, Muslims, Native Americans, Hindus, and many others. Therefore, it should not be forbidden by the establishment clause of the First Amendment.

Creationism is not, as the Supreme Court has ruled, a religious belief. It is a scientific theory, and has been articulated by many philosophers and scientists, for example, Aristotle, in a completely secular context.

History has shown that scientific theories are often disproved over time; evolution, thus, should not be considered to be an unassailable truth. In the spirit of scientific inquiry and intellectual skepticism, students should be exposed to competing theories.

CONS

All religions offer a creation story, varying from religion to religion and from culture to culture. A public school might examine all of these beliefs in the context of a history of ideas course, rather than in a science course. In practice, however, creationists are not interested in exploring different beliefs; they are, rather, committed to putting one religious belief on equal footing with prevailing scientific thinking in the science classroom.

A scientific theory is not a theory that has been articulated by a scientist, let alone by a philosopher—a scientific theory is a theory that is supported by evidence. For a scientific theory to be strong enough to be taught to students it must have rigorously tested empirical evidence to support it; creationism clearly does not meet this standard.

If evolution had a competing scientific theory, it should undoubtedly be taught: creationism is not this. Evolution is not taught as an attack on religion; it is taught as the best scientific explanation of available facts. Students are free to pursue their own private religious beliefs.

Sample Motions:

This House favors a curriculum free of creationism teachings in public schools.

This House believes that science education in public schools should not exclude creationist thought.

This House thinks that teaching creationism alongside evolution in public schools is justified.

Web Links:

- Evolution and Creationism in Public Schools. <http://atheism.about.com/library/decisions/indexes/bldec_CreationismIndex.htm> Index of court cases on the issue.
- Evolution vs. Creationism. <http://physics.syr.edu/courses/modules/ORIGINS/origins.html> Information on both sides of the debate as well as links to articles, newsgroups, books, and FAQs.
- PBS. <http://www.pbs.org/wgbh/nova/beta/evolution/intelligent-design-trial.html> Companion site to a television program on the teaching of intelligent design in American schools.

Further Reading:

Berkman, Michael, and Eric Plutzer. *Evolution, Creationism, and the Battle to Control America's Classrooms.* Cambridge University Press, 2010.

Geisler, Norman. *Creation and the Courts: Eighty Years of Conflict in the Classroom and the Courtroom.* Kindle ed. Crossway Books, 2007.

Gunn, Angus M.. and Paul Giesbrecht. *Evolution and Creationism in the Public Schools: A Handbook for Educators, Parents and Community Leaders.* McFarland, 2004.

Scott, Eugene C., and Glenn Branch. *Not in Our Classrooms: Why Intelligent Design Is Wrong for Our Schools.* Beacon, 2006.

■ ■

CURFEW LAWS

More than 300 US towns have passed local curfew laws making it illegal for youths to be out-of-doors between certain publicized times. In most cases cities imposed nighttime curfews, but a 1997 survey indicated that approximately one-quarter had daytime curfews as well. All curfews are aimed at proactively reducing juvenile crime and gang activity. Officials also see curfews as a way of involving parents and keeping young people from being victimized. Opponents say the curfews violate the rights of good kids to prevent the actions of a few bad ones.

PROS

Youth crime is a major and growing problem, often involving both drugs and violence. Particularly worrying is the rise of youth gangs, which can terrorize urban areas and create a social climate in which criminality becomes the norm. Imposing curfews on minors can help solve these problems. They keep young people off the street and out of trouble. Curfews are easy to enforce compared to other forms of crime prevention and are therefore effective.

The use of curfews can help protect vulnerable children. Although responsible parents do not let young children out in the streets after dark, not all parents are responsible. Inevitably their children suffer, both from crime and in accidents, and are likely to fall into bad habits. Society should ensure that such neglected children are returned home safely and that their parents are made to face up to their responsibilities.

Children have no good reason to be out alone late at night, so a curfew is not really a restriction on their liberty. They would be better off at home doing schoolwork and participating in family activities.

Child curfews are a form of zero-tolerance policing. The idea of zero tolerance comes from the theory that if the police ignore low-level crimes they create a permissive atmosphere in which serious crime can flourish and law

CONS

Curfews are not an effective solution to the problem of youth crime. Research finds no link between reduction in juvenile crime and curfews. Although some towns with curfews did see a drop in youth crime, this often had more to do with other law-enforcement strategies, such as zero-tolerance policing, or with demographic and economic changes in the youth population. In any case, most juvenile crime takes place between 3 p.m. and 8 p.m., after the end of school and before working parents return home, rather than in the hours covered by curfews.

Youth curfews infringe upon individual rights and liberties. Children have a right to freedom of movement and assembly, which curfews directly undermine by criminalizing their simple presence in a public space. This reverses the presumption of innocence by assuming all young people are potential lawbreakers. They are also subject to blanket discrimination on the grounds of age, although only a few young people commit crimes. Furthermore, curfews infringe upon the rights of parents to bring up their children as they choose. Just because we dislike the way some parents treat their children does not mean that we should intervene. Should we intervene in families whose religious beliefs mean girls are treated as inferior to boys, or in homes where parents practice corporal punishment?

Children in their mid-teens have legitimate reasons to be out at night without adults. Many have part-time jobs. Others participate in church groups or youth clubs. Requiring adults to take them to and from activities is unreasonable. It will ensure many children do not participate in after-school activities either because adults are unwilling or are unable to accompany them. On a more sinister note, some children are subject to abuse at home and actually feel safer out on the streets.

Youth curfews have great potential for abuse, raising civil rights issues. Evidence suggests that police arrest far more black children than white for curfew violations. Curfews tend to be imposed in inner cities with few places for

PROS

and order breaks down entirely. Child curfews can help the police establish a climate of zero tolerance and create a safer community for everyone.

Child curfews can help change a negative youth culture in which challenging the law is seen as desirable and gang membership an aspiration. Impressionable youngsters would be kept away from gang activity on the streets at night, and a cycle of admiration and recruitment would be broken. By spending more time with their families and in more positive activities such as sports, which curfews make a more attractive option for bored youngsters, children will develop greater self-esteem and discipline.

We should try other ways of reducing youth crime, but they will work best in conjunction with curfews. If a troubled area develops a culture of lawlessness, identifying specific youngsters for rehabilitation becomes more difficult. A curfew takes the basically law-abiding majority off the streets, allowing the police to engage with the most difficult element. Curfews are a tool in the struggle to improve lives in rundown areas. They are likely to be used for relatively short periods to bring a situation under control so that other measures can be put in place and given a chance to work.

CONS

children to amuse themselves safely and legally. Curfews compound the social exclusion that many poor children feel with physical exclusion from public spaces. This problem is made worse by the inevitable deterioration in relations between the police and the young people subject to the curfew.

Imposing curfews on children would actually be counterproductive because it would turn millions of law-abiding young people into criminals. More American children are charged with curfew offenses than with any other crime. Once children acquire a criminal record, they cross a psychological boundary, making it much more likely that they will perceive themselves as criminals and have much less respect for the law. This can lead to more serious offenses. At the same time, a criminal record decreases the chances for employment and so contributes to the social deprivation and desperation that breed crime.

A number of alternative strategies exist that are likely to do more to reduce youth crime. Rather than a blanket curfew, individual curfews could be imposed upon particular troublemakers. Another successful strategy is working individually with young troublemakers. For example, authorities can require them to meet with victims of crime so that they understand the consequences of their actions. Youths can also be paired with trained mentors. Overall, the government needs to ensure good educational opportunities and employment prospects so that youngsters feel some hope for their futures.

Sample Motions:

This House would introduce child curfews.

This House would lock up its daughters.

This House believes children should be neither seen nor heard.

Web Links:

- CBS News. <http://www.cbsnews.com/stories/2004/02/03/national/main597788.shtml> Discussion of the US debate over curfew laws, with brief descriptions of the main arguments.
- McKinney, James. <http://www.time.com/time/nation/article/0,8599,1837634,00.html> Describes the growing trend of local governments implementing curfew laws in attempts to fight juvenile crime.
- National Youth Rights Association. <http://www.youthrights.org/issues/curfew/> Resources and frequently asked questions on US curfew laws.

Further Reading:

Jensen, Gary F., and Dean G. Rojek. *Delinquency and Youth Crime.* 4th ed. Waveland Press, 2008.

McNamara, Robert Hartmann. *The Lost Population: Status Offenders in America.* Carolina Academic Press, 2008.

Urban, Lynn S. *The Deterrent Effects of Curfews: An Evaluation of Juvenile Probationers.* LFB Scholarly Publishing, 2007.

..

DEEP-SEA DRILLING

Deep-sea drilling is the process of extracting oil from reservoirs thousands of feet below the seabed. Particularly after the April 2010 Deepwater Horizon disaster, in which the collapse of an oil rig in the Gulf of Mexico killed 11 men and caused the largest offshore oil spill in US history, deep-water drilling has come under much criticism for its negative environmental and economic impacts, as well as the immense costs of cleaning up the oil. Opponents insist that such drilling should not be allowed; supporters claim that this method of extracting oil is vital to a world highly dependent on oil and that improvements in extraction technology have made spills very rare.

PROS

Although accidents can always happen, drilling in the United States is very safe. According to the Mineral Management Service, as of 2008, only about one one-thousandth of the oil transported or drilled for in US waters is spilled. Indeed, a study conducted by the organization from 2002–06 found that most blowouts occur in shallow, not deep, water. Technology and safety standards have improved over the years, making drilling for oil extremely safe.

The United States is facing high unemployment—deepwater drilling can create much-needed jobs. According to the National Ocean Industries Association, each deepwater rig creates (directly and indirectly) 1,400 jobs. In a fragile economy, we cannot afford to lose jobs.

Deepwater drilling and research in alternative energy are not mutually exclusive. The United States consumes enormous amounts of oil, so even though weaning ourselves from nonrenewable resources is necessary, in the short term we should ensure that everyone's energy needs are provided for.

CONS

Granted, spills may be rare, but the costs and environmental impact of them are so great that drilling for oil in deep waters remains very risky. Spills can cause long-lasting harm to wildlife and ecosystems both fragile and sturdy. Thousands of animals can be killed, with environmental recovery taking decades. The contaminated water and oil exposure resulting from spills are also hazardous to human health. In addition, spills are extremely costly to clean up. Currently, BP is spending about $6 million a day in cleanup in the Gulf of Mexico. David Kotok, director of the Global Interdependence Center, estimates the total cost could be $12.5 billion. Finally, technology is not as advanced as it seems—look at the problems BP has had in trying to rectify the Deepwater Horizon disaster.

While oil rigs may create jobs, oil spills can wreak havoc on a region's economy. A study published by the University of Mississippi in June 2010 predicted that Mississippi could lose $120 million in tourism revenue from May to August due to the Deepwater Horizon oil disaster. Furthermore, investing in alternative energy could also create lots of jobs—without the immense risk attached to the deepwater drilling industry.

Rather than contributing to climate change and risking environmental catastrophe by continuing to rely on petroleum, we should be investing in greener technologies. Furthermore, deepwater drilling is not an effective short-term response to our energy problem because it can take decades from locating an oil trap to extracting the oil. The US Energy Information Administration estimates that drilling in the Pacific, Atlantic, and eastern Gulf regions would not significantly affect natural gas and domestic crude oil production until 2030. Americans must face the unfortunate truth that they need to stop consuming so much oil.

PROS

The United States is currently dependant on a number of nations for oil, including Saudi Arabia, Russia, Venezuela, and Congo. Rather than remaining indebted to nations with which we may not share political, cultural, or moral ideals, the United States ought to work toward energy independence. Increasing deepwater drilling off US shores is an important part of this endeavor. In 2006, the *New York Times* wrote that the most optimistic estimates show a possible 40 billion barrels of undiscovered oil in deepwater areas in the Gulf of Mexico. Given that the United States consumes, according to the Energy Information Administration, about 7.6 billion barrels of oil a year, these reserves could be enormously beneficial.

State and federal laws currently regulate oil drilling and chemical levels. Seismic waves may have some negative effects, but, in general, they lead to less environmental damage because they increase the likelihood that drills will be successful—thus eliminating the need for multiple wasteful drills. And, drilling fluids have become cleaner over the years, according to the US Department of Energy.

CONS

First, because we consume so much oil, deepwater drilling off our coasts will not make our nation more energy independent. According to Robert Kaufman, director of Boston University's Center for Energy and Environmental Studies, the United States produces 5 million barrels and consumes 20 million barrels of oil a day. Even if we could drill for more oil, we would need to drastically increase our production capability to close that 15 million barrel gap. Second, we have no sure way to determine how much oil is actually extractable. Estimates of hidden oil reserves are unreliable; even when we are certain that an oil reserve exists, companies are only ever able to remove some at a cost that guarantees profit. Third, oil prices are set by the global market, so even if we could gain "energy independence," we would not be any better off financially. Finally, the number one exporter of oil to the United States is Canada, a country with which we have strong and friendly ties.

Even when spills do not occur, deepwater drilling has harmful environmental effects. The seismic waves and sounds created by oil searches disrupt marine wildlife; in addition, when oil is extracted, other chemicals and toxins like benzene and arsenic get pulled up as well. Most important, the oil extracted is ultimately used as a source of energy, emitting dangerous greenhouse gases into the atmosphere.

Sample Motions:

The federal government should ban deepwater drilling.

This House would continue to go deep.

This House believes that investigation of alternative energy supplies ought to take precedence over deepwater drilling.

Web Links:

- "Moratorium Won't Reduce Drilling Risks." <http://www.nytimes.com/2010/06/26/business/26nocera.html?pagewanted=1> Article on the necessity of deepwater drilling for US energy needs.
- Savage, Charlie. "Judge Blocks Deep-Water Drilling Morotorium." <http://www.boston.com/news/science/articles/2010/06/23/judge_blocks_deep_water_drilling_moratorium/> Article explaining why President Obama's six-month ban on deepwater drilling was overturned.
- "Worth the Risk? Debate on Offshore Drilling Heats Up." <http://www.usatoday.com/money/industries/ energy/2008-07-13-offshore-drilling_N.htm> Outlines environmental effects of offshore drilling.

Further Reading:

Freudenburg, William R., and Robert Gramling. *Blowout in the Gulf: The BP Oil Spill Disaster and the Future of Energy in America*. MIT Press, 2012.

Reed, Stanley, and Alison Fitzgerald. *In Too Deep: BP and the Drilling Race That Took It Down*. Bloomberg Press, 2011.

Urwellen, Robert H. *Oil Spill Costs and Impacts*. Nova Science Publishers, 2009.

■ ■

DEVELOPING WORLD DEBT, CANCELLATION OF

For many years, poor nations in Asia, Latin America, and particularly Africa, have borrowed heavily to reduce poverty and foster development. Over the years external debt payments increased dramatically, often forcing countries to choose between paying their debt and funding social, health, and education programs. By the beginning of the new millennium the situation had reached a crisis in some countries. Sub-Saharan Africa owed lenders approximately $200 billion, 83% of its GNP. Groups such as the International Monetary Fund (IMF) and the World Bank, with their Heavily Indebted Poor Countries (HIPC) initiative, are working toward a partial reduction or rescheduling of this debt, but demand adherence to strict economic reforms. In 2005 the HIPC initiative was supplemented by the Multilateral Debt Relief Initiative that grants total relief on eligible debts owed to the IMF, the World Bank, and African Development Fund if nations meet certain conditions. Two years later the Inter-American Development Bank developed a similar program for the HIPCs in the Western Hemisphere.

PROS

The burden of debt costs lives. Some of the most heavily indebted poor countries are struggling to pay even the interest on their loans, let alone paying down the principal. This massively distorts their economies and their spending priorities. African nations currently spend four times as much on debt repayments as they do on health. The reforms demanded by the IMF in return for rescheduled debt make this problem even worse. In Zimbabwe, spending on health care has dropped by a third; in Tanzania, school fees have been introduced to raise more money. Progress made in health and education over the past 50 years is actually being reversed in some countries. It is obscene that governments are cutting spending in these vital areas to repay debts. The debts must be cancelled now.

To raise the cash for debt repayments, poor countries have to produce goods that they can sell internationally. Often this means growing cash crops instead of the food needed to support their population. People in fertile countries can find themselves starving because they cannot afford to buy imported food.

Debt repayments often punish those who were not responsible for creating the debt in the first place. In a number of poorer countries, huge debts were amassed by the irresponsible spending of dictators in the past. They have now been overthrown, yet the new government and the people of that country still are required to pay the price for the dictator's actions. This is clearly unfair.

CONS

There are many reasons for the current problems in the world's poorest nations. They may often have heavy debt burdens, but the debt is not necessarily the cause of the problems. Many countries spend huge amounts of money on weapons to fight local wars instead of investing in their people. Many are led by dictators or other corrupt governments, whose incompetence or greed is killing their own population. The money to pay for social programs and, at the same time, repay debt may well exist, but it is being wasted in other areas.

Again, there are many potential causes for starvation—famines are caused by war or by freak weather conditions, not by debt. While growing cash crops can seem to be counterintuitive, the money they bring in helps boost the country's economy. The idea that a nation could and should be agriculturally and industrially self-sufficient is outdated.

This thinking has dangerous implications on an international level. Governments are always changing in democracies, but nations are expected to honor their debts. A crucial element in lending money is the promise that the debt will be repaid. If every new government could decide that it was not responsible for its predecessor's debts, then no one would ever lend money to a country. Developing countries in particular still need loans to invest in infrastructure projects. Canceling debt now would make lenders far less likely to provide loans on good terms in the future and would retard economic growth in the long term.

PROS

All poor countries need is the chance to help themselves. While their economies are dominated by the need to repay debt, it is impossible for them to truly invest in infrastructure and education. By canceling debt, we would give them a fresh start and the opportunity to build successful economies that would supply the needs of generations to come.

The developed world has a moral duty to the developing world because of the historical background of developing world debt. In the rush to invest in the 1970s, many banks made hasty loans, pouring money into pointless projects without properly examining whether they would ever make a profit. Because of these bad investments, some of the world's poorest countries are so burdened with debts that they can now no longer realistically expect to pay them off and are instead simply servicing the interest. An important parallel may be made with bankruptcy: if an individual is unable to repay his or her debts, he or she is declared bankrupt and then allowed to make a fresh start. The same system should be used with countries. If they are unable to repay their debts, they should be given the opportunity to start again. A country making contributions to the world economy is far better than a country in debt slavery. At the same time, banks would be discouraged from making bad loans as they did in the 1970s.

CONS

Reform must come first. Corrupt and incompetent governments and economic systems cripple many poor countries. Canceling debt would therefore make no difference, it would be the equivalent of giving a one-time payment to dictators and crooks, who would siphon off the extra money and become rich while the people still suffer. Even worse, dictators might spend more money on weapons and palaces, thus reincurring possibly even greater debt. A country's government must be accountable and its economy stable before debt reduction or cancellation is even considered.

The parallel with bankruptcy cannot work on a national scale. First, when an individual is declared bankrupt, most assets and possessions are seized to pay as much debt as possible. This is why banks find bankruptcy an acceptable option. In national terms, this would mean the total loss of sovereignty. Foreign governments and banks would be able to seize control of the infrastructure or the resources of the "bankrupt" country at will. No government could, or should, ever accept this. Second, the difference in scale is vitally important. Whereas the bankruptcy of a single individual within a country is unlikely to cause major problems for that country's economy, the bankruptcy of a nation would significantly affect the world economy. The economic plans of banks and nations currently include the interest payments on developing world debt; if this substantial revenue stream were suddenly cut off, economic repercussions could be catastrophic. Even if this debt relief would be helpful to the "bankrupt" countries in the short term, a world economy in recession would be in nobody's best interest.

Sample Motions:

This House would end developing world debt.

This House would kill the debt, not the debtors.

This House would break the chains of debt.

Web Links:

- International Monetary Fund. <http://www.imf.org/external/np/exr/facts/hipc.htm> Offers information on IMF debt-relief programs and progress.
- Jubilee Debt Campaign. <http://www.jubileedebtcampaign.org.uk/?lid=98> Research, analysis, news, and data on international debt and finance presented by an advocacy group dedicated to ending developing world debt.
- Yambwa, Jean-Pierre Nziya. <http://www.tigweb.org/express/panorama/article.html?ContentID=5725> Argues that debt cancellation will not help Africa because it does not solve the real problem—corruption in government.

Further Reading:

Herman, Barry, Jose Antonio Ocampo, Shari Spiegel, eds. *Overcoming Developing Country Debt Crises.* Oxford University Press, 2010.

DNA DATABASE FOR CRIMINALS

DNA evidence is playing an increasing role in criminal cases—both in convicting the guilty and clearing the innocent. The federal government and the states are building interlinked computerized databases of DNA samples. Initially these samples were taken from people convicted of sex crimes and a few other violent offenses, but recently the suggestion has been made to gather the DNA of all convicted criminals. Some officials have recommended expanding the database to include all individuals arrested, while others want the database to include DNA from everyone. Many people view extending the database beyond convicted criminals as an invasion of privacy and a violation of civil liberties.

PROS

DNA detection has considerable advantages over conventional fingerprinting. Fingerprints attach only to hard surfaces, can be smeared, or can be avoided by using gloves. Comparison of even a clear print from a crime scene with a print in the national database requires significant scientific expertise. Scientists can build an accurate DNA profile from very small amounts of genetic data, and they can construct it even if it has been contaminated by oil, water, or acid at the crime scene. The accused should appreciate a "fingerprinting" technique that is both objective and accurate.

The use of a DNA fingerprint is not an affront to civil liberties. The procedure for taking a sample of DNA is less invasive than that required for taking a blood sample. The police already possess a vast volume of information; the National Crime Information Center Computer in the United States contains files relating to 32 million Americans. A forensic DNA database should be seen in the context of the personal information that other agencies hold. Insurance companies commonly require an extensive medical history of their clients. Mortgage lenders usually demand a full credit report on applicants. Many employers subject their employees to random drug testing. If we are prepared to place our personal information in the private sector, why can we not trust it to the police? Law enforcement officials will use the DNA sample only

CONS

Although DNA detection might have advantages over fingerprint dusting, the test is nevertheless fallible. Environmental factors at the crime scene such as heat, sunlight, or bacteria can corrupt any genetic data. DNA evidence must be stored in sterile and temperature-controlled conditions. Criminals may contaminate samples by swapping saliva. There is room for human error or fraud in analyzing samples. In 2003, for example, in Houston, Texas, the police department was forced to close down its crime lab because of shoddy scientific practices that led to inaccuracies in DNA testing. Hundreds of cases were involved, including death-penalty cases. Even a complete DNA profile cannot indicate the length of time a suspect was present at a crime scene or the date in question. The creation of a database cannot be a panacea for crime detection.

DNA fingerprinting would have to be mandatory, otherwise those liable to commit crime would simply refuse to provide a sample. Individuals consent to pass personal information to mortgage or insurance agencies. When citizens release information to outside agencies they receive a service in return. In being compelled to give a sample of DNA, the innocent citizen would receive the scant benefit of being eliminated from a police investigation. Moreover, the storage by insurance companies of genetic information remains highly controversial because of the potential abuse of that information. Finally, creation of the database would change the attitude of government toward its citizens. Every citizen, some from the moment of their birth, would be treated as a potential criminal.

PROS	CONS

in the detection of a crime. In short, the innocent citizen should have nothing to fear.

The creation of a DNA database would not require a disproportionate investment of time or public resources. The requisite computer and laboratory technology is already available. The United States has developed the Combined DNA Index System. The expense of sampling the entire population of most countries would be substantial and is unlikely to be offset by any subsequent saving in police resources, but this is part of the price for justice. Popular support for "law and order" suggests that the public puts a very high premium on protection from crime.

The initial and continuing expense of a DNA database would be a gross misapplication of finite public resources. Public confidence in the criminal justice system will neither be improved by requiring individuals to give time and tissue to the police nor by the creation of a bureaucracy dedicated to administering the database. The funds would be better spent on recruiting more police officers and deploying them on foot patrol.

Persons who create violent crimes are unlikely to leave conventional fingerprints. However, the National Commission on the Future of DNA Evidence estimates that 30% of crime scenes contain the blood, semen, or saliva of the perpetrator. DNA detection can identify the guilty even when the police have no obvious suspects.

The most serious violent crimes, notably rape and murder, are most commonly committed by individuals known to the victim. When the suspects are obvious, DNA detection is superfluous. Moreover, it is harmful to suggest that crimes can be solved, or criminals deterred, by computer wizardry. Unless the DNA is used to identify a genetic cause for aggression, violent crimes will continue.

A DNA database is not intended to replace conventional criminal investigations. The database would identify potential suspects, each of whom could then be investigated by more conventional means. Criminal trials frequently feature experts presenting scientific evidence. The jury system is actually a bastion against conviction on account of complicated scientific facts. If the genetic data and associated evidence is not conclusive or is not presented with sufficient clarity, the jury is obliged to find the defendant not guilty. O. J. Simpson was acquitted of the murders of Nicole Brown Simpson and Ron Goldman in spite of compelling DNA evidence linking him to the scene of the crime.

There is a serious risk that officials will use genetic evidence to the exclusion of material that might prove the suspect innocent. Moreover, there is the possibility that not only the police, but also the jury, will be blinded by science. It seems unlikely that juries will be able to comprehend or, more importantly, to question the genetic information from the database. The irony is that forensic evidence has cleared many wrongly convicted individuals but might now serve to create miscarriages of its own.

The increased use of DNA evidence will minimize the risk of future wrongful convictions. An FBI study indicates that since 1989 DNA evidence has excluded the initial suspect in 25% of sexual assault cases. Moreover, forensically valuable DNA can be found on evidence that has existed for decades and thus assist in reversing previous miscarriages of justice.

We do not need a database to acquit or exclude non-offenders. When the police have identified a suspect they ought to create a DNA profile and compare it to the crime scene data. Likewise, a DNA sample should be taken if there is concern that an individual was wrongly convicted of a crime.

Sample Motions:
This House would have a criminal DNA database.
This House would give away its DNA.
This House would catch a crook by his genes.

Web Links:

- The Economist. <http://www.economist.com/debate/overview/141> An online debate on the issue sponsored by The Economist; it also links to background resources.
- Etzioni, Amitai. "DNA Tests and Databases in Criminal Justice: Individual Rights and the Common Good." <www.hks.harvard.edu/dnabook/Amitai%20Etzioni%20II.doc> Analyzes the conflict between individual rights and the common good raised by the issue.
- Mnookin, Jennifer. <http://articles.latimes.com/2007/apr/05/opinion/oe-mnookin5> Article examining the injustice of a DNA database that is solely for criminals.

Further Reading:

Häyry, Matti et al. The Ethics and Governance of Human Genetic Databases: European Perspectives. Cambridge University Press, 2007.

Krimsky, Sheldon, and Tania Simoncelli. Genetic Justice: DNA Data Banks, Criminal Investigations, and Civil Liberties. Columbia University Press, 2012.

Lazer, David. DNA and the Criminal Justice System: The Technology of Justice. The MIT Press, 2004.

Lynch, Michael, Simon A. Cole, Ruth McNally, and Kathleen Jordan. Truth Machine: The Contentious History of DNA Fingerprinting. University of Chicago Press, 2011.

■ ■

THE DREAM ACT

The Development, Relief, and Education for Alien Minors Act — also known as the DREAM act — is a proposed law, designed to provide a path to legal residency for illegal immigrants brought to the United States as minors. The proposed legislation, which has been introduced in various forms since 2001, includes several conditions to be met by those wanting to pursue legal residency. Most important, applicants would have to prove that they arrived in the United States before the age of 16, and were of "good moral character," meaning they had not been convicted of a felony or a "significant" misdemeanor. In addition, applicants would have to graduate high school and complete two years of military service or two years at either community college or a four-year institute of higher learning. The DREAM Act is a bipartisan proposal, with broad support coming from both Democrats and Republicans. However, critics of the act view it as an "amnesty program" that will encourage further illegal immigration.

PROS

The DREAM Act encourages young undocumented immigrants to work toward permanent residency, proving themselves as productive members of society. Census figures from 2009 indicate that more than 4 million illegal immigrants under 25 live in the United States, yet only 65,000 graduate from high school each year. Those who do graduate high school have limited opportunities when it comes to higher education. Though some colleges do admit illegal immigrants, without access to federal financial aid or the ability to hold down a legal job, few are able to finance further education. As a result, illegal immigrants tend to live in poverty, thus leading to high crime rates and a disproportionate dependence on welfare. By rewarding hard work and determination,

CONS

The DREAM Act does not require illegal immigrants to complete a degree, but merely to attend college for two years. In addition, individuals who have been convicted of numerous misdemeanors — which may have been pleaded down from felonies — will be eligible, allowing criminals to avoid deportation. An individual need only submit a DREAM Act application to halt deportation proceedings; therefore, fraudulent applications will be common, and the burden of proving inaccurate information will be on the Department of Homeland Security. Instead of the DREAM Act, which rewards illegal immigrants who contribute very little to the country, we should adopt "staple" green cards, which allow foreign nationals with PhDs in science, technology, engineering,

PROS

the DREAM Act allows young people to break out of this cycle of poverty, benefiting society as a whole.

Approximately 1.8 million illegal immigrants would be eligible for residency under the DREAM Act—allowing them to work legally would bring significant economic benefits to the country. Not only would these immigrants be more economically productive when allowed to work legally, they would also produce income that is taxable. A 2010 report from the Congressional Budget Office and the Joint Commission on Taxation projected that the DREAM Act would reduce deficits by $1.4 billion and increase government revenues by $2.3 billion over the next ten years. In contrast, it would cost approximately $25.5 billion to deport all the individuals eligible for residency under the DREAM Act.

There is no other viable solution to the problem of children who have been raised in the United States after being brought into the country illegally. Often these children have no memory of, or connection to, their "home country," sometimes not even speaking the language. Under the current system, these children would have to return to their home countries in order to apply for US residency, a process that can take several years and is not guaranteed to be successful. Forcing these individuals, many of whom identify as American, to abandon their lives and move to an unfamiliar country is cruel.

The individuals eligible to apply for residency under the DREAM Act have not broken the law—the adults who brought them into the United States did. It is not fair to punish these children for situations that are beyond their control; they are innocent victims, and the law should be amended to treat them as such.

CONS

or medicine to work in the United States. These are the immigrants who are most beneficial to society.

The DREAM Act will place a huge economic burden on American taxpayers, who will be required to cover the educational costs of illegal immigrants. Under the DREAM Act, illegal immigrants will be eligible for federal student loans and other forms of financial aid, placing them in direct competition with US students. Furthermore, unemployment numbers will rise and American workers will face increased difficulty in finding a job due to the addition of workers to the workforce. Although the DREAM Act would allow the income of over a million illegal immigrants to be taxed, it would also make these immigrants eligible for forms of government assistance, thus acting as a drain on already limited government resources.

There are proper channels for immigrants who wish to come to the United States legally; therefore, there is no reason why these illegal immigrants should be exempt from the rules that all other immigrants are required to follow. The DREAM Act is essentially an amnesty program, rewarding those who have chosen not to follow the law. Every year tens of thousands of immigrants apply for US residency from their home countries, using the process already in place; though this process may be tough, it is the price they are willing to pay to live in the United States. Allowing illegal immigrants to circumvent this process creates an incentive to break the law.

Giving permanent residency to children brought to the United States illegally will benefit their parents too. Immigrants can apply for US residency on the basis of having a family member who is a US resident; the DREAM Act will therefore create a chain of migration for families that send children to the United States illegally, encouraging others to do the same rather than to immigrate legally.

Sample Motions

This House supports the DREAM Act.

This House opposes amnesty for illegal immigrants brought over as minors.

Web Links

- Immigration Policy Center. <http://www.immigrationpolicy.org/issues/DREAM-Act> Articles and research reports focusing on numerous aspects of the DREAM Act.
- CNN. "Paul Ryan Changes Course on DREAM Act". <http://politicalticker.blogs.cnn.com/2013/02/22/paul-ryan-changes-course-on-dream-act/> Overview of Republican stances on the act.
- White House. <http://www.whitehouse.gov/blog/2010/12/01/get-facts-dream-act> Comprehensive list of arguments for the DREAM Act.

- NAFSA: Association of International Educators. <http://www.nafsa.org/uploadedFiles/NAFSA_Home/Resource_Library_Assets/Public_Policy/The%20DREAM%20Act%20T%20and%20M%20-%20Jan%202012(1).pdf> List of myths and facts regarding the DREAM Act.
- New York Times. "Following Her Dream, and Hoping for the Dream Act." <http://www.nytimes.com/2012/11/26/nyregion/pursuing-dream-of-us-citizenship-colombia-native-applies-to-stay.html> Article looking at case studies of people who would benefit from the act.

Further Reading

Bush, Jeb, and Clint Bolick. *Immigration Wars: Forging an American Solution.* Threshold Editions, 2013.

Nicholls, Walter. *The Dreamers: How the Undocumented Youth Movement Transformed the Immigrant Rights Debate.* Stanford University Press, 2013.

Olsen, Laurie. *Made in America: Immigrant Students in Our Public Schools.* New Press, 2008.

Perez, William. *We Are Americans: Undocumented Students Pursuing the American Dream.* Stylus, 2009.

• ■

DRINKING AGE, LOWERING

Teenage drinking has long been a concern of policy makers in the United States. In response to widespread drunk driving fatalities among young people during the 1970s, the United States Congress passed a law in 1984 that effectively increased the legal drinking age from 18 to 21. While individual states are presumably free to maintain a legal drinking age of 18, the law would deny those states important federal funds, and has thus operated as a blanket national policy for nearly 25 years. Recently, university leaders have reinitiated a debate over the logic and effectiveness behind the prohibition, and a movement to lower the drinking age to 18 is gaining momentum. Among other arguments, proponents claim that the current law is discriminatory and has actually contributed to an increase in alcohol abuse within the targeted age group. Opponents of the measure insist that the current law has saved countless lives and is part of an effective strategy to combat alcoholism nationwide.

PROS

The current drinking age arbitrarily discriminates between people who are 21 years old and those who are younger, in violation of the US Constitution. Eighteen-year-olds are equally capable of making adult choices. In fact, US law assumes that 18-year-olds can handle serious responsibility in other contexts, including military service, jury service, voting, marriage, and contract formation. The decision to drink is arguably less weighty than these important responsibilities. Therefore, the line drawn is arbitrary and unjustified.

The current age restriction is not an effective deterrent because it can never be fully enforced. Those under the age of 21 often use fake IDs and/or have older friends purchase alcohol for them. The law is even more difficult to enforce on college campuses, where young people from 18 to 22 years old socialize together and older students regularly purchase alcohol that is consumed by younger students.

CONS

Although the law does distinguish between age groups, it does not violate the US Constitution. While it is true that government allows 18-year-olds greater freedom in other contexts, the government has a legitimate interest in preventing alcohol abuse by young people. Drinking has demonstrated and disastrous consequences and government has a strong interest in preventing these costs to society. Since the law is rationally related to these legitimate goals, it is valid.

The current law is effective because it makes alcohol more difficult to obtain. Just because a law cannot be fully enforced does not mean that it should not be upheld. There are criminal penalties for giving alcohol to minors, and these act as an additional deterrent. The dangers resulting from underage alcohol consumption are great, and countless lives have been saved since the law was implemented. Even partial deterrence is better than none at all.

PROS

Lowering the drinking age makes youth more responsible about drinking and helps to reduce future alcohol problems, including binge drinking. If American youth are allowed to consume alcohol earlier in their lives, as is practiced throughout Europe, they will avoid more destructive behaviors such as binge drinking. Such a culture also ensures that parents have greater oversight of and input into their children's drinking habits.

Lowering the drinking age encourages young people with drinking problems to come forward and seek help. Since selling/providing alcohol to minors is currently criminalized, people with alcohol problems in this age group are unlikely to come forward for fear of punishment, both their own and their friends'.

Individual states should have the right to determine an appropriate drinking age for their residents. The law as it now stands punishes states that lower the drinking age by denying them much-needed federal highway funds. This effectively keeps states from being able to make specific, tailored decisions about what is best for their residents, because they cannot afford to forgo the highway funds. Such a law violates the fundamental principle of federalism.

CONS

Lowering the drinking age does not make young people more responsible about drinking. Studies have shown that students who start drinking at younger ages tend to drink more heavily in college and have more drinking problems generally. Studies have also shown a relationship between younger-age drinking and other serious problems such as drug abuse and depression. Finally, the idea that children who are allowed to drink at earlier ages will drink more responsibly is largely a middle-class myth. In England, where young people often drink alcohol from quite a young age, binge drinking is a serious nationwide problem.

A lower drinking age does not help alleviate alcohol problems among youth, but actually makes them worse. More teenage drinkers inevitably results in more teenagers with alcohol problems. Even if alcoholic teens felt less fearful about seeking help, there would be far more young people with alcohol problems.

States are indeed free to lower the drinking age to 18 if they so choose. However, the federal government has the right to withhold federal funds if a state does not comply with certain federal policies. Preventing alcohol-related problems is an important federal goal, and the federal government can withhold funds to encourage state compliance with that aim.

Sample Motions:

This House would lower the drinking age to 18.

This House supports maintaining the legal drinking age of 21.

Web Links:

- McCardell, John M. <http://www.cnn.com/2009/POLITICS/09/16/mccardell.lower.drinking.age/index.html> Middlebury
- College president argues in favor of lowering the drinking age.
- Mothers Against Drunk Driving. <http://www.madd.org/statistics> Comprehensive list of studies and experts supporting MADD's stance that lowering the drinking age would be dangerous.
- Streeter, Ruth. <http://www.cbsnews.com/stories/2009/02/19/60minutes/main4813571.shtml> Companion site to a news program on the issue; links to video segments containing interviews with a variety of students, organizations, and experts.

Further Reading:

Babor, Thomas, ed. *Alcohol: No Ordinary Commodity: Research and Public Policy.* Oxford University Press, 2010.

Edvin, David, and Samuel Herald, eds. Underage Drinking: Examining and Preventing Youth Use of Alcohol. Nova Science Publishers, 2010.

Kiesbye, Stefan. *Should the Legal Drinking Age Be Lowered?* Greenhaven Press, 2012.

Marcovitz, Hal. *Should the Drinking Age Be Lowered?* ReferencePoint Press, 2010.

▪ ▪

DRIVING AGE, INCREASING

The controversy around increasing the driving age to 18 has swelled over the past several years. Automobile accidents continue to be the leading cause of death among teenagers, and amount to nearly 40% of all teenage fatalities. People who support the age increase point to the fact that 16-year-olds are simply not mature or responsible enough to engage in such an inherently dangerous activity. Opponents counter that increasing the driving age will merely delay consequences, inadvertently punish poorer households, and prevent young people from exercising adult responsibility.

PROS

Sixteen-year-olds are involved in more automobile accidents than 18-year-olds because they are less mature. Therefore, increasing the driving age will save thousands of lives. In a Canadian study, 16-year-old girls were found to have more driving accidents than 17- and 18-year-old girls with the same amount of driving experience. In New Jersey, which has increased the driving age to 17, it is estimated that hundreds of lives are being saved every year. The only way to substantially reduce the risk of automobile accidents for 16-year-olds is to prevent them from driving until they are mature enough to drive more safely.

Saving lives is more important than avoiding economic harm for a small group of people. Automobile accidents are the leading cause of death among teenagers. The fact that poorer families may be economically impacted is unfortunate, but it is not as important as reducing that risk. Furthermore, it is not clear that poorer families would suffer more. Less wealthy households tend to own fewer vehicles and are more likely to use public transportation. Therefore, it is probable that poorer teenagers share vehicles with household members and therefore drive less than their wealthier peers.

Driving is a dangerous activity that 16-year-olds are not responsible enough to engage in. The law limits children's power to make decisions and engage in certain activities in many other contexts. For example, society has decided that 16-year-olds are not prepared to serve in the military or to vote, due to the possible consequences of allowing them to do so. Most of Europe, China, Brazil, and Japan also prohibit driving for children under the age of 18. Sixteen-year-olds can still practice responsibility in many other ways, but the risks of teenage driving are just too great.

CONS

The problem is not maturity, it is lack of experience. Increasing the driving age will merely delay the consequences, not prevent them. First-time drivers will be just as inexperienced at 17 as they are at 16. In New Jersey, where the driving age is now 17, the accident rate among 17-year-old beginners is nearly identical to that of 16-year-old beginners in other states. The solution is not to increase the age threshold, but to require more driving education and practice before licensing. Some states have successfully lowered their teenage driving casualties by requiring more hours of driving lessons and practice with licensed adults.

Increasing the driving age will unfairly impact economically disadvantaged and/or nontraditional families. Not all heads of households are available to drive teenagers to their obligations. Teenagers can legally work at age 16. Many teens between the ages of 16 and 18 work to support themselves and/or their families and need to drive in order to do so. Often in these situations, other family members also work and are not available to provide transportation. If the driving age is raised, more wealthy and/or traditional families (in which a stay-at-home caretaker is available to escort teenagers and other children) will not be affected, but those families who do not fit that economic/social mold will suffer.

Driving is a great way for 16-year-olds to learn responsibility in that it allows them to gain independence from their parents, make autonomous decisions about their behavior and safety, and engage in an important adult activity. Increasing the driving age will limit this opportunity and make it more difficult for young people to transition to adulthood. Furthermore, such a law would be contradictory since our society allows 16-year-olds to work, an activity that often requires far greater responsibility than driving.

Sample Motions:

This House would increase the legal driving age from 16 to 18.

This House would vote to maintain the legal driving age at 18.

Web Links:

- Bowers, Cynthia. <http://www.cbsnews.com/video/watch/?id=4433138n> Video news segment on the debate over the appropriate driving age.
- Gaudiano, Nicole. "Bill Would Raise Unrestricted Driving Age to 18." <http://www.azcentral.com/news/articles/20100702teen -drivers-bill.html> Explains congressional proposal that would create more requirements for state driver licensing laws.
- Insurance Institute for Highway Safety. <http://www.iihs.org/news/rss/pr090908.html> Argues that licensing at later ages reduces car crashes involving teen drivers.

Further Reading:

Wanberg, Kenneth W., David S. Timken, Harvey B. Milkman, eds. *Driving With Care: Education and Treatment of the Under-age Impaired Driving Offender.* Sage, 2010.

■ ■

DRONES, USE OF IN WARFARE

Drones are military vehicles that can be operated from a remote location. Currently, the United States and the United Kingdom are the only two nations that use drones in combat. Also called "unmanned aerial vehicles" (UAVs), drones are most notably used in the war in Afghanistan and in military operations in Pakistan, Somalia, and Yemen. Some UAVs merely scope out an area; however, the most recent UAVs can also identify and hit a target. The major advantage UAVs offer is fewer casualties among pilots. UAVs are controversial because they are prone to error and have caused significant civilian casualties. Under President Barack Obama, the use of military drones by the United States has increased 700 percent, which has killed more than four times the number of those killed by drones under President George W. Bush. In 2011, US drones killed US citizen Anwar al-Awlaki in Yemen, later killing his American-born 17-year-old-son. Since US courts are not involved in approving drone strikes, these killings have led to allegations that the US government was engaged in the extrajudicial killings of citizens; this, combined with the lack of government transparency over the use of drones, has made the issue increasingly controversial.

PROS

Because UAVs are unmanned, pilots' lives are in much less danger. This is advantageous because fewer casualties occur and it prevents plummeting morale. If many pilots die in dangerous flight missions, public opinion may demand an end to military missions that are important to national security.

Because UAVs are both low risk and high tech, they allow the military to hit very specific targets, thus reducing unnecessary deaths and danger to bystanders. UAVs can go into areas that are too dangerous for piloted planes to enter, allowing the military to target remote terrorist camps. Although any military should focus on minimizing civilian casualties during its missions, the first priority must be its own country's safety.

CONS

An ethical military cannot only consider the well-being of its own troops. The use of drones has resulted in high civilian casualties. In pure self-interest, the easiest way to wage war would be to simply drop a nuclear bomb on an entire country. A responsible military must be willing to accept some losses out of respect for civilians.

UAVs have a high error rate. A report compiled by the Brookings Institution estimates that UAVs in Pakistan kill 10 civilians for every Al-Qaeda militant they kill. The 2013 figures, released by the Bureau of Investigative Journalism, estimate that US drones have killed almost 1,000 civilians in Pakistan, Yemen, and Somalia, including up to 209 children. Such a high rate of civilian casualties shows an unacceptable indifference to human life.

PROS	CONS
Civilians check each other against aiding militants. If one neighbor's choice to harbor terrorists results in another losing his home, neighbors and communities are likely to apply pressure to avoid the conflict.	Significant civilian casualties hinder military interests. Such casualties anger civilians and make them more likely to support rogue militant groups.
Apprehending terrorists is not always possible. Al-Qaeda sets up terrorist havens in remote desert areas on the border of Afghanistan and Pakistan; live capture from these areas is virtually impossible. Taking prisoners may be ideal,	UAVs only have the ability to fire, preventing any attempt to capture prisoners rather than kill. High-ranking terrorists are much more useful alive and imprisoned than dead because they have crucial intelligence information.
but killing top militants is better than letting them continue to wreak havoc with civilian populations.	

Sample Motions:

This House protects its soldiers.

This House advocates the use of drones in warfare.

This House holds the military responsible for unnecessary civilian casualties.

Web Links:

- Bergen, Peter, and Katherine Tiedemann. "The Year of the Drone: An Analysis of U.S. Drone Strikes in Pakistan, 2004–2010" <http://www.newamerica.net/publications/policy/the_year_of_the_drone> Policy paper on the United States' drone program in Pakistan.
- Brookings Institution. "Do Targeted Killings Work?" <http://www.brookings.edu/opinions/2009/0714_targeted_killings _byman.aspx> Analysis of the benefits and disadvantages of UAVs in Pakistan.
- Cutting Edge. "60 Minutes Video: Drone Warfare in Iraq." <http://news.cnet.com/8301-11386_3-10064231-76.html> US military strategists in Iraq discuss their use of UAVs.
- Frontline. "The Future of War." <http://www.pbs.org/wgbh/pages/frontline/digitalnation/waging-war/remote-control-war/ thefuture-of-war.html> Military technology expert P. W. Singer discusses the increased use of UAVs in the "war on terror" [video].
- Newsweek. "Drone On: Q&A: A Former Pakistani Diplomat Says America's Most Useful Weapon Is Hurting the Cause in His Country." <http://www.newsweek.com/2009/07/07/drone-on.html> Pakistan's former deputy representative at the UN, S. Azmat Hassan, evaluates US use of UAVs in Pakistan.

Further Reading:

Singer, P. W. *Wired for War: the Robotics Revolution and Conflict in the 21st Century.* The Penguin Press, 2009.

■ ■

DRUG TESTING IN SCHOOLS

The right of schools to randomly test students for drugs has been debated in the courts for years. In a landmark 1995 decision Vernonia School District v. Acton, *the US Supreme Court ruled that schools could test student athletes for drug use. Three years later the US Court of Appeals for the Seventh Circuit (covering Illinois, Indiana, and Wisconsin) extended the right to test all participants in extracurricular activities, but in 2000 the Indiana Supreme Court banned such testing where the student concerned was not suspected of taking drugs. In 2002 the US Supreme Court ruled that drug testing was permissible for students involved in "competitive" extracurricular activities. Does society's desire to combat a growing drug problem override the right to privacy?*

PROS

Drug use among teenagers is a clear and present problem. Current measures to tackle drugs at the source (i.e., imprisoning dealers and breaking the supply chain) are not succeeding. It is especially important to protect teenagers at an impressionable age and at the time when their attitude to education greatly affects their entire lives. Some sacrifice of human rights is necessary to tackle the drug problem.

Students who do not take drugs have nothing to fear.

The purpose of random drug testing is not so much to catch offenders but to prevent all students from offending in the first place.

Peer pressure is the primary cause of experimentation with drugs. Discouraging drug use among athletes, model students, etc., sends a powerful message to the entire student body.

Urine, hair, and breath samples can be used to detect use of most common drugs, including marijuana, cocaine, heroin, and methamphetamines.

CONS

Our justice system is based on the principle that a person is innocent until proven guilty. To enforce random drug testing (thereby invading the privacy of students who are not suspected of drug use) is to view them as guilty until proven innocent. Nothing justifies the sacrifice of the human rights of innocent people.

Innocent students do have something to fear—the violation of privacy and loss of dignity caused by a drug test.

Other methods of preventing drug abuse are less invasive. These include encouraging extracurricular activities, fostering better relations with parents, tackling the problems of poverty and safety, and so on.

Teenagers, especially drug-taking teenagers, are attracted by rebellion and the chance of beating the system. Draconian, Big Brother–style tactics of random drug testing will only provoke resentment and encourage students to break the law. Peer pressure increases as they unite against school authorities.

Drug users will only turn to drugs that are more difficult to test, such as "designer" drugs, or use masking agents before being tested.

Sample Motions:

This House supports random drug testing in schools.

This House believes in a student's right to privacy.

Web Links:

- Creative Education. <http://www.creativeeducation.co.uk/videos/watch-video.aspx?id=59> Video depicting one school's random drug testing policy.
- Gerada, Clare, and Eilish Gilvarry. <http://www.pubmedcentral.nih.gov/articlerender.fcgi?artid=1472793> Article arguing against random drug testing in schools; outlines the effectiveness of testing, methods of testing, and problems with testing.
- Office of National Drug Policy. < https://www.ncjrs.gov/ondcppubs/publications/pdf/drug_testing.pdf> US government brief defending random drug tests in schools.

Further Reading:

Lineburg, Mark. *Random Student Drug Testing in Virginia Public Schools.* VDM Verlag Dr. Müller, 2008.

Schmitt, Nanette. *Drug Testing in Today's Schools: The Relationship Between Drug Testing Policies in Extracurricular Activities and the Incidents of Student Drug Use.* Lambert Academic Publishing, 2010.

United States Congress. *Drug Testing in Schools: An Effective Deterrent?* General Books, 2012.

■ ■

DRUGS IN SPORTS

Over the past decade, the sports world has been rocked by revelations that world-class athletes have used performance-enhancing drugs. During 2002, major league baseball players Jose Canseco and Ken Caminiti claimed that a large percentage of players used steroids to enhance their performance; since 2003, Barry Bonds, who holds the record for most home runs in a season, has continually been dogged by allegations of having used steroids and other performance-enhancing drugs. In 2012, record-breaking cyclist Lance Armstrong was found to have used performance-enhancing drugs and was issued a lifetime ban from all competitive sport; he was also stripped of every title he had won since 1998. In 2013, he admitted to what the US Anti-Doping Agency described as the most "successful doping program that sport has ever seen." The use of steroids has not been confined to professional athletes. Young athletes have died as a result of steroid use, which has led to bans on performance-enhancing drugs in high school and college programs. Some people argue that this whole approach is deeply flawed; these critics believe that eliminating performance-enhancing drugs is unrealistic. Instead, they advocate leveling the playing field by allowing all athletes equal access to performance-enhancing drugs, under the guidance of trained health professionals.

PROS

Using performance-enhancing drugs is an issue of freedom of choice. If athletes wish to take drugs in search of improved performances, let them do so. They harm nobody but themselves and should be treated as adults capable of making rational decisions on the basis of widely available information. We should not forbid them performance-enhancing drugs even if such drugs have long-term adverse effects. We haven't outlawed tobacco and boxing, which are proven health risks.

What is the distinction between natural and unnatural enhancement? Athletes use all sorts of dietary supplements, exercises, equipment, clothing, training regimes, medical treatments, etc., to improve their performance. There is nothing "natural" about taking vitamin pills or wearing whole-body Lycra suits. Diet, medicine, technology, and even coaching already give an artificial advantage to those athletes who can afford the best of all these aids. As there is no clear way to distinguish between legitimate and illegitimate artificial aids to performance, they should all be allowed.

Legalizing performance-enhancing drugs levels the playing field. Currently, suspicion about drug use surrounds every sport and every successful athlete. Those competitors who don't take performance-enhancing drugs see themselves as (and often are) disadvantaged. There are no tests for some drugs, and, in any case, new medical and chemical advances mean that cheaters will always be ahead of the testers. Legalization would remove this uncertainty and allow everyone to compete openly and fairly.

CONS

Once some people choose to use these drugs, they infringe on the freedom of choice of other athletes. Athletes are very driven individuals who go to great lengths to achieve their goals. To some, the chance of a gold medal in two years time may outweigh the risks of serious long-term health problems. We should protect athletes from themselves and not allow anyone to take performance-enhancing drugs.

Where to draw the line between legitimate and illegitimate performance enhancement? Difficult though that may be, we should nonetheless continue to draw a line: first, to protect athletes from harmful drugs; second, to preserve the spirit of fair play and unaided competition between human beings at their peak of natural fitness. Eating a balanced diet and using the best equipment are clearly in a different category from taking steroids and growth hormones. We should continue to make this distinction and aim for genuine drug-free athletic competitions.

Legalization is very bad for athletes. The use of performance-enhancing drugs leads to serious health problems, including "steroid rage," the development of male characteristics in female athletes, heart attacks, and greatly reduced life expectancy. Some drugs are also addictive.

PROS

Legalizing these drugs will provide better entertainment for spectators. Sport has become a branch of the entertainment business, and the public demands "higher, faster, stronger" from athletes. If drug use allows athletes to continually break records or makes football players bigger and more exciting to watch, why deny the spectators what they want, especially if the athletes want to give it to them?

Current rules are very arbitrary and unfair. For example, the Olympics forbids athletes from using cold medicines, even in sports where the stimulants in these medicines would have minimal effects on performance. There is also the possibility that some positive tests are simply the result of using a combination of legal food supplements. Cyclists legally have heart operations to allow increased circulation and thus improve performance, but they would be banned if they were to use performance-enhancing drugs.

In many countries bans on performance-enhancing drugs fail to stand up in court. The legal basis for drug testing and the subsequent barring of transgressors from further participation is open to challenge, both as restraint of trade and invasion of privacy. Sports governing bodies often fight and lose such court cases, wasting vast sums of money.

If drugs were legal, they could be controlled and monitored by doctors, making them much safer. Athletes on drugs today often take far more than needed for performance enhancement because of ignorance and the need for secrecy. Legalization would facilitate the exchange of information on drugs, and open medical supervision will avoid many of the health problems currently associated with performance-enhancing drugs.

CONS

Spectators enjoy the competition between athletes rather than individual performances; a close race is better than a no-contest in a world record time. Similarly, they enjoy displays of skill more than simple raw power. In any case, why should we sacrifice the health of athletes for the sake of public enjoyment?

What about the children? Even if performance-enhancing drugs were legalized only for adults, how would you control the problem among children? Teenage athletes train alongside adults and share the same coaches. Many would succumb to the temptation and pressure to use drugs if these were widely available and effectively endorsed by legalization. Young athletes are unable to make fully rational, informed choices about drug taking, and the health impact on their growing bodies would be even worse than for adult users. Legalization of performance-enhancing drugs would also send a positive message about drug culture in general, making the use of "recreational drugs" with all their accompanying evils more widespread.

Legalization discriminates against poor nations. Far from creating a level playing field, legalization would tilt it in favor of those athletes from wealthy countries with advanced medical and pharmaceutical industries. Athletes from poorer nations would no longer be able to compete on talent alone.

Reform is preferable to surrender. The current testing regime is not perfect, but better research, testing, and funding, plus sanctions against uncooperative countries and sports could greatly improve the fight against drugs in sports.

Sample Motions:
This House would legalize the use of performance-enhancing drugs for athletes.
This House would win at all costs.
This House believes your pharmacist is your best friend.

Web Links:
- Gendin, Sidney. <http://www.mesomorphosis.com/articles/gendin/philosophical-defense-of-steroid-use.htm> Philosophy professor offers a strong defense of steroid use in sports.

- Mehlman, Maxwell J. <http://www.thedoctorwillseeyounow.com/content/bioethics/art1972.html> Lays out arguments for and against the use of drugs in sports.
- Patient UK. <http://www.patient.co.uk/showdoc/40024949/> Comprehensive overview of the use of drugs in sports.

Further Reading:

Magdalinski, Tara. Sport, Technology and the Body: The Nature of Performance. Routledge, 2008.

Moller, Verner. The Ethics of Doping and Anti-Doping: Redeeming the Soul of Sport? Routledge, 2009.

Mottram, David R. *Drugs in Sport.* 5th ed. Taylor and Francis, 2011.

..

ECONOMIC DEVELOPMENT VS. ENVIRONMENT

The issue of economic development versus environmental conservation can also be seen as the First World vs. the Third World. Industrialized nations, ironically those that are most responsible for current environmental problems, fear that unregulated economic development in the Third World will have disastrous long-term environmental effects on the planet. They point out that massive clearing of tropical forests for farmland is threatening biodiversity and may impact world climate, while a reliance on heavy industry to fuel economic growth adds more pollutants to the air, ground, and water. Developing countries counter that they must make industrialization and economic development a priority because they have to support their growing populations. Developing countries must address current problems; they cannot afford to worry about the distant future.

PROS

Taking care of the millions of people who are starving is more important than saving natural resources, most of which are renewable anyway.

The industrialized world's emphasis on protecting the environment shackles developing countries and contributes to and widens the great divide between the First and Third Worlds. By limiting the development of profitable but polluting industries like steel or oil refining, we are sentencing nations to remain economically backward.

Economic development is vital for meeting the basic needs of the growing populations of Third World countries. If we do not permit industrialization, these nations will have to implement measures to limit population growth just to preserve vital resources such as water.

Obviously the world would be better if all nations abided by strict environmental rules. The reality is that for many nations such adherence is not in their larger interests. For example, closing China's massive Capital Iron and Steelworks, which ecologists point to as a major polluter, would cost 40,000 jobs. The uniform application of strict

CONS

We have wasted and destroyed vast amounts of natural resources, and in so doing have put Earth in jeopardy. We must preserve Earth for future generations.

No one wants to stop economic progress that could give millions better lives. But we must insist on sustainable development that integrates environmental stewardship, social justice, and economic growth. Earth cannot support unrestricted growth.

Unchecked population growth has a deleterious effect on any nation and on the entire planet. Limiting population growth will result in a higher standard of living and will preserve the environment.

Nations are losing more from polluting than they are gaining from industrialization. China is a perfect example. Twenty years of uncontrolled economic development have created serious, chronic air pollution that has increased health problems and resulted in annual agricultural losses of billions of dollars. Thus, uncontrolled

PROS	CONS

environmental policies would create insurmountable barriers to economic progress.

Rapid industrialization does not have to put more pressure on the environment. Technological advances have made industries much safer for the environment. For example, nuclear generating plants can provide more energy than coal while contributing far less to global warming. We are also exploring alternative, renewable types of fuel.

The "Green Revolution" has doubled the size of grain harvests. Thus, cutting down more forests or endangering fragile ecosystems to provide more space for crops is no longer necessary. We now have the knowledge to feed the world's increasing population without harming the environment.

growth is not only destructive to the environment, it is also unsound economically.

Technological progress has made people too confident in their abilities to control their environment. In just half a century the world's nuclear industry has had at least three serious accidents: Windscale (UK, 1957), Three Mile Island (US, 1979), and Chernobyl (USSR, 1986). In addition, the nuclear power industry still cannot store its waste safely.

The Green Revolution is threatening the biodiversity of the Third World by replacing native seeds with hybrids. We do not know what the long-term environmental or economic consequences will be. We do know that in the short run, such hybrid crops can indirectly cause environmental problems. The farmer using hybrid seed, which is expensive, must buy new seed each year because the seed cannot be saved to plant the following year's crops. Farmers using hybrid seeds in what once was the richest part of India went bankrupt. As a result, fertile lands lay idle and untilled, resulting in droughts and desertification.

Sample Motions:

This House believes that environmental concerns should always take precedence over economic development in both the First and Third Worlds.

This House believes that economic growth, even at the expense of some environmental degradation, is justified by the need to feed the rising world population.

Web Links:

- The Centre for International Sustainable Development Law. <http://www.cisdl.org/pdf/brief_common.pdf> Explains the concept of "common but differentiated responsibilities."
- International Institute for Sustainable Development. <http://www.iisd.org> Describes the institute's activities and offers reports and research materials on different aspects of sustainable development.
- McManus, Kelly. "The Principle of 'Common But Differentiated Responsibility' and the UNFCCC." <http://www .climaticoanalysis.org/wp-content/uploads/2009/12/kmcmanus_common-responsibilities.pdf> Discusses the concept of common but differentiated responsibility, including its impact on the UNFCCC, Kyoto Protocol, and present-day legal frameworks.
- The Pew Charitable Trusts. <http://www.pewtrusts.org/our_work_report_detail.aspx?id=32716> Detailed report explains why developed countries, in particular the US, have the greatest responsibility to fight climate change.
- World Bank. <http://news.mongabay.com/2006/0510-worldbank.html> Describes the rapid increase in the amount of greenhouse gases China and India are emitting.

Further Reading:

Adams, W. M. *Green Development: Environment and Sustainability in a Developing World*. Routledge, 2008.

Sinha, Ajit, and Siddharta Mitra, eds. *Economic Development, Climate Change and the Environment*. Routledge India, 2007.

Wilson, Gordon et al. *Environment, Development and Sustainability: Perspectives and Cases From Around the World*. Oxford University Press, 2009.

■ ■

ECONOMIC SANCTIONS VS. ENGAGEMENT

Economic sanctions are one of the most controversial ways whereby the international community seeks to influence a nation's internal policy and democratize countries. Sanctions helped end apartheid in South Africa, but the 50-year-old US embargo of Cuba has not brought down its communist government. China has a terrible human rights record, nevertheless sanctions have not been imposed on it. The question of whether to use trade to effect change is a subject of continuing debate.

PROS

Free trade brings about democratization in three ways: it permits a flow of information from Western countries; it raises a nation's standard of living; and it facilitates the growth of a middle class. These factors generate internal pressure and consequent political change—economic freedom leads to political freedom. Free trade helped bring about the downfall of communism in Eastern Europe and is beginning to increase freedoms in China. When the United States linked most favored nation (MFN) status to improvements in human rights, China made only token gestures to improve its rights record to maintain MFN status. Deep structural changes in human rights in any country come only with unlimited free trade.

Sanctions are ineffective. For example, France and Russia currently have openly breached international sanctions against Iraq because of their complete failure. Sanctions against Cuba and Burma have also proved useless because many nations do not recognize them. In addition, once sanctions are in place, the government of the country being sanctioned keeps all available resources, ensuring that sanctions adversely affect only the people. In the case of Iraq, sanctions led to terrible suffering.

Sanctions block the flow of outside information into a country, thus permitting dictators to use propaganda to strengthen their own position. People cannot believe such propaganda is false when there are no competing external claims.

CONS

Most dictatorial oligarchies welcome free trade as it usually increases their wealth. The West no longer has any leverage over them once they have been accepted into the free trade arena. Although the international community chose not to impose sanctions on China because it is a valuable economic and strategic partner, trade, specifically MFN status, can still be used to force China to improve human rights. Believing that free trade can lead to democratization is naïve. Governments against which sanctions are imposed will not permit the growth of a middle class or let wealth filter down to the people. In reality free trade has worsened Chinese living standards by putting domestic industries out of business and forcing people to work for multinational corporations that pay little.

Sanctions are effective as a long-term tool. They worked in South Africa and they worked in the former Rhodesia. Granted, they can lead to mass suffering of the very people they are designed to help, as they did to the black population of South Africa. However, Nelson Mandela has said that the suffering was worthwhile because it helped end apartheid.

Sanctions send a strong message to the people of a country that the Western world will not tolerate an oppressive regime.

Sample Motions:

This House would put trade relations above human rights.

This House believes in free trade.

This House would make money, not war.

This House would engage, not estrange, nondemocratic nations.

Web Links:

- Cato Institute Center for Trade Policy Studies. <http://www.cato.org/research/trade-immigration> Site advocating free trade; includes essays on China, the Cuban embargo, and the failure of unilateral US sanctions.
- Colvin, Jake, and Simon Cox. <http://www.cfr.org/publication/13853/are_economic_sanctions_good_foreign_policy.html> Two economists debate the merits of different types of economic sanctions.
- USA*Engage. <http://usaengage.org> Information on current US sanctions and potential sanctions by a coalition of American businesses, trade associations, and agriculture groups that oppose unilateral US action.
- Winkler, Adam. <http://muse.jhu.edu/journals/human_rights_quarterly/v021/21.1winkler.html> Uses the principles of Just War to justify trade sanctions in very specific circumstances.

Further Reading:

Gordon, Joy. *Invisible War: The United States and the Iraq Sanctions.* Harvard University Press, 2010.

Hufbauer, Gary Clyde et al. *Economic Sanctions Reconsidered.* 3rd ed. Peterson Institute for International Economics, 2009.

Krustev, Valentin. *Bargaining and Economic Coercion: The Use and Effectiveness of Sanctions.* VDM Verlag, 2008.

■ ■

ELECTORAL COLLEGE, ABOLITION OF

The US Electoral College is the assembly of representatives and senators, known as "electors," who formally elect the president and vice president of the United States. Each state chooses its electors through a popular vote and is apportioned the same number of electors as it has members of Congress. This means that voters in less populous states tend to have a disproportionately large influence over the election—for example, California has one electoral vote for every 679,000 people while Wyoming has one for every 189,000 people, so one vote in Wyoming is worth almost four votes in California. The presidential election of 2000 gave new prominence to the Electoral College system. Although Al Gore received more popular votes than George W. Bush, Bush won the election because his victory in Florida gave him a majority of electoral votes. To some observers, this outcome demonstrated clearly that the Electoral College should be abolished. They feel it is an anachronism that has outlived its usefulness. To others, however, the result demonstrated that the Electoral College is both good and necessary, and that the system had worked as it was designed to do. The debate over the Electoral College was reignited in 2012, when it became a distinctly partisan issue. Influential Democrats—most notably Al Gore—publicly called for a popular vote system, while the 2012 Republican National Convention passed a platform opposing any move to abolish the Electoral College. Since the current Electoral College system advantages the small rural states that tend to vote Republican, and disadvantages the large urban states that tend to vote Democratic, this debate is increasingly a point of contention between the two parties.

PROS

The president should be the person chosen by the greatest number of Americans, via the popular vote. The Electoral College violates this mandate in principle and sometimes in practice.

The Electoral College was established at a time when the people were not trusted to choose wisely; senators, too, were initially not chosen by popular vote. The system should be changed to trust the wisdom of the American people.

CONS

The Electoral College ensures that the person elected president has broad support throughout the country. Without the college, candidates could win by appealing only to heavily populated urban areas.

The principle behind the Electoral College is similar to the principle that determines the composition of the Senate, wherein every state is deemed equal, no matter its size. The college is an integral part of the system of federalism, which gives the states distinct and important rights.

PROS

The Electoral College system gives greater weight to votes cast in lightly populated states. The result is that a vote cast for the president by a New Yorker counts less than a vote cast by a North Dakotan; this inequality is inherently unfair.

The lightly populated states that are privileged by the Electoral College system are overwhelmingly white. In effect, the system discounts the worth of votes cast by minorities living in urban areas and exacerbates the racial imbalance of power in the country.

The current winner-take-all system effectively eliminates third-party candidates, as they cannot win enough Electoral College votes to gain office. The result? The electoral process is predisposed to the status quo, and change and progress are discouraged.

Too much latitude is given to electors in the present system; in some states, electors are not required to cast their votes for the candidates who have won the popular vote in their states. Electors should not have the power to disregard the will of the people.

CONS

The Electoral College forces candidates to campaign broadly throughout the country to gain the electoral votes of as many states as possible. If it is eliminated, candidates will spend all their time campaigning in the states with the greatest number of voters and ignore smaller states.

Minority voters could be safely ignored by candidates in a national election that depended only on receiving a popular majority. But because these voters can determine who wins a majority—and the electoral votes—in a given state, their influence is significant in the present system.

Because no candidate can win the presidency without an absolute majority of electoral votes, the Electoral College promotes the strength of the two-party system and that system promotes the political stability of the country.

The Constitution designed the US government to include a series of checks and balances, and the Electoral College is part of that system. The Electoral College is meant to limit the "tyranny of the majority" that is possible in unrestrained democracy.

Sample Motions:
This House supports the abolition of the Electoral College.
This House values the democratic will over states' rights.

Web Links:
- Herald Tribune. <http://www.heraldtribune.com/article/20090110/OPINION/901100323?p=1&tc=pg> Argues for abolition of the Electoral College.
- NPR. <http://www.npr.org/templates/story/story.php?storyId=4127863> Two radio segments, one featuring George Edwards (see below) arguing against the Electoral College and the other with a political scientist who believes that the Electoral College ensures that the winner has support from many different factions.
- Samples, John. <http://www.cato.org/publications/commentary/defense-electoral-college> Think-tank article arguing in favor of retaining the Electoral College.
- United States Government. <http://www.archives.gov/federal-register/electoral-college/index.html> Offers a thorough explanation of how the Electoral College functions.

Further Reading:
Bugh, Gary. *Electoral College Reform (Election Law, Politics and Theory)*. Ashgate, 2010.
Edwards, George C., III. *Why the Electoral College Is Bad for America*. Yale University Press, 2005.
Ross, Tara. *Enlightened Democracy: The Case for the Electoral College*. 2nd ed. Colonial Press, 2012.

EMBRYO SCREENING

Francis Galton coined the term "eugenics" in 1883 during his work on the genetic basis of intelligence. Literally meaning "good breeding," the term referred to the restructuring of the characteristics of the human race through selective mating (and subsequent reproduction) of the higher echelons of society. Some people, including Theodore Roosevelt, embraced the idea at the turn of the nineteenth century, but it lost favor as a result of its association with Nazi Germany, which took the idea to its extreme. Today, as a result of advances in biotechnology, we can screen fetuses to determine their predisposition to certain congenital disorders. In 2000, a baby boy, Adam Nash, was born after having been genetically screened as an embryo, from several embryos created by in vitro fertilization by his parents. They chose that embryo because tests showed that it was genetically healthy and the baby would be able to act as a bone marrow donor for his sister, who had a genetic disease. The case sparked heated moral debate.

PROS

Testing embryonic cells can help to identify potentially debilitating illnesses or inherited disorders. It can also determine the sex of a baby, allowing parents who carry a sex-linked genetic disorder to have children without passing on the disorder to their children. It is eminently sensible to use this technology to ensure that children are as healthy as possible.

We have a duty to give a child the best possible start in life, and if the technology is available to determine whether a baby will have a genetic disease such as Huntington's we should use it. This is not a case of engineering a child.

When a number of embryos are created through in vitro fertilization, the embryos not chosen after screening may be offered up for "adoption." Human life will not be thrown away, and childless couples can benefit.

CONS

Embryonic testing could become a slippery slope for future exploitation of the process. It must not develop into the widespread abuse of screening to create "designer babies" chosen for aesthetic or other qualities considered desirable. This is morally wrong.

Are we not presuming that those born with physical or mental defects or genetic predispositions to certain diseases do not enjoy a quality of life as high and a life as fruitful as those born without? To suggest that they be bred out of society is presumptuous and abhorrent. More to the point, many "defective" genes confer advantages of a different nature, e.g., the sickle cell anemia allele protects somewhat against malaria.

The proposition holds sinister overtones of treating embryos like commodities. Even more morally dubious is the idea of disposing of those embryos that do not conform to the requirements of health.

Sample Motions:

This House would choose its babies.

This House would genetically engineer its children.

This House calls for more genetic screening.

Web Links:

- DNA Genetic Testing: Screening for Genetic Conditions and Genetic Susceptibility. <http://www.genetics.edu.au/Information/Genetics-Fact-Sheets/DNAGeneticTestingTestingforGeneticConditionsandGeneticSusceptibilityFS21> Explains the process of genetic testing and its effectiveness.
- Smithsonian Magazine. "Henrietta Lacks' 'Immortal Cells.'" <http://www.smithsonianmag.com/science-nature/82414557.html> This interview with Skloot (see Further Reading) summarizes the Henrietta Lacks controversy and its lasting significance.

- The Texas Tribune. "DSHS Turned Over Hundreds of DNA Samples to Feds." <http://www.texastribune.org/texas-state -agencies/department-of-state-health-services/dshs-turned-over-hundreds-of-dna-samples-to-feds/> Article discussing the controversy in Texas over using infant blood samples without parental consent.

Further Reading:

Baily, Mary Ann, and Thomas H. Murray. *Ethics and Newborn Genetic Screening: New Technologies, New Challenges.* Johns Hopkins University Press, 2009.

Cowan, Ruth Schwartz. *Heredity and Hope: The Case for Genetic Screening.* Harvard University Press, 2008.

Skene, Loane, and Janna Thompson. *The Sorting Society: The Ethics of Genetic Screening and Therapy.* Cambridge University Press, 2008.

▪ ▪

ENVIRONMENTALLY LINKED AID

Many parts of the developing world have begun industrializing without regard to the environmental consequences. In light of growing environmental concerns, some individuals and groups have suggested tying aid to environmental goals including curbing emissions of carbon dioxide and chlorofluorocarbon. The international community would still give emergency aid in response to disasters, but it would tie development aid to environmental standards set by the United Nations Environmental Programme (UNEP). Countries with especially low emissions would receive extra aid.

PROS

The scientific community is almost unanimous in believing that emissions are seriously damaging the world ecosystem. The most serious threat is climate change. The effects of global warming include increasing desertification and rising sea levels. In addition, the El Niño phenomenon occurs more often. Air pollution has also resulted in increased acid rain and a growing hole in the ozone layer.

The industrialization of the small number of developed countries caused virtually all the problems laid out above. If developing countries, which have about five times the population of the developed world, were to industrialize unchecked, the effect could be catastrophic. For example, rising sea levels would flood millions of homes in low-lying areas such as Bangladesh. Increased crop failure would kill many more by starvation. Developed countries might be able to protect themselves from these effects, but developing countries would not. The developing world has not acted to prevent environmental disaster and so the developed world must act to save literally billions of lives.

The UN could design initial standards so that all developing countries could meet the goals and receive aid. If they spend this development aid wisely, developing countries

CONS

Environmental pressure groups seriously overstate the evidence for climate change. Even if climate change is occurring, pollution is not necessarily the cause. It may result from natural variations, which the fossil record indicates have occurred in the past.

This is just a new form of imperialism. Developing countries have the right to develop economically and industrially just as developed countries have. Industrialization will improve the living standards of billions of people throughout the globe. In addition, industrialization will lead to economic stability for the world's poorest countries. This, in turn, will increase democratization in these nations.

Developed countries are hypocritical in trying to restrict emissions from developing countries when they do so little themselves. The United States, which is still the world's could industrialize in an environmentally clean way. In the long run, the combined approach of extra rewards for successful countries and serious sanctions for unsuccessful countries should ensure success.

Developed countries should be guardians of the planet expressly because they have a terrible history of polluting. They must prevent unhindered industrialization elsewhere.

Even if environmentalists have exaggerated their claims, the threat from environmental pollution is still great enough to require action. The potential benefit of acting to save the planet's ecosystem far outweighs any downside. (We are not conceding that the claims are exaggerated, merely that it does not matter even if they are.)

biggest polluter, consistently refuses to ratify environmental treaties because its own economic self-interest does not appear to be served by doing so. What right does the developed world have to preach to the developing world about emissions?

Asking the UNEP to set emission standards is unfeasible because both developed and developing countries would try to influence the agency. Developed countries would lobby for very restrictive emission standards to decrease the threat from cheap imports. Developing countries would demand standards so lax that they would have no effect.

This proposal has serious consequences for world stability. First, developed countries would certainly not enforce regulations against China (an important trading partner and the linchpin of regional stability), the world's fastest growing polluter. Second, the developing countries, particularly those that fail to meet the standards, would resent such outside intrusion. In addition, withholding aid could cause economic collapse and the subsequent rise of dictatorships. Rogue nations might form alliances that threatened world stability. In their rush to develop, these states would increase pollution because developed countries would have no influence over them.

Sample Motions:

This House would link aid to emissions reductions.

This House believes that the environment must come first.

Web Links:

- Center for Global Development. <http://www.cgdev.org/section/initiatives/_active/codaid> Discussion of "Cash on Delivery," a foreign aid initiative that withholds aid from developing countries that fail to meet set standards (environmental or otherwise).
- Environmental Defense Fund. <http://www.edf.org/page.cfm?tagID=1475> Advocates using economic incentives to reduce global warming.
- United Nations Environment Programme. <http://www.unep.ch/etb/areas/econInst.php> Explains how financial incentives and economic tools can be used to encourage sustainable development.

■ ■

EXTRAORDINARY RENDITION

"Extraordinary rendition" is the transferring of a person from one jurisdiction to another, without any form of judicial or administrative process ("rendition" in this case means giving something over to someone else). This

makes it different from other rendition methods, such as extradition, which is treaty-based, or deportation, which is based on the expelling country's domestic judicial processes. The term is currently connected to the US government's "war on terror." Ever since President Bill Clinton issued a directive in 1995, the Central Intelligence Agency (CIA) has had the possibility of using extraordinary rendition in the US fight against terrorism. The agency's use of it rose significantly after the 9/11 attacks.

The persons who are "rendered" might be captured outside the United States and then, without legal process, transferred to the US. They also might be captured on foreign soil and then transferred to another country. It is the latter case that has attracted the most criticism: according to critics, the US uses this specific form of extraordinary rendition to torture those suspected of terrorism, without having to do the torturing itself. That is why extraordinary rendition is sometimes also referred to as "torture flights." This discussions focuses on these alleged "torture flights."

PROS

The US government uses "extraordinary rendition" as "torture by proxy." It delivers those suspected of terrorism to countries that are known to practice torture, and expects certain results from those countries, in the form of information extracted. US practice violates both the UN Convention Against Torture (CAT), which forbids countries to render persons to states that practice torture, and US domestic law, which also prohibits this.

CONS

In 2006 Secretary of State Condoleezza Rice reaffirmed that the US government does not render persons to countries with the purpose of having them tortured. The US government may render those suspected of terrorism for "harsh interrogation," but harsh interrogation is legal both under CAT and domestic law, which determines torture as "inducing severe pain." In any case, the main reasons for rendering a terrorist suspect to another country for questioning have more to do with that state's role in the investigation than with particular interrogation techniques practiced there. The destination state may be better placed to interrogate the suspect in his own language, and may have detailed background information to inform the questioning process that the US lacks. The suspect may also be accused of plotting atrocities in the state to which he has been rendered, so it has a legitimate interest in interrogating him first.

Finally, in ratifying the Convention Against Torture in 1994, the US did so with the reservation that it can render persons to countries when it believes that it is more likely than not that a person will not be tortured. Thus, under the US interpretation of CAT, the US can render individuals to countries that practice torture, as long as the US has reason to believe that the country will not torture in this specific case.

How does the US government know the difference between "harsh interrogation" and "torture," and on what grounds does it base its belief that it is "more likely than not" that torture will not take place? By its nature, the work of the CIA is secretive. So, even if the CIA does obtain assurances, the general public can never check whether these agreements are being enforced. Since the CIA is being held responsible for fighting terrorism, they might even have an incentive to bend the rules a bit — as long as they can later show results to the public.

The CIA has a policy in practice whereby it obtains "diplomatic assurance" that torture will not be used. Under customary international law, the US is obliged to act "in good faith." So, when America is given diplomatic assurance by another government, it would be a diplomatic blunder not to trust that guarantee. Also, imagine the consequence if it were one day proved that the CIA rendered a person, knowing they would be tortured: not only would those involved lose their jobs, but also the reputation of the CIA would be severely damaged. That is why the CIA has an incentive to make sure that these assurances are believable.

PROS

What if the CIA makes mistakes? Because the victims are held in detention without recourse to any kind of judge, they have no possible way of getting out. Even worse, if someone is released out of this type of detention, the victim has no way of seeking redress since the operation was covert. An example of this is the case of Khalid El-Masri, a German of Lebanese descent, who suddenly disappeared in 2003. After he resurfaced in Albania in 2004, he claimed he was "kidnapped" by the CIA and tortured under the policy of "extraordinary rendition," until the CIA realized its mistake and released him, without excuse, and without compensation of any kind. Since there is no official record, his attempts to make a case against the CIA have failed. Worse still, a judge dismissed his case, under the argument that pursuing the case would be a severe threat to national security.

For every example of an "effective" rendition, one has to ask: is it worth it? Because for every terrorist successfully caught and convicted after rendition, there may be many more mistakes. For every Ramzi Youssef, there might be dozens of Khalid El-Masris, Abu Omars, Majid Mahmud Abdu Ahmads, Muhammad Bashmilas, and many more. On top of that, consider the loss of reputation that the practice of extraordinary rendition has caused the US to suffer among its chief allies. In 2007 the EU adopted a report condemning this particular US policy, and this was followed by a massive public outcry against the practice. Such American tactics simply play into the hands of terrorists who seek to stir hatred against America and divide it from its allies. And finally, does the pretext of a terrorist threat really justify taking away a person's right to due process? The question is even more relevant in that many experts believe torture is an ineffective method of acquiring reliable intelligence in any case.

The people targeted by extraordinary rendition are citizens, not combatants, and more important, they are human beings. If there is a reasonable suspicion that these people are terrorists, the US should follow the normal route of asking the country where the suspect is living to extradite him. The suspect can then be tried by a regular US criminal court, where the public eye will ensure his right to due process. Even if one views this person as a "combatant," he still has the fundamental human right to due process. The US should not violate the fundamental democratic rights it proclaims to defend in this war on terror.

CONS

To ensure that the CIA does not make any mistakes, it has started researching so-called erroneous renditions. In the case of Khalid El-Masri, the CIA has never admitted kidnapping him. The CIA does suspect, and is trying to apprehend, a German-based terrorist with the name Khalid Al-Masri, and it is possible that this person is using the similarity in names to create a backlash against the CIA. Regardless of the merits of this particular case, it is clearly in the interests of America's enemies to blacken its name and undermine its security forces through accusations of torture. Murky and unsubstantiated stories about rendition should thus not be believed uncritically.

What people should not forget is that extraordinary rendition saves lives. It is used to bring people who are known or believed to be terrorists, to justice. These suspects are often stateless and they hide in places where ordinary processes of law do not work. Extraordinary rendition is then the only possible way of tracking them down, getting the necessary information from them, and bringing them to justice. They carry information that could save thousands of lives. The US would be foolish not to try to extract that from them. An example of this is Ramzi Youssef, who masterminded the 1993 bombing of the World Trade Center and plotted to blow up airlines over the Pacific Ocean. After a rendition to the US, he was convicted and is now serving a life sentence. Without rendition, who knows how many people he would have killed?

We should not forget that the people the US targets for extraordinary renditions should be considered "unlawful combatants" in the war on terror. This term is important, because it identifies the US government as taking part in a war and terrorists as the combatants in that war. The people targeted for extraordinary rendition are "unlawful combatants" since their aim is to kill and terrorize US civilians, not US soldiers. Under international law, that is a very severe war crime, requiring the US to take very severe measures. Moreover, since the US is at war with terrorism, it has the obligation to protect its citizens first—and the obligation to dirty its hands in the process. Mistakes will inevitably be made, but in a time of war, the US cannot afford to risk the lives of its own citizens.

■ ■

FACTORY FARMING, BANNING OF

Factory farming is the large-scale, industrial production of livestock and poultry designed to produce the highest output at the lowest cost. The practice began in the 1920s after the discovery of vitamins A and D and vitamin supplements, which allowed large numbers of animals to be raised indoors without sunlight. Proponents of the practice point to its economic benefits, while opponents say it has led to cruelty and environmental destruction.

PROS

Factory farming is intrinsically cruel. Modern science permits factory farms to raise large numbers of animals indoors with no concern for their physical and emotional needs.

Factory farming sees animals as commodities for production and sale just like bricks or bread. But animals are conscious and know pleasure and pain. We should treat them humanely and with dignity. Factory farming does not. Yes, we are capable of higher thought and animals are not, but this means that we must be good stewards and care for them. How terribly we fail in fulfilling that duty.

CONS

Factory farming involves very little cruelty or suffering—certainly no more than in traditional forms of farming. Animals have always been herded together, confined, branded, killed, and eaten. Furthermore, government regulatory agencies can more easily monitor large factory farms, so the animals often fare better than they would on traditional farms. Activists have ensured that the few isolated incidents of cruelty or bad practice have received publicity greatly out of proportion to their significance.

This is sentimental nonsense. Unless the state is going to impose vegetarianism (and that's not being proposed here), farming will continue to be a business. It should be efficient and make a profit for the producer, while keeping prices low for the consumer. Many animals exist simply as a food source. Animals are not our equals and don't have the capacity for higher thought. We can use them without any moral problem.

PROS

Factory farming does not practice healthier, traditional farming methods that were more in tune with nature and that were the backbone of a rural way of life that is now dying. The countryside that we love was created by traditional farming methods, particularly grazing, not vast sheds full of imprisoned animals.

Factory farming is unhealthy for the environment. The waste from factory farms has contributed to water pollution; large-scale beef farming has produced vast quantities of methane that damages the ozone layer. Factory farming also erodes topsoil at an alarming rate.

CONS

Again, sentimentality is interfering with logic. Farming has always been the imposition of artificial, man-made patterns on nature. As for farmers losing jobs, plenty of people are employed in factory farming. Why is that any less worthy? And many farmers have sold off their land for enormous profits.

Come on! Are we really supposed to believe that cow-produced methane is in the same league as pollution from big business and industry?

The topsoil point is more substantial. But that's an argument for regulations requiring the upkeep and replacement of turf, not for banning a whole industry.

Sample Motions:

This House would ban factory farming.

This House would go free range.

This House prefers low-intensity agriculture.

Web Links:

- FactoryFarming.com. <http://www.factoryfarming.com> Information on specific aspects of the topic by group opposed to factory farming.
- Hurst, Blake. <http://www.american.com/archive/2009/july/the-omnivore2019s-delusion-against-the-agri-intellectuals> A defense of factory farming written by a Missouri farmer.
- Sandy, Jennifer. "Factory Farms: A Bad Choice for Rural America." <http://www.preservationnation.org/forum/library/public-articles/factory-farms.html> Describes rural life in the United States and the effects of factory farming.

Further Reading:

Imhoff, Daniel. The CAFO Reader: The Tragedy of Industrial Animal Factories. University of California Press, 2010.

Miller, Debra A. *Factory Farming*. Greenhaven Press, 2010.

Moby and Miyun Park, eds. *Gristle: From Factory Farms to Food Safety*. New Press, 2010.

Singer, Peter, and Jim Mason. The Ethics of What We Eat: Why Our Food Choices Matter. Rodale Books, 2007.

■ ■

FRACKING

Hydraulic fracturing, or "fracking," is a technique used to extract natural gas from underground formations by creating fractures in the surrounding rock. These fractures are produced by injecting a treated solution into either manmade or naturally occurring cracks, under high pressure, which forces these cracks further open. First introduced in the 1940s, this process is now the predominant form of natural gas extraction in the United States. Its popularity in the natural gas industry has permitted access to greater deposits of gas than ever before, raising US fuel production rates. However, the process is highly controversial. The chemical solution used for fracking contains known carcinogens, which critics allege leak into water supplies and contaminate the surrounding environment. The health risks associated with this contamination have caused numerous countries to ban the practice. Proponents of fracking claim that safety concerns have been exaggerated, and that the technology is rapidly evolving to make it safer still. For them, the economic benefits of fracking far outweigh potential environmental and health concerns.

PROS

Fracking is a safe process that has no negative effect on the environment when properly undertaken. Any past contaminations of groundwater or the surrounding environment were the result of a small number of badly drilled wells; the risk of this has been significantly reduced by the introduction of better regulations at the state level. The contemporary fracking process is undertaken with health and safety as primary concerns. A 2012 study by the University of Wyoming and Penn State University found that fracking was getting safer and should present no major environmental concerns. The lead author of the study said that "state oversight of oil and gas regulation has been effective." Both scientists and politicians are working to minimize any risks associated with this new and evolving technology. It makes no sense to ban a safe and effective process because of a few mistakes made in the past.

Fracking is actually beneficial for the environment in the long term, as it produces natural gas, one of the cleanest forms of fuel. Natural gas releases less atmosphere-warming carbon dioxide than other fuels release. Therefore a process that helps move the US toward natural gas and away from dirtier fuels, such as coal and petroleum, should be encouraged by environmentalists. As natural gas production has soared due to fracking, US carbon dioxide emissions have plummeted. A 2012 report by the International Energy Agency (IEA) found that the US led the world in carbon dioxide cuts, having reduced emissions by 430 million tons since 2006. This coincided with a 13% reduction in coal use, with natural gas—largely obtained by fracking—taking its place. The IEA's Faith Birol stated that "technology making shale gas production viable" is the primary reason that the United States is leading the world in reducing emissions. In considering the environmental effects of fracking, its contribution to reducing carbon dioxide emissions, and therefore global warming, must be paramount.

The development of the natural gas industry has been hugely beneficial to the US economy. Government studies estimate that the natural gas industry has created 622,411 direct jobs in the US, and almost 3 million jobs in total through its secondary effects on the

CONS

Fracking is fundamentally unsafe and no amount of regulation will alter that. Water contamination is widespread in regions with heavy fracking; a 2011 report by the Environmental Protection Agency showed that contamination in Wyoming was a direct result of fracking. Despite claims of improvement, fracking wells in the US still have a 5% leakage rate. Even if these leaks were minimized, fracking would still pollute the air with carcinogens. A three-year study from the Colorado School of Public Health found that these caused respiratory and neurological problems for people in surrounding communities. Furthermore, there is evidence that pumping such vast amounts of water into the earth's crust triggers earthquakes, with several reported near wells in Ohio and Arkansas. Fracking companies hamper attempts to properly investigate health risks, with many refusing to disclose the chemical they use. Without an extensive examination of the consequences of fracking, it is immoral to continue to put people and the environment at risk.

Natural gas is far from a clean fuel source, and when it is obtained by fracking, it may even be dirtier than coal. Although natural gas releases less carbon dioxide than coal, the methane that leaks into the atmosphere during fracking completely negates this benefit. A 2011 Cornell University study explained that methane is significantly more harmful to the environment than carbon dioxide, "with 105 times more warming impact, pound for pound." Even the smallest leaks of methane during fracking can be seriously detrimental to the environment; the study also found that up to 8% of the methane found in natural gas leaks into the air during fracking. The study's author concluded that "shale gas [the gas obtained by fracking] is worse than conventional gas and is, in fact, worse than coal and worse than oil." Efforts to reduce our harmful emissions should focus on truly clean sources of energy, such as hydroelectricity and solar energy; attempting to cast natural gas, and fracking, as good for the environment is severely misguided.

While the introduction of fracking into economically depressed regions could have financial benefits for some landowners and workers, it is not fair to sacrifice the environment and the health of everyone for these short-term economic gains. In addition, gas companies tend economy. Fracking also requires gas companies to lease the land above gas reserves, which they do at very competitive prices, benefiting landowners. In a 2011 study by the University of Texas at San Antonio, researchers found that fracking had huge economic benefits for communities surrounding the Eagle Ford Shale, one of the most actively drilled regions in the United States. The study found that fuel extraction—primarily fracking—at the Shale created 12,601 full-time jobs, in addition to generating over $60 million in state revenues and almost $50 million in local government revenues. Instead of sending money overseas by purchasing imported oil, fracking supports US jobs and US industry.

Fracking is financially beneficial to all Americans, not just energy corporations. Due to fracking, natural gas prices have dropped dramatically, making it the least expensive fuel available; natural gas is now three to five times cheaper than it was ten years ago. This reduction in the price of fuel benefits both consumers and industry through a reduction in energy costs. The Energy Information Administration projected that US manufacturing will increase by 2% per year for the next 30 years due to the cheaper natural gas produced by fracking. Access to affordable fuel is consistently rated as a top concern among Americans; by providing this access, fracking benefits us all.

to bring in their own workers from out of town, limiting the number of jobs created in the actual community that will suffer the consequences of fracking; any local jobs that are created tend to be unskilled and short-term. In the long-term, fracking will have a detrimental economic effect on surrounding communities: property values in the region will plummet, as few will want to move to areas with potential water and air contamination; widespread ill health will also have a negative effect on the local economy. It is fundamentally immoral for the welfare of an entire community, including children, to be sacrificed for financial gains that go primarily to large energy corporations rather than local residents.

Any financial benefits produced by fracking are time limited, while the environmental and health consequences will remain indefinitely. In addition, there is evidence that gas companies have been overstating their ability to produce large quantities of fuel at a low cost; a 2011 *New York Times* article revealed that gas companies were inflating figures over well productivity and gas reserves in order to attract investors. Furthermore, the article found that the amount of gas produced by many wells was falling much faster than energy companies had predicted. With the industry lacking in transparency, it is impossible to forecast how long the economic benefits of fracking will last, but there is no evidence that it is a long-term solution to US energy needs.

Sample Motions:

This House believes fracking should be illegal.

This House would endorse fracking.

Web Links:

- Energy from Shale. <http://www.energyfromshale.org/what-is-fracking?gclid=CIbQpvKQtbECFSUTNAod1yEAiw> Online resource endorsed by the natural gas industry discussing the fracking debating.
- New York Times. <http://www.nytimes.com/2011/06/26/us/26gas.html?pagewanted=1&_r=3&src=rechp> Discussion on the sustainability of fracking.
- NPR. <http://michiganradio.org/post/fracking-natural-gas-benefits-and-risks> Benefits and harms of fracking.

Further Reading:

Graves, John. *Fracking: America's Alternative Energy Revolution*. Safe Harbor, 2013.

McGraw, Seamus. *The End of Country: Dispatches from the Frack Zone*. Random House, 2011.

Rao, Vikram. *Shale Gas: The Promise and the Peril*. RTI Press, 2012.

Wilber, Tom. *Under the Surface: Fracking, Fortunes, and the Fate of the Marcellus Shale*. Cornell University Press, 2012.

■ ■

FREE SPEECH, RESTRICTIONS ON

Freedom of speech is one of the basic tenets of democracy. A fundamental right enshrined in the US Bill of Rights, the UN Declaration of Human Rights, and the European Convention on Human Rights, freedom of speech is, nevertheless, not an absolute. Most nations have laws against sedition, libel, or speech that threatens public safety. Where a nation draws the line between protected and unprotected speech is a continuing subject for debate.

PROS

Free speech is an inherently ambiguous concept that requires definition and interpretation; it is the job of governments to clarify these ambiguities.

As Justice Oliver Wendell Holmes wrote, "the most stringent protection of free speech would not protect a man in falsely shouting fire in a theater and causing a panic." We accept limitations on free speech when it may threaten public safety. Therefore, freedom of speech is never absolute.

Speech leads to physical acts. Pornography, hate speech, and political polemic are linked to rape, hate crimes, and insurrection.

Government must protect its citizens from foreign and internal enemies. Thus, governments should be permitted to curb speech that might undermine the national interest during war.

Some views are antithetical to religious beliefs. To protect the devout, we should ban this type of offensive speech.

We need to protect children from exposure to obscene, offensive, or potentially damaging materials.

CONS

The limits to free speech are too important to be determined by government. If speech is to be regulated, it should be done by an independent body.

The tyranny of the majority is a good reason to resist government censorship. A healthy democracy recognizes that smaller groups must be heard; to guarantee that they have a public voice, no restrictions should be put on speech.

Society is self-regulating. The link between speech and action is a false one. Yes, people who commit hate crimes are likely to have read hate literature, and people who commit sex crimes are likely to have watched pornography. But viewing pornography or reading hate speech does not necessarily lead to crime. In addition, exposing hate speech and extreme political polemic to societal scrutiny increases the likelihood that it will be discredited and defeated, rather than strengthened through persecution.

Regardless of the situation, the public has the right to a free exchange of ideas and to know what the government is doing.

We must defend the right of the nonreligious to express their views.

We all agree that government must protect children, but that does not mean that government should have the right to censor all material.

Sample Motions:
This House would restrict freedom of speech.
This House would muzzle the press.
This House would censor the Internet.
This House would ban books.

Web Links:

- American Civil Liberties Union. <http://www.aclu.org/freespeech/index.html> Coverage of current issues relating to free speech in the United States.
- American Library Association. <http://www.ala.org/ala/aboutala/offices/oif/firstamendment/firstamendment.cfm> Links to court cases and other resources related to the First Amendment.
- Van Mill, David. <http://plato.stanford.edu/entries/freedom-speech/> Philosophical discussion of free speech and democracy.

Further Reading:

Heyman, Steven J. Free Speech and Human Dignity. Yale University Press, 2008.

Lewis, Anthony. *Freedom for the Thought That We Hate: A Biography of the First Amendment.* Basic Books, 2010.

Mill, John Stuart. On Liberty. Nabu Press, 2010.

Warburton, Nigel. Free Speech: A Very Short Introduction. Oxford University Press, 2009.

■ ■

FREE TRADE AND DEVELOPMENT

Economists and politicians have praised the virtues of free trade for over 200 years. By allowing everyone equal access to all markets, the theory goes, you guarantee the most efficient allocation of resources and the cheapest prices for consumers. Can such a theory work in practice? Specifically, could it help the least-developed countries achieve a better quality of life? Western rhetoric says it can and points to international institutions like the World Trade Organization (WTO) and the World Bank that foster free trade and help these nations. However, as long as the West continues to protect its own agriculture and industries from the international market, its position is arguably hypocritical.

PROS

Interlocking trade relationships decrease the likelihood of war. If a nation is engaged in mutually beneficial relationships with other countries, it has no incentive to jeopardize these relationships through aggression. This promotes peace, which is a universal good.

A tariff-free international economy is the only way to maintain maximum global efficiency and the cheapest prices. Efficient allocation of the world's resources means less waste and, therefore, more affordable goods for consumers.

Free trade might lead to domestic layoffs, but the universal good of efficiency outweighs this. We should not subsidize uncompetitive industries; we should retrain workers for jobs in other fields. Subsidizing inefficiency is not sound economic practice. Moreover, the jobs we subsidize in the West are more needed in the developing world, to which they would inevitably flow if free trade were observed.

The growth of the developing world is a universal good because improving the quality of life of millions of people

CONS

Free trade does not promote peace. Trading countries have gone to war against each other. This argument might apply to a good-natured trading relationship, but not necessarily to one that is just tariff free.

International economics isn't as simple as increasing the efficiency of global resource allocation above all else. Tariff revenue is a perfectly legitimate and useful source of government income. Without tariffs governments cannot protect the jobs of their citizens.

Job security is a legitimate concern of governments. The destruction of jobs is clear testimony against free trade serving a "universal good." Free trade supporters fail to factor in the political ramifications of job losses. A starkly utilitarian understanding of "universal good" may dictate that jobs flock to the developing world, but political considerations may dictate a more localized definition of the "good."

Defending pure, unadulterated free trade is a pointless exercise. Textbook ideas are always mediated by practical

PROS	CONS
is clearly a moral imperative. Free trade helps countries by maximizing their comparative advantage in free trade circumstances.	constraints. In reality, the conditions developing countries must meet just to join the "not quite free trade" WTO are stringent and may cost the equivalent of the nation's entire annual humanitarian budget. Poor nations have social and development programs that must take priority over trade issues.
Free trade permits developing countries to gain ready access to capital in liberalized international financial markets. This gives them the opportunity to finance projects for growth and development.	If capital flow were rational, it would be beneficial. In practice, liberalized capital flow can destabilize developing economies, which are prone to speculation based on investor whim rather than economic fundamentals.

Sample Motions:

This House believes free trade serves a universal good.

This House believes free trade is good for the developing world.

Web Links:

- Friedman, Milton, and Rose Friedman. <http://www.hoover.org/publications/hoover-digest/article/7125> A defense of free trade from famed economist Milton Friedman.
- Public Citizen. <http://www.citizen.org/Page.aspx?pid=1328> Nongovernment organization website promoting more protectionism in American trade policy.
- World Trade Organization (WTO). <http://www.wto.org> Offers general information on the WTO, international trade and trade agreements, and WTO programs.

Further Reading:

Fletcher, Ian. Free *Trade Doesn't Work: What Should Replace It and Why*. 2nd ed. U.S. Business and Industry Council, 2011.

Hanson, David. *Limits to Free Trade: Non-tariff Barriers in the European Union, Japan and United States*. Elgar, 2010.

Irwin, Douglas. Free Trade Under Fire: 3rd ed. Princeton University Press, 2009.

Stiglitz, Joseph E., and Andrew Charlton. Free Trade for All: How Trade Can Promote Development. Oxford University Press, 2007.

▪ ▪

GAY ADOPTION

US states are currently divided on the issue of whether a gay couple should be able to adopt a child together. Although all states allow a gay individual to petition to adopt as a single parent, the situation becomes more complex when a gay couple wants to adopt together. Traditional adoption law allows for just one legal parent of each gender, therefore prohibiting same-sex couples from adopting together. Numerous states have amended this law to give gay couples adoption rights equal to those of heterosexual couples. However, several states either prohibit same-sex adoption completely, or allow it only when one partner is the child's biological parent. In states such as Kansas, Kentucky, Nebraska, and North Carolina, a gay person is not allowed to adopt a partner's biological child, unless the partner first relinquishes parental rights over the child. Consequently, an estimated two million children in the United States are unable to establish a legal relationship with both of their parents. Civil rights groups are currently challenging bans on gay adoption in federal courts, but no case has yet reached the US Supreme Court.

PROS

Society is changing, and the traditional idea of the nuclear family, with married mother and father, is no longer the only accepted way to raise a family. Several states now recognize same-sex marriages, or domestic partnerships, meaning that gay couples are increasingly able to lay the foundations of a stable family unit. Many same-sex couples already raise children together, through surrogacy or previous heterosexual relationships; 2011 US census data indicated that one-quarter of all same-sex households were raising children. Furthermore, the vast majority of evidence confirms that same-sex parenting is not harmful to children. Banning same-sex couples from being recognized as joint-parents does nothing other than deny legal rights to a minority group and stigmatize already existing family units.

A child should not be denied a loving home simply because that home does not fit the current social "ideal." If children were denied home lives that were not superficially ideal, they would not be adopted into single-parent families, low-income families, disabled families, step-families, or families with any deviation from the upper-middle-class nuclear model at all. In fact, until recently, interracial families were similarly demonized—up to 1996, US adoption agencies were able to deny the placement of a child solely on the basis of race. Child-rearing ideals are fluid: they are also irrelevant if they do not reflect the reality of the options a child is faced with. Even if studies did show that a married mother–father unit is best, this is meaningless to a child whose only chance at a happy family is with a loving homosexual couple. As long as a child is loved and cared for by a committed guardian, then that guardian is the child's parent and deserves to be legally recognized as such.

Allowing gay people to adopt as single parents but not as committed couples is contrary to the aim of promoting stable two-parent families. Banning gay adoption penalizes the children raised by same-sex couples: not only are they denied the intangible sense of security that comes from being formally connected to a parent, but they also lose out on legal benefits. For example, the child of a same-sex couple would not be entitled to Social Security Survivor benefits or inheritance rights if their second parent died. The child may also be denied any visitation to their second parent in the event of a contentious separation. Rather than simplifying familial relationships, denying adoption rights to same-sex couples actually complicates them, with the child bearing the brunt of these complications.

CONS

The traditional nuclear family is still the ideal. A 2012 study, published in *Social Science Research*, found that children living with both their biological mother and biological father were healthier, happier, better educated, and less prone to criminal activity than those raised by homosexual parents. Obviously, in the case of adopted children, it is not an option for them to be raised by both biological parents, but a maternal and paternal figure is the best approximation of this. The clear benefits of heterosexual parenting need to be kept at the forefront when making legal decisions regarding the welfare of children; the welfare of children must come before the issue of rights for same-sex couples.

Prohibiting gay people from adopting as a couple does not deny a child a loving home; it merely simplifies the parental roles within that home. A child could still be adopted into a household with a homosexual parent—just as a single heterosexual parent could adopt a child—and be raised with the assistance of the parent's partner. The fact is that a child needs a clear-cut "mother" or "father" figure as a primary caregiver; placing a child into a situation with two mothers or two fathers has the potential to be confusing and distressing for a child seeking stability. The situation becomes even more complex when one of the mothers or fathers is a biological parent and the second mother or father is the partner of the biological parent; in this situation, a legal adoption by a second same-gender parent serves no purpose other than to confuse the child and complicate custody arrangements in the event of a separation.

Children are best protected by a system that errs on the side of caution when it comes to granting parental rights; relatives, friends, and the partners of parents, all play vital roles when it comes to raising a child, but this does not make them a child's parent. The law should not function to protect the rights of gay couples to construct family units however they wish, but should instead protect children from being legally bound in confusing relationships with people they are not even related to. If an individual in a same-sex couple wants to include a partner's child in a will, or arrange visitation with that child after the relationship has ended, then that is a matter to be privately negotiated, not mandated by the federal government.

States do not have the right to discriminate against a protected group, which gay people are defined as. Since heterosexual people are allowed to adopt the biological children of their partners, and heterosexual couples are allowed to adopt together, disallowing homosexual couples from these same rights, simply on the basis of their sexuality, is nothing other than discrimination. The Equal Protection Clause of the Fourteenth Amendment to the US Constitution affirms that "no state shall . . . deny to any person within its jurisdiction the equal protection of the laws." Throughout US history, the "states' rights" argument has been used to marginalize and oppress minority groups. It is the proper role of the federal government to intervene when a state passes discriminatory laws; as such, the federal government should override any state bans on gay adoption.

The federal government should have no role in dictating how states define the family unit and oversee the adoption process. The Tenth Amendment to the US Constitution clearly states that "The powers not delegated to the United States by the Constitution, nor prohibited by it to the States, are reserved to the States respectively." Since the right to adopt is not protected in the Constitution, the federal government does not have the ability to override a state's decision on the issue. In addition, not allowing same-sex couples to adopt together does not constitute discrimination; adoption laws include all types of restrictions—such as age limitations and income minimums—that do not equate to discrimination. Furthermore, most states do not even recognize gay marriage, meaning that a federal mandate to allow gay adoption would be completely out of sync with the social climate in these states.

Sample Motions:

This House would allow gay couples to adopt children.

This House would ban adoption agencies from discriminating against gay couples.

Web Links:

- Children of Lesbians and Gays Everywhere. <http://www.colage.org> Site offering sociological information on gay families for children of gay parents.
- Gay Adoption: A New Take on the American Family <http://www.cnn.com/2007/US/06/25/gay.adoption/> Case study on the hurdles gay couples face in starting a family.
- Gay Family Values <http://www.time.com/time/magazine/article/0,9171,1640411,00.html> Article that looks at the legalization of gay adoption and need for homes for abandoned children.
- YouDebate.com. <http://www.youdebate.com/DEBATES/gay_adoption.HTM> Pros and cons of gay adoption.

Further Reading:

Brodzinsky, David. *Adoption by Lesbians and Gay Men: A New Dimension in Family Diversity*. Oxford University Press, 2011.

Sullivan, Ann. *Issues in Gay and Lesbian Adoption*. Child Welfare League of America, 1995.

Tasker, Fiona, and Susan Golombok. *Growing Up in a Lesbian Family: Effects on Child Development*. Guilford Press, 1998.

▪ ▪

GENE PATENTING

The pioneering research of the Human Genome Project has given us the ability to isolate our genes. This has engendered hope that scientists may be able to use genetic research to treat or cure disease. To date, the United States Patent and Trademark Office has granted thousands of patents on human DNA—approximately 20% of our genes are currently patented. The patents are not on DNA in its natural state, but on the process of discovering and isolating certain strings of DNA, and on DNA developed in the laboratory. But legal—and ethical—questions arise when commercial companies attempt to patent genetic research. Many people fear that these companies are coming close to patenting the building blocks of life itself. In June 2013, the Supreme Court ruled that isolated human genes are the product of nature, not human invention; as such, they cannot be patented. However, this decision did not cover manmade DNA molecules, which are still eligible for patents.

PROS

Companies engaged in genomic research are legally entitled to patent genes, so why should they be prevented from doing so?

If companies are not allowed to patent the products of their research, other companies will exploit their findings. Without the safeguards that a patent provides, companies will end their research because they see no future profit.

An inventor must be able to protect his or her invention. Private companies will continue genomic research because it promises to be extremely lucrative. Competitors will be willing to pay royalties to the patent holder for use of the material because they, too, can foresee future profit.

Patents are granted for a limited time in the United States, 17 years. Companies need this time to recoup their investments. If another company wishes to pursue a project in a patented area, it can always consult the patent owner.

Profit has proved to be the most practical means of promoting medical advances. It is unrealistic and ill conceived to criticize an incentive that has brought us such benefits.

CONS

Genes are the very basis of human life, and to claim that anyone has the right to be regarded as the "owner" of a particular gene shows a basic disregard for humanity. Patenting treatments based on genetic research is morally acceptable, but patenting genes is not.

Most genetic research is not conducted by private companies. The publicly funded Human Genome Project has contributed, by far, the greater amount of knowledge in this area. Patenting stifles research. We need to ban patenting in order to protect the public investment in genome research.

Facts do not support this contention; the Myriad Company, which held patents on isolating genes connected with breast cancer, prevented the University of Pennsylvania from using a test for these genes that was substantially cheaper than the company's own screening procedure. It was this controversy that led to the 2013 Supreme Court ruling, which invalidated the Myriad Company's patents. Companies put private profit before public good. Instead of protecting their research investment, companies have a moral duty to facilitate the development of inexpensive treatments and screening procedures.

Patenting discourages research because scientists fear costly lawsuits by patent holders. Medical and biotech patent holders frequently exploit their monopolies, charging what they like for their drugs and treatments. It was only after immense public protest, for example, that companies cut the prices of their AIDS medicines for African countries.

The Human Genome Project makes its research readily available to ensure the free flow of information and stimulate further research. The only barriers to genetic research should be those of conscience.

Sample Motions:

This House would allow the patenting of genes.

This House believes that genes are inventions.

Web Links:

- Caulfield, Timothy. <http://www.scienceprogress.org/2009/10/do-gene-patents-hurt-research/> Argues that gene patents do not hinder research.

- Human Genome Project Information. <http://www.ornl.gov/sci/techresources/Human_Genome/elsi/patents.shtml> Provides overview of pro and con arguments and links to many articles as well as other useful resources.
- Los Angeles Times. <http://articles.latimes.com/2013/jun/14/business/la-fi-court-gene-patents-20130614/2> Details the Supreme Court's 2013 ruling on gene patenting.
- PBS. <http://www.pbs.org/newshour/bb/health/jan-june10/patents_04-02.html> Video report on the debate in light of a 2010 US federal court ruling striking down seven patents on genes linked to breast and ovarian cancers.
- Then, Christoph. <http://www.greenpeace.org/international/Global/international/planet-2/report/2004/6/the-true-cost-of-gene-patents.pdf> Comprehensive overview of the negative social and economic consequences of gene patenting.

Further Reading:

Arezzo, Emanuela, and Gustavo Ghidini, eds. *Biotechnology and Software Patent Law: A Comparative Review of New Developments.* Elgar, 2011.

Gibson, Johanna. *Patenting Lives (Intellectual Property, Theory, Culture).* Ashgate, 2008.

Koepsell, David. *Who Owns You? The Corporate Gold Rush to Patent Your Genes.* Wiley-Blackwell, 2009.

∎ ∎

GENETIC PRIVACY/ETHICS IN MEDICAL RESEARCH

Genetic material is necessary for research aimed at finding treatments and cures for disorders and catastrophic illnesses. However, researchers often use material taken from uninformed and non-consenting individuals. Most famous, Henrietta Lacks's doctor took a sample of her cervical cancer cells to do a biopsy in 1951. He discovered that her cells were "immortal"; they could divide endlessly. "HeLa cells," named after Lacks, were used to develop the polio vaccine and are used today in nearly all biological research labs—though neither Lacks nor her family ever consented to this use or received compensation. Similarly, many US states do a blood panel on infants to test for congenital or genetic disorders and then store the samples for research without parents' knowledge or consent. This issue is controversial because a person's "ownership" of her genetic material is disputed. Even if it is a person's property, many researchers argue that this "property right" can be overruled for the greater good.

PROS

Genetic material is essential to research; such research improves medical understanding and thereby allows scientists to develop protocols and treatments for illnesses, thus saving many lives that otherwise would be cut short. An individual's right to privacy is not absolute. For example, the police can frisk a person on the street if they suspect the person of committing a crime. Similarly, though collection of genetic material without a patient's knowledge or consent may be some perceived violation of privacy, this supposed "violation" is vastly outweighed by the benefits to society of medical research.

Opponents of acquiring genetic material without consent vastly exaggerate the intrusion into a person's privacy. DNA cells are easy to collect; wiping a cotton swab on the inside of the mouth is sufficient. Furthermore, in the most controversial cases of collected genetic material (infant DNA and HeLa cells), the cells were only used for research after they had been collected to run tests for the

CONS

The principle of "double effect" evaluates the morality of using people as a means to an end in a given situation. If the ends could still be attained were that person to be removed from the situation, then using the person is justifiable. If, however, the person is essential to the ends, then the person is being used as a tool—this degrades human worth because it compromises individual rights. If the person whose cells are being used did not exist, the scientist could not obtain that person's genetic material and information. Therefore, this is a case of unjustified use of individuals as the property of society.

A person's genetic material is his property; it comes from his body and our laws generally assume that people have a right to bodily integrity. Society at large would benefit if we killed a healthy person and distributed her organs to five people dying of organ failure. However, we respect an individual's right to bodily integrity and autonomy because we respect each individual's right to govern his life.

PROS

patient's personal benefit. After doctors were done with the samples, they chose to pass them along for research rather than throw them in the garbage. This is not a case of bodily intrusion but making beneficial use of material that would otherwise be wasted.

The medical research community is complex, and, because most discoveries are accidental, researchers cannot anticipate whether they will profit from a particular individual's genetic material. When researchers find something they think is significant, as in the case of Henrietta Lacks, they send the information to many other labs. To force researchers to track the original human source of every piece of research material that ultimately leads to a successful discovery places an unreasonable burden on those who should instead be focused on the pursuit of scientific knowledge that may benefit thousands.

If researchers cannot obtain genetic material legally, unethical researchers will obtain it in any way they can—causing corruption and endangering those involved. Medical research is a highly prestigious, profitable, and competitive field because it is so important; researchers *must* be able to access necessary material. Many individuals misunderstand the use of genetic material in research. Individuals may confuse the use of other cells, such as cancer cells, with the use of stem cells, which many people morally oppose. Furthermore, patients may have an irrational sense of discomfort at the thought that something that had been part of them is being experimented on; vast numbers refuse to permit their organs to be donated upon death, even though they

will clearly not need them. Medical researchers need to collect genetic material and cannot be hindered by irrational squeamishness.

CONS

Medical research companies that patent procedures and medications based on research conducted on genetic material earn large profits on their products. If a researcher is earning a profit as the result of a material supplied by another person, that person has a right to be aware and demand compensation for the benefits derived from study of their genetic material.

People commit murder even though it is illegal—those who choose to violate a law are the reason to enforce the law, not avoid establishing it. Furthermore, researchers would be allowed to have access to genetic material—they simply must make participants aware and gain their consent. Consent is standard when humans are involved in medical testing; requiring consent is not an undue burden. Individuals who refuse to donate organs may be irrational, but society respects their decision because we respect their bodily autonomy. The claim of the "ignorant public" is not an acceptable reason to violate codes of medical conduct—which include getting informed consent; instead, doctors should take the time to explain what kinds of cells are being used, what is being done with them, and what beneficial discoveries may result from a patient's donation.

This allows individuals to make an informed choice rather than be exploited.

Sample Motions:
This House requires medical researchers to obtain patient consent before using a person's genetic material for research.
This House promotes scientific discovery and its benefits to all of society.
This House believes that humans ought not be used as a means to an end.

Web Links:
- Smithsonian Magazine. "Henrietta Lacks' 'Immortal Cells.'" <http://www.smithsonianmag.com/science-nature/82414557.html> This interview with Skloot (see Further Reading) summarizes the Henrietta Lacks controversy and its lasting significance.
- The Texas Tribune. "DSHS Turned Over Hundreds of DNA Samples to Feds." <http://www.texastribune.org/texas-state-agencies/department-of-state-health-services/dshs-turned-over-hundreds-of-dna-samples-to-feds/> Article discussing the controversy in Texas over using infant blood samples without parental consent.

Further Reading:

Elger, Bernice. *Ethical Issues of Human Genetic Databases: A Challenge to Classical Health Research Ethics?* Ashgate, 2010.

Plows, Alexandra. *Debating Human Genetics: Contemporary Issues in Public Policy and Ethics.* Routledge, 2011.

..

GENETICALLY MODIFIED FOODS

The development of genetically modified (GM) foods has precipitated an ongoing debate among consumers, environmentalists, scientists, and even economists. On the one hand, genetic modification has improved crop characteristics—yield, resistance to disease, pests, or drought, etc.—and has contributed to global health. Recently, scientists announced the development of "golden rice"—rice genetically modified to produce greater levels of vitamin A—which can help prevent a variety of diseases in developing countries. On the other hand, the procedure has raised a number of concerns including the long-term risks to humans and the environment. Economists also point out that because biotechnology companies often patent GM crop varieties, farmers will become increasingly dependent on monopolies for seed.

PROS

Genetic modification is unnatural. There is a fundamental difference between modification via selective breeding and genetic engineering techniques. The former occurs over thousands of years and so the genes are changed much more gradually. With change occurring so rapidly, we now have no time to assess the long-term effects of these products on human health and the environment.

Introducing the DNA of one species into the genes of another is wrong. This attempt to play God is short-sighted and unnatural.

Testing GM food is often difficult. Biotechnology companies are often unwilling to submit their results for peer review. Furthermore, in some countries government agencies are often unwilling to stop GM foodstuffs

CONS

Genetic modification is entirely natural. The process of crop cultivation by selective breeding, which has been performed by farmers for thousands of years, leads to exactly the same kind of changes in DNA as modern modification techniques do. Current techniques are just faster and more selective. In fact, given two strands of DNA created from the same original strand, one by selective breeding and one by modern modification techniques, it is impossible to tell which is the "natural" strand. The changes resulting from selective breeding have been just as radical as current modifications. Wheat, for example, was cultivated through selective breeding from an almost no-yield rice-type crop into the super-crop it is today.

It is perfectly natural and safe to introduce genes from one organism into another. We must remember that all DNA is made up of the same four fundamental molecules regardless of which organism the DNA came from originally. DNA from all organisms is very similar. Human DNA is 99% the same as chimpanzee DNA and about 50% the same as grass DNA. Consequently, the addition of genes from one organism into the DNA of another is like using LEGOs to create a structure. Indeed such processes occur all the time in nature in sexual reproduction.

This debate should be decided on the basis of hard facts, not woolly assertions and environmental sentiment. Until scientific tests show that GM food poses a risk to agriculture or health, it should not be banned. GM foods from reaching the shelf because of the clout the companies have with the government.

GM foods are potentially dangerous. Human health is at risk because, despite extensive testing, scientists cannot anticipate all the problems that might occur when food is modified. This risk will increase as biotechnology companies introduce more modifications. GM foods also present a danger to the environment. The use of these crops has resulted in fewer strains planted. If disease wipes out a few these strains, the result could be catastrophic. In addition, removing certain varieties of crops wipes out the organisms that feed on them. Furthermore, pollen produced from GM crops can accidentally fertilize unmodified crops, polluting the natural gene pool. This cross-pollination, in turn, makes labeling foods impossible. Thus consumers will not be able to choose whether to purchase GM crops.

GM food will not help solve hunger in developing countries. The problem in such countries is not one of food production but of distribution (due to wars, for example), the emphasis on cash crops rather than staple crops (to pay off the national debt), and deforestation and desertification. In addition, many GM strains are infertile, forcing farmers to buy seed annually from companies that can charge whatever they want because they have a patent on the strain.

Yes, banning GM food would decrease consumer choice. However, governments have the right and obligation to intervene to prevent harm to both the population and the environment. Besides, the number of consumers who actually want GM food is tiny.

Genetically modifying food is yet another means by which multinational corporations can exercise illegitimate economic power over developing nations. The combination of the patenting of genes and the use of the terminator gene is a recipe for exploiting the developing world and destroying traditional agriculture.

Issues of principle should always come before pragmatic concerns about unemployment. People have jobs that are dependent on illegal trade in endangered species and in drugs and arms. Maintaining or providing employment is not an argument for the continuation of these harmful and immoral practices nor is it an argument in favor of GM foods.

undergo extensive testing before they are placed on the market. This testing takes two forms: peer review by other scientists and testing by the food standards agencies in the countries in which the product is to be marketed. For example, in the United States all GM food must be tested for nine years before being released into the market.

The fears about GM food are a result of media scares about "frankenfood." Few deaths have been directly attributed to genetic modification, and scientists are taking all reasonable precautions to ensure these products are safe. The need for many different strains is not an argument against GM crops. Scientists and farmers cannot produce and plant many different strains. Furthermore, scientists have no evidence that cross-pollination of GM with non-GM varieties is harmful.

The possible benefits from GM food are enormous. Modifications that render plants less vulnerable to pests lead to less pesticide use, which is better for the environment. Other modifications increase crop yield, which leads to lower food prices. This technology is particularly important for developing countries; it can help farmers grow crops in arid soil. More important, it can help prevent diseases, as the introduction of "golden rice" has shown.

Banning GM food results in fewer choices for the consumer. Scientists can prevent crossbreeding between GM and non-GM plants so that foods can be properly labeled.

The question of whether crop varieties should be allowed to be patented is separate from the debate on whether GM food is itself good or bad.

Unemployment in the biotechnology industry would increase dramatically if GM foods were banned.

Sample Motions:

This House would ban genetically modified food.

This House believes that genetically modified foods are not in the public interest.

This House would not eat "frankenfood."

Web Links:

- GM Watch. <http://www.gmwatch.org/ > Links to articles on genetically modified food from an organization dedicated to fighting corporate propaganda on the issue.
- PBS. <http://www.pbs.org/wgbh/harvest/> Offers links to news articles, reports, and other websites related to the controversy surrounding genetically modified foods.
- World Health Organization. <http://www.who.int/foodsafety/publications/biotech/20questions/en/> Questions and answers on genetically modified foods, particularly about their status in international trade.

Further Reading:

Bertheau, Yves, ed. *Genetically Modified and Non-Genetically Modified Food Supply Chains: Co-existence and Traceability.* Wiley, 2012.

Halford, Nigel G. *Genetically Modified Crops.* Imperial College Press, 2011.

Robin, Marie-Monique. *The World According to Monsanto.* New Press, 2012.

Weasel, Lisa H. *Food Fray: Inside the Controversy Over Genetically Modified Food.* AMACOM, 2009.

■ ■

GLOBAL WARMING

Since the 1980s, a growing body of evidence has suggested that industrialization is affecting the planet's climate; scientists studying climate change are warning of its effects on water supplies, agriculture, ecosystems, and coastal communities. Americans are divided on how to respond. Some want the government to take aggressive action to address the problem, while others say "What problem?" Most people remain confused about the issue. Global warming is a particularly difficult issue because it demands a worldwide response. Many developing nations are understandably angry that a problem that seems to have been created by the rich, developed nations will have the most impact on the Third World. They fear that efforts to curb global warming will also curb economic development. A global consensus remains far off.

PROS

Over the past 100 years, humankind has been burning increasing quantities of fossil fuels to provide energy. This has released large volumes of gases into the atmosphere, particularly CO_2. At the same time, the world's remaining large forests, which help absorb CO_2, are being rapidly felled. Overall, the levels of carbon dioxide in the atmosphere have increased by 30% during the last century. When in the atmosphere, CO_2 and other gases are thought to cause a "greenhouse effect": they allow sunlight to pass through, but absorb heat emitted by the Earth, trapping the heat and leading to global warming. Weather records seem to support this theory. Average temperatures have increased by 0.6°C since the nineteenth century; the four hottest years

CONS

Scientists have not yet proved conclusively that humankind is causing global warming. Although average temperatures rose during the twentieth century, temperatures actually dropped slightly between the 1930s and the 1970s. This was not associated with a reduction in fossil fuel consumption; emissions actually increased over this period. If the "greenhouse gases" are responsible for global warming, how do you account for this? Accurate records simply do not cover a long enough period to be useful. The Earth's average temperature varies naturally through time, and we have few good explanations of the Ice Ages. Indeed, there was a "mini–Ice Age" around 400 years ago, during which the River Thames in England repeatedly froze over in winter. This was followed by an since accurate records have been kept have all been in the 1990s. Unusual weather patterns such as floods and droughts have also been on the increase, with the uncharacteristically strong El Niño events of recent years causing widespread disruption. The Intergovernmental Panel on Climate Change (IPCC), an international body set up to study possible global warming, has concluded that "... the balance of evidence suggests that there is a discernible human influence on global climate."

Computer models predict that continued global warming could have catastrophic effects. Changes in temperature could devastate wildlife when local vegetation dies off. Patterns of disease could change. Already isolated cases of malaria have been reported far north of traditional danger zones as warmer weather allows the mosquitoes that carry the disease to spread. Most important, a portion of the polar ice caps might melt and lead to a rise in sea level, which has already increased by between 10 and 25 cm in the last 100 years. Giant cracks have been found in the Larsen ice shelf in Antarctica, which suggest that it is breaking apart; a section 48 miles wide and 22 miles long drifted free and melted as early as 1994. If, as experts believe, temperatures rise a further 3°c over the next century, low-lying areas and even entire countries, such as Bangladesh, could disappear under the waves.

Technology has now reached the point where we can continue to increase standards of living without burning fossil fuels. Renewable sources of energy, such as wind or solar power, are ripe for development, but have yet to see the levels of investment needed to make them truly effective. More efficient use of energy is also vital. Encouraging the development of electric cars or promoting better insulation of houses could make a substantial difference in CO_2 levels in the long run.

Global warming is a worldwide catastrophe waiting to happen. The emission of greenhouse gases affects everyone. It is, therefore, vital that the entire world respond now. The targets set by the Kyoto Protocol will barely scratch the surface of the problem. The developed world agreed to only minimal reductions in carbon dioxide emissions, and no agreement was reached involving the developing world, which is producing a greater percentage of greenhouse gas emissions every year. Gases like CO_2 remain in the atmosphere for centuries. If we wait

intense but natural period of "global warming." We do not have enough information to say that current trends are not simply a natural variation.

Again, our computer models for predicting climate change are far from reliable. Weather is a hugely complex system that we are only beginning to understand. It is affected by many factors, including solar activity, volcanic eruptions, ocean currents, and other cycles that we are gradually discovering. Very slight changes in the computer model result in immense differences in predictions. Some scientists, for example, have suggested that global warming could actually cause a drop in sea level as rainfall patterns and ocean currents shift. Indeed, refinements in the models used by the IPCC have caused it to modify its predictions. In 1990, the IPCC estimated that by 2100 the average temperature would rise by 3°c and the sea would rise by about 65 cm; in 1995, it revised its estimates to 2°c and 50 cm. The more research that takes place, the less catastrophic global warming seems to be. The media always report the predictions of doom most widely.

Of course greater energy efficiency is important. However, most alternative fuels are simply not effective. They can also cause their own problems. Nuclear power creates unacceptable radioactive waste; hydroelectric power projects, such as the Three Gorges Dam in China, lead to the flooding of vast areas and the destruction of the local environment; solar and wind power often require the covering of large areas of natural beauty with solar panels or turbines. Environmentalists often paint an idealistic view of renewable energy that is far from the less romantic reality.

The evidence for global warming is not strong enough to merit this kind of response. The changes over the past century may certainly have been purely natural. Environmentalists in the developed world can afford the luxury of demanding government action because reducing pollution will have a minimal impact on their technology-based economies. Those in the developing world are not so lucky. Industrialization is a key part of building successful economies and bringing prosperity to the world's poorest people; heavy industry is often the only area in which until we can see the results of global warming, it may be too late. The damage will have been done. We must act now, and we must act globally. Developed countries must do all they can to reduce their use of fossil fuels. They must assist developing nations to do the same, by sharing technology or perhaps through "emissions trading," allowing poorer countries to sell their quota of pollution in return for hard cash. International pressure must be exerted against those countries that do not cooperate, even if this slows economic growth. The poorest regions of the world would suffer most from more droughts and floods and rising sea levels. However difficult it may be in the short term, such actions now may save millions of lives in the future.

developing nations can compete. Global action on greenhouse gas emissions would sustain the inequalities of the status quo. The developing world would have to depend on multinational corporations to provide the technology needed to keep pollution levels low, or else they would have to stop expanding their economies. Having apparently caused the problem through the industrialization that made them powerful, developed countries would be pulling the ladder up behind them, depriving other countries of the chance to grow. This is simply unacceptable. In the modern world, one of our first priorities must be to help the poorest people achieve the prosperity they need to support themselves. The current evidence for global warming does not begin to merit endangering this goal.

Sample Motions:

This House believes that the Kyoto Protocol didn't go far enough.

This House calls for urgent action on global warming.

This House fears a global greenhouse.

This House believes that global warming demands global action.

Web Links:

- Intergovernmental Panel on Climate Change. <http://www.ipcc.ch> Offers reports assessing scientific, technical, and socioeconomic information related to human-induced climate change.
- PBS. <http://www.pbs.org/newshour/indepth_coverage/science/globalwarming/> Companion site to a television program on the global warming debate.
- Totty, Michael. <http://online.wsj.com/article/NA_WSJ_PUB:SB10001424052748703819904574551303527570212.html> Overview of climate change skeptics' arguments and the common responses of those who do believe in global warming.

Further Reading:

Archer, David. *Global Warming: Understanding the Forecast.* Wiley, 2011.

Maslin, Mark. Global Warming: A Very Short Introduction. Oxford University Press, 2009.

Spencer, Roy. *The Great Global Warming Blunder: How Mother Nature Fooled the World's Top Climate Scientists.* Encounter Books, 2012.

■ ■

GLOBALIZATION AND POVERTY

Globalization is the process that spreads economic, political, social, and cultural activity across national boundaries and increases the integration of internationally dispersed activities. Foreign media often focus on the spread of American culture (characterized as fast food restaurants, Hollywood movies, etc.), but academic debates center around more fundamental economic issues. While globalization may have benefited industrialized nations and transnational corporations (TNCs), has the trend eroded global and national solidarity and increased the poverty and isolation of developing nations?

PROS

Globalization marginalizes the poor. It is a means of exclusion, deepening inequality and reinforcing the division of the world into core and periphery. It is a new form of Western imperialism that dominates and exploits through TNC capital and global governance by institutions such as the World Bank and the International Monetary Fund (IMF).

Globalization has intensified global and national inequality. The economic and social gaps within countries and between countries are widening, with the rich becoming richer and the poor becoming poorer. Globalization is an uneven process causing world fragmentation. Trade has also seen increasing inequality. Because of increasing globalization the value of world trade is 17 times greater than 50 years ago, but Latin America's share has fallen from 11% to 5% and Africa's from 8% to 2%. The terms of trade have increasingly moved against developing nations.

Globalization exploits developing nations and their poor through TNCs. Globalization is a euphemism for transnationalization, the spread of powerful companies to areas that best suit corporate interests.

Increased global integration means that poorer countries become more vulnerable to world financial markets. The East Asian economic crisis of the 1990s, a direct result of globalization, increased and intensified poverty. The crisis shows that even the strongest developing states are at the mercy of global economic forces that serve the interests of the dominant capitalist powers. Globalization also resulted in the speedy transition of the crisis to the other East Asian countries — the "contagion effect" — with devastating human consequences. The benefits of the global market accrue to a relatively small proportion of the world's population. The strong become stronger and the weak become weaker.

Globalization is a form of disempowerment. Outside interference from the World Bank and the IMF has weakened the economies of poor nations and constrained development. International negotiations to reduce and eliminate foreign debt have led to increasing exports of capital and deeper indebtedness in developing nations.

CONS

Globalization is eroding the differences between developed and developing nations, sometimes called the North-South divide. It is a progressive force for creating global prosperity. Through free trade and capital mobility, globalization is creating a global market in which prosperity, wealth, power, and liberal democracy are being diffused around the globe.

Globalization has increased world prosperity, and organizational efforts to stabilize the world economy have shown significant progress. By historical standards global poverty has fallen more in the last 50 years than in the previous 500, and the welfare of people in almost all regions has improved considerably during the past few decades. Globalization will bring about the end of the Third World. The fall in the developing nations' share of world trade is due to internal economic, social, and political conditions in individual countries.

Globalization promotes development by spreading technology and knowledge to poor nations. The poorest nations are those countries bypassed by globalization.

Globalization has brought about huge benefits. The emergence of a single global market, free trade, capital mobility, and global competition has permitted the diffusion of prosperity, wealth, and power. Globalization has opened up new opportunities and is the harbinger of modernization and development. It was the force that led to the successful development of East Asia and its "economic miracle." Far from making developing nations more vulnerable, increased global integration means that better organizational structures are in place to address world political, economic, and social problems.

The policies of institutions such as the IMF and the World Bank have reinforced the global market. Outside intervention allows the dissemination of effective economic management strategies to less developed areas.

Sample Motions:

This House believes that globalization marginalizes the poor.

This House believes that globalization will bring about the end of the Third World.

This House believes that globalization is a euphemism for transnationalization.

Web Links:

- Bardhan, Pranab. <http://www.scientificamerican.com/article.cfm?id=does-globalization-help-o> Argues that globalization need not harm the poor so long as proper domestic precautions are taken.
- Birdsall, Nancy, and Devin T. Stewart. <http://www.carnegiecouncil.org/studio/multimedia/20130222/index.html> An interview with Nancy Birdsall, founding president of the Center for Global Development.
- Meredith, Robyn, and Suzanne Hoppough. <http://www.forbes.com/forbes/2007/0416/064.html> Argues that globalization benefits the poor.
- Rena, Ravinder. <http://www.africaeconomicanalysis.org/articles/gen/globalisation_0507.html> Argues that globalization hurts less-developed countries.

Further Reading:

Howard-Hassman, Rhoda E. *Can Globalization Promote Human Rights?* Pennsylvania State University Press, 2010.

Kanbur, Ravi, and Michael Spence, eds. *Equity and Growth in a Globalizing World*. World Bank Publications, 2010.

Nissanke, Machiko, and Erik Thorbecke. *The Poor Under Globalization in Asia, Latin America and Africa.* Oxford University Press, 2010.

• •

GOD, EXISTENCE OF

This is the "Big" question, the ultimate metaphysical debate. It has occupied the world's best minds for centuries. Followers of many religions have offered proofs of the existence of God. Below are arguments from within the Judeo-Christian and Islamic traditions.

PROS

The world is so magnificent and wonderful, so full of variety and beauty that it is inconceivable that it could have come about purely by chance. It is so intricate that a conscious hand must have been involved in its creation. Therefore, God exists as the creator of the world.

If you saw a watch lying on the sand, you would think that someone must have made the watch—a watchmaker. Similarly, we human beings are so complicated and amazing that we must conclude that we had a conscious maker.

Only human beings are capable of rational thought. That we are here at all is amazing. One infinitesimal change in the world and life would not have evolved. Getting something so amazing, on such long odds, smacks of intention.

God must be perfect if he exists. But a thing that exists is more perfect than a thing that doesn't exist. But nothing can be more perfect than God. So God must exist.

CONS

You cannot infer from the variety and beauty of the world that God was the creator. The conception of God contains many extra attributes that are not necessary for a world creator. Just because the world is beautiful and varied does not mean it was consciously designed. Why can't beauty happen by accident?

The difference between a watch and humans is that the watch serves a purpose—to tell time. Therefore, seeing something so perfectly serving a purpose suggests design. What purpose do we serve? We don't, we just exist. And even if we were designed for a purpose, the earlier argument applies: a purposeful designer isn't necessarily God.

The argument from probability does not work. It relies on there being something special about us. What is so special about us? We are rational—so what?

This ontological argument can be rebutted by rejecting the idea that existence is perfection. Something either exists or it doesn't. The argument is a disguised conditional. You say "if God exists then he must be perfect, and if he must be perfect he must therefore exist." But all this rests

PROS	CONS
	on the initial "if God exists." If God doesn't exist, we don't have the problem and the argument doesn't work.
Everything in the universe has a cause. It is inconceivable that time is one long chain of cause and effect without beginning, but it must be because we cannot conceive of something happening uncaused. Therefore, God exists as the uncaused first cause.	The cosmological argument doesn't work. For a start, an uncaused first cause still doesn't necessarily have all the attributes it would need to be called God, e.g., omnipotence, benevolence, and omniscience. More important, an uncaused first cause is just as incomprehensible to us as an endless chain of cause and effect. You are just shifting the incomprehension one stage back.

Sample Motions:

This House believes that God exists.

This House believes that reports of God's death have been greatly exaggerated.

Web Links:

- American Atheists. <http://www.atheists.org/religion> Arguments against the existence of God from an organization that lobbies for atheists' civil liberties.
- Counterbalance. <http://www.counterbalance.org> Contains summary of the debate about the existence of God from a cosmological standpoint.
- Craig, William Lane. <http://www.leaderu.com/truth/3truth11.html> Academic paper employing a cosmological argument to help prove the existence of God.
- Hitchens, Christopher, and David Wolpe. <http://cityroom.blogs.nytimes.com/2008/11/03/hitchens-vs-rabbi-on-god> Hitchens and Rabbi Wolpe debate the existence of God.
- New Advent. <http://www.newadvent.org/cathen/06608b.htm> Detailed essay outlining the various proofs for the existence of God.

Further Reading:

Hitchens, Christopher. *The Portable Atheist: Essential Readings for a Nonbeliever.* Da Capo Press, 2007.

Reitan, Eric. *Is God A Delusion: A Reply to Religion's Cultured Despisers.* Wiley-Blackwell, 2008.

Stenger, Victor J. *God: The Failed Hypothesis. How Science Shows That God Does Not Exist.* Prometheus Books, 2008.

▪▪

GREENHOUSE GASES: TRADING QUOTAS

A number of methods have been proposed to reduce the emissions of the so-called greenhouse gases that lead to global warming. The European Union has always favored taxing heavy polluters, while the United States has supported Tradable Pollution Quotas (TPQs). The 1997 Kyoto Protocol laid the foundation for TPQs. Under this agreement developing countries are exempt from the emission standards and cannot take part directly in pollution trading. Each country in the TPQ plan is initially permitted to produce a certain maximum amount of each polluting gas. Countries that want to exceed their quotas can buy the right to do so from other countries that have produced less than their quota. Furthermore, countries can also "sink" carbon (by planting forests to remove carbon dioxide from the atmosphere) to offset some of their pollution quotas. Interestingly, two usually opposing groups are against TPQs. Industries claim that they go too far and that such stringent regulation is unnecessary. Environmentalists maintain that they are too lax.

PROS

The scientific community agrees that something must be done to curb emissions of greenhouse gases that may be the cause of global warming. The possible consequences of global warming include crop failure, mass flooding, and the destruction of entire ecosystems with the possible loss of billions of lives. Other consequences of pollution include acid rain and the enlargement of the hole in the ozone layer.

The TPQ plan is the only practical way to reduce emissions of greenhouse gases globally. It will guarantee that global levels of these gases are kept below strict targets and is more realistic than expecting heavy polluters to cut their emissions overnight.

Emissions are a global problem. The emission of the main greenhouse gas, carbon dioxide, for example, affects the entire planet regardless of where the gas is produced. This validates the use of TPQs, which act to limit the total amount of each polluting gas globally. TPQs are much more effective than the alternative of taxing emissions, because rich companies or countries will be able to pay the tax and still pollute.

TPQs are tried and tested. The United States has used them successfully since they were introduced in 1990. Therefore, we have good reason to expect them to succeed on a global scale.

Progress in the field of emission control is remarkably difficult because of the opposition from the industrial lobby, most notably in the United States, which sees such restrictions as harmful to its economy. TPQs are the one method of control acceptable to these lobby groups and, more significant, to the US government. As the world's biggest polluter, the United States must be included in any meaningful treaty. Therefore, TPQs are the only practical way forward.

TPQs cause less damage to an economy than any other emission control regime. Individual companies and

CONS

The environmental lobby has hugely overestimated the claims for pollution damaging the environment. The fossil record indicates that climate change has occurred frequently in the past, and there is little evidence linking climate change with emissions.

The TPQ plan ensures more pollution in the long run than if limits were strictly enforced for each country and punitive taxes imposed on those exceeding their quotas. Without TPQs, the environment would benefit further if a country kept well below its emissions quota. Adopting the TPQ plan means that this benefit is lost because the right to this extra pollution is bought by another country.

Stating that it does not matter where pollution is produced is simplistic and completely untrue for many gases, which do affect the region in which they are created. Furthermore, to permit developing countries to industrialize, they have been exempted from the protocol. This seriously undermines its efficiency. Furthermore, if taxes on pollution were set high enough, big companies would stop polluting because it would be prohibitively expensive. In addition, the introduction of TPQs will make later reductions in global emissions much harder. Once trading in TPQs has started, countries that have bought extra emission rights would certainly not voluntarily give them up to help reduce global emissions further.

TPQs have had some success in the United States, but they failed in Europe for two reasons. First, the European plans were poorly conceived, as was the Kyoto Protocol. Second, whereas the American solution to pollution was always trading emissions, the main European solution was, and still is, to produce new technology to clean the emissions. Extending the TPQ plan to the entire globe will slow the technological developments needed to reduce greenhouse gases.

The Kyoto Protocol lacks a comprehensive enforcement mechanism and is thus ineffective. In addition, assessing the effect that an individual country's carbon "sink" is having on the atmosphere is impossible. This merely creates a loophole that allows a country to abuse the protocol and produce more than its quota of gases.

TPQs will hit employment hard. Even developed countries are not so rich that they can simply buy enough countries can trade TPQs on the free market until they have struck the right balance between the cost of paying to pollute and the cost of cleaning up their industry.

quotas to avoid pollution; neither can they afford to install the expensive cleaning technology. Growth will consequently decline and with that decline will come a drop in living standards in developed countries.

Sample Motions:

This House would buy the right to pollute.

This House supports tradable pollution quotas.

This House believes that the Kyoto Protocol got it right.

Web Links:

- Daly, Jessica. <http://edition.cnn.com/2008/TECH/science/09/01/carbon.trading.pv/index.html?iref=intlOnlyonCNN> Answers FAQs related to the issue.

Further Reading:

Freestone, David, and Charlotte Streck, eds. *Legal Aspects of Carbon Trading: Kyoto, Copenhagen, and beyond.* Oxford University Press, 2010.

Jackson, Felicia. *Conquering Carbon: Carbon Emissions, Carbon Markets and the Consumer.* New Holland Publishers, 2010.

Labatt, Sonia, and Rodney R. White. *Carbon Finance: The Financial Implications of Climate Change.* Wiley, 2007.

Meckling, Jonas. *Carbon Coalitions: Business, Climate Politics, and the Rise of Emissions Trading.* MIT Press, 2011.

■ ■

GUN CONTROL

Gun control is a highly controversial political issue in the United States, partially because many consider gun ownership an inalienable right. However, the prevalence of gun violence and instances of high-profile mass shootings make gun control the subject of ongoing debate. Though few Americans favor the outright banning of all guns, an increasing number advocate greater gun control, particularly tougher controls over who can buy guns and the type of firearms they can purchase. In 2012, gun control was at the forefront of the national consciousness, with the year being the worst in terms of those killed in mass shootings in US history. Two especially horrific incidents in 2012 captured the public attention: in July, 12 people were killed and 58 were injured in an Aurora cinema by a perpetrator using assault weapons and high-capacity magazines; in December, 20 children and six adults were killed at Sandy Hook Elementary School, again, by a perpetrator using a semiautomatic rifle and high-capacity magazines. In response to this latter tragedy, President Barack Obama proposed greater gun controls. Most controversially, this proposal included a renewed ban on assault weapons—which had been previously banned between 1994 and 2004—and magazines containing more than 10 rounds. Additionally, the proposal required background checks on anybody wanting to purchase a gun, including sales between private individuals, which are currently exempt.

PROS

Increased gun control reduces both gun violence and overall rates of homicide and violent crime. The United States has approximately 310 million privately owned

CONS

Widespread gun ownership actually acts as a deterrent to crime, allowing potential victims to defend themselves. A report by the National Crime Victimization Survey guns, which is by far the highest rate of gun ownership in the world; the United States also has one of the highest homicide rates of all developed nations. In 2011, 8,583 people were murdered by someone using a firearm in the United States, accounting for more than two-thirds of all US murders. Statistics show that among developed nations, countries with easier access to guns also have more gun violence; therefore, controlling access to firearms is a logical way to reduce this gun violence. Furthermore, controlling the numbers of assault weapons in circulation would reduce the ability of single perpetrators to inflict large losses of life. In 2012, *Mother Jones* compiled a list of US mass shootings, which showed that assault weapons were used in 40% of incidents, despite making up only around 1% of all guns owned.

The background checks included in the proposed gun control legislation would not prevent law-abiding citizens from purchasing guns; background checks would only affect those with criminal records. Currently, private sales—which require no background checks at all—are the primary way that guns are transferred from legal owners to illegal owners; legal gun ownership directly channels guns into the hands of criminals. Under the Obama administration's proposal, the only types of firearm that law-abiding citizens will be banned from purchasing are assault weapons, which, given their size and unwieldy rapid-fire discharge, are impractical for self-defense anyway.

The authors of the Constitution did not intend for the general public to be armed with the type of high capacity firearms that we see today. The Second Amendment states: "A well regulated Militia, being necessary to the security of a free State, the right of the people to keep and bear Arms, shall not be infringed." This passage refers to the right of states to keep an armed militia, not the right of individuals to arm themselves with assault weapons. Society has evolved since the Constitution was written; contemporary issues such as increased urbanization, drug-related crime, and gang violence mean that guns no longer have any place on our streets. Furthermore, the argument that gun ownership must be unrestricted so that citizens can defend themselves against a tyrannical government is entirely illogical in an era of nuclear bombs and modern military technology.

Current gun laws have nothing to do with protecting freedom, but are, instead, the result of the economic interests of the firearms industry. For several years, members of Congress have named the National Rifle Association (NRA) as the most powerful lobbying organization in

estimates that guns are used in self-defense between 60,000 and 120,000 times a year. Furthermore, a study of right-to-carry laws in various states found that the implementation of these laws coincided with an 8% reduction in the murder rate. Rather than encouraging violent crime, guns often prevent violence, being used by less physically strong individuals, such as women or elderly people, to protect themselves when confronted with a stronger aggressor. The gun control measures proposed by the Obama administration will make it harder to purchase guns, limiting the number of people that own guns and diminishing the ability of the general population to protect themselves from criminals.

Banning law-abiding citizens from owning assault weapons will put them at a disadvantage if they are confronted by a criminal armed with one. With approximately 4 million assault weapons in the United States, removing all of them is virtually impossible. Because criminals are unlikely to respect a ban on assault weapons and will still purchase them on the black market, the ban directly benefits those who do not obey the law. Furthermore, in high-stress situations, such as home invasions, when people are unable to reload multiple times, assault weapons are necessary for self-defense—banning them compromises the safety of average Americans, while giving criminals the upper hand.

The Constitution explicitly protects the right of Americans to own firearms. The Supreme Court has repeatedly upheld the concept that the Second Amendment refers to an individual's right to bear arms, not an abstract collective right or a right limited to militias. The United States was founded in order to escape the oppressive governments of Europe; the presence of an armed citizenry is key to protecting the people from tyranny. Restricting the types of firearms that Americans can own is akin to restricting the types of books people can read or the thoughts that they can express—inalienable rights cannot be restricted by the government. Any attempts by the government to infringe upon the constitutional right to bear arms should be resisted as it is a complete overreach in the role of the federal government, and a direct attempt to limit freedom.

The firearms industry provides thousands of jobs for Americans and adds millions of dollars to the economy. The 2012 Firearms and Ammunition Industry Economic Impact Report details over 220,000 direct and induced jobs created by the firearms industry in the United States, the United States. Like all other lobbying groups, the NRA opposes any attempts to regulate its industry. Even common-sense regulations, such as those addressing assault weapons and criminal background checks, are framed in terms of "freedom" and "tyranny" in a cynical attempt to protect gun sales.

and over $33 billion in economic activity. Furthermore, NRA lobbying is on behalf of gun owners not gun manufacturers. Nearly half of the NRA's annual revenue comes from membership dues, with the majority of remaining funding coming from voluntary donations—only a small amount of revenue comes from gun manufacturers.

Sample Motions:

This House calls for stricter controls on gun ownership.

This House believes there is no right to bear arms.

This House supports a federal assault weapons ban.

This House would ban the private transfer of firearms between individuals.

Web Links:

- Barnes, Robert, and Dan Eggen. <http://www.washingtonpost.com/wpdyn/content/article/2010/06/28/AR2010062802134 .html> Explains the 2010 Supreme Court decision affirming that the Second Amendment confers on individuals the right to bear arms and explains that ruling's importance in the context of judicial and political debates on the issue.
- Krouse, William J. "Gun Control Legilsation." <http://www.fas.org/sgp/crs/misc/RL32842.pdf> CRS Report for Congress on gun control in the 112th Congress.
- National Rifle Association of America. <http://www.nra.org> America's most powerful pro-gun lobby offers information on campaigns to limit gun control.
- USA TODAY Staff. Where Each State Stands on Gun-Control Legislation <http://www.usatoday.com/story/news/nation/2013 /01/14/state-by-state-gun-report/1834361/> Compilation on each US state's position on gun control.
- Wallace-Wells, Benjamin. <http://nymag.com/news/features/gun-control-newtown-2013-2/> Comprehensive look at growing support for gun control following the shooting in Newtown, Connecticut.
- Gun Violence in America: The 13 Key Questions. <http://www.theatlantic.com/national/archive/2013/02/gun-violence-in -america-the-13-key-questions-with-13-concise-answers/272727/> Provides detailed answers to key questions regarding gun control in the United States.

Further Reading:

Doherty, Brian. *Gun Control on Trial: Inside the Supreme Court Battle Over the Second Amendment.* Cato Institute, 2009.

Horwitz, Joshua, and Casey Anderson. *Guns, Democracy and the Insurrectionist Idea.* University of Michigan Press, 2009.

Lott, John R. *More Guns, Less Crime: Understanding Crime and Gun Control Laws.* 3rd ed. University of Chicago Press, 2010.

▪▪

HABEAS CORPUS, RESTRICTIONS ON

Habeas corpus is a centuries-old legal mechanism that prevents government from arbitrarily detaining its citizens. It is a petition to a state or federal court, on behalf of a prisoner, requesting that the court review the basis of the person's detention. Habeas corpus is considered to be one of the foundations of constitutional democracy and the principle has been adopted by many countries throughout the world. Habeas corpus is fundamental to the US legal system, allowing capital defendants to challenge death penalty rulings and immigrant detainees to challenge the legality of their detentions. It is protected by Article I, Section 9 of the Constitution, which states: "The privilege of the writ of habeas corpus shall not be suspended, unless when in cases of rebellion or invasion the public safety may require it." After the attacks of September 11, 2001, the Bush administration began to challenge the applicability of habeas corpus to those detained on suspicion of being terrorists. The legal and political battles around restrictions on habeas corpus have been fierce. In Boumediene v. Bush (2008), *the Supreme Court held that terror suspects detained at Guantanamo are protected by habeas corpus; two years later, however, a federal circuit court in* Maqalah v. Gates *held that protections did not extend to noncitizens detained overseas—those held by US forces in Afghanistan, for example.*

PROS

The events of September 11 constituted an unprecedented attack against Americans on American soil. The US government must do everything in its power to ensure that the individuals responsible cannot participate in further terrorist activities. Restricting suspected terrorists' rights to challenge their detentions is necessary to achieve that goal. Terror suspects still have recourse to military tribunals, which contain many of the same safeguards as the federal court system.

Unlawful enemy combatants are not US citizens. The only connection they have to this country is the desire to destroy it. As such, they do not fall within the group of people the Constitution is intended to protect.

Global terrorism calls for aggressive responses. We cannot allow our nation to be besieged by terrorists while we stand aside and do nothing. Constitutional freedoms are extremely important, but the security and continued existence of our nation come first. American must make a stand and demonstrate that terrorism will not be tolerated.

There is a longstanding tradition of suspending habeas corpus protections during times of war and conflict. For example, President Lincoln suspended habeas corpus during the Civil War. Habeas was also suspended briefly during World War II, after the attacks on Pearl Harbor. The war on terror may not follow the rules of traditional warfare, but it is a war nonetheless. Current restrictions on habeas corpus are merely an extension of policies enacted in the past during similarly challenging times.

CONS

There is no reason why the US cannot uphold constitutional protections such as habeas corpus and effectively combat terrorism at the same time. The two are not mutually exclusive. In fact, ensuring that suspected terrorists have access to Federal Courts will save much-needed resources and ensure more accurate administration of justice. In the present case, it is unclear which of the Guantanamo detainees actually committed the acts that are used to justify their indefinite detention. Allowing detainees to challenge their detention would bring clarity to this uncertain situation and free up resources in the war against terrorism.

Via legal precedent, habeas corpus protections extend to foreign nationals detained in the US. Furthermore, to focus solely on the immigration status and purported guilt of suspected terrorists ignores the fact that habeas exists to protect us all. Eliminating rights for "bad" people necessarily eliminates them for the innocent, as well.

Restrictions to habeas corpus undermine the war against terror and put our national security further at risk. Habeas corpus legitimizes the war against terror by ensuring that US action against suspected terrorists has some legal basis and is not purely subjective. Furthermore, if the US disregards habeas protections, it sets a dangerous precedent for the rest of the world. If other countries followed suit, US citizens abroad could be indefinitely detained with no legal recourse.

The current war on terror is not comparable to past wars during which habeas was suspended. Both the Civil War and World War II were openly declared wars of limited duration following invasions by hostile forces. The "war on terror" is nebulous and open-ended. In any case, history has harshly judged arbitrary detentions during wartime. Lincoln's Civil War detentions and Roosevelt's Japanese internment camps of the 1940s are embarrassing chapters in our national history. The fact that former presidents improperly suspended habeas corpus is all the more reason to exercise caution now.

Sample Motions:

This House would reaffirm habeas corpus protections for suspected terrorists.

This House would suspend habeas corpus during the war against terrorism.

Web Links:

- Brennan Center for Justice. <http://www.brennancenter.org/content/section/category/detention_habeas_corpus> Contains links to publications, legal briefs, and other web resources about restrictions on habeas corpus post–9/11.
- New York Times. <http://topics.nytimes.com/topics/reference/timestopics/subjects/h/habeas_corpus/index.html> Links to recent articles on the topic.
- NPR. <http://www.npr.org/templates/story/story.php?storyId=14521071> Radio broadcast on 2007 Senate debate on the issue.

Further Reading:

Hafetz, Jonathan. *Habeas Corpus after 9/11: Confronting America's New Global Detention System.* New York University Press, 2011.

King, Nancy J. *Habeas for the Twenty-First Century: Uses, Abuses, and the Future of the Great Writ.* University of Chicago Press, 2011.

Wert, Justin J. *Habeas Corpus in America: The Politics of Individual Rights.* University Press of Kansas, 2011.

■ ■

HATE SPEECH ON CAMPUS

Hate speech is that which creates a climate of hate or prejudice. The term is often used to describe speech that targets a group or an individual on the basis of religion, gender, race, or sexual orientation. In 1969, the Supreme Court ruled that all speech that did not incite "imminent lawless action" is protected under the First Amendment of the US Constitution; in 1992, the Supreme Court further ruled that the prohibition of hate speech was unconstitutional. However, since the 1980s, many universities, both public and private, have implemented "speech codes" designed to restrict hate speech on campus. The Supreme Court has not directly ruled on the constitutionality of speech codes at public universities, but several bans on hate speech have been struck down by lower courts—in 1989, a federal district court determined that the University of Michigan's hate speech code was in violation of the constitutional right to free speech. However, supporters of the code argued that it was essential to protect equal access to education, regardless of religion, race, gender, or sexual orientation. The debate over whether hate speech should be banned on campuses centers on the principles of freedom and equality, and how to mediate when the two come into conflict.

PROS

All rights come with responsibilities. Minorities have a right to be free from verbal abuse and fear. If such rights are not informally respected, the college administration has the right and obligation to adopt codes prohibiting offensive speech.

The constant repetition of hate speech promotes offensive racist, sexist, and homophobic stereotypes. If children and youths grow up hearing such views, they are more likely to become adults who hold them too. Hatred of

CONS

Free speech is one of our basic rights and should be upheld at all costs. College administrations may abuse these speech codes, using them to silence those whom they consider disruptive. Upholding the right to hate speech will protect the free speech of everyone. Colleges should outlaw hate crimes, not hate speech. While we may abhor the views expressed in hate speech, it would be wrong to censor them.

Stereotyping is a result of the underrepresentation of minorities among students, faculty, and administrators on most campuses. University authorities should recruit more members of these minorities, exposing students to a minorities is a learned behavior: preventing hate speech from being passed on to young people is the surest way to ensure that it is not perpetuated and that future generations will live in a society that is inclusive and safe for all.

Adopting a speech code sends a strong message. It shows minorities that the authorities support them and, thus, will help in minority recruitment. It also shows bigots that their views will not be tolerated and helps marginalize and punish them. The primary purpose of a university is to educate students, which involves learning how to engage in reasoned debate—a student who has to resort to hate speech in order to make a point has no place in a university. Hate speech codes underline this important message.

Minority students cannot learn in an environment of fear and hatred. If all students are to achieve their potential, they must be allowed to work without harassment. Allowing hate speech on campus violates minority students' Fourteenth Amendment right to equality.

broad range of role models and authority figures. In addition, universities should ensure that they have a diverse student body—history has shown that integration and communication between different groups is the best way to counter prejudice.

Codes that ban hate speech often lead to resentment, which can cause a backlash against the minorities that they strive to protect. For example, in 1993 a white student at the University of Pennsylvania was charged with violating the campus hate speech code for calling a group of noisy African American students "water buffalo"; this incident, which was widely criticized as an overreach of university authority, actually led to an increase in racial tension between black and white students on campus. This reality undermines any message that a university is trying to send to students.

Ensuring freedom of speech is especially critical in universities. The needs of education are served best in an environment in which free thought and free expression are actively encouraged.

Sample Motions:

This House would censor hate speech on campus.

This House believes that hate speech at universities should be protected as free speech.

This House may not agree with what you say, but will defend your right to say it.

Web Links:

- ACLU. <http://www.aclu.org/free-speech/hate-speech-campus> Information on the issue from a progressive organization strongly opposed to speech codes.
- Halger, Frank. <http://www.policymic.com/articles/28711/oberlin-college-hate-speech-imitates-how-americans-discriminate-as-adults> Argues that college campuses are an indicator that our country has a long way to go to overcome racial intolerance.
- Hudson, David L. <http://www.firstamendmentcenter.org/hate-speech-campus-speech-codes> Outlines the history of restrictions on hate speech and analyzes possible reform; links to relevant cases.
- Lerner, Natan. <http://www.wcl.american.edu/hrbrief/v3i2/lerner32.htm> Argues that generally the government is justified in restricting hate speech.

Further Reading:

Downs, Donald Alexander. *Restoring Free Speech and Liberty on Campus.* Cambridge University Press, 2006.

Lewis, Anthony. *Freedom for the Thought That We Hate: A Biography of the First Amendment.* Basic Books, 2010.

Shiell, Timothy C. *Campus Hate Speech on Trial.* 2nd rev. ed. University Press of Kansas, 2009.

Waldron, Jeremy. *The Harm in Hate Speech.* Harvard University Press, 2012.

■ ■

HUMAN ORGANS, SALE OF

Advances in surgical and diagnostic techniques have substantially increased the success of organ transplant operations. In 2008, over 23,000 organs were transplanted in the United States. However, during the past decade, the waiting list for organs has grown faster than the number of transplants, and thousands of Americans die each year waiting for transplants. The sale of human organs can be considered as a possible solution to the crippling shortage; in 1984, however, Congress passed the National Organ Transplantation Act, which prohibits the sale of human organs from either dead or living donors. However, the overseas market trade in human organs is thriving.

PROS

The seriously ill are entitled to spend their money on saving their lives. It is preferable that some individuals receive organs, and survive, than that they die. The wealthy will not be the sole beneficiaries of a policy of organ purchase. For each successful kidney transplant operation, valuable hours on a dialysis machine will open up. The expense of palliative care for individuals requiring a transplant will be eliminated.

Let the poor do what they have to do to survive. Donating an organ is better than starving.

The donor of an organ, or his family, will benefit considerably from the sale. Both a kidney and a piece of liver can be removed without significant harm to the individual. Any assertion that an individual cannot make a reasoned decision to donate or sell these organs is patronizing. The family of a recently deceased individual also ought to be able to save the life of another and simultaneously receive remuneration.

The Chinese maintain that they do not trade in human organs. They say that the relatives of executed prisoners voluntarily approve of the use of the organs. If an individual is concerned about Chinese practices, they can go elsewhere.

The transplant surgeon, the nursing staff, and even the pharmaceutical companies producing the anti-rejection drugs receive payment for each operation performed. Why should the donor of the organs, arguably the most important actor in any transplant, not also receive remuneration? What is remarkable is that a lifesaving treatment should apparently have no financial value.

CONS

A single kidney has a black market price of $20,000. Consequently, the sale of organs will highlight and support the most egregious discrimination between rich and poor. Those who cannot afford to purchase an organ will have no opportunity to receive one. What family, if prepared to donate the organs of a relative, would decide to decline a payment of tens of thousands of dollars? Donated organs will disappear. The poor will die and only the rich will survive.

Overseas travel for organs is fueling a trade in human organs that exploits the poorest of the poor. We do not want to encourage a system where people want money more than their organs.

The market in organs works in one direction—from the Third World to the First. The relative absence of regulation and the comparative value of the rewards mean that healthy individuals in Asia and Africa fall victim to scavenging organ merchants. The financial rewards make the decision to sell an organ one of compulsion rather than consent. Where colonialists raped the land, the neocolonialist surgeon steals from bodies.

The sale of organs will lead to appalling human rights violations. Chinese judicial officials are reported to have executed prisoners for their body parts. The lawful sale of organs would legitimize human sacrifice.

Putting a price on the human body invites only exploitation by the unscrupulous.

Sample Motions:

This House would legalize the sale of organs.

This House would have a heart — with a price tag.

This House would buy body parts.

Web Links:

- Dubner, Stephen J. <http://freakonomics.blogs.nytimes.com/2008/04/29/human-organs-for-sale-legally-in-which-country/> Describes the success of the organ market in Iran (the only country that has legalized the sale of organs).
- Kahn, Jeffrey P. <http://archives.cnn.com/2002/HEALTH/10/01/ethics.matters.selling.organs/> Article arguing that the human cost of selling an organ exceeds the price organs fetch.
- NPR. <http://www.npr.org/templates/story/story.php?storyId=90632108> Broadcast radio debate between six experts on the pros and cons of legalizing the organ market.
- Shapiro, Robyn S. <http://www.americanbar.org/publications/human_rights_magazine_home/human_rights_vol30_2003/spring2003/hr_spring03_livingdonors.html> Analyzes the legal status quo of organ sales in the United States and proposes potential reform for the future.

Further Reading:

Cherry, Mark. *Kidney for Sale by Owner: Human Organs, Transplantation, and the Market.* Georgetown University Press, 2005.

Farrell, Anne-Maree, David Price, and Muireann Quigley, eds. *Organ Shortage: Ethics, Law and Pragmatism.* Cambridge University Press, 2011.

Territo, Leonard, and Rande Matteson, eds. *The International Trafficking of Human Organs: A Multidisciplinary Perspective.* CRC Press, 2012.

Wilkinson, T.M. *Ethics and the Acquisition of Organs.* Oxford University Press, 2011.

■ ■

HUMAN RIGHTS: EXISTENCE OF

The concept of human rights is central to modern Western culture. But what does "human rights" mean? Do we have such rights, and if we do, why are they needed? The United Nations adopted the Universal Declaration of Human Rights (UDHR) in 1948 in response to the savage inhumanities of World War II. This document sets out a declaration of fundamental entitlements including the political and civil rights common to Western democracies as well as economic, social, and cultural rights that Western nations have not historically considered fundamental. However, the document includes no enforcement mechanism, and states are obliged only to "move toward" a realization of these rights. Thus, while important steps have been made toward an international understanding of rights, there is a long way to go.

PROS

By their nature and birth, human beings possess certain inalienable rights. As Article I of the UDHR states, "All human beings are born free and equal in dignity and rights."

The simple sharing of a common humanity establishes human rights. We extrapolate from this humanity the norms that secure the basic dignity with which we all want to live.

CONS

Do animals have the same inalienable rights by virtue of their nature and birth? Isn't this claim a bit arbitrary? Why should everyone have a "right" just because they are born?

This argument is arbitrary and nebulous. It bases fundamental human rights on extrapolating from "feelings." How accurate can this be? Furthermore, isn't this just a wish list of ways we want to be treated? A desire to be treated in a certain way doesn't give one the right to be so treated.

PROS

Desires are not what grounds human rights. What human rights are based on is the universal need for basic security in our bodies, our possessions, and our relationships within society. This security isn't just desirable; it is vital. Human rights are those things that rationally assure these vital requirements. Thomas Hobbes recognized that all people benefit from this security because human beings are equal in their capacity to harm one another.

Our understanding of human rights has evolved over several hundred years. The rights contemporary Western societies consider basic are more extensive than those found in past societies because these Western societies have a higher standard of living. People often must experience the lack of something to appreciate how vital it is—this is true of human rights.

Human rights are not meant to be subject to artificial, academic analysis. They are practical guides to life, standards of how we should be able to live. They are an objective standard that people can use when calling on their governments for justice.

CONS

If human rights are requirements of reason, then why do we see so much ambiguity and confusion over what they are? There is huge debate over what rights we have, and many people cannot agree that we have basic economic or development rights. This seems odd if human rights are rational requirements that are vital to life.

This is a very subversive trail to start down. These "requirements of reason" are both subjective and dependent on specific circumstances. Does that mean that humans really don't have inalienable rights, but instead transform accepted standards of living into actual rights? In that case, two cultures could have radically different but valid interpretations of a specific human right. Can this be a satisfactory basis for concrete and actual rights?

This all suggests that human rights can be extremely useful. However, something can be useful, indeed necessary, without it being your right. None of these arguments establishes that human beings have inherent "rights."

Sample Motions:

This House believes in fundamental human rights.

This House believes rights are right.

Web Links:

- Nickel, James. <http://plato.stanford.edu/entries/rights-human/> Philosophical discussion of the existence, definition, and recognition of human rights.
- Universal Declaration of Human Rights. <http://www.un.org/Overview/rights.html> Text of the document.
- University of Minnesota Human Rights Library. <http://www1.umn.edu/humanrts/> Provides links to more than 7,000 documents on human rights.

Further Reading:

Clapham, Andrew. *Human Rights: A Very Short Introduction.* Oxford University Press, 2007.

Griffin, James. *On Human Rights.* Oxford University Press, 2009.

Hunt, Lynn. *Inventing Human Rights: A History.* Norton, 2008.

■ ■

ILLEGAL IMMIGRATION AND "SHOW ME YOUR PAPERS" LAWS

An estimated 10 to 20 million immigrants currently live in the US illegally, and approximately half of them come from Mexico. Preventing illegal immigration is a major concern for many Americans, particularly those living close to the Mexican border. To them, illegal immigrants drive up crime and drain financial resources. "Show me your papers" laws, which allow law enforcement to demand documentation from those they suspect of being in the country illegally, are among the more controversial measures used to combat illegal immigration. Arizona's contentious 2010 Support Our Law Enforcement and Safe Neighborhoods Act paved the way for similar laws in Alabama and Georgia, all featuring "show me your papers" provisions. These laws have been subject to extensive legal rulings; in June 2012, the Supreme Court upheld the portion of the Arizona law that allows law enforcement to investigate the immigration status of individuals who are stopped, so long as there is a reasonable suspicion that they are in the country illegally. The connection between this "reasonable suspicion" and racial profiling is key to this debate.

PROS

Because all foreign nationals are required to carry immigration documents, these laws ensure that only those here illegally are targeted by police—all legal residents can be immediately identified and let go. It is already a federal offense for foreign nationals not to carry immigration documents with them; "show me your papers" provisions merely allow this existing law to be enforced. In addition, the laws specifically prohibit racial profiling and require that all stops be based on the "reasonable suspicion" that someone is an illegal immigrant. Furthermore, the Arizona law requires a legitimate law-enforcement incident (e.g., speeding or running a red light) before any individual can be stopped. These laws do nothing to harm law-abiding documented immigrants, but effectively target the illegal immigrants that cause problems for the community at large.

It is an indisputable fact that laws must be enforced; if it is illegal for undocumented immigrants to be in the country, and for any immigrants to be without their papers, the police must be allowed to investigate these offenses. When someone is suspected of any other crime, the police have the right to stop and question the suspect. By treating illegal immigration differently we are condoning it. Illegal immigrants are aware that the police have little authority over them, which decreases their respect for law enforcement in general and encourages further criminal behavior. If we want immigrants to respect our laws, we must allow the police to enforce them.

CONS

These laws will be damaging to all individuals of Hispanic or Latino origin in the US, regardless of their immigration status. By allowing police to stop people and investigate their immigration status on the basis of suspicion alone, we are paving the way for rampant racial profiling. The laws do nothing to define what a "reasonable suspicion" is. Undocumented immigrants cannot be distinguished from documented immigrants by sight alone—anyone who appears to be an immigrant can be arbitrarily stopped and detained until proof of legal residence in the country is produced. In practice, this "suspicion" will be based on one primary characteristic: race. It will become routine for Hispanic and Latino people to be stopped for minor infringements, for the sole purpose of checking documents, with the result of dehumanizing and alienating whole communities.

These laws will worsen relationships between Hispanic communities and local law enforcement. A 2004 Amnesty International study demonstrated that unwarranted stops by the police cause humiliation and emotional distress. If individuals are routinely stopped by police, simply because they look "illegal," they will lose respect for the police force. For young people, who will grow up with the sense that law enforcement is against them, this is counterproductive; if individuals feel that society already views them as criminal, they are more likely to feel that crime is their only option. If we want immigrants to respect our laws, we must show them that the laws are intended to protect them too; this is not achieved by alienating them from the police.

PROS

Crime is endemic among illegal immigrants in border towns; police powers must be strengthened in order to protect Americans from this. Drug cartels, which depend on illegal immigrants to act as drug mules, present a real danger to communities along the border. The immigration law in Arizona drew widespread support following the 2010 murder of Robert Krentz. Krentz, a rancher, was shot dead close to the Mexican border by suspected illegal immigrants and drug smugglers. There were over 15,000 murders in Mexico in 2010, mainly concentrated along the US border; Ciudad Juarez, just across the border from Texas, is consistently named as the most violent city in Mexico. To stop this violence from spilling over the border, we must stop the perpetrators from living in the United States by aggressively pursuing all those who are here illegally.

Illegal immigrants are an economic drain on states—they do not pay their share of taxes and they use public services disproportionately. The state's first obligation is to provide for its citizens—having a population of "free riders" hampers its ability to do this. In fact, the Federation for American Immigration Reform estimated that in Arizona alone illegal immigration costs taxpayers $2.6 billion a year in medical, educational, and incarceration expenses. Illegal immigrants may also lower wages and take jobs from US citizens, in that employers often get away with paying illegal immigrants less than minimum wage. The ability to identify and remove illegal immigrants is vital to states that are still struggling economically since the recession.

CONS

There is no evidence that illegal immigrants are any more criminal than the general population. In fact, the 2008 crime rate in Arizona was lower than it had been in 40 years, with violent crime decreasing as illegal immigration increased. Furthermore, it is other immigrants—not US citizens—who are most likely to be the victims of crimes committed by illegal immigrants. Investigating these crimes, and arresting dangerous offenders, is made more difficult if victims and witnesses do not come forward due to fear of deportation. A survey of Latino attitudes conducted for the National Council of La Raza in May 2010 found that 47% of those surveyed would be less likely to report a crime or volunteer information to the police as a result of the Arizona law. Preventing drug cartel activity is best achieved by strengthening border control, not by police harassment of anyone who looks like an immigrant.

"Show me your papers" laws will generate an enormous number of lawsuits from individuals wrongfully stopped by the police, putting a huge financial burden on states—possibly hundreds of millions of dollars. Furthermore, illegal immigrants do contribute to the economy; although they are often paid lower wages, this props up the economy by providing cheaper goods and services. Economic activity produced by illegal immigrants employs approximately 5% of US workers and the IRS estimates that 6 million tax returns are filed by undocumented workers every year. Furthermore, illegal immigrants subsidize Social Security, as they pay into it but cannot claim benefits. If Arizona successfully deported all illegal immigrants, it would lose an estimated. $26.4 billion in economic activity and 140,000 jobs.

Sample Motions:

This House believes that "show me your papers" laws are just.

This House would deport all illegal immigrants.

This House maintains that, on balance, illegal immigration does more harm than good.

Web Links:

- Immigration Policy Center. "Q&A Guide to Arizona's to New Immigration Law." <http://www.immigrationpolicy.org/specialreports/>.

- Jurist. "Arizona's Immigration Law: Constitutional But . . ." <http://jurist.org/forum/2010/05/arizonasimmigrationlaw.php> A discussion of the legal issues behind Bill 1070.

- New York Times. "Show Me Your Papers." <http://www.nytimes.com/2012/07/02/opinion/keller-show-me-your-papers.html?pagewanted=all> Argues that "show me your papers" laws lead to discrimination and should be replaced with federal immigration reform.

- "Why Arizona Drew a Line." <http://www.nytimes.com/2010/04/ 29/opinion/29kobach.html> An editorial refuting the main arguments in opposition to Bill 1070.

Further Reading:

Ankarlo, Darrell. *Illegals: The Unacceptable Cost of America's Failure to Control Its Borders.* Thomas Nelson, 2010.

Chacon, Justin Akers, and Mike Davis. *No One Is Illegal: Fighting Racism and State Violence on the U.S.–Mexico Border.* Haymarket Books, 2006.

Friedmann Marquardt, Marie. *Living "Illegal": The Human Face of Unauthorized Immigration.* New Press, 2011.

Sterling, Terry Greene. *Illegal: Life and Death in Arizona's Immigration War Zone.* Lyons Press, 2010.

. .

INSTANT REPLAY IN SPORTS

Technological advances allow the option to use instant replay in sports; a referee can immediately observe video footage of a play to aid his decision. Instant replay is used widely in the American National Football League (NFL) and for certain plays in the American Baseball League to allow more accurate decisions. Other sports leagues, including the Fédération Internationale de Football Association (FIFA), reject instant replay as taking the "human factor" out of the sport, "replacing a mind with a machine." These leagues also fear errors that are inevitable when depending on technology. FIFA's refusal to use instant replay created controversy during the 2010 World Cup, which many sport commentators argue may have had a different outcome if instant replay had been used to correct erroneous referee calls.

PROS

Instant replay need not be perfect to be beneficial. While camera shots can be misleading, they are much more accurate than the naked eye. A team should win because it plays a stronger game, not because the referee makes a mistake. During the 2010 World Cup, referees made a variety of significant errors—one ignored a clear goal scored by England against Germany, another ignored an offside violation by Argentina against Mexico. These, and countless other errors, were no doubt unintentional and demonstrate that human error has a significant and undue influence on the outcome of sports contests. The fair outcome of games is important, not only for the sake of the sport itself, but also for those who may receive promotions, endorsements, and have other business interests that depend on the outcome of individual games and the entire season's results.

As discussed below, football and baseball have great numbers of viewers and fans despite constant starting and stopping. Sports games are frequently interrupted to switch players, assist injured athletes, dispute calls, etc. Using instant replay in moderation will not disturb the spirit of the game. If anything, it can add to the experience—spectators wait in anticipation as the referee comes to the most fair and appropriate call.

If used correctly, instant replay would not add a significant amount of time to the game; lengthening the game

CONS

Cameras can be faulty; pictures do lie. Depending on the angle, zoom, timing, lighting, and other factors, cameras may portray a play in a misleading manner. It is unwise to depend on technology as the ultimate arbiter or as a total solution to human error. We should not use instant replay to replace human on-the-spot judgment with an imperfect machine.

Instant replay interferes with the spirit of the game. Excitement builds during the action of a game; stopping to review video footage, besides slowing the game, will bore viewers and break athletes' concentration.

Instant replay slows the game. Constant referrals to a camera will make a game considerably more time-consuming;

PROS	CONS
is unlikely to deter fans from following it. Instant replay need only be used for controversial calls—by its nature, it is immediate and thus quick. Sports fans are often willing to dedicate large amounts of time and money to watch their favorite teams; fans are unlikely to give up watching their favorites if games were slightly longer. In the United States, baseball and football are the most watched sports, despite being relatively slow-paced. We maintain that fans would enjoy the game more because referees would make fewer bad calls.	in a single game, hundreds of moves could be reviewed on camera. This disturbs the continuity of the game and frustrates fans, who will grow bored and stop watching the game before it finishes.
Instant replay does not have to be used for every call. The American NFL uses a "challenge system" whereby coaches may challenge a certain number of calls per game; instant replay can be limited to certain types of calls and can be limited within the context of a single game.	Not all sports decisions are objective; instant replay cannot account for subjective calls. In baseball, two umpires could look at the same pitch on instant replay and come to different conclusions about whether it is a strike. Instant replay diminishes respect for the referee's decision.
When instant replay is not available, it cannot be used—but when it is available, it should be used. Instant replay is used in American outdoor sports without significant impediments due to weather. Furthermore, it is illogical to dismiss an opportunity to improve the game on the basis that it will not always be there. For example, amateurs should not refrain from playing soccer in the park simply because they cannot find a referee, but when referees are available, they improve the game.	Instant replay cannot be universally implemented. In the 2010 World Cup, FIFA decided not to use instant replay—FIFA president Sepp Blatter claimed the technology is flawed and would be vulnerable to weather conditions. Since soccer is played outside, cameras and televisions would be susceptible to rain, wind, and snow. Any game should always be played according to the same rules and guidelines.

Sample Motions:
This House supports instant replay in competitive sports.
This House preserves the human aspect of a sports game.

Web Links:
- ESPN Soccer Net: World Cup 2010. "I'm So Angry I Could Break Glass." <http://soccernet.espn.go.com/world-cup/columns/story/_/id/5333748/ce/us/chris-jones-mad-break-glass?cc=5901&ver=us> Article discussing fans' reactions to a clearly erroneous referee decision that could have been prevented by using instant replay.
- Salon News. "Would Instant Replay Work in Soccer?" <http://www.salon.com/news/feature/2010/06/21/replay_soccer_world_cup> Article discussing the advantages of using instant replay in soccer and considering the logistical difficulties.

■ ■

INTERNET CENSORSHIP

The Internet is the largest tool for mass communication and information distribution in the world. In the past few years concern has increased about the Internet's dissemination of content that is violent and sexual, that gives bomb-making instructions, abets terrorist activity, and makes available child pornography. In response, some have called for censorship. In 1998, the US Congress passed the Child Online Protection Act, restricting access by minors to Internet material that is deemed harmful. However, the courts have blocked implementation, ruling that the act violates constitutional protection of free speech. But even if censorship of the Internet can be morally and legally justified, practical problems with regulation arise. The issue of Internet censorship came to the global forefront in 2011. The 2011 Arab Spring—the term for a wave of civil uprisings across the Arab world—saw citizens using social media to organize protests against authoritarian regimes, thus illustrating the democratizing power of an open Internet. In the United States, two bills—known as SOPA (Stop Online Piracy Act) and PIPA (Preventing Real Online Threats to Economic Creativity and Theft of Intellectual Property Act)—were introduced into the US Congress; both were designed to combat online copyright infringement by allowing the US government and judicial system increased control over online content. Despite receiving bipartisan support, the bills were subject to widespread protests from both the Internet community and free-speech activists and were, subsequently, not passed into law.

PROS

Although democratic nations value freedom of speech, all put some restrictions on the right. Such restrictions usually surround hard-core and child pornography, but some nations restrict hate speech as well. The Internet should be no exception to these basic standards. Truly offensive material is no different because it is published on the web.

Censorship is tailored to the power of the medium. Accordingly, a higher level of censorship is attached to television, films, and video than to newspapers and books: We recognize that moving pictures and sound are more graphic and powerful than text, photographs, or illustrations. Videos are normally more regulated than films seen in theaters because the viewer of a video has control of the medium—the power to rewind, view again, and distribute more widely. The Internet, which increasingly uses video and sound, should be regulated accordingly.

The Internet would be hard to control, but we must not use that as an excuse not to try. Preventing the sale of snuff movies or hard-core pornography is extremely difficult, but some governments do so because they deem it important. A more intractable issue is the anonymity that the Internet provides pornographers and criminals. Asian countries have experimented with requiring citizens to provide identification before posting content on the Web. If universally adopted, such a requirement could be a relatively simple way of enforcing laws against truly offensive and harmful content.

CONS

Censorship is usually immoral. Governments should avoid it wherever possible. Child pornography is an extreme example; sufficient legislation is already in place to handle those who attempt to produce, distribute, or view such material. Other forms of speech may well be offensive, but the only way a society can counter such speech is to be exposed to it and have it out in the open. Without such freedom, these groups are driven underground and can take on the aspect of martyrs.

The distinction between censorship of print and broadcast media is becoming increasingly irrelevant. Print media are comparatively unregulated because they are the primary means of distributing information in society. In the near future, the Internet may become this prime disseminator. Thus the Internet must be allowed the same protections now enjoyed by print media. When English philosopher John Stuart Mill considered freedom of speech and the Founding Fathers of the United States spoke in the Constitution of freedom of the press they were concerned about the primary and most powerful organ of information distribution at that time, the print press. Nowadays they would more likely be concerned with preventing censorship of the broadcast media and the Internet.

Even allowing for the extreme problems surrounding curtailment of freedom of speech, Internet censorship would be more or less impossible. Governments can attempt to regulate what is produced in their own countries but regulating material originating outside national borders would be impossible. What is the point in the US removing all domestic links to hard-core pornography when such material from the UK or Sweden could be readily accessed and downloaded? Individuals could also produce banned material and store it in an overseas domain. True freedom of speech requires anonymity in some cases

PROS	CONS
	to protect the author. Governments that have introduced ID requirements for Internet use also deny many basic rights to their citizens. The Internet allows citizens to criticize their government and distribute news and information without reprisal from the state. These freedoms clearly could not survive Internet ID requirements.
In many countries producing libelous material or material that incites racial hatred incurs multiple liability. Where the author or publisher cannot be traced or is insolvent, the printers can often be sued or prosecuted. The relatively small number of Internet service providers (ISPs) should be made liable if they assist in the provision of dangerous or harmful information.	Internet service providers are certainly the wrong people to decide what can and cannot be placed on the Internet. Big business already controls far too much of this new technology without also making it judge and jury of all Internet content. In any case, the sheer bulk of information ISPs allow to be published is such that reviewing it all would be impossible. Were ISPs to be held liable for allowing such material to be displayed, they would inevitably err on the side of caution to protect their financial interests. This would result in a much more heavily censored Internet.
The issues at stake in this debate—protection of children, terrorist activity, crime, racial hatred, etc.,—are all international problems. If a global solution is required, it can be achieved by international cooperation and treaties. All societies consider censorship justified where harm is caused to others by the speech, words, or art. All the examples cited above are clearly causing harm to various groups in society. By a combination of the initiatives listed above, we could limit that harm.	Many ISPs have shown themselves to be responsible in immediately removing truly offensive content where they have been alerted to it. What is required is self-regulation by the industry, not the imposition of arbitrary and draconian restrictions on Internet content and use. Parents can install software that will filter out offensive sites and sites inappropriate for children.

Sample Motions:

This House would censor the Internet.

This House calls for net filters.

This House would limit freedom of speech.

Web Links:

- American Civil Liberties Union. <http://www.aclu.org/free-speech/internet-censorship> ACLU's page on Internet censorship.
- Center for Democracy and Technology. <http://www.cdt.org/> Offers policy briefs, reports, and articles on issues involved in Internet freedom.
- Electronic Frontier Foundation. <http://www.eff.org/blueribbon.html> Offers summaries of issues involving Internet censorship as well as information on fair use and privacy on the web.

Further Reading:

Ammori, Marvin. *On Internet Freedom*. Elkat Books, 2013.

Deibert, Ronald et al., eds. *Access Denied: The Practice and Policy of Global Internet Filtering (Information Revolution and Global Politics)*. The MIT Press, 2008.

MacKinnon, Rebecca. *Consent of the Networked: The Worldwide Struggle For Internet Freedom*. Basic Books, 2012.

Miles, Jeremy. *The SOPA & PIPA Conspiracy: Taking CONTROL through Internet Censorship*. Amazon Digital Services, 2012.

■ ■

INTERNMENT WITHOUT TRIAL

Internment *can be defined as the indefinite detention of a person by a government and the denial of the normal legal processes that would usually be available to them, such as the right to know the charges and evidence against them, the right to a public trial, the right to appeal to a higher judicial authority, etc. While governments often resort to internment in periods of national emergency, such as a war or during a terrorist campaign, the practice raises questions about the balance between security and liberty. Following September 11, the Bush administration interned hundreds of Al-Qaeda and Taliban suspects in Guantanamo Bay under military authority without appeal to the US legal system. The action generated severe criticism from parts of the international community and prompted a series of legal challenges from civil liberties groups that have resulted in Supreme Court decisions recognizing the government's right to detain illegal combatants but finding illegal the special military commissions established to try such combatants.*

PROS

Governments must have the power to address threats to the nation. Everyone would recognize that laws that apply in peacetime might not be appropriate during war. Captured enemy combatants, for example, should not have the rights of habeas corpus and trial by jury that citizens enjoy. The war on terror is in this respect a war like earlier, more conventional conflicts. Just because our enemies do not wear uniforms or conform to a normal military structure does not make them any less of a threat to our society.

We must reach an appropriate balance between security and freedom. Everyone recognizes the importance of protecting rights and liberties, but this cannot be done at all and any cost. The first duty of our political leaders is to protect us from harm, and the voters will rightly hold them accountable if they fail.

At a time when our society is under threat, protecting our intelligence sources is more important than giving suspected terrorists public trials. Charging and trying terror suspects in open court would require governments to reveal their intelligence sources, thus risking the identification of their spies. These revelations might lead to the murder of brave agents and shut off crucial intelligence channels that could warn us of future attacks. Even if courts made special arrangements for presenting

CONS

The war on terror is not like past, conventional conflicts, and the administration cannot assume wartime powers simply on its own declaration. The September 11 attacks were horrific, but they did not threaten the existence of the nation—the economy rebounded surprisingly quickly, and no one believes that even a successful attack on the White House or the Capitol would have ended American democracy. Nor is the war on terror winnable—there is no likely endpoint at which we will declare victory and so allow detained "enemy combatants" to go home. So these harsh but supposedly temporary wartime measures will become the norm.

Giving the government the power to detain suspects without due process will not make society safer. The proposition's arguments rely on the accuracy of secret intelligence, which supposedly identifies individuals planning terrorist acts but which cannot be revealed in open court. Recent history suggests that such intelligence is often deeply flawed. Intelligence failures in the campaign against Al-Qaeda point to the difficulties Western intelligence services have in penetrating and understanding terrorist groups, while intelligence on Iraq's weapons programs was also clearly flawed. So not only will many innocent people be unjustly interned, many dangerous ones will be left at liberty.

Not only is intelligence often badly flawed, internment simply doesn't work as a strategy to combat terrorism. It is counterproductive, making martyrs of the individuals detained. And, as Britain's experience with the Irish Republican Army has shown, internment can radicalize detainees. Moreover, the harsh measures undermine the confidence of ordinary citizens in their government, reducing their support for the war on terror. Indeed, if we compromise aspects of our free and open societies

PROS

intelligence evidence, terrorists could use the trials to learn more about our intelligence capabilities and tactics. In these circumstances, detention without public trial is the only safe option.

Tough measures are aimed only at very few suspects—only a few hundred are interned at Guantanamo Bay. Exceptional circumstances call for special measures, but these are so limited in scope that they do not threaten our democratic values.

Although a normal public trial is not possible for security reasons, detainees' rights are still respected. Safeguards are built into the internment process so that each case can be considered fairly, with the suspect represented before a proper tribunal and given a right to appeal to a higher authority. If a trial is held (often to standards of evidence and procedure higher than in regular courts in many countries around the world) and a sentence properly passed, then this is not internment as it has been practiced in the past.

CONS

in response to pressure, then the terrorists who hate our values are winning.

Rights protect the few as well as the many. Indefinite detention and lack of a normal public trial undermine the key values of habeas corpus and the presumption of innocence. Try suspects if there is evidence and deport them if they are foreign nationals, but release them if the government cannot make a proper case against them. The British government said that internment in Northern Ireland was aimed only at a tiny minority, but thousands passed through the Long Kesh detention camp in the four years it operated.

Regardless of the procedures that authorities use as window dressing to justify their actions, internment is open to abuse because trials are secret, with the executive essentially scrutinizing itself. Trials are held in secret with crucial evidence frequently withheld from the accused and his defense team or given anonymously with no opportunity to examine witnesses properly. Appeals are typically to the executive (which chose to prosecute them), rather than to an independent judicial body. In such circumstances, prejudice and convenience are likely to prevent justice being done.

Sample Motions:

This House believes that internment is sometimes justified.

This House supports Guantanamo Bay.

This House would detain terror suspects.

Web Links:

- Head, Michael. <http://www.thefreelibrary.com/Detention+without+trial--a+threat+to+democratic+rights-a0155041531> Argues that detention without trial is a threat to democracy.

- Human Rights Watch. <http://www.hrw.org/en/category/topic/counterterrorism/detention-without-trial> Links to articles, reports. and commentaries on detention without trial.

- PBS. <http://www.pbs.org/now/shows/536/index.html> Television program discussing the debate over preventive detention.

Further Reading:

Ferraro, Nicholas A, ed.. *Legal and Trial Issues Stemming from the War on Terror*. Nova Science, 2010.

Margulies, Joseph. Guantanamo and the Abuse of Presidential Power. Simon & Schuster, 2007.

Sulmasy, Glenn. The National Security Court System: A Natural Evolution of Justice in an Age of Terror. Oxford University Press, 2009.

Wittes, Benjamin, ed. *Legislating the War on Terror: An Agenda for Reform*. Brookings Institution Press, 2009.

IRAN'S RIGHT TO POSSESS NUCLEAR WEAPONS

Since the revolution against the US-backed Shah in 1979, the Islamic Republic of Iran has maintained a difficult relationship with the West. A major regional military power, Iran wields considerable influence in the Middle East, and its emerging economy has grown alongside complicated social and political tensions that mark its relations with its neighbors. Iran has declared its intentions of restarting its nuclear technology program, and it has begun to develop centrifuges for refining uranium—the first step not only toward nuclear power but also, the West fears, toward developing nuclear weapons. Because EU-led negotiations with Iran have failed, the UN, the United States and its allies, and the world as a whole must now determine how to deal with Iran's nuclear ambitions.

PROS

Iran is a signatory of the Nuclear Non-Proliferation Treaty, which permits the development of nuclear technology for peaceful purposes. Iran maintains that as it is enriching uranium for peaceful purposes only, it is legally entitled to continue its nuclear program. Iran also draws comparisons between itself and three nuclear powers (Israel, India, and Pakistan) who never signed the treaty.

Iran is a democratic state that has a right to determine its own policies—both about nuclear energy and nuclear weapons. Moreover, religious leaders in Iran have spoken against nuclear armament while still advocating the development of nuclear energy. In August 2005, Iran's supreme political and religious leader, Ayatollah Ali Khamenei, issued a fatwa (a religious edict) declaring that Islam forbids the development, stockpiling, and use of nuclear weapons. He also stated that Iran should never possess nuclear arms. Moreover, Iran has the same right to possess nuclear arms as other countries. As one Iranian soldier said to the BBC, "If America has the right to nuclear weapons after dropping bombs on Hiroshima and Nagasaki, why doesn't Iran have that right?"

Iran, like 116 other developing nations, is a member of the Non-Aligned Movement (NAM). The NAM holds that "all countries have a basic and inalienable right to develop atomic energy for peaceful purposes," and strongly opposes what it sees as a double standard—one for developing nations and another for developed nations. Iran has emerged as a leading member of the NAM, and its fight to develop nuclear technology has become a rallying cry for many NAM states. Many developing nations see the distribution of nuclear arms in the world as reinforcing Western hegemony and promoting the interests

CONS

Nothing prevents Iran from enriching uranium for weapons purposes. Although Iran has permitted inspections of its nuclear facilities in the past, we have no guarantee that it will continue to do so once it has the capacity to create weapons. Iran's track record is poor: it hid its nuclear enrichment program from the world for many years prior to the current crisis. Its ongoing activities to influence politics in other Middle Eastern states and its president's outspoken objection to Israel's existence are all ominous signs that it might pursue developing nuclear weapons if given the chance.

Iran's military and political institutions are unstable and are not accountable to the Iranian public. Real power is in the hands of unelected religious leaders (the ayatollah and the Council of Guardians) who can veto policies and parliamentary candidates by invoking *sharia* (Islamic law). The military also includes Islamic fundamentalists, who, like the clerics, believe that they answer to authorities higher than international law. If these groups are given access to the raw materials of nuclear weapons or to weapons themselves, we have no way of predicting how they might use them.

We must not let nuclear weapons proliferate. Iran has a proven track record of supporting terrorism (including Hezbollah) both in the Middle East and beyond, and the country might provide nuclear arms to such groups. Moreover, just as the rogue Pakistani scientist Abdul Qadeer Khan illegally sold nuclear technology, so Iran might sell such weapons on the black market if given an opportunity. If the world hopes someday to eradicate nuclear weapons, allowing other states, particularly a state like Iran, to acquire them is senseless and dangerous.

of the United States and its allies. By allowing nonaligned states to acquire nuclear arms, the world can help counterbalance US imperialism and give Third World nations more influence in global politics.

Sample Motions:
This House would permit Iran to develop nuclear capabilities as it sees fit.
This House believes that Iran is entitled to possess nuclear weapons.
This House believes that Iran's nuclear program is not a threat to world stability.

Web Links:
- Amayreh, Khaled. <http://www.thepeoplesvoice.org/TPV3/Voices.php/2010/04/01/iran-has-the-right-to-possess-nuclear-we> Argues that Iran has the right to possess nuclear weapons.
- BBC News. <http://news.bbc.co.uk/2/hi/middle_east/4031603.stm> Question and answer document on "Iran and the nuclear issue."
- Bock, Andreas M. <http://archive.atlantic-community.org/app/webroot/files/articlepdf/Bock_Iran%20and%20Nuclear%20Weapons.pdf> Argues that, technically, Iran has the right to possess nuclear weapons.
- Hutchins, Matthew W. <http://www.informationclearinghouse.info/article24973.htm> Describes scholar and activist Noam Chomsky's position that the United States is applying the Non-Proliferation Treaty hypocritically.
- International Atomic Energy Agency. <http://www.iaea.org/NewsCenter/Focus/IaeaIran/index.shtml> Links to documents, reports, and newspaper articles on Iran's nuclear program.

Further Reading:
Jafarzadeh, Alireza. *The Iran Threat: President Ahmadinejad and the Coming Nuclear Crisis.* Palgrave Macmillan, 2008.
Ottolenghi, Emanuele. *Iran: The Looming Crisis.* Profile Books, 2010.
Ronen, Yaël. *The Iran Nuclear Issue (Documents in International Law).* Hart Publishing, 2010.

■ ■

ISRAEL AND THE PALESTINIANS, US POLICY TOWARD

Since it was founded in 1948, the state of Israel has been in conflict with the Arab nations that surround it and with the Arab people living within its own borders—the US has been part of that conflict. The US was one of the first countries to recognize the legitimacy of the Israeli government and has, for more than 50 years, supported Israel militarily, economically, and diplomatically. The United States has also been instrumental in negotiating diplomatic agreements between Israel and the Arab world. The central issue in the conflict today is the creation of a Palestinian state that would give autonomy to the Arabs living under Israeli rule (primarily on the West Bank of the Jordan River). Israel has been reluctant to create this state, which Palestinians regard as their right. The Obama administration has pledged to support "the goal of two states, Israel and Palestine, living side by side in peace and security."

PROS

US policy in the Middle East has been consistently on the side of Israel. Granted, Pres. Barack Obama, unlike George W. Bush, is talking to Palestinian leaders and

CONS

Do not forget that for most of its history, Israel's neighbors said that Israel had no right to exist and must be destroyed. US support has been critical to Israel's survival.

has shown willingness to challenge Israel's policies in the region, but he has done little substantively to change our lopsided policy.

American policy in the Middle East has been guided by politics, not principles. On the one hand, presidents have responded to the pressure from Jewish voters to support Israel. On the other hand, policy toward Arab states has been shaped largely by economic needs: the US has been friendly to countries with large oil reserves, e.g., Saudi Arabia, but has ignored poorer Arabs, e.g., the Palestinians.

The US has claimed that it supports Israel because it is the only democracy in the region—but such support of democracy has not been a firmly held principle and not acted on in other parts of the world. The US has knowingly supported corrupt and unjust authoritarian regimes in Arab countries when their oil policies favored America.

The US has been inconsistent in the application of its moral principles. It has routinely condemned Palestinians and other Arabs for terrorist actions, but it granted immediate recognition to the state of Israel, which engaged in a terrorist campaign against the British.

Throughout the world, the US is committed to the development of open, democratic societies. Israel is the only functioning democracy in the Middle East and shares many of America's political values. It deserves American support.

The US has always acted as an impartial broker, seeking concessions from both sides. The US has used its influence to have Israel consider Arab demands and to have Arab nations and negotiators consider Israel's demands.

The US has acted in good faith with the Palestinian people, but negotiations have faltered because Hamas, which governs Gaza, is classified as a terrorist organization by many governments, including those of the EU and the US.

Sample Motions:

This House supports US sponsorship of a Palestinian state.

This House would value democracy more than votes and oil.

Web Links:

- Eland, Ivan. <http://www.independent.org/newsroom/article.asp?id=2772> Argues that the US should not involve itself more in the Israeli-Palestinian conflict.
- If Americans Knew. <http://ifamericansknew.org/> Organization opposed to US policy regarding Israel.
- Macleod, Scott. <http://www.time.com/time/world/article/0,8599,1873859,00.html> Discusses whether President Obama will be able to broker peace in the Middle East.
- Palestine Facts. <http://www.palestinefacts.org/index.php> Pro-Israel organization.

Further Reading:

Gerteiny, Alfred G. *The Terrorist Conjunction: The United States, the Israeli-Palestinian Conflict and al-Qu'ida (Praeger Security International)*. Praeger, 2007.

Kurtzer, Daniel C., and Scott B. Lasensky. *Negotiating Arab-Israeli Peace: American Leadership in the Middle East*. United States Institute of Peace Press, 2008.

Mearsheimer, John J., and Stepehn M. Walt. *The Israel Lobby and US Foreign Policy*. Farrar, Straus and Giroux, 2010.

▪ ▪

JUDGES, ELECTING

In the United States, federal judges are appointed while individual states decide whether to elect or appoint state judges. Each state's constitution determines the selection system by its interpretation of and attempt to balance the competing goals of judicial independence and judicial accountability. If independence had greater weight, then judges are appointed; if accountability was deemed more important, the state elects its judges. This issue is important because many citizens believe that the judiciary's decisions do not reflect their values. The issue was highlighted at the federal level in 2010 when the Supreme Court in Citizens United v. Federal Election Commission *struck down restrictions on corporate contributions to political campaigns, leading to fears that corporations could effectively "buy" the election of justices favorable to their interests.*

PROS

Public accountability keeps judges in line and ensures that courts take into consideration and reflect the public will. Remember, judges are as capable of corruption and laziness as any other government functionary and should face the consequences of incompetence.

The public should not be prevented from electing judges because some feel that ordinary citizens are too ignorant to decide correctly—the same fallacious argument could be made for having executive or legislative officials appointed rather than elected, but government officials tend to be less corrupt and more responsive to public interests when they are elected. An educated public understands that a judge's responsibility is to interpret law and will elect those it thinks will best carry out that mandate.

The law is subjective and should reflect the public's interpretation. Citizens are completely capable of understanding legal interpretation, and they are entitled to judges who reflect the interpretations the public thinks best. For example, the Second Amendment has been interpreted in at least two ways—so, why is one judge more qualified to decide which is right than the entire American public?

Some good law is better than consistent bad law. Allowing the public to evaluate judicial review and choose judges will bring the judicial system closer to the ideal legal review. The public will sometimes elect bad judges, but these judges will not be reelected and will be replaced by better judges. The "replacement" judges will change judicial review but will change it to the benefit of society.

CONS

A judge's job is not to please the public. Courts often hand down extremely unpopular decisions that reflect the court's genuine interpretation of the law. If judges face reelection, they are more likely to decide according to what the public wants rather than what justice and the law require.

Elections tend to play on citizens' emotions. While this may be acceptable for politics, where arguably one should follow the heart, law should not be subject to whims or the pleadings of special interests. Per Aristotle, "Law is reason free from passion." Executive and legislative officials are supposed to act as representatives of the public, so elections are the best way to ensure they remain responsible to that duty. Judges, however, are responsible to the law and thus should be appointed on the basis of their legal qualifications.

Legal interpretation is extremely nuanced; the average citizen has neither the time nor expertise to evaluate the quality of a judge's legal review. Citizens tend to evaluate judicial candidates by how closely the individual citizen's political views are supported by the judge's rulings—even though decisions are supposed to be determined by legal interpretation rather than personal political opinion. Because of this disconnect between the average citizen and the law, elected judges are bound to either rule improperly or disappoint voters.

"Liberty finds no refuge in the jurisprudence of doubt." These words are cited frequently in Supreme Court decisions. Consistent precedent is essential because citizens need to be able to make decisions knowing the legal consequences of their actions. If new judges are constantly elected and according to swings in public sentiment, precedent will be inconsistent.

PROS

Judges have a direct and tangible effect on the lives of citizens, thus, more so than for any other government position, they must be directly accountable to the public. Judges hear the appeals of the accused, determine trial proceedings, overrule abusive legislation, and set the legal precedents that every citizen lives by. In a democracy, officials with such a tangible effect on citizens' lives should be held directly accountable.

This problem is not unique to judges; Citizens United affects all elections, yet the United States continues to function as a democracy. The outcome of *Citizens United v. Federal Election Commission* emphasizes the importance of allowing citizens to elect their judges; a *New York Times* poll found that 58% of Americans disagree with the decision. The preferable solution to a potentially unfair election is to allow Americans to elect judges who reflect-their interpretations of the First Amendment rather than declare elections problematic and limit public influence in and on government.

CONS

Plenty of unelected government officials have a more direct impact on citizens than elected ones. A citizen is more affected by her teacher than the elected school board, the employees at the DMV, IRS, or other government agencies than the representatives who establish and these agencies. Nevertheless, we do not elect every civil servant. Executive leaders and legislative representatives are elected because they create the law and establish government responsibilities; judges and other civil servants merely respond to these actions and thus are less directly responsible to the public.

Elections are influenced by wealth; candidates who receive more campaign donations have a greater ability to get their message out in the media—thus gaining an unfair advantage. The influence of moneyed interests is exacerbated by 2010 Supreme Court decision in *Citizens United v. Federal Election Commission*, which removed restrictions on corporations' ability to broadcast "electioneering communications." Corporations have vast resources that grassroots organizations cannot compete with; judicial elections under this system would result in judges who are much more sympathetic to business interests than to individual ones, making individual civil suits against large companies (already extremely difficult) almost impossible.

Sample Motions:

This House supports the election of judges.

This House believes judicial appointments are preferable to elections.

This House fears corporate influence over elections.

Web Links:

- Dallas Morning News. "Why Not Elect Judges on Merit, Not Whim?" <http://www.baumbach.org/b2evolution/blogs/index.php/2009/03/16/dmn_wallace_b_jefferson_why_not_elect_ju> Texas Chief Supreme Court Justice Wallace Jefferson argues that the public puts little thought into judicial elections.
- Frontline, PBS. "How Did We Come to Elect Judges?" <http://www.pbs.org/wgbh/pages/frontline/shows/justice/howdid/> This page contains links to several articles discussing the gradual transition from appointed to elected judges in many states.
- New York Times. "Justices, 5–4, Reject Corporate Spending Limit." <http://www.nytimes.com/2010/01/22/us/politics/22scotus.html?_r=1&scp=1&sq=citizens%20united&st=cse> This article explains the effects of the Supreme Court's decision in Citizens United v. Federal Election Commission, which will have a major impact on future electoral campaigns.

▪ ▪

JUST WAR

War is always evil, but some thinkers have maintained that under limited circumstances it may be the lesser evil. From Cicero to St. Augustine, Thomas Aquinas to Hugo Grotius, philosophers and theologians have proposed numerous criteria for determining if a war is just. According to contemporary Just War Theory, a war is just only if it meets the six conditions presented in the following debate. The theory has been formulated to prevent war, not justify it. A nation must satisfy all six conditions or the war is not just. The theory is designed to show states the rigorous criteria they must meet to justify the use of violence and prompt them to find other ways of solving conflicts.

PROS

A Just War satisfies six criteria:

1. Wars are just if the cause is just. Nations should be allowed to defend themselves from aggression, just as individuals are permitted to defend themselves against violence.

2. The war must be lawfully declared by a lawful authority. This prevents inappropriate, terrorist-style chaos, and ensures that other rules of war will be observed. For example, when states declare war, they generally follow specific legislative procedures; a guaranteed respect for such procedures is likely to ensure that the nation will respect other rules of war, such as the Geneva Convention.

3. The intentions behind the war must be good. States have the right to use war to restore a just peace, to help the innocent, or to right a wrong. For example, the US and NATO were justified in using force in Bosnia. Waging war was far more ethical than standing by and permitting genocide.

4. War must be a last resort. The state is justified in using war after it has tried all nonviolent alternatives. Sometimes peaceful measures—diplomacy, economic sanctions, international pressure, or condemnation from other nations—simply do not work.

CONS

The criteria for Just War present several problems:

1. Just cause is an elastic concept. Who determines what is "aggression"? Could violating a border or imposing economic sanctions be aggression? And if a state is unable to defend itself, can another state intervene militarily on its behalf? These borderline cases make invoking this criterion very problematic.

2. Many nations wage war without an official declaration. Moreover, who is to decide which entities can and cannot issue calls to arms? Legitimate authorities have sanctioned some of the most horrific wars in history.

3. Reality is a lot murkier than theory. How are we to determine a state's intent? Sometimes good intentions are bound up with bad. And who is to determine if a peace is just or a wrong has been committed? The nation initiating the war will use its own values to justify its intentions, and these values may be at odds with those of the other party in the conflict. Furthermore, the best way to protect innocent lives is by peaceful means, not by endangering them further through armed conflict.

4. Sometimes going to war before all alternatives are exhausted is the most moral action. For example, a nation might decide to go to war if it determines that waiting would enable the enemy to increase its strength and to do much more damage than an early war would have inflicted. Waiting might allow an invading state to entrench itself so that far greater force would be necessary to remove it at a later date.

PROS	CONS
5. The war must have a reasonable chance of success. War always involves a loss of life, but expending life with no possibility of achieving a goal is unacceptable. Thus, if a fighting force cannot achieve its goal, however just, it should not proceed. Charging an enemy's cannons on horseback or throwing troops at a pointless occupation are clearly not just actions.	5. Sometimes it is morally imperative to fight against overwhelming odds, as resistance fighters did in World War II. Also, this condition may give large nations free rein to bully small ones because they could not win a war. It also may cause a country to surrender in a war it might actually win. Weak countries have won wars against powerful ones—look at the American Revolution.
6. The goal of the war should be proportional to the offense and the benefits proportional to the costs. For example, when an attacker violates a nation's border, a proportionate response might extend to restoring the border, not sacking the attacker's capital. A war must prevent more suffering than it causes.	6. We have seen that a proportional response frequently doesn't work. Suicide bombers continue to blow up victims in the Middle East despite the response. Why should a nation tolerate continued aggression for the sake of proportionality? And if a nation knows it is likely to be attacked, why should it wait to disarm the aggressor? Is not preemptive action justified to prevent the loss of innocent life?

Sample Motions:

This House believes that war is sometimes justified.

This House believes swords are as necessary as plowshares.

This House believes that justifying war is unjustifiable.

Web Links:

- BBC Religion and Ethics. <http://www.bbc.co.uk/ethics/war/just/introduction.shtml> Excellent discussion of Just War Theory.
- JustWarTheory.com. <http://www.justwartheory.com> Overview of the Just War Theory with links to other sources for more in-depth treatment.
- Moseley, Alexander. <http://www.iep.utm.edu/j/justwar.htm> Summary of Just War Theory with review of the literature.
- Orend, Brian. <http://plato.stanford.edu/entries/war/> Philosophical analysis of war in general and Just War in particular.

Further Reading:

Fotion, Nicholas. *War and Ethics: A New Just War Theory (Think Now)*. Continuum, 2008.

Hensel, Howard M. *The Prism of Just War (Justice, International Law and Global Security)*. Ashgate, 2010.

Walzer, Michael. *Just and Unjust Wars: A Moral Argument with Historical Illustrations*. Basic Books, 2006

■ ■

JUVENILE OFFENDERS, STRICTER PUNISHMENT FOR

Most US states have separate justice codes and justice systems for juvenile offenders. Traditionally, the main goal of these systems has been rehabilitation rather than punishment; courts have frequently sentenced young offenders to probation or counseling rather than jail. During the 1980s and early 1990s, the United States experienced an unprecedented wave of juvenile crime; although juvenile crime had dropped by the mid-1990s, a series of high-profile school shootings and murders by children as young as six kept the issue in the news. In response, nearly every state passed laws that made trying and incarcerating juveniles as adults easier. The result: a 208% increase in the number of offenders under 18 in adult prisons between 1990 and 2004. The Campaign for Youth Justice estimates that annually about two hundred thousand juveniles are prosecuted as adults—the majority of them for nonviolent offenses.

PROS

The primary purpose of a justice system is the prevention of crime and the protection of the innocent. It is to achieve these purposes that children should not be entitled to lenient punishment. The purposes of punishment are proportional retribution, deterrence, and prevention of crime. Rehabilitation should at best be a secondary aim.

The "just desserts" theory of punishment argues that the retribution society takes against an offender should be proportional to the harm he has caused the victim. For example, a person who kills is more culpable than a person who robs or hurts. Because the harm children cause is the same as that caused by adults committing a similar offense, children should not receive special treatment. The assumption that children are not as morally culpable as adults is false.

Treating children more leniently than adults undermines the deterrent value of punishment. A 1996 survey in Virginia, for example, showed that 41% of youths have at various times either been in a gang or associated with gang activities. Of these, 69% said they joined because friends were involved and 60% joined for "excitement." This clearly shows that young adults do not take crime seriously because they think the justice system will treat them leniently.

The best way to prevent crime in the short run is to lock up the offenders. This stops them from immediately harming society. In the long term, these children will be reluctant to return to crime because of their memory of harsh punishment.

Rehabilitation (counseling and psychiatric treatment) is too lenient. It will make children believe that they are spending short periods of time at camp. In the US, more than half the boys who were ordered to undergo counseling rather than sentenced to detention committed crimes while in therapy. Rehabilitation programs should take place in a detention facility. Young offenders should be separated from hardened adult criminals, but they should not be given lighter sentences than adults who committed the same crimes.

CONS

Child crime is different from adult crime. In most legal systems the offenders are not deemed to be fully functioning as moral agents. Thus, the best way to handle them is through rehabilitation rather than punishment.

Subjective culpability should play as important a part in punishment as the harm principle. That is why murder is punished more severely than negligent manslaughter, even though both cause the same harm. Children are not capable of making the same moral judgments as adults. It is the inability of children to form moral judgments that makes them less culpable and therefore worthy of lighter punishment.

The deterrence theory assumes that all crime is committed as a result of rational evaluation. If, indeed, 8- or 10-year-old children are capable of making rational calculations, then the prospect of spending several years in reform school should be no less a deterrent then spending the time in jail. It is still a curtailment of their liberty, and if they were rational, they would not want their liberty curtailed. The real problem is that most crimes are committed by people who do not make rational decisions.

This is an argument that would justify imprisoning people for life because that is the surest way to prevent them from harming anyone. Because this is plainly ridiculous, it must be accepted that locking a person up is at best a short-term remedy. The long-term answer lies in rehabilitation.

The only long-term solution to juvenile crime is reform of the child. Children's characters are less formed and thus they are more amenable to reform. The rate of recidivism for child offenders in counseling in the US is significantly lower than that of adult offenders. Some children who have had counseling do return to crime, but a significant proportion does not. Putting children in prison with hardened adult offenders is likely to increase recidivism because they will be influenced by and learn from the adults.

Sample Motions:

This House would lower the age of criminal responsibility.

This House would punish children as if they were adults.

This House believes that sparing the rod spoils the child.

Web Links:

- Coalition for Juvenile Justice. <http://www.juvjustice.org/fp.html> Links to fact sheets and position papers on different aspects of the juvenile justice system.
- PBS. <http://www.pbs.org/wgbh/pages/frontline/shows/juvenile/> Companion to a television program exploring juvenile justice and the debate about the proper treatment of child offenders.
- Schwartz, Robert. <http://www.cnn.com/2010/OPINION/02/18/schwartz.kids.trials/index.html> Argues that children should never be tried as adults.

Further Reading:

Bartollas, Clemens, and Stuart J. Miller. Juvenile Justice in America. 5th ed. Prentice Hall, 2007.

Feld, Barry C., and Donna M. Bishop, eds. *The Oxford Handbook of Juvenile Crime and Juvenile Justice.* Oxford University Press, 2011.

Mays, G. Larry, and Rick Ruddell. *Do the Crime, Do the Time.* ABC-CLIO, 2012.

Scott, Elizabeth S., and Laurence Steinberg. Rethinking Juvenile Justice. Harvard University Press, 2008.

■ ■

LANDMINES, US PRODUCTION AND USE OF

The 1997 Ottawa Convention (the Mine Ban Treaty) was signed by 135 nations. It banned the use and stockpiling of antipersonnel mines. The United States is not a signatory. The Ottawa Convention requires signatories to abandon the use of landmines within ten years and also requires the destruction of the signatory's stockpile of landmines. The convention's aims became official UN policy in 1998 with the adoption of General Assembly Resolution 53/77. In 2004, the United States announced that it would eliminate persistent landmines from its arsenal and seek a worldwide ban on their sale or export. However, it continued to develop nonpersistent (self-destructing/self-deactivating) landmines that would not pose a humanitarian threat after use in battle.

PROS

Landmines do great harm to people, but so do all weapons of war. Landmines are not uniquely unpleasant, and the debate about them has distorted public perception. In truth, they are little different from a hundred other types of weaponry that remain legal under the Ottawa ban.

Landmines are an excellent way of defending a wide area for very little money and with very few military personnel.

CONS

Landmines are a terrible, immoral tool of war. America should neither practice nor condone this kind of warfare. Unlike other weaponry, landmines remain hidden long after conflicts have ended, killing and maiming civilians in some of the world's poorest countries years, even decades later. Just because other weaponry has similar effects, doesn't mean that landmines are acceptable—it means that other weapons are unconscionable, too. But we must start somewhere. We can make a difference by capitalizing on the global movement against landmines and we should.

The usefulness of landmines is significantly overstated. They are easily removed by quite low-technology military

PROS

This is a legitimate aim in warfare, when military personnel are spread too thinly to protect all civilians, and in peacetime, when poor countries want to invest in infrastructure rather than in defense. In the future, nations may not need landmines, but while armies still depend on conventional weapons, using landmines to defend borders is highly appropriate. Landmines can slow or stop an advance, delaying or even halting conflict; they can deter invasion in the first place. By protecting wide areas from a swift military advance on civilians, they can prevent genocide.

The use of landmines is a totally separate issue from removing them. We can do the latter without banning the former. The proposition accepts that those who use landmines must fund clean-up efforts, and the United States is doing this. The attention of the very humanitarian organizations calling for a ban will ensure that this obligation is met.

Banning landmines disproportionately punishes underdeveloped countries unable to acquire the higher-technology military capacity that has made mines less useful to richer nations. Banning landmines harms precisely the nations most likely to need them for defensive purposes.

The ban on landmines has an asymmetric effect: it only stops nations that honor the ban. Nations that want to use landmines will do so regardless of the US position (or that of any other nation)—as demonstrated by the current prolific use of mines despite the large number of signatories to the Ottawa Convention. In addition, if we might one day face an enemy deploying landmines, we

must expose our soldiers to their use in training so that they learn how to deal with them.

The ban fails to distinguish between different kinds of mines. The Americans have mines that can deactivate themselves and can self-destruct. America manufactures only nonpersistent "smart mines"; since 1976, the US has tested 32,000 mines with a successful self-destruction rate of 99.996%. The ban also fails to distinguish between responsible and irresponsible users. Under American deployment, only smart mines are used, and they are used responsibly.

CONS

equipment, which means that they are not very dangerous to armed forces, but are incredibly harmful to civilians.

Suggesting that the use and removal of landmines are two separate issues is absurd—the two are inextricably interlinked. Most nations that deploy landmines, including those manufactured in the US, never remove them. As history has shown, relying on goodwill or trust to remove landmines is folly. Simply put, if landmines are deployed, innocent people inevitably die. The United States should not dirty its hands by trading in these wicked weapons.

Landmines provide a false sense of security. Nations often use them in lieu of negotiating with their neighbors. Landmines are the symbol of exactly the wrong approach to international affairs. Underdeveloped countries should channel their efforts into improving their economies. The US should not encourage them or frighten them into to buying US military equipment.

Obviously only those nations that stand behind their commitments will honor their commitments. That is a rationale for never entering into international treaties. Certainly some nations will ignore the ban—but as a ban gains acceptance, such nations will eventually succumb to pressure, especially if US diplomatic and moral might is behind it. Even if other nations ignore such a ban, doing

the right thing in and of itself is very important. Ultimately, this debate is about what kind of global society you want to live in. Do you want to live in a society that tries hard to stop the use of such horrible weapons and occasionally fails, or one that never even bothers to try?

Faith in these so-called smart mines is hugely misplaced. Testing cannot duplicate battlefield conditions, in which areas of deployment are often not properly recorded or marked. Even if smart mines work as claimed, regimes that use them may not want to deactivate them upon a cease-fire, particularly if their dispute still smolders. The equipment required for deactivation may be lost or destroyed. The best way to ensure that these weapons are not left in the soil is never to put them there in the first place. That some users might be responsible is not good enough, since if anyone uses landmines everyone will.

Used in peacekeeping initiatives, these mines protect US troops and present little danger to civilians. Stopping their use would endanger the lives of peacekeepers and make the United States less likely to enter into such operations. This is one reason why the US refused to sign the Ottawa treaty in 1997 and has declined to do so since.

Suggesting that landmines are the prime protector of US forces, or even an important one, is absurd. The principal protection US troops (as opposed to those of other nations) have in peacekeeping is the threat of using overwhelming force if defied. The damage done to relations with the civilian community from using landmines far outweighs any narrow military benefit garnered from landmine deployment.

Sample Motions:

This House believes the US should cease production and export of landmines and sign the Ottawa Convention.

This House would sign the Ottawa Convention.

This House would ban landmines.

Web Links:

- Human Rights Watch. <http://www.hrw.org/backgrounder/arms/arms0805/> 2005 brief on the production and export of American landmines.
- United States Campaign to Ban Landmines. <http://www.banminesusa.org/> Coalition working to change US policy on landmines.
- US Department of State. <http://www.state.gov/t/pm/wra/c11735.htm> Official US government position on landmine production and use.
- Williams, Jody. <http://articles.latimes.com/2009/dec/01/opinion/la-oe-williams1-2009dec01> Opinion piece that expresses regret about President Obama's decision not to join the Mine Ban Treaty.

Further Reading:

Björk, Kjell. *Ridding the World of Landmines: The Governance of Mine Action.* BrownWalker Press, 2012.

Harpviken, Kristian Berg. The Future of Humanitarian Mine Action. Palgrave Macmillan, 2004.

Maslen, Stuart. Mine Action After Diana: Progress in the Struggle Against Landmines. Pluto Press, 2004.

Rutherford, Ken. *Disarming States: The International Movement to Ban Landmines.* ABC-CLIO, 2011.

Sigal, Leon. Negotiating Minefields: The Landmines Ban in American Politics. Routledge, 2006.

■ ■

LOBBYING: GOOD OR BAD?

Political dialogue in America is frequently peppered with accusatory references to "special interests." These special interests are organized groups that play active political roles, either through making contributions to parties and candidates, or through lobbying government officials in an attempt to influence legislation and public policy. Many of these groups have millions of dollars at their disposal. The question is whether this money corrupts the political system—that is, are legislators more concerned with pleasing donors and lobbyists than they are with responding to the will of average citizens?

PROS

No person who is financially dependent on someone else is truly free to serve the public good in a disinterested way. When a politician depends on huge sums of money contributed by an organization, his or her vote is inevitably influenced by the wishes of that organization rather than by what is best for the country.

The size of contributions has become so large that donors certainly expect some kind of payback. A manufacturers' association will not give $100,000 away just as a gesture of good will; it expects to see its concerns favorably addressed in legislation.

For generations, lawmakers have recognized that the power of special interests can lead to corruption; more than 50 years ago, for example, Congress forbade unions from acting to influence federal elections. But the creation of political action committees (PACs) and the proliferation of soft money have allowed special interest groups to violate the spirit of the law while obeying its letter.

Money purchases access to politicians, who are more willing to make time for donors than for average citizens. Access leads naturally to influence. The average citizen is shortchanged by the current system, which favors cash-rich organizations.

Organizations often spend hundreds of millions of dollars to lobby politicians. They would not spend such sums if they did not think such expenditures were effective in helping them get what they want. Again, money clearly is shaping legislation.

CONS

If a politician were dependent on only one source of funding, undue influence might be a possibility. But so many special interest groups are active in Washington that politicians get contributions from dozens, if not hundreds, of them. The influence of any one group, therefore, is negligible; even a contribution of $10,000 is only a "drop in the bucket" when campaigns cost millions.

Accusations of undue influence are often vague and unsupported by facts. Watchdog organizations like to make statistical correlations between donations and votes, but that is not real evidence that votes have been "bought." Don't forget that actually buying votes is a crime and is vigorously prosecuted.

Special interests are condemned for having too much influence, but the causal logic of the accusers is fundamentally flawed. When the National Abortion and Reproductive Rights Action League (NARAL) makes contributions to politicians, it does not buy the votes of legislators who would have voted differently on reproductive issues. Rather, NARAL gives money to candidates who have already indicated their support for policies in line with NARAL's position.

People who want to kill special interest groups are usually thinking of groups that support a position they oppose. Special interest groups span the political spectrum and represent many points of view. Indeed, the variety of groups with competing interests is an indication of a healthy and vigorous political system.

Individuals should organize themselves into groups to represent themselves more effectively. Congress passes laws that affect the daily lives of teachers, for example; surely, teachers have the right to have their voices heard—through their unions—when those laws are drawn up.

Sample Motions:

This House would change campaign finance laws to allow contributions from individuals only.

This House would lobby Congress to advance its interests.

Web Links:

- Brookings Institution. <http://www.brookings.edu/topics/campaign-finance.aspx> Collection of resources on campaign finance in the United States.
- New York Times. <http://topics.nytimes.com/top/reference/timestopics/subjects/c/campaign_finance/index.html> Links to recent articles on campaign finance.

- Public Campaign. <http://www.publicampaign.org/> Organization dedicated to reducing role of special interest money in American politics.

Further Reading:

Grossmann, Matt. *The Not-So-Special Interests: Interest Groups, Public Representation, and American Governance.* Stanford University Press, 2012.

Levine, Bertram J. *The Art of Lobbying: Building Trust and Selling Policy.* CQ Press, 2008.

Moss, Alan L. *Selling Out America's Democracy: How Lobbyists, Special Interests and Campaign Financing Undermine the Will of the People.* Praeger, 2008.

Rozell, Mark J. *Interest Groups in American Campaigns: The New Face of Electioneering.* Oxford University Press, 2011.

■ ■

LOCAL FOOD MOVEMENT

Over the past decade, the politics of food has assumed increasing importance in Western countries. Organic farming has become a mainstream movement, bringing in billions of dollars a year, and fair-trade goods are now sold in most supermarkets. The Slow Food movement, which celebrates the authenticity of regional cuisine, seasonal changes in the availability of produce, and the labor of small-scale producers, has spread from its origins in Italy to become influential in the United States, Britain, and beyond. Part of this upsurge of interest in where food comes from has been a recent emphasis on buying foods from crops grown and livestock raised by nearby farmers.

Farmers markets—local producers selling directly to consumers—have taken off, providing producers with an alternative to selling the fruits of their labors to hard-bargaining supermarket chains. Locally produced foods are also sold directly from farm shops and through delivery plans such as weekly vegetable boxes. Supporters of "shopping local" argue that it offers great advantages—from economic support for the area's farmers and greater community cohesion to environmental and health benefits. While nobody takes the extremist position that you should never buy locally grown foods, critics have begun to question whether many of the benefits claimed for shopping local actually exist and to point out that some disadvantages may actual arise from too much emphasis on local purchasing.

PROS

Shopping locally supports nearby farmers and the local economy—not huge multinational corporations. Typically farmers are forced to sell to middlemen or enormous wholesalers, such as huge supermarket corporations. Thus, growers see only a small fraction of the price the public eventually pays in a store (as little as 18 cents of every dollar in the United States). Such economics drive down farm incomes and are forcing many farmers off the land as they can no longer make a living. By selling directly to the public at farmers markets and farm shops instead, producers can ensure that they get a fair price for their crops and livestock. The income this provides is particularly crucial for small producers and for farmers committed to more sustainable, less intensive cultivation methods, such as organic production. Consumers who want to support their local producers and sustainable

CONS

Buying only local produce will result in paying much more for your groceries. Two hundred and fifty years ago, Adam Smith demonstrated the economic law of comparative advantage, which states that each country or region should focus on producing those crops and manufactures to which it is best suited, exporting them, and using the income to purchase goods that others can produce more cheaply and efficiently. Everyone prospers, gaining the most profit from their specific areas of efficient production, while spending less to buy goods that others excel at producing. Deciding to buy only local produce flies in the face of economic reality because much of the food that can be produced nearby would be vastly cheaper if imported from another country with lower-cost land and labor, a more suitable climate, and greater economies of scale. The bottom line is that shopping locally can only farming over big agribusiness and retailers should therefore commit to shop locally wherever possible.

Local shopping benefits the environment. At the moment, most food in the stores has been transported huge distances. Even locally sourced food may be trucked hundreds of miles to a big distribution center before being sent back to a store near its point of origin. These "food miles" incur an enormous environmental cost in terms of carbon emissions and are a major contributor to climate change. This is especially true of food that has been air-freighted, a very environmentally damaging practice. In addition, shopping for locally produced food reduces unnecessary and environmentally damaging packaging

Local shopping is good for the whole community. Rather than the impersonal experience of visiting a huge corporate-controlled supermarket, shopping for local produce brings consumers into contact with a whole range of different people. Buying from those who actually grew the food and moving from booth to booth turns shopping into a real social event—more conversation forges social bonds, thus creating sustainable communities and linking urban areas to the countryside surrounding them. Consumers also get a chance to learn about where their food comes from, to inquire about animal welfare standards or pesticide use, and to raise environmental concerns—all the while gaining an appreciation of the concerns of local farmers.

Locally produced food is much fresher and thus healthier. Typical supermarket fruits and vegetables are often picked four to seven days before they make it to the shelves and so may be nearly two weeks old before they are actually eaten—by which time much of their nutritional value will have long departed. To handle these long delays, many fruits are picked unripe so that they do not start to rot in transport or on supermarket shelves. Accordingly, their full flavor has never developed. By buying locally, consumers can ensure that they get the tastiest, healthiest food. Experience also suggests that people are more likely to vary their diet by trying new foods if they come from local producers, who can offer tastings and recipe advice.

Shopping for local produce is also part of a wider movement to rediscover and celebrate local food cultures. The

ever be an indulgence of the rich—ordinary working families must follow the rules of comparative advantage and buy their food cheaply from supermarkets, which can seek out the cheapest and most efficient sources for each foodstuff.

Buying local is not actually environmentally friendly. The idea of food miles sounds wonderfully green, but the concept is deeply flawed. Often much more energy (for heated greenhouses and specific fertilizers) is needed to grow fruit and vegetables locally than is required to grow them in a country with a more suitable climate and then transport them by road, sea, or air. Most of the food miles traveled by products originate with consumers driving to and from stores. Indeed, the carefully packed trucks of the huge supermarkets are a more energy efficient way of distributing food than having lots of small producers driving pick-up trucks to farmers markets.

Buying local produce from farmers markets may be a wonderful social experience, but it also acts as a form of protectionism. In addition to artificially increasing family food bills in developed countries, the cult of localism also hits farmers in the developing world by denying them an export market. Over the past decade or so, countries like Kenya and Peru have begun to develop their way out of poverty by exploiting their comparative advantages in agriculture. Farms growing crops like beans, broccoli, plums, and cherries have provided good jobs for hundreds of thousands of the poor and brought their countries valuable income and investment. We should not sacrifice this massive benefit to the pursuit of protectionist "localism."

Buying local foods from farmers markets does not necessarily guarantee fresher produce. Today, supermarkets' efficient supply chains have green beans on US shelves within 24 hours of being harvested in Kenya or Peru. As most farmers markets only operate once or twice a week, often their produce is no fresher than imported fruits and vegetables. In addition, farmers markets are a great marketing brand, but are no guarantee of local origin of the foodstuffs being sold. Farmers markets often feature such items as olives and coffee beans, which cannot accurately be described as local. And, if no source for a particular product exists within 20 miles or so of the market, a producer from much farther away will be allowed to come in and take a booth.

We should be grateful for the advances of transport and economic globalization that have brought such a wide

PROS

Slow Food movement emphasizes the cultural importance of local cuisines based on the range of foods that are available within a particular region. By treating the whole world as our larder, we have gained an enormous choice of foods but at the cost of our own culinary heritage and folk traditions. We have also lost a sense of seasonality, expecting asparagus and strawberries all year round. Local food restores this connection with the rhythm of the seasons, and connects us to the land around us and to our ancestors who helped shape it.

By creating a market for a wide variety of agricultural produce, shopping locally will encourage a region's farmers to grow and rear a wide variety of crops and animals. Intensive modern farming often consists of huge agribusinesses growing monocultures of wheat, corn, barley, or soy over vast areas, with little room left for nature. Even livestock farming can impose one type of farming practice on the environment and drive out plants and animals that cannot adapt. More varied farming practices are valuable for promoting biodiversity, encouraging a whole range of birds, animals, and plants to establish themselves in field margins and adjacent wild areas. Local variety is also good farming practice, as it means that any disease or pest infestation will not be able to spread quickly to devastate a whole region.

CONS

range of foods to our shops. Our grandparents ate largely local produce, giving them a very dull diet with a very limited choice of fruits and vegetables. They understood the importance of seasonal variation all right, but also had little access to vitamins in the cold winter and spring months. Our diet today is much healthier and more varied as a result of globalization, and we should not try to turn the clock back to the bad old days when only local produce was available.

Other, better ways exist to be environmentally friendly—insisting on shopping for local produce is not the sole "right" path. Locally grown food may be very intensively cultivated, so if sustainability is important to you, buy organic food regardless of its origin. If you have a garden, grow your own vegetables and fruit. And, if you truly care about the environment, eat less meat as raising livestock involves much more carbon emissions than does farming.

Sample Motions:

This House would shop local.

This House believes we should support local farmers markets.

This House would tax food miles.

Web Links:

- Revkin, Andrew C. "Energy, an Ingredient in Local Food and Global Food." <http://dotearth.blogs.nytimes.com/2007/12/11/energy-an-ingredient-in-local-food-and-global-food/> Article discussing the role of environmental concerns in local food movements.
- Time Magazine. "The Local-Food Movement: The Lure of the 100-mile Diet." <http://www.time.com/time/magazine/article/0,9171,1200783,00.html> Article on the growing movement to eat locally.
- Treehugger. "Earthtalk: Why Eat Locally." <http://www.treehugger.com/files/2006/10/earthtalk_why_e.php> Article in support of the movement.

Further Reading:

Cobb, Tanya Denckla. *Reclaiming Our Food: How the Grassroots Food Movement Is Changing the Way We Eat.* Storey, 2011.

Francis, Amy. Local Food Movement. Greenhaven, 2010.

Paarlberg, Robert. *Food Politics: What Everyone Needs to Know.* Oxford University Press, 2010.

Sharzer, Greg. *No Local: Why Small-scale Alternatives Won't Change the World.* John Hunt, 2012.

MANDATORY PAID MATERNITY LEAVE

Paid parental leave provides time off work to care for a child. It is most commonly used by women, in the form of maternity leave, during the late stages of pregnancy and following childbirth. The United States is one of only three countries in the world, along with Swaziland and Papua New Guinea, not to make paid maternity leave mandatory for new mothers. Under the Family Medical Leave Act of 1993, US women are offered 12 weeks of leave following childbirth, though there is no guarantee that this will be paid; consequently, many low-income women are unable to use this maternity leave. Critics of mandatory paid maternity leave argue that it is up to employers and their female employees to negotiate leave, not the government. However, as an increasing number of countries make paid maternity leave a guaranteed right, pressure is mounting for the US government to do the same.

PROS

All women should have the right to maternity leave without financial hardship. Women need time to recover emotionally and physically from childbirth, which requires paid leave—a fact that has been acknowledged by almost every other nation in the world. A study by the National Institute of Child Health and Human Development found that women with three-month-old infants who worked full time reported higher levels of stress, depression, and illness than those who stayed home with their infants. Further studies show that stress and depression in mothers has an adverse effect on the health and cognitive development of children. Women should not be forced to sacrifice their well-being and the well-being of their children because they cannot afford not to.

Lower-income women do not have the same options regarding child care that high-income women have and therefore need paid maternity leave to care for infants. Working mothers like Marissa Mayer, who can afford full-time nannies, are the exception, not the rule. Most new mothers are not able to afford help when they return to work. Furthermore, increasing numbers of new mothers are either single parents or the primary income earners in their families. These women simply cannot afford to have children without paid maternity leave.

Mandatory paid maternity leave is essential for women to have careers. Without it, women would be forced to leave skilled positions for which they are trained in order to find part-time positions that allow them to spend sufficient time with their infants. This leads to widespread underemployment among mothers. While childless women make 94¢ for every $1 made by men without children, mothers earn just 60¢ for every $1 that fathers earn. According to Michelle Budig, an associate professor of sociology at the University of Massachusetts Amherst, lack of paid maternity leave is the reason for this gap.

CONS

All women are different and have unique needs following childbirth. Yahoo! CEO Marissa Mayer took just a few weeks' maternity leave, and Benazir Bhutto gave birth while in office as Pakistan's prime minister. As medical care improves and childbirth becomes an increasingly low-risk process, many women find themselves returning to full health, and therefore to work, very quickly. Extended maternity leave is not essential to a woman, but is instead an option, and, as such, is something to be decided on between an individual woman and her employer. Thus, the government has no role mandating that an employer must provide this.

Having a child is a financial decision, and factoring in leave from work should be part of this decision. Prospective parents are able to borrow and accumulate time off to spend with newborns, and many employers have "leave bank" schemes in which employees deposit days they have not used to contribute toward maternity leave for others. Furthermore, for low-income women who have not factored maternity leave into their decision to have a child, public assistance is often available.

Mandatory paid maternity leave is bad for working women and gives them a competitive disadvantage in the workplace; this is particularly crucial in the current job market. After long absences from work, women will struggle to catch up with changes in the workplace, while also missing out on pay raises and opportunities for career advancement. Furthermore, small firms will avoid hiring women of childbearing age because of the potential costs involved in paid maternity leave. Rather than helping working women, mandatory paid maternity leave actually holds them back.

PROS

When left up to employer discretion, most do not provide any paid maternity leave at all; in fact, the number of employers that do offer it is dropping. While 27 percent of employers reported offering paid maternity leave in 1998, that proportion was down to 16 percent in 2008. A 2011 study reported that 17 percent of public workers and only 11 percent of private sector workers had access to paid maternity leave through their employers. Even when paid maternity leave is offered, the average amount of time given is just six weeks—a fraction of what is mandated by all other developed nations. With employers unwilling to provide the paid maternity leave that women need, it is necessary for the government to legislate it.

Making motherhood compatible with work is financially beneficial to businesses in the long term. The Institute for Women's Policy Research found that the decline in productivity and costs associated with finding and training replacements when women are forced to leave work in order to have children result in significant financial losses. It is therefore in an employer's best interest to accommodate the demands of motherhood. Paid maternity leave functions to keep women in the workforce, actually saving money over the long term.

CONS

Paid maternity leave is an optional benefit that companies will provide if they feel it is in their financial interest to do so. Even without a mandate, many leading companies actually offer a generous amount of paid maternity leave. The Bank of America, for example, offers 12 weeks of paid parental leave for mothers, fathers, and adoptive parents. Employers need the freedom to negotiate policies that work for both them and their employees; many implement other family-friendly policies instead of paid leave, such as flexible hours or working from home. If employers see paid maternity leave as essential to attract and retain workers, then they will provide it, without the need for government intrusion into the work lives of women.

Many businesses simply cannot afford an expensive new benefit such as paid maternity leave. During a period of recession and rising health care costs for employers, the government should be incentivizing businesses to employ more workers; mandating paid maternity leave does the opposite of this. In the event of a mandate, many employers will have to choose between discriminating against females of childbearing age and risking huge financial losses. Struggling businesses could be forced to do whatever necessary to avoid paying for maternity leave, including discriminating against women of childbearing age.

Sample Motions:

This House believes that employers should be required to provide paid maternity leave.

This House supports an employer's right to refuse to provide paid maternity leave.

Web links:

- Bloomberg. "America Last Among Peers With No Paid Federal Maternity Leave." <http://www.bloomberg.com/news/2011-02 -22/america-last-among-peers-with-no-paid-federal-maternity-leave.html> Comprehensive look at a bill introduced to provide federal employees with paid maternity leave.
- New York Magazine. "The Maternity Leave Arms Race" <http://nymag.com/thecut/2012/10/new-power-maternity-leave.html> Argues for mandatory paid maternity leave for men and women.
- New York Times. "Taking a Positive Approach to an Employee's Maternity Leave." <http://www.nytimes.com/2010/07/22/ business/smallbusiness/22sbiz.html?pagewanted=all&_r=0> Article on paid maternity leave and small businesses.

Further Readings:

Crittenden, Ann. *The Price of Motherhood: Why the Most Important Job in the World Is Still the Least Valued.* Picador, 2010.

Gordon, Victoria. *Maternity Leave: Policy and Practice.* CRC Press, 2013.

Kamerman, Sheila, and Peter Moss. *The Politics of Parental Leave Policies: Children, Parenting, Gender and the Labour Market.* Policy Press, 2009.

MANDATORY SENTENCING: THREE STRIKES

Early in the 1980s, national legislators became concerned that the criminal justice system had become inconsistent across the country. Similar crimes were being punished with dramatically different sentences, even though the same laws applied. Accordingly, Congress began to craft rules for mandatory prison sentences in federal cases; these rules were intended to ensure that similar crimes would be punished in similar ways, no matter where these cases were tried. Many state legislatures drafted parallel rules for lower courts. Over time, mandatory sentences in state courts evolved to include "three strikes" rules: if a newly convicted felon had a criminal record of two prior felony convictions, the judge was obligated to impose the maximum sentence for the third crime. At their height, in the late 1990s, 24 states had some form of three-strikes law; California's 1994 law was the strictest, imposing a mandatory prison sentence of 25 years to life for a third felony conviction, even if the crime was nonviolent. Between 1980 and 2008, the US prison population went from 500,000 to 2.3 million people, with mandatory sentencing laws cited as a contributing factor. This overcrowding, coupled with numerous examples of life sentences handed down for minor crimes, led to concerns that three-strikes laws are not simply severe, but may constitute cruel and unusual punishment and, thus, be unconstitutional. In recent years, legislators have sought to relax mandatory sentencing guidelines—in 2011 alone, 15 states passed significant sentencing reform legislation. In 2010, the Fair Sentencing Act was signed into law by President Barack Obama, eliminating the mandatory minimum sentence for crack cocaine possession. In November 2012, Proposition 36 passed in California, revising the three-strikes law to impose a life sentence only when the new felony is "serious or violent." However, these moves are not without opposition: proponents of mandatory sentencing and three-strikes laws see them as the best method of fighting serious crime and deterring habitual offenders.

PROS

One of the fundamental principles of criminal justice is that the punishment should fit the crime. That principle is negated when a life sentence is automatically imposed for a third felony—whether that felony is serious and violent, or minor and nonviolent. Because there is only one sentence possible for many kinds of crimes, it follows that the sentence does not necessarily correspond to the gravity of the offense.

It often happens that the third felony—that is, the one that triggers the automatic sentence—is relatively minor. For example, life sentences have been imposed for possessing cannabis, stealing socks, and attempting to shoplift videotapes. In California, more than 4,000 inmates are serving life sentences for nonviolent crimes. A life sentence for such a crime is "cruel and unusual," and, as such, is forbidden by the Eighth Amendment to the Constitution.

Historically, judges have had discretionary powers when sentencing criminals; this practice recognizes that sentencing should take into account the circumstances of the crime, the character of the criminal, and the amount of harm caused by the crime. Mandatory sentences rob judges of those discretionary powers that are properly theirs. Indeed, mandatory sentences are imposed, in

CONS

It is a primary obligation of the criminal justice system to establish clear and certain penalties for crime. The three-strikes laws offer such clarity, and their mandatory nature makes punishment certain. These laws prevent inconsistency in the criminal justice system.

Historically, judges have abused the discretion that they have been given by the criminal justice system. Too often, judges have imposed light sentences on criminals, even when those criminals have been repeat offenders. The mandatory sentences imposed by three-strikes laws ensure that recidivists are punished appropriately.

The fundamental purpose of the criminal justice system is to protect the rights and the safety of law-abiding citizens. But these citizens are not protected by "revolving door justice," which allows criminals back on the street after repeat offenses. According to the US Department of Justice, more than 50% of prisoners will be back behind bars within three years of being released, showing that short effect, by the legislative branch—thus violating the independence of the judiciary and the separation of powers outlined in the Constitution.

Defenders of the three-strikes laws claim that these laws have a powerful deterrent effect, and reduce the occurrence of crime. Statistics show, however, that recidivism has not been reduced by the presence of such laws. Furthermore, although crime has decreased across the nation since the introduction of three-strikes laws, this is coincidental: research by the University of California found that crime levels in states with three-strikes laws had decreased at similar rates to crime levels in states without these laws. The recent drop in crime cannot, therefore, be attributed to three-strikes laws.

The three-strikes laws are, in effect, ex post facto laws: that is, criminal sentences can take into account—as first and second strikes—crimes that were committed before the law was passed. Moreover, the imposition of mandatory maximum sentences because of past history constitutes "double jeopardy": criminals are being punished again for crimes for which they already served time. For these reasons, three-strikes laws are unconstitutional.

Mandatory sentences are applied with a racial bias. African Americans are imprisoned under three-strikes laws much more frequently than their white counterparts. Although African Americans make up only 6.5% of the population in California, they make up 45% of those given a life sentence under three-strikes laws. Despite the fact that judges have no discretion in sentencing, prosecutors have a enormous leeway when it comes to the charge they apply to a crime: many crimes can be prosecuted as either a felony or a misdemeanor. Data show that prosecutors display a racial bias when deciding whether or not to seek a third felony conviction and life sentence, or go for a lesser charge. Under mandatory sentence guidelines, judges are unable to reverse this bias and must sentence African Americans to life sentences at higher rates than they do whites.

Three-strikes laws do not target the most sophisticated criminals, instead incarcerating low-level criminals, often with mental health issues. A 2005 report from the Legislative Analyst's Office found that out of 7,575 inmates convicted for a third strike, 46% were convicted of a nonviolent or nonserious offense. Furthermore, a 2011 study by Stanford Law School found that nearly 40% of those sentenced to life imprisonment under the three-strikes law in California were mentally ill—these are people who should be given medical treatment and rehabilitated, rather than incarcerated for life.

sentences simply do not deter some criminals. Three-strikes laws remove repeat offenders from society, and prevent them from committing further crimes.

Since three-strikes laws have been introduced across the nation, crime has dropped dramatically. The reason for this decline is obvious: convicted recidivists are not free to commit more crimes, and felons with one or two strikes on their records are deterred by the punishment that they know will follow a third offense.

In 2003, the US Supreme Court upheld California's three-strikes law as constitutional. The Constitution's double jeopardy clause states that someone cannot be tried or punished for the same crime twice—it does not say that someone's past behavior, and therefore their risk of recidivism, cannot be considered during sentencing, which is what three-strikes laws do.

Mandatory sentences are less open to bias than sentences that allow the judge discretion. Unlike traditional sentencing, where judges can use personal biases to give harsher or more lenient sentences, mandatory sentencing does not allow biases to affect the punishment that is handed down: anyone found guilty of committing a particular crime, regardless of their race, will receive the same sentence. Though a disproportionate number of African Americans are given a life sentence under three-strikes laws, this is the unfortunate result of socio-economic disparities between races—and perhaps racial biases in policing—rather than the result of biases in the laws themselves.

Someone who has been convicted of three felonies is not a minor criminal. There are three types of crime: infractions, misdemeanors, and felonies. Felonies are the most serious type of crime. Felony crimes include rape, assault, and burglary. Though drug possession can be classed as a felony, this is usually only in cases where an individual is found to have a large quantity of illegal drugs in their possession. In addition, drug use usually goes hand in hand with other criminal activities, so it is unlikely that someone would be convicted of a felony for drug possession alone. Furthermore, mentally ill criminals can be treated in prison; their mental state does not lessen the severity of their crimes.

Three-strikes laws have contributed to a huge increase in incarceration levels, placing a massive financial burden on state governments. Between 2004 and 2007, the budget for California's Department of Corrections and Rehabilitation more than doubled, rising from $4.7 billion to $10 billion. The economic effect of this on California has been devastating; the state now spends almost twice as much on incarceration as it does on higher education. In the current economic climate, state governments simply cannot afford to spend billions of dollars every year to incarcerate nonviolent low-level criminals.

Crime reduction is consistently ranked as a top priority for Americans and, therefore, spending on corrections should be a priority for governments. Furthermore, although incarceration does cost the taxpayer a significant amount, the decline in crime that resulted from three-strikes laws actually saved taxpayers money overall. When crime is reduced, it not only leads to fewer victims of crime but also reduces the amount of money that is needed for police investigations, public defenders, and prosecutions.

Sample Motions:

This House supports mandatory minimum sentences for federal crimes.

This House believes that criminal punishments should be decided on a case-by-case basis.

This House supports three-strikes laws.

Web Links:

- Brown, Brian, and Greg Jolivette. <http://www.lao.ca.gov/2005/3_strikes/3_strikes_102005.htm> Study by a nonpartisan group on the effects of California's three-strikes legislation.
- FACTS: Families to Amend California's Three-Strikes. <http://facts1.live.radicaldesigns.org/http://www.facts1.com/> Advocacy group that focuses specifically on California laws. Includes history and links to key texts and other resources.
- New York Times <http://www.nytimes.com/2013/02/19/opinion/unjust-mandatory-minimum-prison-sentences.html?_r=0 > Summarizes the US Sentencing Commission's 2013 report recommending an end to unjust mandatory sentencing.
- Prison Policy. <http://www.prisonpolicy.org/scans/jpi/Racial%20Divide.pdf> Examines the racial disparities in California's three-strikes law.
- Taibbi, Matt. <http://www.rollingstone.com/politics/news/cruel-and-unusual-punishment-the-shame-of-three-strikes-laws-20130327> Outlines the injustices of California's three-strikes law.
- Three Strikes. <http://www.threestrikes.org/> Web site of an advocacy group that strongly supports California's three-strikes legislation.

Further Reading:

Alexander, Michelle. *The New Jim Crow: Mass Incarceration in the Age of Colorblindness.* The New Press, 2012.

Domanick, Joe. *Cruel Justice: Three Strikes and the Politics of Crime in America's Golden State.* University of California Press, 2005.

Goldman, Ivan G. *Sick Justice: Inside the American Gulag.* Potomac Books, 2013.

Walsh, Jennifer E. *Three Strikes Laws.* Greenwood Press, 2007.

■ ■

MARIJUANA, LEGALIZATION OF

The debate about the legalization of drugs, particularly soft drugs like marijuana, could be characterized as pitting freedom of the individual against a paternalistic state. Advocates of legalization argue that marijuana is not only less harmful than legal substances like alcohol and tobacco, but also has been proved to possess certain *medicinal properties. Twenty states and the District of Columbia currently permit the use of marijuana to treat conditions such as multiple sclerosis, insomnia, and chronic pain. However, in 2005, the US Supreme Court ruled that the Justice Department has the authority to prosecute state-authorized medicinal cannabis patients for violating the 1970 federal Controlled Substances Act. Though medical marijuana remains illegal at the federal level, new guidelines, implemented in 2009, state that prosecuting medical marijuana patients would no longer be a priority for federal law enforcement. Following this move, many have called for the federal government to legalize marijuana use for both medicinal and nonmedicinal purposes; a 2010 study by the Cato Institute predicted that this would generate $8.7 billion every year in federal and state taxes, not to mention the resources saved by not policing or prosecuting marijuana use. However, many remain opposed to marijuana legalization, fearing its addictive qualities and its role as a "gateway drug," encouraging harder drug use and increased criminal behavior.*

PROS

Although marijuana does have some harmful effects, it is no more harmful than legal substances like alcohol and tobacco. Research by the British Medical Association shows that nicotine is far more addictive than marijuana. Furthermore, the consumption of alcohol and cigarette smoking cause more deaths per year than does marijuana. The legalization of marijuana will remove an anomaly in the law whereby substances that are more dangerous than marijuana are legal, while the possession and use of marijuana remains unlawful.

In recent years, scientists and medical researchers have discovered that marijuana possesses certain beneficial medicinal qualities. For instance, marijuana helps to relieve the suffering of patients with multiple sclerosis. The latest research that was conducted by the Complutense University in Madrid indicates that marijuana has the potential to kill some cancerous cells. Governments should acknowledge such findings and legalize marijuana.

Individuals should be given the freedom to lead their lives as they choose. Of course, such freedom is not absolute, and laws should intervene to limit this freedom, especially when the rights of others are infringed. In the case of the use of marijuana, it is a victimless crime—only the user experiences the effects of the substance. The state should not act paternalistically by legislating against something that harms only the actual user.

Where is the empirical evidence that the use of marijuana will certainly lead users into more dangerous narcotic substances? There is none. Undeniably, a large number of people use the drug despite it being illegal. Rather than turn away from this problem, the government should face

CONS

Unlike alcohol and tobacco, marijuana has an inherently dangerous hallucinatory effect on the mind. Furthermore, many individuals addicted to marijuana resort to crime to fund their addiction. The legalization of marijuana will lead to the drug becoming more readily available, which in turn will mean that many more people will gain access to it and become addicted. The crime rate will inevitably rise. Data from the Netherlands show that the decriminalization and eventual legalization of marijuana did lead to an increase in crime.

The US has supported scientific research into the medical benefits of marijuana. Although evidence may show that marijuana may have some medicinal benefits, we should exercise caution about legalizing it because its use also has harmful side effects. More important, the legalization of marijuana will give rise to a host of social problems. The negatives of legalization far outweigh its benefits. We can thus safely say that the present approach represents the most sensible and evenhanded response to the issue at hand.

The state is justified in introducing legislation to prevent individuals from causing harm to themselves. For instance, many countries have laws requiring the wearing of seatbelts in cars. Moreover, the use of marijuana does lead to medically and socially harmful outcomes that affect other members of society.

The legalization of marijuana will lead to users moving on to harder drugs like morphine and cocaine. This would ultimately bring about an increase in social ills as well as the need to spend more government funds on rehabilitation programs.

reality. The legalization of marijuana will enable the government to regulate its use, thereby protecting its many users from harmful abuse of the substance.

Presently, organized crime sells marijuana. The legalization of marijuana will help facilitate the sale of the drug in establishments like Amsterdam's "coffee houses." This will shift the sale of marijuana away from the criminal underworld. Severing the "criminal link" will ensure that the users no longer need to come into contact with organized crime.

The same criminal elements that now sell marijuana might, when the drug is legalized, diversify and set up "coffee houses" themselves. Legalization will do nothing to separate the sale of marijuana from the criminal underworld. Conversely, it will give criminals a legitimate base from which to continue their activities.

Sample Motions:

This House believes that marijuana should be legalized.

This House supports the legalization of drugs.

This House advocates change in our present drug policy.

Web Links:

- CBS News. <http://www.cbsnews.com/video/watch/?id=6391267n> A televised debate between two experts on California's proposed legalization of marijuana.
- Joffe, Alain, and Samuel Yancy. <http://pediatrics.aappublications.org/cgi/content/full/113/6/e632> Discusses the potential harms to adolescents of legalizing marijuana.
- National Organization for the Reform of Marijuana Laws. <http://www.norml.org> Information on marijuana facts, laws, and medical use from the oldest US organization supporting legalization.
- Office of National Drug Control Policy. <http://www.whitehousedrugpolicy.gov> Provides information on US government drug policy, statistics on drug use, news stories, and publications from an anti-legalization perspective.
- Szalavitz, Maia. <http://www.time.com/time/health/article/0,8599,1893946,00.html> Describes the positive effects of Portugal's decriminalization (distinct from legalization) of all drugs.

Further Reading:

Earleywine, Mitch. *Pot Politics: Marijuana and the Cost of Prohibition.* Oxford University Press, 2006.

Gerber, Rudolph J. *Legalizing Marijuana: Drug Policy Reform and Prohibition Politics.* Praeger, 2008.

Room, Robin et al. *Cannabis Policy: Moving Beyond Stalemate.* Oxford University Press, 2010.

■ ■

MULTICULTURALISM VS. INTEGRATION

One of the biggest questions facing societies today, particularly in light of the rise of fundamentalist Islam, is how to deal with a culturally diverse citizenry. Different religions and traditions exist side by side in many cities. Historically, the United States has had a continuing debate about how completely immigrants should adopt the dominant language and culture. Facing growing immigrant communities determined to retain their identity, Europe has had to address the issue. On one side are those who want to enforce a certain degree of integration—a basic knowledge of the national language, the national history, and civil customs. On the other are those who believe that a multicultural society is strong enough to accommodate numerous cultures within it and that it might even gain from the diversity this entails.

PROS

Multiculturalism is clearly better; how can you expect people to give up their heritage? Immigrants do not leave a country to leave their cultural identity behind.

If a society claims to be tolerant of personal choice, it must respect the choice of immigrants to retain their heritage. Anything less smacks of social engineering.

Clinging to an idea of monolithic, national identity is anachronistic. The nation-state model for society is crumbling and is being outstripped by transnational models, such as the European Union. As a result, there is less emphasis on national identity. Such exclusive nation-alism is destructive, and history shows it to be so.

Perpetuating a national identity inevitably leads to the alienation of those who for religious or other reasons choose not to conform. If the national identity does not include the wearing of a turban, headdress, or robe, then those who do wear these garments are excluded from the mainstream. Such exclusion gives rise to the notion of the "other" and leaves those perceived as the "other" open to physical assault.

We should embrace the fact that people can support both their old and new nations. It shows that we have moved beyond the divisive national stereotyping that causes conflict. The more tolerance of difference and embrace of other cultures we can achieve, the less conflict there will be.

CONS

If you decide that you want to live in a country, you have to respect its traditions. Expecting new citizens or residents to conform to certain national norms is not unreasonable.

What some people call social engineering, integrationists call ensuring that society is as harmonious and conflict-free as possible. If difference breeds contempt, then the least difference the better.

We totally reject the notion of the demise of the nation-state. It is still the primary mode of national identity. As US history has shown, a nation can absorb millions of immigrants and yet maintain a unique identity.

There is a middle point between denying anyone the right to practice their religion openly and denying any sort of national identity or conformity. A shared sense of belong-ing and purpose is vital for national coherence and serves the nation and the nation's peoples well in times of war. In addition, we want everyone to cheer their favorite ball team.

This is naïve and presumes, arrogantly, that we have moved beyond the point where we are at risk from ene-mies. As the rise in extremism and its support from some of our own citizens show, we have been too liberal. We have forgotten why nationhood is important and why we all need to feel a communal belonging and affinity with the basic values of our society.

Sample Motions:

This House would be multicultural.

This House believes in multiculturalism.

This House believes that the nation-state is dead.

Web Links:

- Australian Department of Immigration and Citizenship. <http://www.immi.gov.au/media/publications/multicultural/issues97/macpape3.htm> The benefits of multiculturalism in Australia and the policies to control it.
- Berliner, Michael S., and Gary Hull. "Diversity & Multiculturalism: The New Racism." <http://www.aynrand.org/site/PageServer?pagename=objectivism_diversity> Critique of multiculturalism by the Ayn Rand Institute.
- UNESCO. <http://portal.unesco.org/shs/en/ev.php-URL_ID=2552&URL_DO=DO_TOPIC&URL_SECTION=-465.html> Several articles about multiculturalism and integration in modern nation-states.

Further Reading:

Ivison, Duncan. The Ashgate Research Companion to Multiculturalism. Ashgate, 2010.

Rattansi, Ali. *Multiculturalism: A Very Short Introduction.* Oxford University Press, 2011.

Rubin, Derek, and Jaap Verheul, eds. *American Multiculturalism After 9/11: Transatlantic Perspectives*. Amsterdam University Press, 2010.

Taras, Ray, ed. *Challenging Multiculturalism: European Models of Diversity*. Edinburgh University Press, 2013.

▪ ▪

NATIONAL TESTING

Responding to mounting concerns that the US educational system was failing its students, Congress passed the No Child Left Behind Act (2001), which mandates that states develop annual assessments (tests) of learning and skills mastered. The scores on these state tests are then compared with those from a sampling of state students who have taken the National Assessment of Educational Progress (NAEP). The intent is to use the results of these tests to chart national academic progress and provide extra help for schools and students who are falling behind. Education in the United States has historically been the responsibility of states and localities; this measure vastly expands federal involvement in education. Many advocates believe this approach to improving the nation's schools is wrong and will not accomplish its objective. Others argue that the only way to know how schools and students are performing is to measure them against other schools and other students in other states.

PROS

A national curriculum for most core subjects already exists without school boards and local communities even realizing it. Most high school students are preparing for standardized college entrance exams and therefore study what is needed to do well on these tests. Also, only a few textbook companies produce texts for high school students. When localities select one of these textbooks, they are, in effect, agreeing to what amounts to a national curriculum. Besides, students across the country should learn the same skills.

As long as school boards and localities follow the national curriculum, student success on the test will follow. Drilling and "teaching to the test" occur only when schools make a decision to test without altering their curriculums. Students undeniably need to have certain basic skills and subject mastery when they graduate. The National Assessment of Educational Progress and the state-developed assessments will test those; the school day affords plenty of time for students to learn the basics and still participate in additional activities and attend classes that go beyond the basics.

The entire reason that public education in America was founded was to develop a more productive workforce. Although education by itself is a worthy goal, ultimately what we want for our children is for them to be successful

CONS

The mandate for a national test makes every locality teach the same curriculum. Each state and locality should be able to determine its own curriculum as schools across the country are very different and should be able to make decisions at the local level on what will be taught within their classrooms. Requiring national testing removes the traditional rights of localities to adapt to community standards and desires when making curriculum decisions.

Mandating a national test will result in teachers "teaching to the tests." Students will face days of learning how to take tests at the expense of learning skills and knowledge that will help them become good citizens and contribute in meaningful ways to society. They will become good test takers but will miss out on the joy of learning for learning's sake. Subjects like art and music that are not covered on the standardized tests could be cut. Our children's education would become narrowly focused on a yearly test.

Using a national test to determine if schools and students are working oversimplifies education. Advocates of national testing use terms that are more specific to business, as if children are simply widgets coming out at the individuals who are able to earn a living when they graduate from high school or college. Focusing on word choices that may also be used in the business world is just a distracter, used by opponents of national testing to shift the debate away from what really needs to happen in our nation's schools.

In a society where education is so important to success, we must make sure our schools are performing for our nation's children. The primary reason for national standards and assessment is to make schools and teachers accountable for what goes on in the classroom. If schools and teachers are doing a good job, they have nothing to fear as we move to a national system of accountability through assessment.

Developing acceptable national standards is not easy, but other countries have demonstrated that creating good standard tests that motivate students and teachers is possible. Excellence is created by bringing together the right people, examining textbooks, and looking at standards already put in place by many national teachers associations. In the United States, the quality of education that students receive depends on what state, county, and town they live in and even in what part of town they reside. This violates the principle of equality that is fundamental to the values of our country. If all teachers are expected to achieve the same standards, the quality of education for all children can go up.

end of an assembly line. Proponents of national testing use terms like "setting objectives," "getting results," and "the bottom line" when talking about our nation's children. We cannot let the unethical, corrupt, and profit-driven world of business encroach into our nation's classrooms.

Using a national test to determine if students are mastering material is unfair and will drive good teachers out of our classrooms, making existing problems worse. A better alternative is a broad-based assessment, which looks at multiple measures of what a student has learned. Instead of testing a student on one day, a multiple-measure assessment uses teacher evaluations, teacher-created tests, and student demonstrations that occur over the entire school year. This would especially benefit students who are not good test takers.

The idea of national standards may seem like a good one until you start to actually try to create the standards that teachers must teach to. Agreeing what must be taught is difficult enough in a local setting; nationally such agreement is probably not achievable. Which historic figures should all students learn about? What parts of history are most important? Also, good standards are difficult to craft. Standards are either too vague so the test makers and teachers do not know what material to focus on, or they are too detailed so that teachers and students are overwhelmed by the sheer number of subjects that must be mastered.

Sample Motions:

This House would ban national testing.

This House believes that national standards are more valuable than locally developed curriculums.

This House believes that national standards will have a detrimental effect on education.

This House believes that national standards promote equality in education.

Web Links:

- Fair Test. <http://www.fairtest.org/facts/howharm.htm> Arguments against standardized testing as an educational tool.
- National Education Association (NEA). <http://www.nea.org/home/NoChildLeftBehindAct.html> Site maintained by the major national organization that opposed national standards; currently focuses on the implementation of the initiative.
- PBS. <http://www.pbs.org/wgbh/pages/frontline/shows/schools> This companion website to the PBS show *Frontline* presents a balanced overview of the issue of national testing.

Further Reading:

Au, Wayne, and Melissa Bollow Tempel. *Pencils Down: Rethinking High-stakes Testing and Accountability in Public Schools.* Rethinking Schools, 2012.

Gorlewski, Julie A., Bradley J. Porfilio, and David A. Gorlewski, eds. *Using Standards and High-Stakes Testing for Students: Exploiting Power with Critical Pedagogy.* Peter Lang, 2012.

Harris, Phillip, Bruce M. Smith, and Joan Harris. *The Myths of Standardized Tests: Why They Don't Tell You What You Think They Do.* Rowman and Littlefield, 2011.

■ ■

NUCLEAR ENERGY

Since the mid-1980s, nuclear power has been a major source of electricity in the United States—second only to coal. Yet the future of nuclear power in the United States and the rest of the world is uncertain. Although the United States has the most nuclear capacity of any nation, the US Department of Energy predicts that the use of nuclear fuel will have dropped dramatically by 2020, by which time more than 40% of capacity will have been retired. Some support nuclear expansion, emphasizing its importance in maintaining a diverse energy supply, but currently the United States has only one new nuclear plant under construction, located in Tennessee. Many fear nuclear energy because of accidents such as those at Chernobyl, Three Mile Island, and, most recently, Fukushima. There is also ongoing concern about the disposal of nuclear fuel. However, with the reduction of carbon emissions becoming increasingly urgent, and renewable energy remaining a distant reality, many argue that nuclear energy is the only viable alternative we have.

PROS

Currently, the majority of the world's electricity is generated using fossil fuels. Although estimates vary greatly about the world's supply of fossil fuels, some estimates suggest that oil could be exhausted within 50 years and coal within 25 years. Thus we must find a new source of energy. We must start to convert to nuclear energy now so there is not a major crisis when fossil fuels do run out.

Nuclear energy is clean. It does not produce gaseous emissions that harm the environment. Granted, it does produce radioactive waste, but because this is a solid it can be handled easily and stored away from population centers. Burning fossil fuels causes far more environmental damage than using nuclear reactors, even if we factor in the Chernobyl catastrophe. Consequently, nuclear energy is preferable to fossil fuels. Furthermore, as new technologies, such as fast breeder reactors, become available, they will produce less nuclear waste. With more investment, science can solve the problems associated with nuclear energy, making it even more desirable.

Unfortunately, the nuclear industry has a bad reputation for safety that is not entirely deserved. The overwhelming majority of nuclear reactors have functioned safely and

CONS

Estimates of how long fossil fuel resources will last have remained unchanged for the last few decades. Predicting when these fuels will be depleted is virtually impossible because new deposits may be discovered and because the rate of use cannot be predicted accurately. In addition some experts estimate that the world has 350 years of natural gas. We have no current need to search for a new power source. Money spent on such exploration would be better spent on creating technology to clean the output from power stations.

Even apart from the safety issues, nuclear power presents a number of problems. First, it is expensive and relatively inefficient. The cost of building reactors is enormous and the price of subsequently decommissioning them is also huge. Then there is the problem of waste. Nuclear waste can remain radioactive for thousands of years. It must be stored for this time away from water (into which it can dissolve) and far from any tectonic activity. Such storage is virtually impossible and serious concerns have arisen over the state of waste discarded even a few decades ago.

The nuclear industry has a shameful safety record. The effects of nuclear accidents, such as Chernobyl, on the local people and environment are devastating. The fallout from effectively. The two major nuclear accidents, Three Mile Island and Chernobyl, were both in old style reactors, exacerbated in the latter case by lax Soviet safety standards. We are advocating new reactors, built to the highest safety standards. Such reactors have an impeccable safety record. Perhaps the best guarantee of safety in the nuclear industry is the increasing transparency within the industry. Many of the early problems were caused by excessive control due to the origin of nuclear energy from military applications. As a civilian nuclear industry develops, it becomes more accountable.

We must examine the alternatives to nuclear energy. For the reasons explained above, we can rule out fossil fuels immediately. We also see enormous problems with other forms of energy. The most efficient source of renewable energy has been hydroelectric power. However, this usually creates more problems than it solves. Building a large dam necessarily floods an enormous region behind the dam, displacing tens of thousands of people. Dams also cause enormous damage to the ecology and incur enormous social and cultural costs. Solar energy has never lived up to expectations because it is hugely inefficient. Wind energy is only marginally better, with an unsightly wind farm the size of Texas needed to provide the energy for Texas alone. The great irony is that not only are most renewable sources inefficient but many are also ecologically unsound! The opposition to building wind farms in certain areas has been just as strong as the opposition to nuclear power because wind farms destroy the scenery.

Chernobyl can still be detected in our atmosphere today. Despite assurances from the nuclear power industry that safety standards had improved, 2011 saw another nuclear meltdown, this time in Fukushima, Japan. This disaster was the second, after Chernobyl, to measure Level 7 on the International Nuclear Event Scale. In addition to these catastrophic failures, nuclear power stations have had a number of "minor" accidents. The industry has told us that these problems will not happen again, but time and time again they recur. In addition, the nuclear industry has had a terrible impact on those living around power plants. The rate of occurrence of certain types of cancer, such as leukemia, is much higher in the population around nuclear plants.

Although alternative energy is not efficient enough to serve the energy needs of the world's population today, it could, with investment in all these methods, be made efficient enough to serve humankind. We are not advocating a blanket solution to every problem. Many dam projects could have been replaced by solar power had the technology been available. In addition, most countries usually have at least one renewable resource that they can use: tides for islands, the sun for equatorial countries, hot rocks for volcanic regions, etc. Consequently, any country can, in principle, become energy self-sufficient with renewable energy. The global distribution of uranium is hugely uneven (much more so than for fossil fuels); accordingly, the use of nuclear power gives countries with uranium deposits disproportionate economic power. Uranium could conceivably become subject to the same kind of monopoly that the Organization of Petroleum Exporting Countries has for oil. This prevents countries from achieving self-sufficiency in energy production.

Sample Motions:

This House would look to the atom.

This House would go nuclear.

Web Links:

- New York Times. <http://topics.nytimes.com/top/news/business/energy-environment/atomic-energy/index.html> Links to recent articles on nuclear energy.
- Nuclear Information and Resource Service. <http://www.nirs.org/nukerelapse/background/toptenreasons.htm> Lists 11 reasons to oppose nuclear energy; contains many links to other resources and websites that also present arguments against nuclear energy.
- World Nuclear Association. <http://www.world-nuclear.org/why/biosphere.html?ekmensel=c580fa7b_8_0_32_1> Information on the need for nuclear power by an organization seeking to promote the global use of peaceful nuclear energy.

Further Reading:

Caldicott, Helen. *Nuclear Power Is Not the Answer.* New Press, 2006.

Hopley, George W., and Alan M. Herbst. *Nuclear Energy Now: Why the Time Has Come for the World's Most Misunderstood Energy Source*. Wiley, 2007.

Tucker, William. *Terrestrial Energy: How Nuclear Energy Will Lead the Green Revolution and End America's Energy Odyssey*. Bartleby Press, 2008.

■ ■

OBAMACARE

The Patient Protection and Affordable Care Act of 2010, often referred to as "Obamacare," constituted one of the most extensive overhauls of the US health care system ever signed into law. It was also one of the most controversial laws passed in recent years, sparking allegations of government overreach, unconstitutionality, and even socialism. The provision of health care to the citizens of the United States has been a contentious issue for decades. Though almost every other industrialized country has a system of universal health care, the United States has kept health care largely in the hands of private insurance companies. The Affordable Care Act did not introduce universal health care to the United States, as some would have liked. Rather, it introduced a system of regulations and mandates designed to increase access to private health care and reduce the overall cost. Many proponents of universal health care argue that the Affordable Care Act is inadequate to deal with the injustices of the US health care system. Opponents of universal health care see the Affordable Care Act as a step in the wrong direction, and want the law repealed.

PROS

The Patient Protection and Affordable Care Act of 2010 placed effective regulations on an industry that was in urgent need of being reigned in. The result of years of policies favoring insurers was that hardworking Americans were deprived of affordable health care. Before the act passed, insurance companies routinely denied people coverage, citing "preexisting conditions"; a government report predicted that this practice could be used to discriminate against up to 50% of all nonelderly Americans. In addition to ending this, the act also prohibited insurance companies from canceling coverage when a patient gets sick, and from limiting lifetime benefits for policy holders, which often left patients without coverage during periods of catastrophic need.

Almost 17% of the US population, including those who are fully employed, are without health insurance. Prior to the Affordable Care Act, millions of Americans could not afford coverage, but were also not eligible for government assistance. The act expands Medicaid to include all Americans under 65 whose income is up to 133% of federal poverty guidelines. Under the act, the government will also provide subsidies to help lower-income Americans purchase private insurance. In total, this will

CONS

Like all other services, health care is best governed by free market principles. It is too much government regulation, rather than too little, that led to failures in the industry. Consumers should have a broad range of provider's to choose from, and the freedom to switch easily if their current insurer's policies are unfavorable. Federal regulations against purchasing insurance out of state, and state-level regulations on the types of benefits that must be covered in plans, have hampered the health care industry's ability to evolve according to free market principles. If all government regulation were removed, insurance providers that are unable to supply a product that consumers want will be quickly replaced by those who can.

All families and individuals who legitimately cannot afford health care are already covered by Medicaid. Expanding the program to cover middle-income people, who could afford health insurance themselves if the costs of coverage were reigned in, is simply overextending the government and draining its limited resources. The government is not in a financial position to pay for health insurance for such a large portion of the population. The fact is that the Affordable Care Act will cost the US extend health insurance to an additional 30 million people. Reducing the number of uninsured Americans is not just beneficial to those receiving insurance: it is beneficial to society as a whole. Everyone suffers from high rates of mental illness and disease in the population. In addition, the cost of treating the uninsured is passed on to the insured through increased premiums.

The Affordable Care Act reduces the cost of health care for average Americans, not just for the poorest. In 2008, Americans paid an average of $7,000 each on health care—twice what people in Japan and the UK spent for equivalent results. A huge chunk of this expenditure goes toward company profits in the insurance industry. In 2009, despite the recession, the profits reported by health insurance companies rose by 56%, to $12.2 billion. Under the act, insurance companies now have to spend 80% of premiums on care or improvements to care, rather than on administration or profit—in the first year this went into effect it saved consumers an estimated $1.5 billion.

The Obama administration never claimed that health care costs would go down immediately, but that cost increases would begin to slow, before eventually declining. A study by the Kaiser Family Foundation showed that health care costs increased an average of 8.7% per year during the ten years preceding the Affordable Care Act; the study also found that costs rose by 3.8% in 2010, 4.6% in 2011, and an estimated 4.0% in 2012, showing a significant decrease in growth. In 2014, when tax credits and other provisions come into effect, average Americans will begin to see a reduction in costs. According to the nonpartisan Congressional Budget Office, people who get coverage through their employers today will likely see lower premiums in the future. Seeing premiums actually go down is a massive improvement for a country that is used to an average annual increase of 8.7%.

The Affordable Care Act will expand the coverage of those in full-time employment. The majority of people without health insurance are from low-income working families. By not providing coverage, employers are effectively leaving it up to the taxpayers to provide health care for their low-and middle-income workers, who have no means of purchasing it themselves. While the act does not include a mandate for employers to provide health care, it does require large employers that do not provide health care to pay a fee. The act exempts firms with fewer than 50 full-time employees, more than 96% of which already provide health care for their workers, and provides tax credits for small businesses that choose to provide health insurance.

taxpayer about $1,168 billion over 10 years, according to the Congressional Budget Office. Many middle-income people who claim to be unable to afford health insurance find a way to afford other optional expenses, such as vacations and evenings out; it should not be up to taxpayers to subsidize the lifestyles of others.

Health insurance premiums have not decreased at all since the reforms; in 2012, two independent studies found that health care spending had actually risen since the act, with premiums climbing $2,370 for the average family during President Obama's first term. The CEO of health insurer Aetna warned that consumers would face an additional "premium rate shock" with costs rising 20–50% on average, following the introduction of further regulations in 2014. Instead of attempting to reduce the cost of health care by limiting the profit the businesses can make, the government should lift regulation and allow free market competition to drive prices down.

In focusing on regulating the health care industry, the Obama administration has ignored other more effective ways to reduce costs. In addition to encouraging free market competition, medical malpractice laws need to be reformed. This litigation costs doctors up to $250,000 per year in insurance, which is then passed on to patients. It also encourages "defensive medicine," which is the overtreatment of patients in order to avoid lawsuits. The American Medical Association, which estimates that defensive medicine costs up to $151 billion each year, advocates capping awards in malpractice suits to reduce health care costs; President George W. Bush endorsed this legislation. Northwestern University's Kellogg School of Management concluded that these reforms would lower overall health care costs by up to 2.3%—significantly better than just a small decrease in growth.

The act will not improve the health care of those who are employed. Instead, the requirement for businesses to provide government-approved health insurance or pay a federal tax if they do not will actually cost jobs and hurt working Americans. Small companies will be disinclined to hire above the 50-employee threshold, and may even lay off workers in order to avoid paying for employee health insurance. In addition, for larger companies it would make better financial sense for them to simply pay the federal tax rather than continuing to provide employee insurance, which can average around $5,000 for an individual and around $14,000 for a family. Not only will the Affordable Care Act cause many working

PROS

Hardworking Americans should not have to go without health care, and the Affordable Care Act works to prevent this from happening.

The act's individual mandate means that insured Americans will no longer have to carry the financial burden of those who decide not to purchase insurance. In 2009, uninsured Americans cost approximately $40 billion in unpaid hospital bills, which was passed on through increased premiums. Under the act, individuals are not forced to buy health insurance; they simply have to pay an additional tax, to offset potential hospital visits, if they choose to go uninsured. There is a precedent for this: Americans who drive cars must, by law, purchase motor vehicle insurance—in many areas, driving a car is a necessity, not something that an individual can opt out of; particular homeowners are required to buy flood insurance; and certain employers and landlords must purchase safety equipment.

In June 2012, the Supreme Court ruled that the individual mandate was not an overextension of government power, but was, instead, a constitutional tax. In doing this, it upheld the constitutionality of the Affordable Care Act. While the Constitution does not allow the government to force anyone to purchase a private product, this is not what the Affordable Care Act does. The act imposes a tax on those who do not take responsibility for their own health care, something authorized by Congress's mandate to tax individuals. Deciding to go without health insurance is a taxable behavior, just as numerous other actions are, such as purchasing alcohol or importing goods.

CONS

Americans to lose their existing health care, it will also cause many working Americans to lose their jobs.

The individual mandate functions to compel Americans to purchase an expensive private product, regardless of whether or not they want it. Personal responsibility is fundamental to American citizenship; if individuals want to take the risk of not having health insurance, and to deal with the consequences, it should be their right as free citizens. While the Emergency Medical Treatment and Active Labor Act, which requires hospitals to treat patients with emergency conditions regardless of ability to pay, does unfairly push the burden of the uninsured onto those with insurance, an unprecedented government mandate is not the solution. Instead, those who can pay their bills should be aggressively pursued, and those who genuinely cannot should be covered by government programs. The individual mandate represents a dramatic overextension of government power.

Though the Supreme Court ruled in favor of the individual mandate by a slim majority of just 5–4, numerous federal judges found it unconstitutional, and the majority of Americans are opposed to it. The threat to individual liberty inherent in the government's ability to levy a tax on anyone who does not purchase a government-approved product is clear—this is a dangerous precedent to set. If the government can compel individuals to purchase health insurance for the reason that it may benefit society, the scope of what the government can force an individual to purchase is huge.

Sample Motions

This House believes that Obamacare is on balance beneficial for public health.

This House would repeal Obamacare.

This House believes Obamacare's individual mandate is unconstitutional.

Web Links

- Heritage Foundation. <http://www.heritage.org/research/projects/impact-of-obamacare> Information and arguments against Obamacare.
- Huffington Post. <http://www.huffingtonpost.com/bob-burnett/defending-obamacare-5-bas_b_1653703.html> Argument in favor of Obamacare.
- New York Times. <http://topics.nytimes.com/top/news/health/diseasesconditionsandhealthtopics/health_insurance_and _managed_care/health_care_reform/index.html> Links to articles about health care reform.
- Slate. <http://www.slate.com/articles/news_and_politics/jurisprudence/2012/03/supreme_court_and_obamacare_what _donald_verrilli_should_have_said_to_the_court_s_conservative_justices_.html> A constitutional defense of Obamacare.

Further Reading

Gibson, Rosemary, and Janardan Prasad Singh. *The Battle over Health Care: What Obama's Reform Means for America's Future.* Rowman and Littlefield, 2012.

Jacobs, Lawrence R., and Theda Skocpol. *Health Care Reform and American Politics: What Everyone Needs to Know.* Oxford University Press, 2012.

McDonough, John E. *Inside National Health Reform.* University of California Press, 2012.

Starr, Paul. *Remedy and Reaction: The Peculiar American Struggle over Health Care Reform.* Yale University Press, 2013.

■ ■

OPEN ADOPTION

Historically, virtually all adoptions in the United States were "closed," meaning that the birth parents had no contact with their child or the adoptive parents following an adoption. In recent years, many adopted children, as well as children conceived as a result of anonymous sperm donations, have challenged this policy, insisting that they have a right to know who their biological parents are. Some biological parents have contended that forcing them to reveal their identity infringes on their rights.

PROS

The reassurance that comes from knowing one's parentage is a valuable source of psychological security. The child's desires and wishes must take precedence over the wants of anonymous parents.

Biological parents should not have to raise a child if they do not wish to, but children should have the right to learn the identity of their biological parents. Neither the biological nor the adoptive parents should make this choice on the child's behalf.

Children who do not know their biological parents are medically disadvantaged. Knowing parents' medical background and genetic profile is increasingly important in preventing and treating disease.

CONS

The most important factor in raising a child is a secure and loving home environment. Whether biological or adoptive parents provide this is unimportant. If the genetic parents wish to remain anonymous, then they should retain a right to privacy. Removing the right to anonymity from a sperm donor will greatly reduce the number of men willing to become donors—for fear of unwanted contact or even financial responsibility in later life.

Giving adopted children the right to know the identity of their biological parents would simply cause greater emotional distress for all concerned. The child may resent his or her biological parents and even seek revenge. The adoptive parents may see their role undermined as the child tries to connect with his or her biological parents. Adopted children may end up feeling that they do not truly belong anywhere. Similarly, when sperm donation has been used to achieve pregnancy, the child's contact with his or her biological father may undermine role of the mother's partner, who is acting as the father.

Predicting disease through reviewing an individual's genetic heritage is wrong and will likely result in higher insurance premiums and medical discrimination for the child. Gathering and holding medical information on parents who give up their children for adoption will create a genetic underclass whose DNA will be stored for no good reason.

PROS	CONS
Parents will not abandon a child to preserve their anonymity. The right to know parentage does not equal the right to contact or depend on biological rather than adoptive families, so parents are unlikely to act in these irresponsible ways.	Parents who do not wish their identity known would simply abandon a child rather than formally give him or her up for adoption and have their identity recorded. The child may well die of exposure or starvation before it is found. In addition, some expectant mothers may fear identification so much that they do not seek vital medical support when they give birth, but do so alone with all the risks to mother and child that implies.

Sample Motions:

This House believes in the right to know parentage.

This House believes the rights of the child come first.

This House wants to know its parents/children.

Web Links:

- adoption.com <http://www.openadoptions.com/information/pros-cons.html> Pros and cons of open adoptions.
- Child Welfare Information Gateway. "Openness in Adoption: Building Relationships Between Adoptive and Birth Families." <https://www.childwelfare.gov/pubs/f_openadopt.pdf> Document detailing the procedure and benefits of open adoption.
- Crary, David. "Open Adoption: New Report Details Increase." <http://www.huffingtonpost.com/2012/03/21/open-adoption-increase_n_1371122.html> Article reflecting recent increases in open, rather than shrouded, adoptions.
- FindLaw. <http://family.findlaw.com/adoption/adoption-types/open-adoption-comparison.html> Discussion of pros and cons of open and closed adoption.

Further Reading:

Elkins, Russell. *Open Adoption, Open Heart: An Adoptive Father's Inspiring Journey.* Aloha, 2012.

Holden, Lori, and Crystal Hass. *The Open-Hearted Way to Open Adoption: Helping Your Child Grow Up Whole.* Rowman and Littlefield, 2013.

■ ■

OPEN PRIMARIES

Typically, states allow political parties to hold their own primary elections to select a candidate to run in the general state election. In most states, such elections are open only to registered members of the party. However, three states—California, Louisiana, and Washington—hold open primary elections, in which all candidates, and voters, can participate. Candidates need not denote official party affiliations on the ballots, and parties cannot officially nominate candidates (although they can still show their support for or even endorse specific individuals). The top two vote-getters, even if they are from the same party, then run in a general election. California elected to implement this system in 2010, when voters passed Proposition 14. The proposition was adopted because of increasing concerns that partisan gridlock was preventing California from passing important legislation (in particular, financial reform to address California's growing deficit). However, the measure was controversial within California, with critics alleging that it has not solved the problem and that, instead, it has created problems that are just as serious. In September 2011, following a lengthy court case, a California appellate court ruled that the open primary system is constitutional. On a national level, this ruling has increased the likelihood that more states will adopt a similar system.

PROS

An open primary system forces candidates to adopt more moderate positions because they must appeal to all voters, not just party members. A more moderate government will be less susceptible to gridlock.

In an open primary system, candidates are not required to run on an official ticket or a party's platform; thus, they will be free to express positions that differ from the party's stand and may appeal to a broader segment of the electorate than the party base. Under the new system, politicians can represent the interests of the people rather than the party. Special interests will also have less power as candidates will have to appeal to a broad base and will not be able to rely on single-issue voters.

Higher voter turnout is good for democracy. In many states, independents are not allowed to vote in partisan primaries. An open primary would broaden the elections to allow many more voters. Greater numbers may vote in general elections if both candidates are from the same party since there would be less certainty of victory for a particular candidate than in races where one of the candidates is from a party not favored in the state.

States that use an open primary system also mandate that information about candidates' party preference history be posted online, so voters will need to expend only a small amount of effort to learn de facto party affiliation. Blindly toeing the party line is not in anyone's interest; it is exactly this mentality that contributes to the partisanship between US political parties. If we want our politicians to compromise more, we need to be more willing to look at other points of view. We should research issues important to our lives and take the time to objectively analyze our positions.

Open primaries do not stop parties from endorsing or supporting candidates; it simply prohibits parties from nominating them. Open primaries free politicians to run without party affiliation. Furthermore, politicians are always forced to appeal to different types of people. Elections would be pointless if politicians never had to engage citizens with varying points of view.

CONS

Election reform is not the only way to solve this problem: gerrymandering by politicians has caused the majority of partisan gridlock. Redrawing district lines to create more politically diverse districts is the better way to encourage politicians to take more moderate positions. Furthermore, having a government made up of politicians with varying viewpoints is not bad. It can be very dangerous when one particular political party maintains too much power. With government officials representing a wide range of views, state governments can create more inventive state policy and ensure that all political positions are heard and understood.

Open primaries limit voter choice. In fact, they would be a return to the old "smoke-filled rooms" in which party leaders chose candidates. Because the general election would involve only the top two candidates, party leaders may discourage some individuals from running in the primary and focus their resources on one or two individuals they think can win the general election.

Even if more people vote in primary elections, voter choice will be drastically limited in general elections. If the election is between only two candidates, many voters' views will not be represented, thus actually decreasing voters' power. Voters will also be unable to cast protest votes if the two candidates are from the same party. Giving more citizens the incentive or ability to vote is not helpful if their choices ultimately are more limited.

Some individuals do not have the time to research candidates before an election, thus accurate party designations can help them make better decisions about who is most likely to serve their needs. Because partisan candidates can choose not to declare a party preference on the ballot under Proposition 14, less-informed voters will not know which candidates represent their interests. Such voters may be left not only confused but also more susceptible to media manipulation because campaigns characterize partisan voters as "independents."

Denying political parties the right to nominate candidates violates their right to freedom of association. When the Ninth Circuit Court ruled unconstitutional the blanket primary of Washington state, which operated similarly to the primary outlined in Proposition 14, it wrote that "[T]hose who actively participate in partisan activities . . . have a First Amendment right to further their party's

PROS

Although candidates will have to spend more money, presumably they will also be able to raise more money, since their voter (and donor) base will be drastically expanded. Furthermore, an extremely high financial barrier to entry already exists in US politics; the way to solve this problem is through campaign spending limits or shorter election seasons. We need to directly address the problem of money in US politics, not limit voter choice as a "Band-Aid" solution.

CONS

program for what they see as good governance. Their right to freely associate for this purpose is thwarted because the Washington statutory scheme prevents those voters who share their affiliation from selecting their party's nominees." Candidates should not have to appeal to members of the opposite party to win nomination.

Candidates will be forced to spend more money in both primaries and general elections. They will have to launch primary campaigns that reach their state's entire population, rather than just the voters from a designated party. Then, if the general election is between two candidates of the same party, candidates may need to spend more money distinguishing themselves. Such financial concerns may create a larger barrier to entry in the political process and favor wealthy politicians.

Sample Motions:

This House would eliminate partisan primary elections.

This House would continue to allow political parties to hold their own primaries.

Web Links:

- Open Primaries and Top Two Elections. <http://policyarchive.org/handle/10207/bitstreams/95923.pdf> Comprehensive study by the Center for Governmental Studies on the likely ramifications of Proposition 14.
- Protect Voter Choice. <http://www.stoptoptwo.org/> Website outlining arguments against top two primary systems.

Further Reading:

Abramowitz, Adam. *Voice of the People: Elections and Voting in the United States.* McGraw-Hill, 2003.

Bibby, John F. *Politics, Parties and Elections in America.* Wadsworth, 2007.

Thurber, James A., and Candice J. Nelson. *Campaigns and Elections American Style.* Westview Press, 2009.

■ ■

OVERPOPULATION AND CONTRACEPTION

Despite scientific advances, no amount of technological innovation will solve the problem that Earth has only finite resources. Attention has therefore turned to the question of population growth; preserving the environment would be far easier if natural resources were shared among fewer people. Environmental degradation will accelerate if the rate of global population increase is not slowed. Over the years, much debate has been heard about whether widespread use of contraception is the solution to the population explosion in the developing world.

PROS

Population is a major problem today; the world population of over 7 billion is expected to reach 9.4 billion by 2050. Given the current strain on global resources and

CONS

Many population forecasts are exaggerated and do not take into account the different phases of population growth. A nation's population may grow rapidly in the

the environment, an environmental disaster is clearly waiting to happen as the population time bomb ticks on. While reproduction is a fundamental human right, rights come with responsibilities. We have a responsibility to future generations, and population control is one method of ensuring that natural resources will be available for our descendants.

Contraception is an easy and direct method of slowing population growth. The popularity and success of contraception in the developed world is testament to this.

Contraception can reduce family size. With smaller families, a greater proportion of resources can be allocated to each child, improving his or her opportunities for education, health care, and nutrition.

Contraception empowers women by giving them reproductive control. Delaying pregnancy gives opportunities for education, employment, and social and political advancement. Birth control can therefore be a long-term investment in political reform and offers some protection of women's rights.

Contraception can help save the lives of women in the developing world. The lack of obstetric care and the prevalence of disease and malnutrition contribute to a high rate of mortality among pregnant mothers and their newborn children. This risk can be over 100 times that of mothers in developed countries.

Supporting contraception is an easy way for the developed world to help the developing world cope with the

early stages of development, but with industrialization and rising levels of education, the population tends to stabilize at the replacement rate. Even if the quoted figure of 9.4 billion by 2050 is true, this is likely to remain steady thereafter, as the developing nations of today achieve maturity. Developed nations can use alternative methods to solve the environmental and social problems arising from overpopulation. All available options should be exhausted before making the drastic decision to curb reproductive rights.

Implementing widespread contraception presents technical difficulties. The cost can be prohibitive, especially when considered on a national scale. Large numbers of trained workers are required to educate the public on the correct use of contraceptives. Even with an investment in training, birth control methods may be used incorrectly, especially by the illiterate and uneducated.

Many agricultural families need to have as many children as possible. Children's farm work can contribute to the family food or be a source of income. In an undeveloped nation without a good social welfare system, children are the only security for old age. Furthermore, having a large number of children usually ensures that some reach adulthood; child mortality is very high in the developing world. Until the child mortality rate is reduced, families will not use contraception.

Women may not have the choice to use contraceptives. In many developing nations, males dominate in sexual relationships and make the decisions about family planning. Religious pressure to have as many children as possible may also be present. Birth control may not even be socially acceptable. Are women's rights advanced by contraception? We don't really know. In reality, contraception typically is one element of a national population control policy. Such policies (e.g., China's one-child policy), when considered as a whole, often violate women's rights.

While birth control should be a priority of many developing nations, such nations often need to address other, more pressing, issues. Providing basic health care and proper sanitation can improve the health of an entire family, in addition to reducing child mortality (often a major reason for parents wanting to have a large number of children). Spending on such infrastructure and services is a far better long-term investment than providing contraception.

Contraception is a controversial issue in both developed and developing nations. Some religions prohibit it. This

PROS	CONS
population crisis and the consequent stifling of development. Contraceptives, compared to monetary aid, are less likely to be misdirected into the pockets of corrupt officials.	can reduce the success of birth control programs in the developing world and diminish the political appeal of (and thus funding for) pro-contraception policies in the developed world.

Sample Motions:

This House supports contraception in developing nations.

This House would cap population growth in the developing world.

This House believes that there are too many people.

Web Links:

- OverPopulation.com. <http://www.overpopulation.com/> Extensive site with information on a wide variety of population issues. Includes a good overview essay on the overpopulation controversy.
- Population Reference Bureau. <http://www.prb.org> Provides a comprehensive directory of population-related resources.
- United Nations Population Information Network. <http://www.un.org/popin/> Offers links to population information on UN systems websites.

Further Reading:

Angus, Ian, and Simon Butler. *Too Many People?: Population, Immigration, and the Environmental Crisis.* Haymarket Books, 2011.

Brown, Lester R. *Full Planet, Empty Plates: The New Geopolitics of Food Scarcity.* Norton, 2012.

Connelly, Matthew. *Fatal Misconception: The Struggle to Control World Population.* Harvard University Press, 2009.

Mosher, Steven. *Population Control: Real Costs, Illusory Benefits.* Transaction, 2009.

.. ■

OVERSEAS MANUFACTURING

In the new era of globalization, American companies often locate their manufacturing operations in countries outside the United States. Many countries are eager to attract American industries and the employment they bring; overseas factories usually can be run at substantially lower costs largely because wages for foreign workers are much lower than wages for American workers. The treatment of these foreign employees has engendered many questions and raised many issues. Their working conditions may not be safe; they may be asked to work unreasonable hours; they may be paid less than a living wage. In some parts of the world, many factory workers are school-age children. Increasingly, the public is putting pressure on American corporations to improve the treatment of their foreign workers and to provide the same kind of safeguards that protect American workers.

PROS	CONS
Companies build factories overseas for one primary reason: foreign workers are cheaper. When companies are driven by the profit motive, they have an incentive to pay as little as possible and to skimp on equipment and procedures that would provide comfort and safety to workers. Workers need to be protected from corporations that care more about profits than people.	Manufacturers know that mistreating workers does not pay in the long run. They know that a healthy and a happy workforce is going to be more productive and give their operation long-term stability. Certainly manufacturers care about the bottom line, and it is precisely that concern that motivates them to treat their workers well.

PROS

Some foreign governments are so eager to attract American investment that they favor management over labor. They do not protect their own citizens with strong labor laws, and they do not guarantee workers the right to form unions. Workers are at the mercy of their employers.

American companies located in foreign countries have no incentive for making commitments to the local community. If the workers become too expensive, or if the companies are forced to spend money to improve conditions, they simply pull out and move to another country with cheaper workers and lower standards.

Because they have no union protections, workers are often asked to work absurdly long hours, with no extra pay for overtime, and in dangerous conditions with hazardous materials. They fear that if they complain, or refuse to work when demanded, they will be fired and replaced by someone who is desperate for a job.

Child labor is condoned in many countries where American companies do business, but American companies should refuse to take part in this abuse. There is little hope for the future of countries where a child must provide labor, instead of getting an education.

CONS

The presence of American companies has a direct benefit on the economies of their host countries. Workers are taught skills and exposed to new technology. Moreover, a strong industrial economy has been proved to be the best way to lift people out of poverty. In time, foreign workers will achieve wages and working conditions comparable to those enjoyed by American workers today.

Wages may be low compared to US standards; however, the cost of living in these countries is also low. It is absurd, therefore, to expect American companies to pay the standard minimum US wage in a country where that wage has ten times the buying power that it has in America.

Activists like to say that factory jobs in foreign countries are intolerable and undesirable, but the facts do not support that assertion. People are eager to work in a factory, when their alternative is making less money for a full day of backbreaking agricultural work. To the workers, jobs in American factories represent opportunities to gain a higher standard of living.

The American objection to child labor is founded on the idealistic notion that children should be in school. But in many countries where the factories operate, universal schooling is nonexistent, and the child who is thrown out of a factory job goes back on the street. In many cases, the child who does not work in a factory will simply work someplace else; in poor families, it is expected that anyone who is able to work will earn a wage to support the family.

Sample Motions:
This House will not buy materials made in foreign sweatshops.
This House would force American companies to let foreign workers unionize.

Web Links:
- Ending Sweatshops. <http://www.sweatshops.org> This website, sponsored by the activist organization Co-op America, discusses "sweatshop" conditions in foreign countries and encourages citizens to take action to eliminate them.
- New York Times Magazine. <http://query.nytimes.com/gst/fullpage.html?res=9D02E6D6163BF937A1575AC0A9669C8B63&sec=&spon=&pagewanted=all> Article defending sweatshops.
- PBS. <http://www.pbs.org/now/politics/outsourcedebate.html> Links and information on the outsourcing debate.

Further Reading:

Locke, Richard M. *The Promise and Limits of Private Power: Promoting Labor Standards in a Global Economy.* Cambridge University Press, 2013.

Marsh, Peter. *The New Industrial Revolution: Consumers, Globalization, and the End of Mass Production.* Yale University Press, 2012.

Pisano, Gary P., and Willy C. Shih. *Producing Prosperity: Why America Needs a Manufacturing Renaissance.* Harvard Business Review Press, 2012

Ross, Robert. *Slaves to Fashion: Poverty and Abuse in the New Sweatshops.* University of Michigan Press, 2004.

■ ■

PACIFISM

Pacifism has a long history in the United States. Although their numbers have been small, pacifists have opposed every American war from the Revolution to the Iraq War. Occasionally their voices have contributed to policy changes, as was the case in the Vietnam War. The debate between nonviolent objection and the use of force to achieve a goal brings up issues like morality vs. practicality: Is violence ever constructive; and, does pacifism in the face of a threat serve to increase or diminish evil? The debate also contrasts the lives lost in war with the liberty that might be lost if war is avoided and thus raises the difficult issue of sacrificing lives to preserve a principle.

PROS

Violence is never justified under any circumstances. Life is sacred, and no cause or belief allows a person to take the life of another.

Neither side in a war emerges as a victor. War rarely settles issues. (For example, World War I created the conditions that led to World War II.) War always creates suffering on both sides. Often the innocent suffer, as in the case of the firebombing of Dresden or the dropping of the atomic bomb on Hiroshima in World War II.

Pacifists believe that violence begets violence. Pacifists do not have to retreat completely from world and domestic affairs. During World War I, conscientious objectors stood up against the militarism and cynical diplomacy that had led to the conflict. In many countries they were executed for their beliefs.

When war is inevitable, pacifists can protest the cruelties of war, such as torture, attacks on civilians, and other contraventions of the Geneva Convention, in an attempt to curb violence's excesses.

Great religious leaders, such as Jesus and Gandhi, have always advocated pacifism. They believe that "He who lives by the sword dies by the sword." For thousands of years the wisest thinkers have believed that violence does not end suffering, but merely increases it.

CONS

We are not arguing that violence is of itself a good thing. We are saying that when others are using violence to endanger principles as fundamental as human rights, people have a duty to stand up against them. Not to do so would merely allow evil to spread unchecked.

Disputes do sometimes persist after wars, but often wars can lead to the resolution of some issues. For example, World War II prevented fascism from taking over Europe, and the Persian Gulf War led to Saddam Hussein's withdrawal from Kuwait. In these cases, the failure to act would have led to the oppression of millions and permitted an aggressor to triumph.

Pacifism is a luxury that some can practice because others fight. Pacifists claim moral superiority while enjoying the liberty for which others have died. We fought both world wars to combat aggression and injustice. We did our moral duty in resisting tyranny.

This type of protest is not true pacifism, which rejects war outright. By admitting that war is sometimes inevitable, you are acknowledging that sometimes people cannot sit by and do nothing.

In practice, most world religions have adopted violence, in the shape of crusades or holy wars, to serve their ends. And does not the Bible advocate "an eye for an eye"? When an aggressor endangers liberty and freedom, humanity must use violence to combat him.

Sample Motions:
    This House would be pacifist.
    This House rejects violence.
    This House would turn the other cheek.

Web Links:
- Fiala, Andrew. <http://plato.stanford.edu/entries/pacifism/> *Stanford Encyclopedia of Philosophy* entry on pacifism.
- Hoekema, David A. <http://www.religion-online.org/showarticle.asp?title=115> Discussion of Christianity and pacifism.
- PBS. <http://www.pbs.org/itvs/thegoodwar/story.html> Website of a PBS film on pacifists throughout history; contains links for further research.

Further Reading:
    Atack, Iain. *Nonviolence in Political Theory.* Edinburgh University Press, 2012.
    Cortright, David. *Gandhi and Beyond: Nonviolence for an Age of Terrorism.* Paradigm Publishers, 2006.
    Gelderloos, Peter. *How Nonviolence Protects the State.* South End Press, 2007.
    Nepstead, Sharon E., and Lester R. Kurtz, eds. *Nonviolent Conflict and Civil Resistance.* Emerald Group, 2012.

■ ■

PORNOGRAPHY, BANNING OF

Most adult pornography is legal in the United States, where it is protected by the First Amendment guarantee of freedom of speech. Nevertheless, many campaigns to restrict it have been mounted. Initially such suggested restrictions were based on moral grounds, but in recent years women's groups have urged a ban because some studies have shown that pornography contributes to violence against women.

PROS

Pornography debases human interactions by reducing love and all other emotions to the crudely sexual. Sex is an important element in relationships, but it is not the be all and end all of them. Pornography also debases the human body and exploits those lured into it. It also encourages unhealthy, objectifying attitudes toward the opposite sex. Pornography is not a victimless crime. The victim is the very fabric of society itself.

Pornography helps to reinforce the side of our sexual identity that sees people as objects and debases both their thoughts and bodies. We have seen evidence of this in the way pictures of seminaked women (hardly ever men) are used in advertising. Society's acceptance of pornography leads to the objectification of women and thus directly to sexual discrimination.

CONS

Freedom of speech is one of our most cherished rights. Censorship might be justified when free speech becomes offensive to others, but this is not the case with pornography. It is filmed legally by consenting adults for consenting adults and thus offends no one. Pornography injures no one and is a legitimate tool to stimulate our feelings and emotions in much the same way as music, art, and literature do.

Pornography is a legitimate exploration of sexual fantasy, one of the most vital parts of human life. Psychologists have confirmed the important, if not driving, role that sexual impulses play in shaping our behavior. Repressing or denying this part of our personalities is both prudish and ignorant. Consequently, pornography should be available for adults to vary their sex lives. Indeed, far from "corroding the fabric of society," pornography can help maintain and strengthen marriages by letting couples fully explore their sexual feelings.

Society's apparent tolerance of legal pornography encourages illegal forms, such as child pornography. Are we to allow pedophiles the "legitimate sexual exploration" of their feelings? The opposition cannot let human impulses override societal rules that protect children.

This is not true; no "slippery slope" scenario exists. People interested in child pornography will obtain it regardless of its legal status. Human sexuality is such that mere exposure to adult pornography does not encourage individuals to explore child pornography.

Many rapists are obsessed with pornography. It encourages them to view women as objects and helps justify their contention that women are willing participants in the act. Indeed, feminists have proposed that pornography is rape because it exploits women's bodies. Pornography serves only to encourage brutal sex crimes.

Sadly, rape will exist with or without pornography. Rapists may use pornography, but pornography does not create rapists. The claim that pornography is rape is invalid. Our legal system depends on the distinction between thought and act that this claim seeks to blur. Pornography is a legitimate form of expression and enjoyment. Government should not censor it in the interests of sexual repression and prudery.

Sample Motions:

This House believes pornography does more harm than good.

This House would ban pornography.

This House believes that pornography is bad for women.

Web Links:

- Bradley, Gerard V. <http://www.socialcostsofpornography.org/Bradley_Moral_Bases_for_Legal_Regulation.pdf> Offers nuanced policy proposals for regulating pornography.
- Council for Secular Humanism. <http://www.secularhumanism.org/library/fi/mcelroy_17_4.html> Several articles on feminism and pornography.
- West, Caroline. <http://www.science.uva.nl/~seop/entries/pornography-censorship/> *Stanford Encyclopedia of Philosophy* entry on pornography and censorship.

Further Reading:

Bronstein, Carolyn. *Battling Pornography: The American Feminist Anti-Pornography Movement, 1976–1986.* Cambridge University Press, 2011.

Kammeyer, Kenneth. *A Hypersexual Society: Sexual Discourse, Erotica, and Pornography in America Today.* Palgrave Macmillan, 2008.

Langton, Rae. *Sexual Solipsism: Philosophical Essays on Pornography and Objectification.* Oxford University Press, 2009.

Levin, Abigail. *The Cost of Free Speech: Pornography, Hate Speech and Their Challenge to Liberalism.* Palgrave Macmillan, 2010.

■ ■

PORTION SIZES, GOVERNMENT CONTROL OF

Obesity poses a serious health risk in many developed countries, and is now the leading cause of preventable death in the United States. As obesity levels have increased in the United States, so too have portion sizes, with numerous food companies now using larger sizes as selling points. Some public policy advisors suggest that placing government restrictions on portion sizes will help to reduce obesity levels. In 2012, New York City Mayor Michael Bloomberg restricted sales of sugary drinks in portions exceeding 16 ounces. This policy is controversial, as it infringes upon individuals' right to make informed decisions about their own diet.

PROS

Large portion sizes are bad for your health. Obesity now claims an estimated 400,000 lives a year in the United States—this is a direct result of excessive calorie consumption. Oversized portions are a growing source of these excess calories. The 7-Eleven Double Gulp, a 64-ounce soda, contains nearly 800 calories, which is ten times the calories found in the original 6.5 ounce Coca-Cola bottle when the drink was introduced. A 2002 study by Lisa Young and Marion Nestle found that portion sizes are consistently larger than they were in the past, and that these portions "not only contain more energy but also encourage people to eat more." Limits on portion size allow individuals to consume whatever food they like, while reducing the adverse effects on health of high-calorie foods.

Restrictions on harmful products are a key function of government. For example, the Controlled Substances Act of 1970 regulated the use and distribution of numerous substances that were deemed harmful to health. Even legal products, such as alcohol and tobacco, are sold with government restrictions. Because excessive calorie consumption also has a detrimental effect on health, it makes sense that the government would regulate this too.

Large portions are decreasing the health and life expectancy of children, who are not able to make responsible decisions regarding portion control by themselves. Research has shown that if children are served larger portions, they consume more calories without realizing it. Furthermore, a study conducted by Johns Hopkins Bloomberg School of Public Health found that parents have only a weak influence over their child's diet, meaning that they are unable single-handedly to control the portion sizes of children. With approximately one-third of all US children overweight or obese, it is clear that parents need assistance.

Food manufacturers that sell large portion sizes will be able to adapt their businesses to fit government restrictions. As public attitudes to health have evolved, so have food products. In 2003, leading fast food restaurant McDonald's introduced healthier food items on their menu. Following this move, the company announced a 13% rise in profits. All leading soda manufacturers now produce low-calorie alternatives to their sugary drinks. In 2011, the low-calorie drink Diet Coke surpassed Pepsi as the second most popular soda in the United States, after Coca-Cola. Government regulations on food, just as public health attitudes to food, do not hurt business, but inspire new approaches to food manufacture and sale.

CONS

Large portions are not bad for your health, as long as they are combined with exercise and a well-balanced diet. Consuming large portions is not a problem, if an individual then eats fewer calories and subsequent snacks. Furthermore, many people require a large amount of calories; a tall active young male, for example, can need around 4,000 calories a day—four times what a small inactive female would need. People should be allowed to adjust their own diets according to their needs, and it cannot be assumed that everyone needs to restrict their calorie intake. Rather than banning large portion sizes, the government should provide information that enables consumers to make their own decisions. Food labels, helping people to better understand portion sizes, are a much better option than government restrictions.

In a free market, the sale of goods should be governed by supply and demand and not the government. Government restrictions on food quantity set a dangerous precedent for allowing excessive government intrusion into our lives. If politicians can limit portion size in order to reduce obesity, what will stop them from banning whole food groups, or even mandating exercise? The government should focus on encouraging personal responsibility when it comes to diet.

Parents, not the government, are responsible for overseeing the diets of their children; government should not intrude into our private family lives. If parents do indeed have a limited influence over the diets of children, more could be done to strengthen this, such as regulating fast-food advertising to children or educating parents in healthy eating. Furthermore, research has consistently pinpointed inactivity as a leading factor in producing overweight children. Rather than restricting the food that we all consume, the government should target children specifically with policies that increase exercise in schools.

Government restrictions on portion size will negatively affect businesses, and cost jobs. Following Mayor Bloomberg's restrictions on large servings of sugary drinks, industry groups filed suit against the city, stating that these limits place an unfair burden on small businesses, as larger convenience stores—such as 7-Eleven—are exempt from the restriction. The reality is that government restrictions are never fairly applied, but instead are rife with exemptions and loopholes for certain companies. If a business is unable to provide a particular product, customers will simply take their business elsewhere. In the current economic climate, government should be encouraging businesses to grow, not putting restrictions on them.

PROS

Restrictions on consumer behavior are effective. Over the past decade, smoking in public areas has been restricted by law in much of the United States and Europe. When the United Kingdom became a smoke-free zone in 2007, critics predicted that smokers would continue smoking in alternative venues, such as private residences. However, within the first year, the Department of Health reported that 400,000 people had quit smoking. If government restrictions on a highly addictive behavior such as smoking have been effective, there is no reason to feel that government restrictions on portion sizes will not work too.

Obesity rates are disproportionately high among blacks and Hispanics, and therefore, limiting portion sizes will be particularly beneficial to these groups. A 2011 paper, published in the *Temple Political and Civil Rights Law Review*, found that snack and soft-drink industries specifically target minority groups, with advertising for high-calorie products being much more prevalent in these communities than in white communities. Prohibiting large portion sizes of high-calorie foods will help to counter this imbalance and increase the health and life expectancy of minority groups.

Obesity affects society as a whole and is therefore an issue for government regulation. The burden that obesity places on society is continually increasing, with health insurance premiums and taxpayer-supported health care costs rising as a direct result of obesity in patients. In addition, obese individuals suffer more health issues, meaning that they take significantly more time off from work—on average obese women take 9.4 more sick days a year and obese men take 5.9 more sick days a year. According to a 2012 Reuters article, obesity costs the US economy $30 billion per year in lost productivity. With US society suffering the consequences of obesity as a collective, obesity is not a personal matter and is, therefore, absolutely a problem for the government to solve.

CONS

Restrictions on consumer behavior will not be effective. The free market depends upon supply and demand; cutting off supply does nothing to address demand, and consumers will simply find alternative means to maintain a high-calorie diet. For example, when alcohol was banned during Prohibition, those wanting to drink simply found alternative means, usually purchasing alcohol through illegal bootleggers. To successfully reduce the amount of high-calorie foods that individuals consume, the government should focus on reducing demand through education, rather than attempting to restrict supply.

Minority groups would be unfairly affected by restrictions on portion sizes, as they tend to consume more of the high-calorie products that would be targeted. Restrictions would harm low-income individuals, many of whom rely on inexpensive drink options as part of their diet. In fact, the National Association for the Advancement of Colored People (NAACP) and the Hispanic Federation filed suit against Mayor Bloomberg in January 2013, claiming that his ban on high-sugar drinks in excess of 16 ounces restricts "freedom of choice in low-income communities." Restrictions that affect one group of people more than others are inherently unfair.

An individual's weight is a personal matter, and is not something that government, or society, should have any control over. If an individual would prefer to be obese and suffer the health consequences associated with this, then that is his or her choice. Likewise, if someone takes a lot of leave from work, they will suffer a competitive disadvantage in the workplace, which is also a personal choice. The list of behaviors that can lead to health problems is endless: from spending too much time in the sun to experiencing stress from working too hard. The government cannot regulate all of these, and so needs to leave decisions regarding preventative health care up to the individual. Furthermore, the cost of obesity to the health care system can be offset through alternative means, such as higher insurance premiums for overweight individuals.

Sample Motions:
This House would restrict the portion sizes of certain high-calorie foods.
This House believes that an individual's consumption habits should be a subject of government interest.
This House believes that the state should regulate the sale of unhealthy foods.

Web Links:

- Centers for Disease Control and Prevention. <http://www.cdc.gov/obesity/data/adult.html> Provides data on obesity rates and medical costs in the US.
- Forbes. "NYC's Soda Ban Is a Good Idea, But a Tax Would Be Better." <http://www.forbes.com/sites/natesadeghi/2012/09/13/nycs-soda-ban-is-a-good-idea-but-a-tax-would-be-better/> Looks at taxation, rather than a ban, as a method to reduce portion size.
- Young, Lisa, and Marion Nestle. <http://steinhardt.nyu.edu/nutrition.olde/PDFS/young-nestle.pdf > Discusses the increase in portion size in the US.

Further Reading

Forth, Neal. *Food Regulation: Law, Science, Policy, and Practice*. Wiley, 2007.

Lusk, Jayson. *The Food Police: A Well-Fed Manifesto About the Politics of Your Plate*. Crown Forum, 2013.

Nestle, Marion. *Food Politics: How the Food Industry Influences Nutrition, and Health*. University of California Press, 2007.

Schwartz, Barry. *The Paradox of Choice: Why More Is Less*. Harper Perennial, 2005.

■ ■

PRIESTLY CELIBACY, ABOLITION OF

One of the requirements set by the Roman Catholic Church for priests is that they remain celibate. Celibacy is the renunciation of sex and marriage for the more perfect observance of chastity. This vow of celibacy has been propelled to the forefront of public discussion by charges, which began arising in 2002, that the church conspired to protect priests accused of child molestation. The vow of celibacy is seen by some as a cause of the pedophilia that seems to be rampant within the Catholic Church in America. The Vatican has not changed its stance on celibacy in the wake of the controversy, but some within the church have called for the elimination of the requirement to be celibate.

PROS

Until 1139, priests in the Western church were permitted to marry. The Bible does not mandate celibacy and, in fact, St. Peter, the first pope, was married. The true history and traditions of the Roman Catholic Church include the option for priests to marry.

The number of priests in America is on the decline, and many parishes are without a priest. The prohibition on marriage pushes some men away from the priesthood. The requirement of celibacy drastically reduces the pool from which the church can select priests and means that the church is not always getting the "best and the brightest."

Protestant clergy successfully balance their work in the church and their families. Were priests permitted to marry and have families, their families could serve as

CONS

The earliest church fathers, including St. Augustine, supported the celibate priesthood. In the fourth century, church councils enacted legislation forbidding married men who were ordained from having conjugal relations with their wives. We do not know if any of the apostles, other than Peter, were married, but we do know that they gave up everything to follow Jesus. More important, Jesus led a celibate life.

Protestant churches, which do not require celibacy, also are having problems recruiting clergy. Worldwide, the number of new priests is increasing. Only the developed world has seen a decline in priestly vocations. A recent study showed that vocations were on the rise in dioceses in the US that were loyal to the teachings of the church, including priestly celibacy.

A celibate priest can devote all his time to his parishioners. A married priest must spend time with his family. Protestant clergy have balanced their work for the church with examples to others. In addition, marriage can provide a priest with increased social support and intimacy.

their family responsibilities only with difficulty. Many wives and families of Protestant clergy report feeling second to the congregation.

Priestly celibacy is outdated. It sets the priest apart from the world and the experiences of his parishioners.

The priest is set apart from the world. He has a unique role: he represents Christ to his parishioners. Just as Jesus led a life of chastity dedicated to God, a priest must offer his life to God's people.

Celibate priests can never experience the intimate and complicated marital relationship. They lack credibility when conducting marital and family counseling. Married priests can better serve their parishioners because of their marital and family experiences.

The celibate priest has a unique understanding of the power of self-control and the giving of the self, which are key ideas in marriage. The priest is married to the church and can counsel couples and families using that knowledge.

The prospect of celibacy draws sexually dysfunctional men to the priesthood. They hope that by totally denying their sexuality, they will not engage in pedophilia, but unfortunately they often cannot overcome their deviant desires. Permitting priests to marry would bring men with healthy sexual desires to the priesthood.

Celibacy and pedophilia are not connected. Sexual abuse also occurs in religions where clergy are permitted to marry. Studies have shown that sexual abusers account for less than 2% of Roman Catholic clergy, a figure comparable to clergy in other denominations.

Sample Motions:

This House would permit priests to marry.

This House would have the Vatican stop requiring priestly celibacy.

This House believes that a married priest is a better priest.

Web Links:

- Carroll, James. <http://www.boston.com/bostonglobe/editorial_opinion/oped/articles/2010/05/16/celibacy_and_the_catholic _priest/> Argument against priestly celibacy written by a practicing Catholic.
- Hudson, Deal. <http://www.catholicity.com/commentary/hudson/00199.html > Clear presentation of arguments against celibacy—with refutations.
- Thurston, Herbert. <http://www.newadvent.org/cathen/03481a.htm> Offers a detailed article on the history and theology of priestly celibacy.

Further Reading:

Bordisso, Lou A. *Sex, Celibacy, and Priesthood: A Bishop's Provocative Inquisition.* iUniverse, 2011.

Cavadini, John C., ed. *The Charism of Priestly Celibacy: Biblical, Theological, and Pastoral Reflections.* Ave Maria Press, 2012.

Kasomo, Daniel W. *Arguments for Priestly Celibacy.* Lambert Academic, 2011.

■ ■

PRISON PRIVATIZATION

Prison privatization refers to the construction and operation of jails and detention centers by for-profit companies. In the United States, the private prison movement began in the 1980s, promoting privatization as a cost-effective solution to widespread prison overcrowding. As US incarceration rates skyrocketed throughout *the 1990s and 2000s, the private prison industry grew. By 2011, the two largest private prison companies in the United States, CCA and GEO Corrections Corporation of America and the GEO Group), earned a total of $3.3 billion a year. This debate intersects with the broader debate over the privatization of government functions: Does privatization encourage better value through free market competition, or a reduction in standards as companies cut costs in the pursuit of profit? Critics of prison privatization also argue that it is immoral for people to profit from the incarceration of others.*

PROS

Privatizing prisons saves taxpayers money. According to the Bureau of Justice Statistics, private prisons cost less to operate than their government-run counterparts. Government-run facilities are subject to extensive regulations, such as the requirement that they provide medical and mental health services to all inmates, regardless of the seriousness of their condition. Consequently, medical costs were an average of $2.44 a day more for inmates in publicly run prisons than for those in private prisons—a difference of almost $900 a year per inmate. With approximately 2.3 million people currently incarcerated in the United States, this difference in costs has the potential to translate into huge savings for taxpayers. In this struggling economy, with state and federal budgets stretched to the breaking point, any means of reducing expenditure must be pursued.

Private prisons are beneficial to the surrounding community. Many of the private prisons built during the industry's boom in the 1980s and 1990s were located in economically depressed communities, in some of the poorest counties in the US. These prisons provided jobs for the unemployed and revenue for the towns to tax. Nearly 800,000 people currently work in the US prison system, with an increasing share of them being employed by private companies. Job creation has been cited by many politicians as the primary benefit of private prisons. When introducing a bill to facilitate the construction of a private prison in Milo, Maine, Sen. Douglas Thomas said, "I could pretend that this bill is about reducing the high costs of running Maine prisons. . . . Let's not pretend, because this bill is really about jobs for a town that desperately needs them."

Privatized prisons emerged as a solution to overcrowding, and the consequent dangerous conditions, in government-run facilities. By 1988, more than two-thirds of the states in the US were facing serious prison overcrowding, with many facilities operating at least 50 percent over capacity. The growth of private prisons functioned

CONS

The argument that private prisons save money does not stand up to scrutiny. Research from the Arizona Department of Correction indicates that private prisons have lower operational costs only because they cherry-pick the healthiest prisoners, leaving the most expensive ones to be housed at the taxpayer's expense. Furthermore, investigations by the Associated Press, the Sentencing Project, and the American Friends Service Committee have all found that, even though privately run prisons steer clear of the costliest inmates, they actually cost more to operate. Private prisons have an interest in increasing the numbers of people behind bars; to really save taxpayer money, governments should focus on reducing the numbers of people incarcerated, by examining cheaper alternatives.

Private prisons have damaged surrounding communities. Many small towns have opted to become "prison towns," investing in expensive constructions in the belief that it would boost their economy; however, studies have consistently shown that the economic benefits promised by private prisons have rarely materialized. Any jobs created are low-paying, and often local residents are unqualified for these, so prisons bring in their own workforce. Researchers at Washington State University found that local job growth is often actually impeded in surrounding communities. The study revealed that the money used to construct private prisons was often diverted from educational resources, such as community colleges, limiting the educational attainment and employability of locals. In addition, the incentives offered to private prisons—such as tax subsidies, water and road maintenance, and municipal services—actually burden local taxpayers, outweighing any scant benefits.

Privatizing prisons encourages overcrowding and potentially dangerous conditions. By their very nature, private prisons function by generating more money than they spend. Since they get paid on a per inmate basis, this requires them to squeeze in as many inmates as possible, in addition to cutting costs however possible. One

PROS	CONS

PROS

to alleviate this overcrowding. Private prisons provide better quality services than public prisons, as evidenced by the higher number of accredited private facilities. To become accredited, a prison must demonstrate high standards with regard to both living conditions and safety. In 2005, 44% of private prisons had met the standards for accreditation, while only 10% of public prisons had.

Private prisons provide a straightforward extension of the services that public prisons provide. There is nothing immoral about a private company doing what the state would be doing anyway. Private prisons incarcerate only individuals who have been found guilty of crimes and assigned sentences through the proper legal channels. Private prisons have no say in who is incarcerated and for how long; they merely implement the judgments of the legal system. Incarceration is a widely accepted method of punishment, and as long as private companies have no say in who is incarcerated, there is no conflict of interests.

CONS

way costs are reduced is by slashing staff wages, leading to a high turnover rate and guards who lack the proper experience to deal with dangerous situations. Unsurprisingly, inmate uprisings in private prisons have become common. A nationwide study reported that assaults on guards by inmates were 49% higher in private prisons than in government-run prisons. This suggests that a for-profit business model is incompatible with safe conditions in prisons.

It is immoral for one group of people to profit from the incarceration of another group of people. A study by the Justice Policy Institute found that, through donations to politicians, private prison companies have contributed to strict sentencing policies in order to boost their profits. The US incarceration rate is already the highest in the world, fracturing communities—particularly minority communities—and exacerbating the problem of intergenerational poverty. With private prison companies profiting from increased incarceration, and therefore lobbying for stricter sentencing, it is clear to see how their interests will have a detrimental effect on society.

Sample Motions:

This House would stop the use of private prisons.

This House believes that prison privatization does more good than harm.

Web Links:

- Corrections Corporation of America (CCA) <http://www.cca.com/> Website of the largest private prison corporation in the US.
- Lee, Suevon. <http://www.propublica.org/article/by-the-numbers-the-u.s.s-growing-for-profit-detention-industry> Article with statistics about the growth of private prisons.
- Segal, Geoffrey. <http://www.burnetcountytexas.org/docs/6-Segal-Commission-on-PrisonAbuse.pdf> Compares the quality of public and private prisons.
- Zito, Matthew. <http://www.ifpo.org/articlebank/prison_privatization.html> Article detailing the history of private prisons up to the present.

Further Readings:

Coyle, Andrew, Allison Campbell, and Rodney Neufeld. *Capitalist Punishment: Prison Privatization and Human Rights*. Zed Books, 2003.

Herivel, Tara, and Paul Wright. *Prison Profiteers: Who Makes Money from Mass Incarceration*. New Press, 2007.

Selman, Donna, and Paul Leighton. *Punishment for Sale: Private Prisons, Big Business, and the Incarceration Binge*. Rowman and Littlefield, 2010.

■ ■

PRIVACY VS. SECURITY

In the aftermath of the terrorist attacks of September 2001, Congress passed the Patriot Act, which gave new rights and powers to law enforcement agencies. For example, the act gives the FBI greater latitude in wiretapping and in the surveillance of material transmitted over the Internet. Legislators have also proposed national identification cards, facial profiling systems, and tighter restrictions on immigration. All of these measures are aimed at protecting Americans from further terrorist attacks. But this increased security comes at a cost: the government will be able to gather more information about the private actions of individuals. To some observers, this invasion of privacy is unwarranted and represents an attack on fundamental freedoms guaranteed in the Constitution.

PROS

The primary function of government is to "secure the general welfare" of its citizens. Security is a common good that is promised to all Americans, and it must take primacy over individual concerns about privacy.

Electronic surveillance—of financial transactions, for example—is an essential tool for tracking the actions of terrorists when they are planning attacks. The government cannot stand by and wait until criminal acts are committed; it must stop attacks before they happen.

Tighter security controls at airports and borders will help prevent damage and loss of life. In addition to their deterrent effect, they will enable officials to stop attacks as they are happening.

Tighter immigration laws and more rigorous identification procedures for foreigners entering the country will reduce the possibility of terrorists entering the country.

The right to privacy is by no means absolute, and Americans already allow the government to control some of their private actions. (The government can require drivers to wear safety belts, for example.) Any intrusions on privacy for the sake of security would be minimal, and fundamental rights would still be respected.

CONS

The right to privacy underlies the Fourth Amendment to the Constitution, which prohibits unreasonable "search and seizure." When the government collects and shares information about its citizens, it is conducting an electronic version of such prohibited searches.

Any proposal that increases the power of government agencies should be dismissed. Historically, government agencies (e.g., the IRS) have abused their power over citizens. Increased power means a greater potential for abuse.

Tighter security controls can be used to target specific ethnic and religious groups in a way that is unfair and discriminatory.

Preventive measures affect the innocent as well as the guilty. This is especially true in the case of foreign nationals: tighter immigration controls may exclude foreigners whose presence in America would be beneficial to the country.

History has shown that the invocation of national security has often led to the restriction of fundamental rights. For example, Japanese-American citizens were interned during World War II to increase security. We should not allow the government to take even small steps in a direction that can lead to something worse.

Sample Motions:

This House supports the creation of a national identity card.

This House would give the government more power in time of war.

Web Links:

- Electronic Privacy Information Center. <http://privacy.org/> Web site devoted to gathering information on privacy issues and links to privacy Web sites.
- Privacy vs. Security: A Bogus Debate? <http://www.businessweek.com/stories/2002-06-04/privacy-vs-dot-security-a-bogus-debate> In an interview for Business Week, David Brin, author of *The Transparent Society*, argues that the conflict between privacy and security is a false dichotomy.
- Rotenberg, Marc. <http://www.huffingtonpost.com/marc-rotenberg/privacy-vs-security-pr_b_71806.html> Argues in favor of privacy protection when in conflict with security measures. Contains link to opposing viewpoint by K. A. Taipale.

Further Reading:

Akpeninor, James Ohwofasa. *Modern Concepts of Security*. AuthorHouse, 2012.

Darmer, M. Katherine B., ed. *National Security, Civil Liberties, and the War on Terror*. Prometheus Books, 2011.

Rule, James B. *Privacy in Peril: How We Are Sacrificing a Fundamental Right in Exchange for Security and Convenience*. Oxford University Press, 2009.

Solove, Daniel J. *Nothing to Hide: The False Tradeoff between Privacy and Security*. Yale University Press, 2011.

■ ■

PRIVATE MILITARY FIRMS

Private military firms are for-profit corporations that conduct activities traditionally performed by state militaries. Though they are not a recent development, public awareness of private military firms has increased since the US-led wars in Iraq and Afghanistan. Both of these US military campaigns relied heavily on private military firms — in 2006, the United States had approximately 100,000 private contractors in Iraq, 10 times as many as were used in the Persian Gulf War 10 years earlier. This growth in private military firms has been controversial, with concerns over the lack of accountability of private contractors at the forefront; because private firms are not operated by a particular national government, they may function under less regulation than state military organizations. However, proponents of private military firms see them as indispensable, providing specialized services and rapidly mobilized forces that are essential to modern military campaigns.

PROS

Privatizing military operations can save taxpayer money, with both training and post-operation costs being significantly lower for private firms. According to Paul Cerjan, vice president of Halliburton's worldwide military affairs, military outsourcing cuts the cost of training because many subcontractors are already experienced military veterans. Furthermore, because most subcontractors are hired on a per contract basis, essentially rendering them freelance soldiers, there are no ongoing costs once the contract is fulfilled. While subcontractors are usually paid more than enlisted US soldiers, their overall cost is far lower when compared to lifetime military workers who require training bases, deployment costs, and post-operations benefits such as pensions and health care. With the wars in Iraq and Afghanistan estimated to cost US taxpayers a total of $2.4 trillion by 2017, it is crucial that military spending be reduced — private military firms are essential to achieving this without compromising security.

CONS

Spending on private military firms is largely unchecked, and there is no evidence that any taxpayer money is saved by using them. It is nearly impossible to obtain precise data on how much is spent on private military firms, but estimates place it at around 40% of all military spending. Since these organizations are strictly for-profit, a portion of this spending goes directly to the owners of large corporations, rather than toward national security. The cost of private contractors far exceeds the cost of traditional military personnel: while an enlisted US soldier makes $18–24,000 a year, private contractors make an average of four times that. The result of this inflated salary is that soldiers are trained by the US army, at the taxpayer's expense, before "going private" rather than reenlisting. Particularly at the top echelon of the US army, this has drained talent and resulted in bonuses of up to $150,000 being offered by the army in an attempt to retain expensively trained personnel. Private military firms essentially funnel resources away from the state military in order to produce vast profits for a few.

Private military firms help to provide veterans with viable employment. Many soldiers return to the United States with few employment prospects, often lacking the education and training needed to compete in the current job market. In January 2013, the unemployment rate for veterans was estimated to be 10.8%, far above the national average of 7.9%; this has cost the military almost $1 billion per year in unemployment benefits. Private military firms offer a solution to the problem of veteran unemployment, providing well-paid jobs that value military experience. Consequently, thousands of veterans have found employment in private military firms. Private military firms mitigate problems for US veterans while simultaneously making the war effort run more smoothly and effectively.

Private military firms ease the burden of war for the regular armed forces. Many private contractors are not actual soldiers or even armed security agents. Instead, they provide support to the US military in terms of transportation, intelligence, food preparation, and other duties that free up military personnel. As Congressional Research Service defense expert, Moshe Schwartz, testified before Congress, "Contractors can provide significant operational benefits to DOD [Department of Defense], including freeing up uniformed personnel to conduct combat operations." During simultaneous military operations in Iraq and Afghanistan, the US armed forces simply did not have the numbers to undertake every duty involved in both military campaigns; if contracting private military firms were not an option, the government would have had to implement drastic policies, such as conscription.

Private military firms are able to undertake missions that state militaries cannot. They provide security and support in areas that are politically more difficult for the US military to operate in. For example, in the 1960s private military firms dismantled African and Asian governments operating under colonial rule. Private military firms can enter conflict zones with greater ease than large governmental organizations, and operate with more efficiency, secrecy, and stealth. In addition, private military firms that are local to an area can be contracted for particularly sensitive operations, allowing the military to draw on their knowledge of regional geography, language, customs, and culture. The use of private contractors allows the military greater flexibility and specialization, making

Private military firms exploit US veterans, putting them in dangerous situations, in jobs that lack financial security. Due to an absence of regulation and oversight, private contractors are often put in situations too perilous for the military. Private firms are not required to report casualties; however, almost 2,000 private contractors are estimated to have been killed in Iraq alone. Furthermore, private military firms do not offer secure employment to veterans. Veterans are employed for short contracts, often paid by the day, and are provided with no benefits for them or their families back home. Despite the dangers they face, private contractors often receive no health care, life insurance, disability insurance, or other veteran services. This dangerous temporary work does not offer a long-term solution to the problem of veteran unemployment.

Private corporations are concerned with profit, which can negatively affect quality. During war, quality can directly relate to safety. Retired Colonel Thomas X. Hammes of the US Marine Corps stated, "Wartime is not about efficiency; it's about effectiveness." Too many levels of subcontracting in order to maximize efficiency results in a bloated, inefficient system that neither saves money nor accomplishes much on the battlefield. The problem, he argues, is that "We're working toward efficiency rather than effectiveness . . . it certainly seemed to me there were a lot of layers and a lot of wasted money," when private military firms were contracted. Even noncombat military functions, such as transport and intelligence, have a huge influence on the effectiveness of a military campaign; by contracting these to companies committed to driving down costs in the pursuit of profit, the US military is compromising both safety and effectiveness.

Though they are now referred to as "contractors," private military personnel are no different from mercenaries, making up loosely regulated and largely unwatched militias. According to Global Research, "Private military and security companies operate in a legal vacuum: they pose a threat to civilians and to international human rights law." Consequently, private military firms have been involved in torture, public executions, and other violations of human rights, all without the accountability required of official US organizations. Local contractors can be hired to perform duties that are illegal for the military to undertake, such as torture or "enhanced interrogation." At Abu Ghraib—the Iraqi prison where torture and prisoner abuse by US forces were widespread—50%

PROS	CONS
it indispensable for modern military objectives, such as counterinsurgency and counterterrorism.	of interrogators at the time of the abuse were found to be private contractors. A US military officer at the prison reported that many of these interrogators were untrained and originally contracted as cooks or drivers.

Sample Motions:

This House supports the use of private military firms.

This House believes that the use of private military firms is unjust.

Web Links:

- Dinucci, Manlio. "The Privatization of War." Voltaire Network, March 12, 2012 <http://www.voltairenet.org/article172962.html>. Describes statistics from Iraq and Afghanistan that show an increased emphasis on private military firms in the United States.
- Gomez Del Prado, Jesse L. "The Privatization of War: Mercenaries, Private Military and Security Companies (PMSC)." Centre for Research on Globalisation, March 5, 2013 <http://www.globalresearch.ca/the-privatization-of-war-mercenaries-private-military-and-security-companies-pmsc/21826>. Summarizes the historical appearance of private military firms, their tasks, and how they are defined within international law.
- Isenberg, David. "Contractors in War Zones: Not Exactly 'Contracting.'" Time Magazine, October 9, 2012 <http://nation.time.com/2012/10/09/contractors-in-war-zones-not-exactly-contracting>. Discusses the growth of private military companies in Iraq and Afghanistan and the subsequent decline of US troops. Offers figures on the number of contractors placed by the US in different war zones around the world.
- PBS. <http://www.pbs.org/wgbh/pages/frontline/shows/warriors/contractors/ceff.html>. Interviews with five experts with varying opinions over the cost-efficiency of private military firms as compared to that of a standing army. Linked to PBS Frontline's show "Private Warriors."

Further Readings:

Hughes, Solomon. *War on Terror, Inc.: Corporate Profiteering from the Politics of Fear.* Verso, 2007.

Singer, P. W. *Corporate Warriors: The Rise of the Privatized Military Industry.* Cornell University Press, 2008.

Uesseler, Rolf. *Servants of War: Private Military Corporations and the Profit of Conflict.* Soft Skull Press, 2008.

■ ■

PROGRESSIVE INCOME TAXATION

A government tax on the money that people earn is known as an "income tax." The amount paid is usually determined as a percentage of an individual's overall annual income. Numerous income tax systems exist, with a progressive income tax being one of the most widely used. Under a progressive income tax, high-income earners pay a higher percentage of their income in tax than do low-income earners. The United States currently has a progressive income tax. In 2010, individuals earning less than $8,375 per year paid 10% tax, while those earning more than $373,650 paid 35%. Though the US tax system has been progressive for almost 100 years, critics view it as fundamentally un-American. For them, a flat tax system, which imposes the same tax rate on everyone, is fairer.

PROS	CONS
Progressive taxation increases equality by asking everyone to pay what they can afford. The unfortunate reality	Equality of opportunity, not outcome, should be the guiding principle of our democracy. Government should

is that we live in a deeply unequal society, in which some individuals struggle to provide basic necessities for their children, while others accumulate vast amounts of disposable wealth. Requiring everyone to pay a flat tax rate places an unfair burden on low-income families. For example, someone earning $10,000 a year would suffer significant financial hardship if taxed at 15%—their annual income would be reduced to just $8,500. In contrast, someone earning $500,000 a year would suffer no hardship at all through a 15% tax, which would still leave them with $425,000 a year. This discrepancy in the impact of a flat tax upon high- and low-income individuals makes it fundamentally unfair; a progressive tax, which aims to have an equivalent impact on everyone, redresses this imbalance.

Wealthy people do not become successful in a vacuum, but, instead, become successful due to the contributions of society at large; therefore, high-income individuals have a duty to pay back to society. As President Obama said, "If you were successful, somebody along the line gave you some help. There was a great teacher somewhere in your life. Somebody invested in roads and bridges. The Internet didn't get invented on its own. Government research created the Internet so that companies could make money off the Internet." A progressive income tax system does not penalize success, but acknowledges the diffused and interconnected efforts that make individual success possible.

A progressive tax rate does not unfairly target the rich. In fact, the wealthy benefit greatly under the current progressive tax system in the United States. Deductions under the current system allow for high-income Americans to obtain tax breaks on charitable giving, business ventures, retirement savings, and home ownership. Consequently, federal, state, and local governments give billions in tax breaks to the wealthiest Americans every year. These numerous rewards, which are all geared toward high-income Americans, more than compensate for the higher tax rate. In addition, the corporate subsidies provided under the current progressive system reward socially useful actions, such as employing veterans or implementing energy efficient policies, with tax credits. Replacing the progressive tax system with a flat tax rate would not reduce the amount of tax that most wealthy Americans pay—it would merely remove their incentives to use their wealth in responsible and socially beneficial ways.

extend equal protection under the law to all. By its very definition, progressive income tax is unequal, because it demands that a certain sector of society pay a disproportionate amount of their income. No one is arguing that wealthy people should not pay more in taxes—under a flat tax rate high-income individuals would still pay more than low-income individuals: 15% of $500,000 is clearly more than 15% of $10,000. Under this flat rate system, wealthier people would pay more tax than poorer people, while being treated equally. Under the progressive tax system, wealthy people are treated unequally and their success is something that is punished rather than rewarded.

Requiring successful people to "pay back" to society is a means of wealth redistribution and a distinctly socialist policy. Social welfare programs, which are disproportionately funded by the taxes of high earners, are almost exclusively used by low-income people; this involves a government-mandated transfer of money from those who have earned it, to those who have not. Requiring wealthy people to pay a higher portion of their income in taxes than poorer people has nothing to do with acknowledging the collective contributions underpinning individual success; high-income people acknowledge these contributions in their everyday lives. They pay road taxes to use roads, and they pay Internet service providers to use the Internet. Instead, progressive income taxation is about the government attempting to raise funds by taking from the rich.

Progressive systems are so complicated that often the very wealthy are able to evade their obligations through exploiting loopholes. A flat tax would eliminate this unfair tax avoidance. The deductions—or loopholes—found in the progressive tax system often have the result that very high-income individuals pay a lower tax rate than poorer Americans; billionaire Warren Buffett famously reported that his middle-income secretary paid a higher tax rate than he did. A flat tax would benefit the large majority of middle-income Americans, who are unable to exploit loopholes and are therefore hardest hit by the progressive system. In addition, Americans spend approximately 6.1 billion hours working out their taxes each year—one estimate indicates that a flat tax could save more than $200 billion a year in man hours. Furthermore, a flat tax would increase taxpayer privacy, as individuals would no longer have to submit details about their personal finances to the Internal Revenue Service. Replacing the progressive system with a flat tax would be fairer, quicker, and easier.

PROS

Governments have a mandate to raise funds through taxation; taxation on income, with varying rates, is firmly within this mandate. The US government, in particular, is authorized to tax income by the Sixteenth Amendment to the Constitution. Furthermore, it was authorized to levy a progressive tax by the Revenue Act of 1913, which mandated an income tax of 1% on income exceeding $3,000, increasing to 7% on incomes greater than $500,000. The Supreme Court upheld this as constitutional in 1916 in the case of *Brushaber v. Union Pacific Railroad Company*. The Constitution makes no mention of the particular tax rates that high- and low-income individuals should pay and therefore does not prohibit a progressive income tax system.

CONS

Progressive income taxation violates the Constitution, which promotes equal rights for all citizens. Though the Sixteenth Amendment authorizes income taxation, Article 1, Section 8, Clause 1 of the Constitution specifically instructs that "[A]ll duties, imposts and excises shall be uniform throughout the United States." Since "uniform" means "always having the same form, manner, or degree: not varying or variable," a progressive taxation is in clear violation of this. Taxing one group of individuals at a higher rate than others is the antithesis of equal treatment. Progressive taxation, therefore, sets a dangerous precedent in allowing the government to treat individuals unequally and penalize portions of society through increased taxes.

Sample Motions:

This House believes that higher earners should pay a higher tax rate.

This House believes that the progressive income tax is unjust.

Web Links:

- CNN. "Let's Kill the Progressive Tax Rate System." <http://www.cnn.com/2012/04/17/opinion/brown-progressive-tax-rates> Looks at the benefits of a flat tax system.
- Huffington Post. "Raising Top Tax Rate Is a Very Big Deal." <http://www.huffingtonpost.com/robert-creamer/raising-top-tax-rates-is_b_2395825.html> Argues that the tax rate of the wealthiest should be raised in order to benefit the US economy.
- New York Times. "Combating Inequality May Require Broader Tax." <http://www.nytimes.com/2012/11/28/business/combatting-inequality-may-require-broader-tax.html?pagewanted=all> Article arguing for raising taxes among the middle class, rather than a more progressive tax system.

Further Readings:

Bartlett, Bruce. *The Benefit and the Burden: Tax Reform — Why We Need It and What It Will Take*. Simon and Schuster, 2012.

Burman, Leonard, and Joel Slemrod. *Taxes in America: What Everyone Needs to Know*. Oxford University Press, 2012.

Slemrod, Joel, and Jon Bakija. *Taxing Ourselves, 4th ed.: A Citizen's Guide to the Debate over Taxes*. MIT Press, 2008.

■ ■

PROSTITUTION, LEGALIZATION OF

Prostitution has long been opposed on moral grounds, but recently concerns about sexually transmitted diseases, particularly AIDS, and about the violence that surrounds prostitution have contributed to renewed demands to stop the selling of sex. Criminalizing prostitution has not worked, and some nations have moved to regulate or legalize it to protect prostitutes and monitor the conditions under which they work. In Singapore and Denmark, selling sex is legal; the Dutch city of Amsterdam and the Australian state of New South Wales have no laws for or against prostitution. Nevada has made prostitution lawful in a limited number of licensed brothels. This arrangement also has enjoyed notable success in the Australian state of Victoria.

PROS

Prostitution is an issue of individual liberty. The control of one's own body is a basic human right. We do not impose legal penalties on men and women who choose to be promiscuous. Why should the exchange of money suddenly make consensual sex illegal?

Prostitution has existed in all cultures throughout history. Governments should recognize that they cannot eradicate it. Consequently they should pass legislation that makes prostitution safer, rather than persist with futile and dangerous prohibition.

Prostitutes have performed a valid social function for thousands of years. Prostitution actually helps maintain marriages and relationships. A purely physical, commercial transaction does not jeopardize the emotional stability of a relationship. In Italy, for example, visiting a prostitute does not violate the law against adultery.

Many libertarian feminists believe that prostitution reflects the independence and dominance of modern women. The majority of prostitutes are women. Once the danger of abuse from male clients and pimps is removed, the capacity of women to control men's sexual responses in a financially beneficial relationship is liberating. Furthermore, many campaigners for the rights of prostitutes note that the hours are relatively short and the work well paid. Prostitutes are paid for services other women must provide without charge.

Some studies suggest that prostitution lowers the incidence of sex crimes.

Legalization would improve the sexual health of prostitutes and, as a result, that of their clients. The sexual transaction would occur in a clean and safe environment rather than on the street. In areas where prostitution is legal, prostitutes have regular health checks as a condition of working in the brothels. Furthermore, the use of contraception is compulsory and condoms are freely available.

CONS

Prostitutes do not have a genuine choice. They are often encouraged or forced to work in the sex industry before they are old enough to make a reasoned decision. Many have their reasoning impaired by an unhappy family background, previous sexual abuse, or drugs. They may be compelled to enter prostitution by circumstances beyond their control, such as substance addiction or the necessity to provide for a family.

Governments have a duty to protect the moral and physical health of their citizens. Legalizing prostitution would implicitly approve a dangerous and immoral practice. Prostitution is never a legitimate choice for a young girl.

Prostitution harms the fabric of society. Sexual intercourse outside of marriage or a relationship of love shows disregard for the sanctity of the sexual act and for the other partner in a relationship. Emotional commitment is inextricably linked to physical commitment.

Feminists overwhelmingly oppose prostitution. The radical feminist school that emerged in the 1990s supports the idea that prostitution leads to the objectification of women. Men who use women's bodies solely for sexual gratification do not treat them as people. This lack of respect dehumanizes both the prostitute and the client and does not represent a victory for either sex.

How can you prove that some individuals who visit prostitutes would otherwise have committed violent offenses? Psychological therapies that recommended the use of prostitutes have been widely discredited. The number of reported attacks on prostitutes and the considerably greater number of such crimes that go unreported suggest that prostitutes are the victims of the most serious crimes. In Victoria, where prostitution is legal, two rapes of prostitutes are reported each week.

More sexual health problems are inevitable. When prostitution is lawful and socially acceptable, a greater number of men will use prostitutes. Medical studies show that the condom is only 99% effective. Moreover, during the period between each health check, a prostitute could contract and transmit a sexually transmitted disease. Consequently, the legalization of prostitution will result in the transmission of more potentially fatal diseases.

PROS

Legalizing prostitution would break the link between prostitutes and pimps. Pimps physically abuse prostitutes and often threaten greater violence; they confiscate part, if not all, of their earnings, and often encourage the women to become addicted to drugs. Providing a secure environment in which to work frees men and women of pimps.

Licensed brothels will improve the quality of life for people who live and work in areas currently frequented by prostitutes. Regulations can require brothels to locate in areas away from homes and schools.

Existing legal prohibitions against prostitution do not work. Prostitutes are regularly arrested and fined. To pay the fines, they must prostitute themselves. The laws banning prostitution are counterproductive.

Legalizing prostitution would give governments economic benefits. A tax on the fee charged by a prostitute and the imposition of income tax on the earnings of prostitutes would generate revenue.

The problem of a high concentration of "sex tourists" in a small number of destinations will disappear once a larger number of countries legalize prostitution. Supporting this motion, therefore, will reduce the problem of sex tourism.

CONS

The legalization of the Bunny Ranch in Nevada did not prevent the majority of prostitutes from continuing to work outside of the licensed brothel and remain dependent on pimps. Licensed brothels are expensive for prostitutes to work in and for clients to visit. A legal business has to pay for rent, health checks and security; prostitutes working outside the "system" need not worry about such expenses. Some prostitutes use private apartments, while others work on the street. Legalizing prostitution will not remove the street market or the dangers associated with it. The dangerous street environment is a consequence of economics, not legal controls.

Prostitutes will continue to work on the streets and are unlikely to work near the competition offered by the licensed brothels. Furthermore, will local governments want to create "ghettos" of prostitution in certain areas?

Merely because some individuals break a law does not mean that the law itself is at fault or that it should be abolished. The ease with which prostitutes can return to work suggests that penal sanctions should be more severe rather than removed altogether.

An economic benefit cannot offset social harms that result from the legalization of certain prohibited activities. Otherwise we would encourage governments to become involved in other unlawful trades including trafficking in drugs. Moreover, sex workers are unlikely to declare their true earnings from what is a confidential relationship between the worker and client. Thus the amount of revenue generated is likely to be slight.

Legalizing prostitution would render the country in question a destination for sex tourists. Relaxed legal controls on prostitution in Thailand, the Philippines, and the Netherlands have made these countries attractive to these undesirable individuals.

Sample Motions:

This House would legalize prostitution.

This House would legalize brothels.

This House would decriminalize prostitution.

Web Links:

- Bazelon, Emily. <http://www.slate.com/id/2186243> Presents research and arguments both in favor of and against legalizing prostitution.
- Liberator, Mark. <http://www.liberator.net/articles/prostitution.html> Article in favor of legalizing prostitution.
- Raymond, Janice G. <http://action.web.ca/home/catw/attach/Ten%20Reasons%20for%20Not%20Legalizing%20Prostitution.pdf> Ten reasons for not legalizing prostitution.

Further Reading:

de Marneffe, Peter. Liberalism and Prostitution. Oxford University Press, 2009.

Matthews, Roger. Prostitution, Politics & Policy. Routledge-Cavendish, 2008.

Weitzer, Ronald. *Legalizing Prostitution: From Illicit Vice to Lawful Business*. New York University Press, 2011.

Weitzer, Ronald, ed. *Sex For Sale: Prostitution, Pornography, and the Sex Industry*. Routledge, 2009.

▪ ▪

REBUILDING AFTER DISASTERS, GOVERNMENT ROLE IN

Over the past decade, the United States has been buffeted by a series of disasters, from 9/11 to Hurricane Katrina, and, more recently, Hurricane Sandy. Traditionally, Americans have looked to government to play a major role in rebuilding efforts, but following allegations of corruption and inefficiency in reconstructing the Gulf Coast after Katrina, citizens began to reevaluate the roles of the public and private sectors in recovery. Hurricane Sandy hit the heavily populated US East Coast in October 2012, leaving approximately $50 billion of damage in its wake. The aftermath of this hurricane, which occurred just days before the US general election, was, understandably, politicized. While many viewed the response of the Federal Emergency Management Agency (FEMA) as illustrative of exactly why federal government is essential to disaster management, some politicians, and political commenters, disagreed. These critics suggest that individual states, or even private insurance companies, are better equipped to deal with disasters.

PROS

Because of its immense resources, only the federal government can help regions recover from massive disasters quickly and efficiently. Most states do not have the financial ability to rebuild nor do they have the expertise to coordinate a massive reconstruction campaign. Hurricane Sandy affected over 50 million people in the United States, dispersed across 24 different states. At that scale, the federal government was essential for coordination. States must rely on federal entities like FEMA that have experience in dealing with overwhelming and continuing crises.

One of the most important government responsibilities is to provide for the protection and welfare of its citizens, and this includes crisis and recovery management. When a tornado, earthquake, or hurricane strikes, the government bears primary responsibility for restoring citizens' lives to order. Financing rebuilding efforts is necessary to help individuals recover from incredible personal loss and community tragedy.

The government has an obligation to promote the economic redevelopment of regions hit by natural disasters. Rebuilding homes and business ensures that communities

CONS

Government-sponsored rebuilding efforts are notoriously inefficient and prone to fraud. In the wake of Katrina, millions of dollars of government assistance were given to "victims," who spent the money on frivolities ranging from exotic dancers to diamond rings. Government rebuilding efforts, because of their scale and scope, are bureaucratic and ponderous, and do not necessarily respond to cases of greatest need. In contrast, the private sector has a vested financial interest in efficiency and fraud prevention.

Government rebuilding programs are not the answer to disaster recovery efforts; this is why individuals and businesses buy and maintain fire, home, building, and flood insurance. Private insurance agencies, which specialize in emergency management and disaster recovery, are the only organizations fully prepared to take on such huge tasks. They can work efficiently and effectively to manage the rebuilding process because for them, time is money. They have no reason to delay the rebuilding effort.

The government certainly has a responsibility to fix destroyed infrastructure; however, individuals should rely on their insurance to rebuild their homes. Individuals return to work and their normal lives as quickly as possible. We all contribute to each other's well-being when we pay taxes and should expect to get something in return when we are in need. Individuals, families, and businesses affected by disasters are taxpayers, and if a disaster were to strike another region, their tax money would go to support citizens in those areas. Citizens must accept this fact if they are to expect the benefits for themselves one day.

who cannot afford disaster insurance should not live in high-risk areas such as flood plains or other low-lying areas that could be negatively affected by natural disasters. They should not look to government (and the taxpayers) to bail them out because they made the poor decision to live in a potentially dangerous location.

Many communities were established long before they were known to be in locations that are vulnerable to disaster. Changes in climate, and subsequent incidences of dangerous weather events such as floods and hurricanes, are a consequence of collective behavior, and therefore should be dealt with collectively. Living in an area afflicted by disaster is usually not a result of poor decision making—individuals are completely unable to predict one-off disasters, such as terrorist attacks. Making communities responsible for events entirely outside of their control is both unfair and illogical.

Communities that are located in areas prone to flooding or other natural disasters should not be repeatedly rebuilt at the public's expense; this constant rebuilding is a futile waste of money. Instead of being rebuilt, these communities should relocate, or disperse, to areas that are more suitable. Throughout history, settlements have been abandoned once they were shown to be inappropriate places to live; by refusing to face this reality, communities that remain in disaster-prone areas are merely delaying the inevitable and wasting huge amounts of government resources as they do so.

Sample Motions:

This House believes that the federal government bears primary responsibility for rebuilding after a disaster.

This House believes that when disaster strikes, government should employ all means necessary to assist affected areas.

This House believes that taxpayers should not be responsible for disaster relief outside of their community.

Web Links:

- <http://www.fema.gov/safer-stronger-protected-homes-communities>. Educates the public about how to protect homes and communities. Different teams and programs offered by FEMA are discussed.
- <http://www.fema.gov/disaster-process-disaster-aid-programs>. FEMA covers the steps in response to a disaster.
- <http://www.wilsoncenter.org/publication-series/after-the-disaster-rebuilding-communities>. Links to seminar papers highlighting different approaches to disaster relief and arguments for and against heavy government involvement in community rebuilding.

Further Reading:

Birch, Eugenie et al. *Rebuilding Urban Places After Disaster: Lessons from Hurricane Katrina.* University of Pennsylvania Press, 2006.

Cooper, Christopher. *Disaster: Hurricane Katrina and the Failure of Homeland Security.* Times Books, 2006.

Davidson, Colin, Gonzalo Lizarralde, and Cassidy Johnson. *Rebuilding After Disasters: From Emergency to Sustainability.* Routledge, 2009.

Hackler, M.B. *Culture after the Hurricanes: Rhetoric and Reinvention on the Gulf Coast.* University Press of Mississippi, 2013.

Seidman, Karl F. *Coming Home to New Orleans: Neighborhood Rebuilding After Katrina.* Oxford University Press, 2013.

■ ■

REDISTRICTING, CONGRESSIONAL

In the United States, determining boundaries for electoral districts for the House of Representatives has always been controversial. Those controlling the process of drawing district lines have generally been politicians themselves. In a majority of states, state legislatures still draw these boundaries, but a number of states are gradually moving to make redistricting the responsibility of independent commissions. Much litigation has resulted from fights over redistricting, although courts have been reluctant to intervene except when redistricting impinges on the federal Voting Rights Act, which seeks to remove racial impediments to voting. In recent years, computer technology has been utilized to plot likely voting patterns on a street-by-street basis, allowing legislators to redraw boundaries with increased accuracy, and ensure continued partisan advantage. Critics view this as undemocratic, with politicians essentially picking their own voters, rather than voters freely choosing their representatives. Partisan redistricting can often lead to distorted electoral results, with the popular vote going to a losing candidate. For example, Republicans swept into power in state legislatures in 2010 and redrew House district boundaries in their favor in several key states—subsequently, in 2012, Republicans retained their majority in the House of Representatives despite Democratic candidates having received more votes nationwide. Ultimately the debate over whether districts should be redrawn by an independent authority or by state legislatures is about the allocation of institutional and electoral power. Thus, it is necessary to determine what principles should drive the process. The linking of communities of interest, the preservation of districts as geographically contiguous and compact, and the maintenance of electoral competition within a district are the three principles that advocates of reform suggest should be given priority.

PROS

When politicians control the process of drawing electoral boundaries, the result is always having district boundaries drawn to maximize the partisan advantage of those who control the redistricting process. Thus, electoral districts often do not reflect discrete geographic and cultural communities of interest; instead, they are gerrymandered along partisan lines. In Texas, for example, following gains in the state legislature in 2002, Republicans' creative redrawing of legislative districts changed the makeup of their congressional delegation from 17 Democrats and 15 Republicans to 21 Republicans and 11 Democrats after the 2004 election.

The process of redistricting in the United States has resulted in the creation of the "majority–minority" districts where state legislatures seek to devise districts where national ethnic minorities are in the majority, notably African American districts. This is bad not only because it favors one section of the population over another, but also because it sends the message that ordinary electoral districts are incapable of representing all constituents. In addition, grouping black voters together in one, often very irregularly shaped, district removes them from several neighboring districts that, in consequence, contain clear white majorities. In Southern states, some have characterized this as conservative politicians allowing black voters to be represented by a few

CONS

Granting state legislatures the power to draw districts boosts their ability to craft districts that appropriately reflect what they feel are communities of interest within their state. Statisticians and demographers should not be the ones deciding who should be classed together, the representatives of the people should be making those decisions. The public's confidence in electoral institutions is confirmed when their elected representatives are clearly in control. Californians, when faced with the opportunity to vote for an independent commission in a 2006 ballot initiative, rejected the change.

The "majority–minority" district was an appropriate response to the enormous prejudice and historical discrimination that African American candidates faced and continue to face in running for office. These districts have guaranteed a consistent legislative voice on issues concerning African Americans—we cannot confidently maintain that African Americans would otherwise have a voice in governance. In the "winner-takes-all" simple plurality system used in most US elections, the only way for minorities to gain representation is for districts to be created that give them the electoral voice they would otherwise be deprived of.

token black Democratic representatives, while ensuring that several safe Republican seats are created in the surrounding "white" districts.

Allowing politicians to control redistricting results in districts changing more than they otherwise would. This impedes democratic accountability because voters lose their sense of what district they are a part of and who is representing them. Putting redistricting under the control of a neutral commission would ensure that changes occur only when population shifts require that new boundaries be drawn.

Party political control of redistricting often serves to reduce competition. Invariably districts are drawn to protect incumbents, thus reducing the level of electoral competition. In the 2004 congressional election, more than 99% of House members seeking reelection won. This is in contrast to countries that have independently drawn districts. In the 2007 federal election in Australia, approximately 25% of lower house seats changed hands. The easy reelection of incumbents in the United States reduces the incentive for representatives to address constituent issues and energetically advocate for their communities. At a national level, party political control of redistricting reduces the ability of the electorate to hold legislators to account and to shape the country's future direction.

Oddly shaped partisan districts create a range of administrative difficulties. First, challengers must conduct a more difficult and expensive campaign in the district because the district's residents are not a logical community or communities of interest. Second, given that local counties are responsible for administering elections, more expense is incurred when districts straddle county lines. Third, uncertainty about the districts is made worse in jurisdictions where state legislatures cannot agree on boundaries and battles over districts head to the courts.

Federal districts drawn by state legislatures upset the relationship between the different levels of government. State politicians have an unfair advantage over their federal counterparts as they have the power to redraw district boundaries to make federal seats either safer or more marginal for an incumbent. This often leads to federal politicians meddling in state politics and trying to engineer district changes through local loyalists.

If voters are too lazy to read a map or to research who their representative is, then their participation in the process of choosing a government would not be informed and thus not promote democratic accountability. In any case, officials can widely disseminate information about electoral changes or relax absentee voting rules to ensure the franchise of these citizens is protected.

The fact that incumbents are reelected testifies more to the power of incumbents to raise money and sustain a strong media profile than to the need for independent redistricting. No amount of partisan redistricting ever removes competition. In 1990, Democrats in Georgia attempted to redraw districts to reduce electoral competition from Republican rivals. This strategy was only briefly successful: a 9:1 delegation favoring Democrats after the 1992 election became an 8:3 delegation favoring Republicans after the 1994 elections. At the national level, a good number of House seats changed hands in the 2010 midterm elections, allowing the Republicans to gain control of the House.

Administrative difficulties occur only if you assume that legislature-drawn districts never reflect communities of interest. Often, legislators are in a better position than bureaucrats to recognize distinct political and cultural communities and draw district lines to include them. Also, debates about redistricting and redistribution occur in every democracy regardless of whether independent commissions or legislatures create the districts.

State control of the process of determining district boundaries is the very essence of federalism. Ensuring that the districts reflect a distribution of interests as determined by the state itself is necessary for effective federal representation. Encouraging federal politicians to take an interest in state-level issues also probably benefits public policy development.

This House would end the gerrymander.

This House would draw its districts straight.

This House believes that the United States should introduce an independent redistricting commission.

This House maintains that politicians should lose control over electoral redistricting.

Web Links:

- Brookings Institution. "Redistricting Reform." <http://www.brookings.edu/articles/2005/0601politics_mann.aspx> Overview of the issue.
- Common Cause. "Redistricting." <http://www.commoncause.org/site/pp.asp?c=dkLNK1MQIwG&b=196481> Summary of recent reform efforts.
- United States Election Project. "Redistricting." <http://elections.gmu.edu/Redistricting.html> Overview of reform efforts.

Further Reading:

Bullock, Charles S., III. *Redistricting: The Most Political Activity in America*. Rowman & Littlefield, 2010.

Levitt, Justin, with Bethany Foster. *A Citizen's Guide to Redistricting*. Brennan Center for Justice, 2008.

Mann, Thomas E. *Redistricting: A Guide for Reformers*. Brookings Institution Press, 2008.

■ ■

RELIGION IN POLITICS

Secularism, the principle that government and state institutions should be kept separate from religion, is a cornerstone of the modern Western democracy. While some nations, such as France, keep this division strict and absolute, most allow some degree of religious expression to enter the political sphere. In the United States, the degree to which this should be allowed is fiercely debated. The First Great Awakening made Christianity deeply personal to most Americans, fostering a sense of spiritual conviction that often translated to political conviction. The political force of this religious conviction can be observed in movements such as the Temperance Movement and the Civil Rights Movement. While few advocate an official US state religion—the Constitution expressly prohibits this—religious belief permeates contemporary US politics, used as a means to evaluate politicians and frame policy debates. Critics of this practice believe that inserting religion into politics is fundamentally un-American, and a potential route to discrimination and religious tyranny. However, others view religious belief as inextricable from personal morality, and therefore essential to political discourse.

PROS

The use of religious speech in political debate is exclusionary, as these arguments are inaccessible to anyone outside of that particular religion. Civil discourse should be rational and comprehensible to all; it should provide a platform whereby all citizens can engage with political issues. Therefore, a politician must be able to explain his or her stance on political issues without discussing religion. Every political debate, even those regarding social policy, can be framed in nonreligious terms, using fiscal, ethical, or scientific explanations, all of which stem from rational discourse that will not alienate citizens outside a particular religion. Fully removing religion from politics is essential to ensure the full inclusion of all citizens, which is the foundation of a healthy democracy.

CONS

Religious arguments in politics are no different from moral arguments. Politicians often justify their political positions using personal moral beliefs—such as justice or equality—that transcend rational explanation; religion simply provides a clear basis for these moral positions. Though the specific beliefs and practices of religions may differ, the values derived from religion unite us. Any voter who can understand a moral argument about harm or fairness should be able to evaluate a religious argument. Furthermore, voters are free to discard any religious argument that does not concur with their own moral beliefs; religious language and teachings are used to enhance moral arguments, not replace them. Prohibiting religious speech from political discussion merely impedes communication between citizens and politicians.

Religious beliefs are not empirical—that is, based on observable evidence—and therefore, are not open to modification as our understanding of the world develops. While moral beliefs can evolve—for example, changing views of homosexuality or the rights of women—religious beliefs stagnate. Basing political discussion and policy decisions on beliefs that, by their very nature, refuse to adapt, despite evidence to the contrary, is incompatible with a society that wants its laws to reflect the best understanding of human nature and the world around us.

The Constitution explicitly bans any religious test for holding public office; by allowing the religious beliefs of politicians to be explored publicly, we essentially make certain religious beliefs a prerequisite to office, which functions as a religious test. Despite the broad range of different religions in the United States, there has never been a non-Christian US president, and there are very few non-Christians in government at all. In 2012, Mitt Romney, a Mormon, was the Republican candidate for president. Despite the strong links between Mormonism and Christianity, and the large Mormon demographic in the United States, one in five Americans reported that they would not vote for a Mormon even if he were qualified for office. By including religious discussions in the political sphere, qualified candidates are discarded simply because they fail a religious test.

The First Amendment to the Bill of Rights was designed to prevent organized religion from influencing government and vice versa. In the words of Thomas Jefferson, the framers intended to create a "wall of separation between church and state"— this clearly prohibits religious language and debate in the political sphere. By allowing the government to make political decisions for expressly religious reasons, this wall of separation has been breached.

If politicians are permitted to publicly align themselves with a religion, the government, and therefore the state, will inevitably adopt the religious beliefs of the majority. By allowing the majority religion to essentially become the state religion, minority religions are left open to persecution, as happened in Europe throughout the eighteenth century. James Madison recognized that "a majority . . . united by a common interest or a passion cannot be constrained from oppressing the minority." By

Religious beliefs are not incompatible with progressive thought or open-minded discussion; most scientists and visionaries throughout history have grounded their work in religious belief. In fact, religious movements often drive developments in morality and serve to advance society's views on right and wrong. For example, most leading figures in the Civil Rights Movement were motivated by their religious faith. A politics infused with religious teachings allows for developments in human understanding, while retaining the core values that direct these developments.

The Constitution forbids an official state religious test, it does not prevent voters from voting on whatever basis they choose. Voters choose candidates based on a broad range of characteristics, many of which are discriminatory; if voters are able to discriminate against candidates because of gender or ethnicity, there is no reason why they should not also be able to base their decision on religious beliefs. It is also a fallacy that religious political discussions only lead to discrimination for non-Christians—during the 2008 presidential campaign, vice presidential nominee Sarah Palin was routinely asked about her religious beliefs, with many voters discounting her for being "too Christian." Furthermore, a 2011 report by the Pew Research Center found that many small religious groups, including Jews, had a greater representation in Congress than in the general population, while others, including Muslims and Buddhists, were equally represented in Congress and the population.

The First Amendment was not designed to exclude religion from the political sphere—it was designed to prevent the establishment of a state religion. The Free Exercise and Establishment clauses of the First Amendment protect a politician's right to hold any religious belief; the First Amendment also protects an individual's right to free speech, allowing politicians to discuss their religion as they see fit. The Jeffersonian "wall of separation" was intended to allow all Americans freedom *of* religion, not to guarantee them freedom *from* religion.

The US system of government, based around a separation of powers, already limits the force of the majority, making a "tyranny of the majority" unfeasible. The Constitution includes several super-majoritarian checks on simple majorities, in addition to a comprehensive set of inalienable rights, which prevents a religious majority from oppressing minority religious groups. Though Protestants make up the majority of the US population, they have never used this majority to oppress other

PROS	CONS
permitting politicians to unite around religious belief, the United States risks a tyranny of the religious majority.	denominations; in fact, in 1960, the United States—a nation with a Protestant majority—elected John F. Kennedy, a Catholic, as president.

Sample Motions:

This House would keep church and state separate.

This House supports the inclusion of religious values and dialogue in the political sphere.

Web Links:

- Americans United for Separation of Church and State. < http://www.au.org/> Educational organization promoting the constitutional separation of church and state.
- New York Times. "A Church–State Solution" <http://www.nytimes.com/2005/07/03/magazine/03CHURCH. html?pagewanted=all> Overview of the US separation of church and state, and a look at the current issue of evangelical Christians in politics.
- New Yorker. "Tea with Simon Critchley: The Separation of Church and State Is Impossible." <http://www.newyorker.com/online/blogs/books/2012/02/simon-critchley-faith-of-the-faithless.html> Argues that true secularism is unattainable.
- Salon. "Avenging Angel of the Religious Right." <http://www.salon.com/2004/01/06/ahmanson/> Article about Howard F. Ahmanson, a leading campaigner for the conservative Christian political movement.

Further Readings:

Griffith, Marie, and Melani McAlister. *Religion and Politics in the Contemporary United States.* Johns Hopkins University Press, 2008.

Hamburger, Philip. *Separation of Church and State.* Harvard University Press, 2004.

Miller, Nicholas. *The Religious Roots of the First Amendment: Dissenting Protestants and the Separation of Church and State.* Oxford University Press, 2012.

■ ■

RELIGION: SOURCE OF CONFLICT OR PEACE?

Religion has always been one of the most influential forces in the world. It has been a force for peace, but it also has served as a cause, if not a genuine reason, for some of the greatest wars. Today, with the growth of Muslim fundamentalism in Islamic areas, the Western world views religious extremism as the great threat. The events of September 11, 2001, proved that such concerns were justified; however, the war on terror led by the West caused resentment among those for whom Islam was a peaceful source of spiritual stability. So what is religion today? Is it harmful or good? If it can be a source of conflict, can it serve as an instrument of resolution as well?

PROS

Religion is a stronger force than any material incentives. It is far better at directing behavior toward social betterment than either laws or physical force. For example, both Gandhi and Martin Luther King, Jr., conducted nonviolent protests based on religious values.

CONS

Religion is extremely dangerous because it can be used to justify brutal actions. The Inquisition carried out its torture in the name of God. Hitler's followers, among them the so-called German Christians, were also believers in their Führer. Religion should never be involved in politics because it can be used as an instrument of control or to achieve a ruler's aims.

PROS

The very existence of theocratic states, e.g., Iran, proves that religion can be a legitimate source of political power. Governments in theocratic states are much more stable than in secular countries because leaders are viewed as appointed by God. Political stability, in its turn, leads to economic welfare.

Biblical commandments are the basis of Western ethical and legal systems. Religion teaches us tolerance for people of other races and religions. Usually believers are more peaceful and tolerant than nonbelievers.

In the states where religion develops freely and people have free access to places of worship, churches have always served as a shelter for the poor. Some of the greatest works of art were created in the name of God. Furthermore, Woodrow Wilson suggested that a strong affinity exists between religious commitment and patriotism. Love of country, just like love of God, certainly inspires good deeds.

Most wars are not started by religion, although religion often serves to justify them. Most wars are started for economic reasons or for territorial gain.

Western states grew as a result of religion and religious philosophy. Western European and North American societies are still based on Protestant ideals of diligence, thrift, and moderation.

CONS

Theocratic states become totalitarian regimes because they are based on obedience to a ruler who is seen as God's representative rather than on a democratic constitution.

Religions like Islam justify "holy" wars against the "unfaithful," meaning people of other religions. Religious convictions like these paved the way for the terrorist attacks of September 11.

Religion has led to the creation of great art but it has also led to its destruction. Remember the Taliban's destruction of the great Buddhas in Afghanistan? Still worse, religion can be a source of extreme nationalism. In Islam, Christianity, and Judaism, God is described as "mighty warrior," "just king," or "righteous judge." He punishes the unjust, the unrighteous, and the disobedient. The idea that a nation is the instrument of God's will has led to war and the subjugation of people viewed as ungodly.

Whether religion is a genuine reason for war or only its pretext is not important. What is vital is that religion can be and is often used to make people fight in the name of high ideals to further aims of hatred. Thus, religion causes more harm than good.

North American nations emerged only because of economic factors: the existence of famine and overpopulation in Europe on the one hand, and the free markets of the United States on the other. The realities of capitalism, not the tenets of religious faith, prompt people to be diligent and thrifty.

Sample Motions:

This House believes that religion is a positive influence on people.

This House believes that church and state must be kept separate.

Web Links:

- Berkley Center for Religion, Peace and World Affairs. <http://berkleycenter.georgetown.edu/programs/religion-conflict-and-peace> The website of Georgetown University's Religion, Peace and World Affairs program; contains links and resources on a variety of relevant issues.
- Catholic New Times. <http://www.highbeam.com/doc/1G1-133410990.html> Rabbi Dow Marmur's remarks on whether faith is a source of conflict or peace.
- Journal of Religion, Conflict and Peace. <http://religionconflictpeace.org/archive> Archive of a journal that addresses the problems and possible solutions that religion creates.

Further Reading:

Beck, Ulrich, and Rodney Livingstone. A God of One's Own: Religion's Capacity for Peace and Potential for Violence. Polity, 2010.

Leiter, Brian. Why Tolerate Religion? Princeton University Press, 2013.

Pearse, Meic. The Gods of War: Is Religion the Primary Cause of Violent Conflict? IVP Books, 2007.

Ross, Jeffrey Ian. Religion and Violence: An Encyclopedia of Faith and Conflict from Antiquity to the Present. M. E. Sharpe Reference, 2010.

■ ■

RELIGIOUS GARB/SYMBOLS IN PUBLIC PLACES, BAN ON

Turkey, a secular state with a predominantly Muslim population, has traditionally banned headscarves in public buildings, such as schools and courts. In 2004, France introduced a ban on religious symbols in public schools; though the ban prohibited all symbols, it was created primarily in response to the wearing of headscarves by Muslim schoolgirls. Such bans are intended to maintain a secular society and ease cultural assimilation of religious minorities. These bans are controversial because, rather than ease tensions, they have made minority groups feel targeted, apparently repressed religious freedom, and exacerbated cultural tensions.

PROS

Religious garb makes others uncomfortable and alienates them from the wearer. Wearing such symbols indicates that the individual's identity is dictated by religion. This puts off those who are not members of that religion. Religious symbols communicate: "I follow this religion and its beliefs" and thus also communicate any xenophobic hostility associated with that religion.

If the government does not ban religious garb, many who do not wish to wear such symbols will feel socially pressured to do so. For example, a schoolgirl may not wish to wear a headscarf, but if all of her classmates do, she will feel pressured to conform to avoid being ostracized.

Religious symbols and clothing in public hinder the state's ability to remain secular. Religious garb serves as a constant reminder that the individual is acting not only based on his own judgment, but according to the rules of a particular faith. When religious symbols are commonplace, they serve as a constant reminder that society is not being governed by the rule of law made by human beings.

A government cannot avoid imposing some values on its citizens. Murder is condemned by the Sixth Commandment, yet no one would claim that banning homicide

CONS

Religious garb promotes diversity and cultural awareness, reducing discomfort and hostility between people of differing beliefs. Banning religious symbols simply perpetuates ignorant contempt for the unfamiliar. When people interact with a person wearing religious garb, they are better able to appreciate that person's multidimensional identity and are less likely to assume that a particular religion breeds hate or endorses other perverse values.

A ban on religious symbols and garb is the "quick-fix" in this situation; it will not ease an underlying culture clash. The government would more effectively promote universal free religious expression by penalizing harassment and launching awareness campaigns about respect for individual religious choices.

The choice to wear religious symbols does not render a person incapable of functioning in a secular society. A religious person in a secular society may develop ethics according to his religion, letting them guide how he lives his life without expecting others to abide by his values. Furthermore, we should not underestimate the personal benefit a religious person receives from wearing religious symbols; such symbols function as a constant reminder to the individual of her religious beliefs, aiding her in her goal of consistent adherence to her faith.

A ban on religious garb prevents a government from being truly secular. Religious garb is often not only a form of expression; in the case of headscarves, for example, it establishes a religious government. Many governments require children to be vaccinated and/or attend school, or prevent businesses from discriminating on the basis of race or gender, even though these practices are contrary to the tenets of certain religions. As long as the ban prohibits all religious symbols, it avoids passing judgment on specific religions.

A ban on religious symbols in public creates a gradual societal change. Although religious individuals may initially react negatively and withdraw from the public, most will adapt to the idea of a secular public, thus reducing, in general, the use of oppressive religious garb.

Laws should not be dismissed simply because they are difficult to enact correctly; more thought should be put into such legislation. Certainly we can create legislation that bans all religious symbols and then scrutinize enforcement to ensure it is consistent. Furthermore, a clear line exists between religious garb and clothes with political slogans. When an individual wears a cross, another person would reasonably assume that person to be a Christian. An individual wearing a shirt related to a political debate or espousing philosophical wisdom is communicating an opinion, but no one would assume that person is proclaiming affiliation with a particular religion.

is essential to practicing a belief in modesty. A secular state ought not impose beliefs or practices upon citizens. Interfering with religious practices that do not harm others is to claim particular religious ideas wrong or bad, thereby indirectly claiming that other religions are better. To be truly secular, the state cannot pick and choose which practices are acceptable.

A ban that seeks to liberate citizens from oppressive religious practices will oppress them even more. Some religious people will forgo their symbols—others will remove themselves from public places. Turkey instituted a headscarf ban in an attempt to liberate women; in 2008, the Turkish Parliament voted to lift the ban because many women were not seeking higher education or careers because of their religious convictions. The adverse effects of such a ban are exacerbated for women who are externally pressured to wear a scarf; such women are even more oppressed if they must depend on their husbands and male relatives to conduct any public business on their behalf.

A ban on religious garb will inevitably be enforced unfairly. A universal ban will only be enforced against controversial symbols; in 2004, France banned religious symbols in public schools. However, schools generally do not penalize Christian students for wearing crosses or Jewish boys for yarmulkes, rather, they target Muslim girls for wearing headscarves. More generally, "religious garb" is a vague category, especially because religious beliefs are intertwined with philosophy and politics. Should Quakers be allowed to wear shirts with antiwar slogans? Their opposition is rooted in their faith. If a shirt bears a quote by Confucius, is it a religious symbol? To ban all garb that can be associated with religious beliefs would have the overwhelming effect of stifling expression and curtailing public debate.

Sample Motions:

This House bans religious symbols and garb.

This House protects free expression of religion.

This House seeks a secular country.

Web Links:

- The Huffington Post. "France Burqa Ban: French Parliament Approves Ban on Face Veils." <http://www.huffingtonpost.com/2010/07/13/france-burqa-ban-french-p_n_644433.html> Article discussing France's proposition to ban burqas and the social tensions underlying the debate.

- Time Magazine. "Turkey at Odds over Headscarf Ban." <http://www.time.com/time/world/article/0,8599,1711292,00.html> Article addressing the political debate in Turkey over its headscarf ban; discusses both the advantages and dangers of allowing headscarves in public buildings.

Further Reading:

Elver, Hilal. *The Headscarf Controversy: Secularism and Freedom of Religion.* Oxford University Press, 2012.

Evans, Malcolm David. Manual on the Wearing of Religious Symbols in Public Places. Council of Europe Publishing, 2009.

Gerdes, Louise. *Should Religious Symbols Be Allowed on Public Land?* Greenhaven Press, 2011.

Howard, Erica. *Law and the Wearing of Religious Symbols: European Bans on the Wearing of Religious Symbols in Education.* Routledge, 2011.

■ ■

SAME SEX MARRIAGE

American society increasingly supports equal rights for gays and lesbians in areas such as housing, employment, public accommodations, and so on. Nevertheless, many continue to oppose granting homosexuals the right to marry or to formally register their unions with the state. In 2000, Vermont became the first state to grant gay and lesbian couples marriage-like status; in 2004, Massachusetts became the first state to recognize same-sex marriage. During the 2012 election campaign, President Obama spoke out in favor of same-sex marriage, marking a shift in his position on the issue. By early 2013, same-sex marriage was legal in 12 states and the District of Columbia. However, under the 1996 Defense of Marriage Act (DOMA), other states are not required to recognize these marriages; thirty-six states have constitutional amendments or statutes defining marriage as only between a man and a woman. Additionally, DOMA granted federal recognition only to marriages between a man and a woman, meaning that same-sex spouses were excluded from all federal benefits granted to married couples. However, on June 26, 2013, the Supreme Court declared this section of DOMA to be "a deprivation of the equal liberty of persons that is protected by the Fifth Amendment," therefore ruling it unconstitutional. This ruling made all marriage equal in the eyes of the federal government. On the same day, the Supreme Court also dismissed an appeal regarding Proposition 8—California's referendum banning same-sex marriage—making California the thirteenth US state to legalize same-sex marriage.

PROS

The refusal of governments to permit gays to marry is one of the last areas of discrimination against gays. The state should permit gay couples to marry as a means of professing their love to and for each other. Societal views ought to change with the times.

Permitting gay couples to marry would enable them to take advantage of the various financial benefits accorded to heterosexual married couples.

We must modify religious attitudes to reflect changes in society. Many religious views are no longer justifiable (e.g., the notion that women are inferior to men). Conversely, if religious institutions oppose gay marriage as against their beliefs, they should accept civil marriages.

Marriage is not merely an institution for raising children. Many married couples do not have children. In addition, the number of single-parent families is increasing. In any case, many countries permit gay singles and couples to adopt. Advances in medical science also enable gay

CONS

While contemporary society should reject discrimination in general, some forms of discrimination can be objectively justified. Society has always viewed marriage as a heterosexual institution, the religious and/or civil union between a man and a woman.

Many of the financial benefits that married couples enjoy are not designed to encourage marriage per se but to promote the conventional family.

Historically marriage has been a religious institution. Because most major world religions frown on homosexuality, they would find gay marriage unacceptable.

Historically society has viewed child rearing as the major purpose of marriage. Because gay couples are unlikely to have children, they have no need for marriage.

PROS	CONS
couples to have children through artificial insemination and the use of surrogate mothers.	
A "registered union" is an alternative to gay marriage. However, this arrangement is unacceptable because gay couples still would not enjoy the same rights as married heterosexual couples. Moreover, registering would imply that gay couples had an inferior status to married heterosexual couples, thus leading to discrimination.	Numerous countries, including Germany, Ireland, and Switzerland, permit the registered union of gay couples. Registered couples are entitled to joint insurance coverage and enjoy inheritance and tenants' rights. Registration makes no incursions into the sanctity of the institution of marriage. Consequently, it should prove acceptable to the religious sections of society.

Sample Motions:

This House would allow gay couples to marry.

This House would give homosexuals equal rights.

This House believes that discrimination can never be justified.

Web Links:

- Baker, Joshua. <http://www.marriagedebate.com/pdf/iMAPP.May2008.pdf> Provides an overview of important court cases related to gay marriage.
- Kolasinski, Adam. <http://tech.mit.edu/V124/N5/kolasinski.5c.html> Presents a secular argument against gay marriage.
- The Pew Forum on Religion and Public Life. <http://pewforum.org/Gay-Marriage-and-Homosexuality/An-Argument-Against-Same-Sex-Marriage-An-Interview-with-Rick-Santorum.aspx#why> Interview with former US senator opposed to gay marriage; links to an opposing article.
- Pinsky, Drew. <http://larrykinglive.blogs.cnn.com/2010/08/04/dr-drew-prop-8-tramples-on-basic-civil-rights/> Argues against a California constitutional amendment (overturned in 2010) that defined marriage as only between a man and a woman.
- Soller, Kurt. <http://www.newsweek.com/2008/12/15/the-good-book-and-gay-marriage.html> Debate between two religious experts on the religious permissibility of gay marriage.

Further Reading:

Babst, Gordon A. *Moral Argument, Religion, and Same-Sex Marriage: Advancing the Public Good.* Lexington Books, 2009.

Myers, David G., and Letha Dawson Scanzoni. *What God Has Joined Together: The Christian Case for Gay Marriage.* Harper San Francisco, 2006.

Sullivan, Andrew. *Same Sex Marriage: Pro and Con.* Rev. and updated ed. Vintage, 2004.

■ ■

SCHOOL UNIFORMS

Traditionally, students in American parochial schools and some private schools have worn uniforms. Only a smattering of public schools had uniform policies until the mid-1990s, when Long Beach, California, mandated uniforms in an effort to stop school crime. The apparent success of the measure combined with studies indicating that students in many schools with uniform policies performed better academically than those without, opened a floodgate of uniform adoption. Currently, around one in four schools, both public and private, has a policy of mandatory uniforms. The average cost of this to parents is $249 per year. To avoid legal challenges, school districts now make provision for students who cannot afford uniforms or for parents to opt out of the uniform requirement.

PROS

Uniforms help create a strong sense of community, thus promoting discipline and helping raise academic standards. Creating a sense of belonging within the larger group does not alienate students based on socioeconomic gaps, but, rather, is a great equalizing force and pushes students to look at their similarities rather than their differences. Educators frequently adopt uniforms when trying to revive failing schools in order to develop these important attributes in students. Though it is important to encourage cultural diversity in a student body, it is also important for students to assimilate with their peers, promoting social inclusion—school uniforms help to accomplish this.

Wearing uniforms acts as a socioeconomic equalizer not just with fellow students but with teachers and administrators as well; all students are equal in the eyes of the school and of each other. In institutions without uniforms, students are often competitive in dress and worry endlessly about their appearance. Pupils without expensive, trendy clothes may become social outcasts. Many parents prefer uniforms because they save money.

Uniforms have practical benefits outside the school building. If students are identified with a particular institution, they may be more aware of their behavior. They also may be more considerate of others while traveling to and from the school. On organized trips, teachers find it easier to keep track of and monitor the behavior of students when they can be identified through uniforms.

Uniforms make it easy for teachers to monitor dress codes fairly. School administrators and students constantly battle about what clothing is appropriate in schools without uniforms.

Uniforms prepare students for life after graduation. Even in work environments where there is not a standard, company-issued dress uniform, businesses often expect a business or business casual dress code that requires employees to look professional at all times.

CONS

Uniforms suppress individualism and discourage students from accepting responsibility for aspects of their own lives. They encourage teachers to view students as a group rather than as individuals with different personalities and abilities. Uniforms were better suited to an age of rote learning and military-style discipline. They do not belong in modern education, which encourages the imagination and intellectual exploration that is becoming increasingly important in the wider economy. Many schools, indeed many countries, manage to maintain high standards of discipline, community, and academic performance without adopting uniforms.

Students always find ways to tease or bully others regardless of what clothes are worn. Teachers are professionals and do not judge their students based on clothing. In fact, having a school uniform policy interferes with the ability of school staff to focus on teaching and asks them to enforce yet another nonacademic policy. Furthermore, parents often find some uniform items, such as jackets, very expensive and complain that they can never be worn outside the school.

Uniforms make students very identifiable, which has largely negative consequences. Uniforms emphasize the divisions between schools, increasing the possibility of bullying and fights between students from rival institutions. They can also lead to discrimination, with the uniforms functioning as social markers; students who are identified as being from private schools are given preferential treatment over those who are identified as being from schools in low-income communities.

Often it is the uniform that is inappropriate—not warm enough in winter or too hot in summer—largely because it is badly designed and cheaply produced. Girls complain about being forced to wear skirts even in the coldest months. Some groups, such as conservative Muslims, may oppose specific uniform styles for cultural reasons.

The business world is increasingly relaxed about dress codes, thus making the schools that insist on uniforms archaic and out of touch. There is no evidence that adults who attended schools without uniforms struggle in the workplace. Furthermore, if a school wants to prepare students for the workplace, they can implement a dress code, which reflects an office setting much more closely than a uniform does.

■ ■

SCHOOL VOUCHERS

Over the past decades, Americans have been increasingly concerned about the quality of public education, particularly in inner-city neighborhoods, where many public schools are failing. One of the most controversial suggestions for improving education for all children is to establish school voucher programs. Although the specifics of these programs vary with locality, all would distribute monetary vouchers to parents who could then use them to help pay the cost of private, including parochial (religious), schools. Critics fear that vouchers would further damage public schools and argue that they subvert the separation of church and state. Supporters say they will help the children most in need.

PROS

The current public education system is failing countless students, particularly in inner-city neighborhoods. In an era where education is the key to success, these children are not being provided with the chance to develop the skills necessary to compete in the modern world. Vouchers give poor parents the ability to send their children to better schools. These children should not be sacrificed while we wait for public school reform.

The competition for students will force all schools to improve. They will have to use their resources to educate their students rather than squander them on bureaucracies as many do today. Eventually, the unsalvageable

CONS

The American public education system has been central to American democracy. It has provided education for all children regardless of their ethnic background, their religion, their academic talents, or their ability to pay. It has helped millions of immigrants assimilate and provided the civic education necessary for future citizens to understand American values. Establishing a voucher system is saying that we are giving up on public education. Instead of giving up, we should put our efforts into reforming the system.

The competition for students would destroy inner-city public schools. Much of their student body would flee to "better" private schools, leaving inner-city schools with little to no funding. Most states' funding of public schools will close and the others will grow stronger, producing an overall better learning environment. The market will regulate the education produced.

schools is determined by number of students enrolled. If enrollment lags, then the school is not as well funded as it was the previous year. If enrollment booms, then funding increases. Thus, even if urban schools are motivated to improve they will lack the resources to do so.

The money would help some families, and that is worth the risks. Not all students in nonperforming schools will be able to attend a private school. However, after the students who can afford such an opportunity leave nonperforming schools, more resources will be available at those nonperforming schools to educate the remaining students. Private schools would have no reason to change admission standards or tuition, nor is there reason to think that a great swell in private school enrollment would result.

The government vouchers are not monetarily substantial enough to give true financial aid to students. They are not large enough to help poor students go to private schools. The vouchers make private education more affordable for people who could already afford it. In addition, private schools may not be willing to accept all students with vouchers. They could always raise tuition or standards for admission, neutralizing any impact vouchers would have.

Vouchers will eventually lead to a school system that is liberated from bureaucrats and politicians, enabling educators and parents to determine how best to educate children.

Voucher programs would set up a school system that is not accountable to the public. Investigations of current programs in Milwaukee, Wisconsin, and Cleveland, Ohio, have found unlawful admissions requirements, illegally imposed fees, and even fraud.

No violation of the separation of church and state would occur. No student would be forced to enter a religious school. Only families and students interested in a private or religious education would use the vouchers. Any students who desired a more traditional curriculum would be allowed to study in public schools.

Vouchers involve the indirect giving of public funds to religious schools. This transfer of funds amounts to a violation of the doctrine of separation of church and state.

Sample Motions:

This House believes that the government should cease the use of school vouchers.

This House recommends that educational vouchers be used for private and parochial schools.

This House believes that the issuing of vouchers by the government is justified.

Web Links:

- Anti-Defamation League. "School Vouchers: The Wrong Choice for Public Education." <http://www.adl.org/vouchers/vouchers_main.asp> An anti–school voucher website containing a detailed report outlining many reasons why vouchers are a poor policy option.
- BalancedPolitics.org. "Should Government Vouchers Be Given to Pay for Private Schools, Even if They're Religious Schools?" <http://www.balancedpolitics.org/school_vouchers.htm> Discussion of the pros and cons of school vouchers.
- Snell, Lisa, and David Tokofsky. "The Great Voucher Debate." <http://www.latimes.com/news/opinion/la-op-dustup13feb13,0,7261921.story> Two experts debate whether or not school vouchers are beneficial.

Further Reading:

Barrera-Osorio, Felipe et al. *Emerging Evidence on Vouchers and Faith-Based Providers in Education: Case Studies from Africa, Latin America and Asia.* World Bank Publications, 2009.

Gill, Brian P. *Rhetoric Versus Reality: What We Know and What We Need to Know About Vouchers and Charter Schools.* RAND Corporation, 2007.

Howell, William G., and Paul E. Peterson. *The Education Gap: Vouchers and Urban Schools.* Brookings Institution Press, 2006.

Ramirez, Al. *Financing Schools and Educational Programs: Policy, Practice, and Politics.* Rowman and Littlefield Education, 2012.

■ ■

SEX EDUCATION IN SCHOOLS

For years conservatives and liberals in the United States debated whether schools should teach sex education or whether this responsibility is that of the parents. With the rise of teenage pregnancies and sexually transmitted diseases, particularly AIDS, the focus has shifted to what should be taught, rather than where. Should schools advocate sexual abstinence (refraining from sexual activity until the age of consent or marriage), or should society assume that the students will be sexually active and therefore encourage teaching safe sex?

PROS

The primary cause of unwanted pregnancies and the spread of sexually transmitted diseases (STDs) is ignorance about safe sex. The AIDS crisis of the 1980s and 1990s has shown that sex education must be a vital part of the school curriculum and may be supplemented by frank discussion at home.

As the US Guidelines for Comprehensive Sexuality Education (1991) state, "all sexual decisions have effects or consequences" and "all persons have the . . . obligation to make responsible sexual choices." While Hollywood promotes casual, thoughtless sex as the norm, teacher-led discussions can encourage responsible attitudes about sexual relationships.

Abstinence is an outdated approach based on traditional religious teaching. Some young people may choose it, but we cannot expect it to be the norm. Teenagers express their sexuality as part of their development. Having sex is not the problem; having unsafe sex or hurting people through sexual choices is.

CONS

Judging by the number of teenage pregnancies and the continuing spread of STDs, teenagers are not getting the message. Sex education in schools can be counterproductive because teens find it fashionable to ignore what teachers advocate. The most effective channel for sex education is the media, particularly TV, films, and magazines.

This is the wrong approach. Sex education in the classroom encourages young teenagers to have sex before they are ready and adds to peer pressure to become sexually active. In addition, any class discussion may lead to ridicule, thus devaluing the message. Sexual responsibility should be discussed in a one-to-one context, either with older siblings or parents.

Classroom education should promote abstinence. Sex education encourages sexual promiscuity. Advocating both safe sex and restraint is self-contradictory. Children are at risk of severe psychological and physical harm from having sex too young and should be encouraged to abstain.

Sample Motions:

This House believes that sex education should take place at home.

This House would rather not discuss it with its parents.

Web Links:

- Masland, Molly. "Carnal Knowledge: The Sex-Ed Debate." <http://www.msnbc.msn.com/id/3071001/> Article discussing sex education debate in the United States.
- NPR. "Sex Education in America." <http://www.npr.org/templates/story/story.php?storyId=1622610> Report on sex education in the United States.
- Thomson, Alice. "Sex Education: Why the British Should Go Dutch." <http://www.human-being.nl/Library/sex_education .htm> Article on why England should liberalize sex education programs in state schools.

Further Reading:

Fields, Jessica. *Risky Lessons: Sex Education and Social Inequality.* Rutgers University Press, 2008.

Kendall, Nancy. *The Sex Education Debates.* University of Chicago Press, 2012.

Luker, Kristin. *When Sex Goes to School: Warring Views on Sex — and Sex Education — Since the Sixties.* Norton, 2007.

■ ■

SINGLE-SEX SCHOOLS

Studies have shown that boys gain more academically from studying in coeducational schools, but that single-sex schools promote greater achievement in girls. But academic results are not the only criterion on which to judge the success of the education system. In 1996, a long-standing controversy over the Virginia Military Institute's male-only policy resulted in a landmark US Supreme Court ruling that the Institute must admit women. However, the Court left room for private (i.e., not state-run) single-sex institutions and for the establishment of such schools where needed to redress discrimination.

PROS

Women benefit from a single-sex education. Research shows that girls in single-sex schools participate more in class, develop much higher self-esteem, score higher in aptitude tests, are more likely to choose "male" disciplines such as science in college, and are more successful in their careers. In *Who's Who*, graduates of women's colleges outnumber all other women. The United States has only 83 women's colleges.

Children in the formative years, between 7 and 15, gravitate to their own sex. They naturally tend toward behavior appropriate to their gender. Thus implementing an education strategy geared specifically toward one gender makes sense. Certain subjects, such as sex education or gender issues, are best taught in single-sex classrooms.

Boys and girls distract each other from their studies, especially in adolescence as sexual and emotional issues arise. Too much time can be spent attempting to impress or even sexually harass each other. Academic competition between the sexes is unhealthy and only adds to unhappiness and anxiety among weaker students.

Single-sex schools (such as the Virginia Military Institute) are a throwback to the patriarchal society of the past; historically in many cultures, only men were allowed an education of any sort. Such single-sex institutions both remind women of past subservience and continue to bar them from full social inclusion.

Teachers themselves are often discriminated against in single-sex schools; a boys' school will usually have a largely male staff where women may feel uncomfortable or denied opportunity, and vice versa.

CONS

A 1998 survey by the American Association of University Women, a long-time advocate of single-sex education, admitted that girls from such schools did not show academic improvement. That women from single-sex schools are more inclined to study math and science is of questionable importance to society. As the report noted, "Boys and girls both thrive when the elements of good education are there, elements like smaller classes, focused academic curriculum and gender-fair instruction." These conditions can be present in coeducational schools.

The formative years of children are the best time to expose them to the company of the other gender so that they learn each other's behavior and are better prepared for adult life. The number of subjects benefiting from single-sex discussion is so small that this could easily be organized within a coeducational system.

In fact boys and girls are a good influence on each other, engendering good behavior and maturity, particularly as teenage girls usually exhibit greater responsibility than boys of the same age. Academic competition between the sexes is a spur to better performance at school.

Single-sex schools for women are a natural extension of the feminist movement; men have had their own schools, why shouldn't women? If single-sex schools existed only for men, then that would be discriminatory; however, as long as both genders have the choice of attending a single-sex institution (or a coeducational one), you cannot call it discrimination.

Teachers frequently favor their own gender when teaching coeducational classes; for example, male teachers can undermine the progress and confidence of girl students by refusing to call on them to answer questions.

Sample Motions:

This House believes in single-sex education.

This House believes that boys and girls should attend separate schools.

This House would educate boys and girls separately.

Web Links:

- Asthana, Anushka. "Single-Sex Schools 'No Benefit for Girls.'" <http://www.guardian.co.uk/uk/2006/jun/25/schools.gender> Article discussing the lack of benefits for girls from single-sex education.
- Garner, Richard. "Single-Sex Schools 'Are the Future.'" <http://www.independent.co.uk/news/education/education-news/singlesex-schools-are-the-future-1023105.html> Article discussing the future of single-sex education.
- National Association for Single Sex Public Education <http://www.singlesexschools.org/> Arguments in support of single-sex schools.
- Zelon, Helen. <http://www.citylimits.org/news/articles/3971/inside-schools-designed-for-black-and-latino-boys> Discusses the benefits of single-sex schools specifically for black and Hispanic boys.

Further Reading:

Chadwell, David W. *A Gendered Choice: Designing and Implementing Single-Sex Programs and Schools.* Corwin, 2009.

Rivers, Caryl, and Rosalind C. Barnett. *The Truth About Girls and Boys: Challenging Toxic Stereotypes about Our Children.* Columbia University Press, 2011.

Spielhagen, Frances R. *Debating Single-Sex Education: Separate and Equal?* R&L Education, 2007.

Wiens, Kathryn L. *Boys Who Achieve: An Examination of Single-Sex Schools in a Coeducational College Preparatory School.* VDM Verlag Dr. Müller, 2008.

· ·

SMOKING, TOTAL BAN ON

Although most countries place age restrictions on the purchase of tobacco, over a billion adults smoke legally every day. Supplying this demand is big business. By the 1990s, major tobacco companies had been forced to admit that their products were addictive and had serious health consequences, both for the user and for those subject to secondhand smoke. In the developed world, public opinion shifted against smoking. Many governments substantially increased taxes on tobacco to discourage smoking and to help pay for the costs of smoking-related illness. In addition, most US states and European nations implemented some type of smoking ban in enclosed public spaces. Though these restrictions were often controversial at first, they are now widely accepted: a 2009 poll of EU citizens found that 84% supported bans on smoking in offices, while 65% supported smoking bans in bars and clubs. However, anti-smoking campaigners do not think that these bans go far enough, and would like to see further restrictions, including an outright ban on all tobacco products.

PROS

Smoking is extremely harmful to the smoker's health. The American Cancer Society estimates that tobacco causes up to 400,000 deaths each year—more than AIDS, alcohol, drug abuse, car crashes, murders, suicides, and fires combined. Worldwide some 3 million people die from smoking each year, one every 10 seconds. Estimates suggest that this figure will rise to 10 million by 2020. Smokers are 22 times more likely to develop lung cancer than nonsmokers, and smoking can lead to a host of other health problems, including emphysema and heart

CONS

While a government has a responsibility to protect its population, it also has a responsibility to defend freedom of choice. The law prevents citizens from harming others. It should not stop people from behavior that threatens only themselves. Dangerous sports such as rock climbing and parachuting are legal. No laws have been passed against indulging in other health-threatening activities such as eating fatty foods or drinking too much alcohol. Banning smoking would be an unmerited intrusion into personal freedom.

disease. One of the main responsibilities of any government is to ensure the safety of its population; that is why taking hard drugs and breaking the speed limit are illegal. Putting a ban on smoking would therefore be reasonable.

Of course, personal freedom is important; we should act against the tobacco companies, not individuals. If a company produces food that is poisonous or a car that fails safety tests, the product is immediately taken off the market. All cigarettes and other tobacco products are potentially lethal and should be taken off the market. In short, smoking should be banned.

Smoking is not a choice because nicotine is an addictive drug. Evidence suggests that tobacco companies deliberately produce the most addictive cigarettes they can. Up to 90% of smokers begin when they are under age 18, often due to peer pressure. Once addicted, continuing to smoke is no longer an issue of free choice, but of chemical compulsion. The government should ban tobacco just as it does other addictive drugs like heroin and cocaine because it is the only way to force people to quit. Most smokers say that they want to kick the habit, so this legislation would be doing them a favor.

Most smokers are law-abiding citizens who would like to stop. They would not resort to criminal or black market activities if cigarettes were no longer legally available; they would just quit. Banning smoking would make them quit and massively lighten the burden on health resources.

The effects of smoking are not restricted to smokers. Secondhand smoke jeopardizes the health of nonsmokers as well. Research suggests that nonsmoking partners of smokers have a greater chance of developing lung cancer than other nonsmokers. Beyond the health risks, smoke also can be extremely unpleasant in the workplace or in bars and restaurants. Smoking causes discomfort as well as harm to others and should be banned.

At the very least all tobacco advertising should be banned and cigarette packs should have even more prominent and graphic health warnings.

Cigarettes are very different from dangerous cars or poisonous foods. Cigarettes are not dangerous because they are defective; they are only potentially harmful. People should still be permitted to smoke them. A better comparison is to unhealthy foods. Fatty foods can contribute to heart disease, obesity, and other conditions, but the government does not punish manufacturers of these products. Both cigarettes and fatty foods are sources of pleasure that, while having serious associated health risks, are fatal only after many decades. They are quite different from poisonous foods or unsafe cars, which pose high, immediate risks.

Comparing tobacco to hard drugs is inaccurate. Tobacco is not debilitating in the same way that many illegal narcotics are, it is not comparable to heroin in terms of addictiveness, and it is not a mind-altering substance that leads to irrational, violent, or criminal behavior. It is much less harmful than alcohol. Many other substances and activities can be addictive (e.g., coffee, physical exercise) but this is no reason to make them illegal. People are able to abstain—many give up smoking every year—if they choose to live a healthier life. Nevertheless, many enjoy smoking as part of their everyday life.

Criminalizing an activity of about one-sixth of the world's population would be insane. As America's prohibition of alcohol during the 1920s showed, banning a popular recreational drug leads to crime. In addition, governments would lose the tax revenue from tobacco sales, which they could use to cover the costs of health care.

The evidence that passive smoking causes health problems is very slim. At most, those who live with heavy smokers for a long time may have a very slightly increased risk of cancer. Smoke-filled environments can be unpleasant for nonsmokers, but reasonable and responsible solutions can be found. Offices or airports could have designated smoking areas, and many restaurants offer patrons the choice of smoking and nonsmoking sections. Allowing people to make their own decisions is surely always the best option. Restricting smoking in public places may sometimes be appropriate; banning it would be lunacy.

Where is the evidence that either of these measures would affect the rate of tobacco consumption? Cigarette companies claim that advertisements merely persuade people to

PROS	CONS
	switch brands, not start smoking. People start smoking because of peer pressure. Indeed, forbidding cigarettes will make them more attractive to adolescents. As for health warnings, if the knowledge that cigarettes have serious health risks deterred people from smoking, then no one would smoke. People start and continue to smoke in the full knowledge of the health risks.

Sample Motions:

This House would ban tobacco.

This House would not smoke.

This House would declare war on the tobacco industry.

Web Links:

- Center for Disease Control and Prevention: Tobacco. <http://www.cdc.gov/tobacco/index.htm> Research, data, and reports relating to tobacco as well as tobacco industry documents and campaigns for tobacco control.
- Phillip Morris. <http://www.philipmorrisusa.com> Major tobacco company site offering government reports on tobacco as well as information on tobacco issues, including the marketing of tobacco products.
- Smoking From All Sides. <http://smokingsides.com/docs/stat.html> Links to statistics and hundreds of articles on both sides of the argument.
- The Tobacco Homepage. <http://www.tobacco.org> Provides recent information on tobacco-related issues as well as documents, timelines, and links to all aspects of the tobacco controversy.
- World Health Organization. "Tobacco Free Initiative." <http://www.who.int/toh/> Information on WHO's worldwide program to stop smoking, as well as background information on the economic, health, and societal impact of tobacco and smoking.

Further Reading:

Bearman, Peter S., Kathryn M. Neckerman, and Leslie Wright. *After Tobacco: What Would Happen If Americans Stopped Smoking?* Columbia University Press, 2011.

Boyle, Peter et al. *Tobacco: Science, Policy and Public Health.* Oxford University Press, 2010.

Kluger, Richard. *Ashes to Ashes: America's Hundred-Year Cigarette War, the Public Health, and the Unabashed Triumph of Philip Morris.* Random House Digital, 2010.

▪ ▪

SPACE EXPLORATION

The space programs of both the US and the USSR were the most important prestige projects of the Cold War. From the launch of the first artificial satellite, Sputnik, in 1957, through to the first human space flight by Yuri Gagarin in 1961, the first moon landing in 1969, and beyond, both superpowers invested huge amounts of money in outdoing each other in the Space Race. After the end of the Cold War, however, future space exploration projects became more international. Russia shifted its focus to providing space for international passengers aboard its Soyuz rockets, and NASA gradually shut down its shuttle program. Furthermore, the European Space Agency and China are quickly rising as important members of the space exploration community. That said, the future of space exploration is falling increasingly in the hands of private corporations. Private enterprise is now heavily involved in pioneering work, such as asteroid mining, which seeks to extract valuable minerals from space, and sending the first manned mission to mars. Mars One, a Dutch company, has secured substantial private investment in order to establish the first human presence on Mars by the early 2020s, and, in 2012, a group of Internet entrepreneurs announced the formation of a venture to mine asteroids. The shift of space exploration away from state governments is controversial, as many believe that space is a common good and should not be exploited by individuals for private gain.

PROS

Humankind always struggles to expand its horizons. The curiosity that constantly pushes at the boundaries of our understanding is one of our noblest characteristics. The exploration of the universe is a high ideal; space truly is the final frontier. The instinct to explore is fundamentally

human; already some of our most amazing achievements have taken place in space. No one can deny the sense of wonder we felt when for the first time a new man-made star rose in the sky, or when Neil Armstrong stepped onto the Moon. Space exploration speaks to that part of us that rises above the everyday.

The exploration of space has changed our world. Satellites allow us to communicate instantaneously with people on different continents and to broadcast to people all over the world. The Global Positioning System allows us to pinpoint locations anywhere in the world. Weather satellites save lives by giving advance warning of adverse conditions; together with other scientific instruments in orbit they have helped us gain a better understanding of our world. Research into climate change, for example, would be almost impossible without the data provided by satellites.

Space exploration has had many indirect benefits. The space program has brought about great leaps in technology. The need to reduce weight on rockets led to the microchip and the modern computer. The need to produce safe but efficient power sources for the Apollo missions led to the development of practical fuel cells, which are now being explored as possible power sources for cleaner cars. The effects of zero gravity on astronauts have substantially added to our knowledge of the workings of the human body and the aging process. We can never know exactly which benefits will emerge from the space program in the future, but we do know that we will constantly meet new obstacles and in overcoming them will find new solutions to old problems.

Space exploration is an investment in the future. Our world is rapidly running out of resources. Overpopulation could become a serious worldwide threat.

CONS

High ideals are all well and good, but not when they come at the expense of the present. Our world is marred by war, famine, and poverty, with billions of people struggling simply to live from day to day. Our dreams of exploring space are a luxury we cannot afford. Instead of wasting our time and effort on prestige projects like the space program, we must set ourselves new targets. Once we have addressed the problems we face on Earth, we will have time to explore the universe, but not before then. The money spent on probes to distant planets would be better invested in the people of our own planet. A world free from disease, a world where no one lives in hunger, would be a truly great achievement.

Satellite technology has benefited humankind. However, launching satellites into Earth orbit differs significantly from exploring space. Missions to other planets and into interstellar space do not contribute to life on our planet. Moreover, most satellites are commercial; they are launched and maintained by private companies. Space exploration requires huge government subsidies and will never be commercially viable. For example, the Voyager missions alone cost almost $1 billion. This money could be better spent elsewhere.

These auxiliary advantages could have come from any project. They are a result of giving people huge amounts of money and manpower to solve problems, not a result of a specific program. For example, many of the advances in miniaturization were the result of trying to build better nuclear missiles; this is not a good reason to continue building nuclear weapons. Similar resources would be far better devoted to projects with worthier goals, for example, cancer research or research into renewable energy sources. These, too, could provide many side benefits, but would tackle real problems.

Space exploration is a waste of resources. If we want to tackle the problems of overpopulation or of the depletion of resources, we must address them on Earth instead of

PROS

Consequently, ignoring the vast potential of our own solar system — mining resources on asteroids or other planets, or even colonizing other worlds — would be foolish. If we fail to develop the ability to take advantage of these possibilities, we may find it is too late.

CONS

chasing an elusive dream. We can deal with the problems of our planet in practical ways, and we must tackle them with all the resources and all the political will we have.

Sample Motions:

This House would explore the universe.

This House would explore the Final Frontier.

This House would reach for the stars.

Web Links:

- Cornwell, Rupert. "The Big Question: Is Manned Space Exploration A Waste of Time and Money?" The Independent–Science. <http://www.independent.co.uk/news/science/the-big-question-is-manned-space-exploration-a-waste-of-time-and-money-8035031.html> Pros and cons of space exploration.
- Dubner, Stephen J. "Is Space Exploration Worth the Cost? A Freakonomics Quorum." <http://freakonomics.blogs.nytimes.com/2008/01/11/is-space-exploration-worth-the-cost-a-freakonomics-quorum/> Several experts discuss whether space exploration is worth the cost.
- Silver, Matt. "In Defense of Space Exploration." <http://tech.mit.edu/V123/N66/mattsilver.66c.html> Argues that space exploration has important social and scientific value.

Further Reading:

Solomon, Lewis D. *The Privatization of Space Exploration: Business, Technology, Law and Policy.* Transaction, 2011.

Schmitt, Harrison H. *Return to the Moon: Exploration, Enterprise, and Energy in the Human Settlement of Space.* Springer, 2006.

Tkatchova, Stella. *Space-Based Technologies and Commercialized Development: Economic Implications and Benefits.* IGI Global, 2011.

United States Astronautics. *The Practical Values of Space Exploration.* General Books, 2010.

▪ ▪

STEM CELL RESEARCH

Stem cells are biological cells that can develop into specialized cells, such as muscle tissue or brain cells. Research has shown that these cells are able to repair diseased or damaged tissues; doctors and researchers believe that stem cells have the potential to cure conditions such as diabetes, heart disease, paralysis, Parkinson's disease, and Alzheimer's disease. However, ethical issues surround stem cells as they are obtained from embryos that are destroyed in the process. Though stem cells can be derived from adult cells, most of these stem cells are not able to develop into any other specialized cell, thus limiting their usefulness. Ethical objections to stem cell use center on the belief that an embryo is a human life that should not be destroyed under any circumstances — in this sense the debate echoes the debate on abortion, with those who are antiabortion tending to oppose stem cell use. To limit the destruction of embryos, the US government only permits researchers to use embryos discarded during in vitro fertilization treatments — embryos that would be destroyed anyway. However, those who believe that an embryo is equivalent to a human life still consider this immoral. In 2008, President Barack Obama lifted a 2004 ban on government funding for stem cell research, leading to an upsurge in scientific developments. Despite these achievements, many remain uncomfortable with the use of embryonic stem cells and call for a ban on any stem cell research or treatment that uses embryos.

PROS

Although stem cell research involves the creation and destruction of thousands of embryos, the benefits are so great as to outweigh moral considerations. Once the research goals have been achieved, the use of embryo treatments can be greatly reduced. Scientists are already reaping important medical benefits from stem cells. In April 2013, a two-year-old girl received a new windpipe that had been engineered using stem cells.

We already accept the creation and destruction of "spare" embryos for cycles of in vitro fertilization (IVF). IVF facilitates the creation of human life. Stem cell treatments will save existing human lives. The infertile will still survive. The sufferers of Huntington's chorea or Alzheimer's disease will not. If we accept the morality of IVF, we must accept the morality of stem cell treatment.

The creation, storage, and destruction of embryos can be strictly controlled. There should be no fear of "Frankenstein science."

The moral status of the embryo is distinct from that of the fetus. What reason is there to assert that life begins at the stage of embryo creation? The accepted test for clinical death is the absence of brain stem activity. The fetus first acquires a functioning brain six weeks after the embryo has been created. We cannot condone the "wastage" of human embryos. However, we must be wary of regarding the loss of an embryo as the loss of human life.

We cannot equate human embryos with human beings just because they could develop into adults. Between 50% and 70% of embryos are lost naturally through failure to implant in the wall of the uterus. The potential of an embryo to develop does not of itself make the embryo human.

Further research requires the use of the stem cells found in embryos. Research done with adult cells has yielded very little progress because of the difficulty of "reprogramming" an adult cell to develop as the particular neuron or tissue cell required. The greater understanding of human cells that scientists will gain from research with embryo stem cells may increase the utility of adult cells in the future. For the present, resources should be concentrated on research with stem cells harvested from embryos.

CONS

Merely hoping for a good outcome does not make immoral actions acceptable. Medical research should be governed by moral and ethical concerns. No matter how much sympathy we feel for sufferers of terminal diseases, we cannot tolerate the use of human embryos as means to an end. Stem cell research is inherently contradictory: lives would be created and then destroyed in order to save other lives.

The loss of embryos in IVF is a reason to condemn IVF treatment. It is not a reason for allowing another procedure that will sacrifice much more potential life.

Media fears of mad scientists free to manipulate and destroy human life may be overstated. However, research projects carry a significant risk that thousands of embryos will be destroyed for little or no scientific gain.

The embryonic human should have the same moral status as the fetus or the child or the adult. At what physiological point do we declare an embryo "human?" Are we to base a declaration of being human on physical appearance? That the embryo looks different from the fetus and from the adult does not prove that the embryo is not a human being.

The proper test of humanity should be whether the embryo has the potential to organize itself into a "living human whole." Every embryo has this capacity. The fact that embryos are lost naturally does not imply that the destruction of embryos is morally acceptable.

Researchers have no need to use embryo stem cells. Research has continued for many years into the use of adult stem cells. These cells are replaceable and could be used for the purposes of treatment and research without the destruction of embryos.

Sample Motions:

    This House would prohibit stem cell research.

    This House supports the use of embryo stem cells when adult cells cannot be used.

    This House believes that the state should support stem cell research.

Web Links:

- American Catholic. "Stem-cell Research and the Catholic Church." <http://www.americancatholic.org/news/stemcell/> Presents religious and moral arguments against stem cell research.
- International Society for Stem Cell Research. <http://closerlookatstemcells.org/Top_10_Stem_Cell_Treatment_Facts.html> Basics of stem cell science.
- NOVA Online. <http://www.pbs.org/wgbh/nova/miracle/stemcells.html> Article by a member of the National Institutes of Health Human Embryo Research Panel in support of embryonic stem cell research.

Further Reading:

    DeGrazia, David. *Creation Ethics: Reproduction, Genetics, and Quality of Life.* Oxford University Press, 2012.

    Kumar, Dhavendra. *Genomics and Health in the Developing World.* Oxford University Press, 2012.

    Peters, Ted. *Sacred Cells? Why Christians Should Support Stem Cell Research.* Rowman & Littlefield, 2008.

■ ■

TARGETED KILLING

Targeted killing is the intentional killing, by a government or its agents, of an individual outside of their custody or legal jurisdiction. The term "targeted killing" is not defined under international law; it gained currency in 2000 after Israel instituted a policy of targeted killing against suspected terrorists in Palestine. Though not a new practice, targeted killing has become more prevalent following the terrorist attacks of September 11, 2001. Employing methods such as cruise missiles, drone strikes, and special operations raids, targeted killings are a central component of US counterterrorism efforts. Perhaps the highest-profile US military victory of recent times, the May 1, 2011 killing of Al-Qaeda head, Osama bin Laden, was the result of a special operations raid. Targeted killing is a controversial practice, with critics alleging that it violates international law. However proponents see it as necessary for national security in an era of unconventional warfare.

PROS

Targeted killing is the most effective method of countering terrorism. Some of the greatest threats to US national security, including Osama bin Laden and Anwar al-Awlaki, have been eliminated by targeted killings. Both of these terrorist leaders were hiding in ally territories at the time of their deaths and therefore could not have been neutralized using traditional military practices. The success of these high-profile killings extends beyond the deaths of dangerous individuals. By targeting and killing terrorist leaders, the US is projecting its military might and dissuading others from engaging in terrorism.

By using targeted killings, instead of traditional warfare, the US has improved its image abroad and strengthened relations with allies. President Barack Obama,

CONS

Targeted killing exacerbates terrorism by contributing to the sense of injustice that fuels it. According to Pir Zubair Shah, of the Council on Foreign Relations, anti-Americanism in Pakistan is incited by the widespread belief that US drone attacks are a "scourge targeting innocent civilians." This anger is the foundation upon which anti-US terrorism grows. Rather than countering terrorism, targeted killing intensifies the problem. Instead of focusing on targeted killings, which simply creates more terrorists for every individual eliminated, antiterrorist efforts should seek to build bridges with the communities in which terrorists recruit.

Targeted killings have stressed US relations with key allies in the "war on terror." Following the US invasion of Afghanistan, many key terrorist leaders fled across who has relied heavily on targeted killings, is one of the most internationally respected US presidents of recent times, as evidenced by his 2009 Nobel Peace Prize. In contrast, President George W. Bush's more traditional military efforts, specifically his invasions of Iraq and Afghanistan, drew widespread international condemnation. With numerous nations falling victim to international terrorism, targeted killings benefit the global community in its entirety. The 2011 killing of bin Laden was celebrated as a global victory against terrorism; state leaders from Italy, France, Kenya, and Israel, to name just a few, released statements praising the action. Targeted killings have united the world behind the US antiterrorist campaign.

Targeted killing greatly reduces civilian deaths. According to a US government official, 1,300 militants and only 30 civilians have been killed by drone strikes since mid-2008, with no civilian fatalities since August 2010. These numbers are broadly reflected by *The Long War Journal*, a blog that tracks terrorist groups, which calculated that 1,114 militants and 94 civilians had been killed in Pakistan since 2006. By comparison, the wars in Iraq and Afghanistan resulted in the deaths of several hundred thousand civilians, though exact estimates vary. As precision weaponry technology develops, the civilian casualties associated with targeted killings will only decrease. While no military tactic is perfect, targeted killing is far superior to all of the alternatives.

Targeted killing is fully in accord with international law. Though the specific term "targeted killing" is not defined under international law, Article 51 of the UN Charter states that all countries have the inherent right to self-defense; targeted killings are simply a way of exercising this right. Countries have used targeted killing as a counterterrorism tool for many years and the international community has come to accept this practice.

Targeted killings are not illegal under US law. Though Executive Order 12333, issued by President Ronald Reagan in 1981, prohibits assassinations, this legislation is concerned with the killing of foreign leaders during peacetime. The order's use of the term "assassination" denotes a type of murder—distinct from targeted killings, which are done in self-defense. As former federal judge, Abraham Sofaer, wrote: "killings in self-defense are no

the border into Pakistan, making Pakistan a vital ally in the fight against terrorism. Rather than strengthening this essential relationship, targeted killings, and particularly the US's heavy use of drone strikes, have weakened it. Following a November 2011 clash between American and Pakistani troops along the Afghan/Pakistan border, Pakistan threatened to shoot down any US drones in their airspace. In April 2012, the Pakistani parliament voted unanimously to demand an end to US drone strikes on its territory, labeling the actions a violation of their state sovereignty. A Pew Research Center poll reported that the majority of people from every country polled, apart from the United States, opposed targeted killing. Terrorism is a global problem and to successfully fight it the United States should be nurturing international cooperation, rather than alienating itself.

Targeted killing does not adequately reduce civilian death, as most targets operate within civilian populations. The numbers of civilian deaths reported by the US government are manipulated by the use of an unreasonably narrow definition of who constitutes a civilian; all military-age males in a strike zone are considered combatants unless they are proved innocent, which is hard to do and can only happen after they are already dead. Official Pakistani sources claim that 700 civilians were killed in 2009 alone. In fact, rather than avoid civilians, many strikes seem to target them. Ben Emmerson, a UN special investigator, reported that "[It is] alleged that since President Obama took office at least 50 civilians were killed in follow-up strikes when they had gone to help victims and more than 20 civilians have also been attacked in deliberate strikes on funerals and mourners."

Targeted killing violates international human rights law, which permits lethal force outside conflict zones only to prevent an imminent attack that cannot be stopped by any other means. Killing suspected terrorists, who could be captured and put on trial, does not meet this criterion. Instead, targeted killings constitute "extrajudicial executions," which are illegal.

Targeted killing violates US law. Executive Order 12333 states that no "person employed by or acting on behalf of the United States Government shall engage in, or conspire to engage in, assassination." Assassination is the intentional killing of a targeted individual—a definition that clearly encompasses targeted killing. The term "targeted killing" was coined by the Israeli government to legitimize the assassination of Palestinian leaders; in

PROS	CONS
more 'assassinations' in international affairs than they are murders when undertaken by our police forces against domestic killers." If it is agreed that the targeted killings of terrorists are done to defend civilian lives, then the killings cannot be termed assassinations, or deemed illegal.	practice the two terms are synonymous, and, therefore, targeted killing violates the US ban on assassination.

Sample Motions:

This House believes that targeted killing is the most effective counter-terrorism strategy.

This House believes that targeted killings are effective at minimizing civilian deaths.

This House believes that targeted killings improve US sentiment abroad.

This House believes targeted killing violates US and international law.

Web Links:

- Jaffer, Jameel and Nathan Wessler. <http://www.guardian.co.uk/commentisfree/2012/jun/06/targeted-killing-campaign-propaganda> Criticizes the secrecy of the US government about targeted killing.
- Masters, Jonathan. <http://www.cfr.org/counterterrorism/targeted-killings/p9627> Presents both sides of the argument.
- Ofek, Hillel. <http://www.thenewatlantis.com/publications/the-tortured-logic-of-obamas-drone-war> Talks comprehensively about targeted killing from both sides.
- Statman, Daniel. <http://philo.haifa.ac.il/staff/statman/papers%20in%20english/E23.pdf> Discusses Just War Theory in the context of targeted killing.

Further Reading:

Altman, Andrew, Claire Finkelstein, and Jens David Ohlin. *Targeted Killings: Law and Morality in an Asymmetrical World.* Oxford University Press, 2012.

Hunter, Thomas. *Targeted Killing: Self-Defense, Preemption, and the War on Terrorism.* BookSurge, 2009.

Scahill, Jeremy. *Dirty Wars: The World Is a Battlefield.* Nation Books, 2013.

■ ■

TERRORISM, JUSTIFICATION FOR

In the wake of the shocking events of September 11, 2001, terrorism and the "war on terror" became the number one issue for the US government. But terrorism has a far longer, more global history. Political, religious, and national/ethnic groups have resorted to violence to pursue their objectives—whether full recognition of their equal citizenship (in Apartheid South Africa), a separate national state of their own (Israelis in the 1940s, Palestinians from the 1970s onward), or the establishment of a religious/ideological state (Iranian terrorism against the Shah). In some cases former terrorists have made the transition to peaceful politics—for example, Nelson Mandela in South Africa and Gerry Adams in Northern Ireland. Is it possible to justify the use of terrorist tactics if they result in the deaths of innocent civilians in bombings and shootings? This is an issue that calls into question the value we put on our ideals, beliefs, and human life itself.

PROS	CONS
In extreme cases, in which peaceful and democratic methods have been exhausted, it is legitimate and justified to resort to terror. In cases of repression and suffering,	Terrorism is never justified. Peaceful and democratic means must always be used. Even when democratic rights are denied, nonviolent protest is the only moral action.

PROS	CONS

PROS

with an implacably oppressive state and no obvious possibility of international relief, it is sometimes necessary to resort to violence to defend one's people and pursue one's cause.

Terrorism works. In many countries terrorists have succeeded in bringing governments to negotiate with them and make concessions to them. Where governments have not been willing to concede to rational argument and peaceful protest, terrorism can compel recognition of a cause. Nelson Mandela moved from perceived terrorist as head of the African National Congress' armed wing to president of South Africa. In many other countries we see this trend too—in Israel, Northern Ireland, recently in Sri Lanka, and in the Oslo peace process that led to the creation of the Palestinian Authority. Therefore, terrorism is justified by its success in achieving results when peaceful means have failed.

Terrorism can raise the profile of a neglected cause. The hijackings of the 1970s and 1980s publicized the Palestinian cause, helping to bring it to the world's attention. States can use their wealth and media to convey their side of the story; their opponents do not have these resources and perhaps need to resort to terrorism to publicize their cause. In this way, limited and focused use of violence can have a dramatic international impact.

Ideals such as "freedom" and "liberty" are more important than a single human life; they give meaning to the lives of hundreds of thousands of people. Of course, peaceful methods should be tried first, but when all else fails, a nation/ethnic community or other group must be able to fight for its freedom and independence.

Actions should be judged by their consequences. In bringing hope, popular recognition, and ultimately relief to the plight of a group, terrorism is aimed at laudable objectives and can achieve sufficient good to outweigh the evil of its methods.

CONS

And in the most extreme cases, in which subject populations are weak and vulnerable to reprisals from the attacked state, it is especially important for groups not to resort to terror. Terrorism merely exacerbates a situation, and creates a cycle of violence and suffering.

Terrorism does not work. It antagonizes and angers the community that it targets. It polarizes opinion and makes it more difficult for moderates on both sides to prevail and compromise. A lasting and peaceful settlement can be won only with the freely given consent of both parties to a conflict or disagreement. The bad feeling caused by the slaughter of hundreds, perhaps thousands, of innocent people by terrorists makes such consent desperately difficult to give.

Furthermore, states or institutions created in concession to terror are often corrupt, dominated by men of violence with links to organized crime. Nothing is achieved to improve the lives of the people in whose name terror has been used.

All publicity is definitely not good publicity. Powerful images of suffering and death will permanently mark the terrorists' cause, and cause them to lose the battle for public approval around the world. Furthermore, groups that resort to terrorism play into the hands of their opponents; states being subjected to terrorism can win powerful support from similarly affected nations, such as the US, in combating this threat.

Abstract ideals are insignificant when compared with the value of even a single life. Life is sacred, and to murder anyone in pursuit of an idea—or even the improvement of other people's lives—is shocking, abhorrent, and wrong. No one has the right to say another person's life is worthless, or worth less than the cause that is pursued through terrorism.

The end does not justify the means. The consequences of any action are by no means clear. The success of terrorism is not guaranteed; it is an immoral gamble to kill people in the hope of achieving something else. And even if the goal were realized, the price paid is literally incalculable. Those who use violence in the pursuit of "higher" aims presume to be able to calculate suffering. But the fear, suffering, and death caused by terrorism damage millions of people. Not just the victims are affected, with their families and fellow citizens, but people in many different countries are also put at risk because terrorists from other countries are inspired by these atrocious acts.

PROS

The definition of terrorism depends very much upon one's point of view. The affirmative does not need to defend every atrocity against innocent civilians to argue that terrorism is sometimes justified. A broad definition would say terrorism was the use of violence for political ends by any group that violates the Geneva Conventions (which govern actions between armies in wartime) or ignores generally accepted concepts of human rights. Under such a broad definition, states and their armed forces could be accused of terrorism. So could many resistance groups in wartime or freedom fighters struggling against dictatorships, as well as participants in civil wars—all irregular groups outside the scope of the Geneva Conventions. Effectively, such a definition says that the armies of sovereign states should have a monopoly on violence, and that they can only act in certain ways. Some exceptions to this are surely easy to justify—for example, the actions of the French resistance to German occupation in World War II, or of American patriots against the British in the 1770s. A narrower definition would say that terrorism was the use of violence against innocent civilians to achieve a political end. Such a definition would allow freedom fighters and resistance groups with a legitimate grievance to use force against dictatorship and occupation, providing they targeted only the troops and other agents of oppression. Yet even this tight definition has gray areas—what if the soldiers being targeted are reluctant conscripts? Are civilian settlers in occupied territories not legitimate targets as agents of oppression? What about their children? Does it make a difference if civilians are armed or unarmed? Do civil servants such as teachers and doctors count as agents of an occupying or oppressive state?

CONS

States that ignore the Geneva Conventions, for example, by mistreating prisoners or deliberately attacking civilian targets, are guilty of terrorism. Nor are the Conventions applicable only to warfare between sovereign states. Their principles can be clearly applied in other kinds of conflict and used to distinguish between legitimate military struggle and indefensible terrorism.

Nor is it reasonable to argue that there are gray areas and that civilians are sometimes legitimate targets. Once such a claim has been made, anything can eventually be "justified" in the name of some cause. All too often the political leaderships of protest movements have decided that "limited physical force" is necessary to advance their cause, only to find the violence spiraling out of control. The "hard men" who are prepared to use force end up in control of the movement, which increasingly attracts criminals and others who love violence for its own sake. This alienates the original base of support for the movement in the wider population and internationally. The authorities against whom the movement is struggling also respond by using increasingly repressive measures of their own, generating a spiral of violence and cruelty.

Sample Motions:

This House can justify terrorism.

This House cannot justify the use of terrorism under any circumstances.

This House believes that extremism in the pursuit of liberty is no vice.

Web Links:

- Kapitan, Tomis. "Can Terrorism Be Justified?" <http://www.niu.edu/phil/~kapitan/pdf/CanTerrorismbeJustified.pdf> Argues that terrorism can be justified under specific circumstances.
- United Nations. "Terrorism Can Never Be Justified, Participants at Joint UN Conference Conclude." <http://www.un.org/apps/news/story.asp?NewsID=24725&Cr=terror&Cr1> Summary of UN conference condemning terrorism.
- Valls, Andrew. "Can Terrorism Be Justified?" <http://www.cuyamaca.edu/courtneyhammond/pdf/valls.pdf> Discusses terrorism within the context of Just War Theory.

Further Reading:

Mahan, Susan G., and Pamala L. Griset. *Terrorism in Perspective*. SAGE, 2012.

Primoratz, Igor. *Terrorism: A Philosophical Investigation*. Polity, 2012.

Steinhoff, Uwe. *On the Ethics of War and Terrorism*. Oxford University Press, 2007.

Wellman, Carl. *Terrorism and Counterterrorism: A Moral Assessment*. Springer, 2013.

..

TORTURE IN INTERROGATION

One of the most heated controversies of the US war on terror is the use of torture on suspected terrorists. Many policy makers contend that torture is, at times, the most effective method for obtaining critical information that might help maintain national security. Noted jurists such as Alan Dershowitz have argued that regulated torture may be a necessary way to protect Americans. Opponents, however, counter that such interrogation methods violate the basic human rights provisions of the Geneva Conventions and binding UN protocols concerning the laws of waging war (to which the US is a party), as well as the UN Convention Against Torture. In 2006, leaks of the so-called White House torture memos, incidents such as the Abu Ghraib prison scandal, and the debate over the use of waterboarding put the media spotlight on US treatment of detainees.

PROS

Many experienced interrogators have found that aggressive tactics are the best, and sometimes the only, way to obtain information—information that might lead to the arrest or conviction of other terrorists or might protect the US against a future attack. Often such information is needed quickly, so that more subtle means of interrogation are untenable. Moreover, the US has a track record for using aggressive interrogation in a regulated, studied way that does not constitute torture in the conventional sense (defined as methods that will cause permanent damage to vital organs or permanent emotional trauma). The US government has never sanctioned methods that would cause such harm.

The US uses aggressive interrogation only against those it has strong reason to believe have engaged in terrorist activities against Americans. Such extralegal activity requires a strong response. These are bad people, trained terrorists who will stop at nothing to kill innocent US civilians. Those who would heavily restrict interrogation methods would have the US lose the war on terror.

The Geneva Conventions do not apply to the interrogation of terrorists and suspected terrorists held by the US because they are not prisoners of war. They are illegal enemy combatants, outside the scope of such protection.

CONS

Information obtained by torture is suspect at best. Studies have shown that individuals will say anything to stop the abuse. Moreover, bringing terrorists to justice is important for closure and safety, but evidence obtained from torture may be inadmissible in the courtroom.

Every human being has human rights, no matter how heinous a crime he or she is suspected of committing. Article 5 of the Universal Declaration of Human Rights reads: "No one shall be subjected to torture or to cruel, inhuman, or degrading treatment or punishment." Moreover, the US Constitution prohibits torture.

Verbal sleight of hand should not obscure the fact that individuals captured in the war on terror are prisoners of war. Moreover, in many cases they are merely suspected of links to criminal activity (and, as past experience has indicated, often wrongly so). Extralegal military tribunals conducted behind closed doors without proper due process leave the US on shaky moral ground.

PROS	CONS
The US is hardly alone in its use of such interrogation practices and has a good record compared with other nations. Moreover, "torture" is a loaded word that does not accurately differentiate between the studied interrogation practices of US forces and the human rights abuses prevalent in many developing nations.	The US should set the standard for international human rights, rather than strive only for the average. Furthermore, permitting low-level and undertrained US troops to engage in unsupervised interrogation is a recipe for disaster. Incidents like the abuses at Abu Ghraib prison demonstrate how quickly America's reputation can suffer from such illicit treatment of prisoners.

Sample Motions:

This House believes that the US has the right to use torture to protect national security.

This House believes that torture is sometimes necessary in time of war.

This House believes that the US has the right to use torture against suspected terrorists.

Web Links:

- Inskeep, Steve. "The Drawbacks of Fighting Terror with Torture." <http://www.npr.org/templates/story/story.php?storyId=5519633> Transcript of radio broadcast discussing the problems of using torture to battle terrorism; links to related NPR stories.
- PBS. "Debating Torture." <http://www.pbs.org/newshour/bb/military/july-dec05/torture_12-02.html> Transcript of news show discussing torture.
- Miller, Seumas. <http://www.science.uva.nl/~seop/entries/torture/> *Stanford Encyclopedia of Philosophy* entry on the justifications for torture.

Further Reading:

Cohn, Marjorie. *The United States and Torture.* New York University Press, 2012.

Ginbar, Yuval. Why Not Torture Terrorists?: Moral, Practical and Legal Aspects of the 'Ticking Bomb' Justification for Torture. Oxford University Press, 2010.

McCoy, Alfred W. *Torture and Impunity: The U.S. Doctrine of Coercive Interrogation.* University of Wisconsin Press, 2012.

Rejali, Darius. *Torture and Democracy.* Princeton University Press, 2009.

■ ■

TWO-PARTY SYSTEM

Nations such as Australia, the United Kingdom, and the United States have two-party political systems. Other countries have de facto two-party systems: two parties dominate governance, and one or two smaller third parties ensure that one or the other major party maintains power (Germany is a good example). In contrast, nations with multiparty parliamentary systems, Israel, Japan, some Eastern European countries, and some of the Latin American democracies, regularly experience shifting alliances and coalitions among their political parties.

Which system is preferable? Strong voices can be heard on both sides: advocates of the multiparty system extol its diversity and the fact that it forces coalition building; advocates of the two-party model argue that such governments are more stable and have a larger group of members experienced in governing.

PROS	CONS
Two-party systems have emerged either as the result or the reflection of the will of the electorate. Often the	While ideology and the will of the electorate may have been a factor at one stage in the development of a two-

two parties represent key ideological divisions in society over the direction of policy, e.g., between left and right, small government and activist government, liberalism and authoritarianism. Most voters have little interest in the minutiae of policy, but they can understand the broad political choices presented to them by the two distinct parties and make their decisions at election time accordingly.

party democracy, these are factors that limit political progress today. The Cold War with its divisions of left and right is over and ideological labels are increasingly meaningless. Such historical precedents make the creation of third parties difficult. The dominant parties tend to shape electoral rules to exclude smaller parties, and the more dominant parties tend to be the most successful at fund-raising. Thus a two-party system limits the choice of the electorate.

Governments in two-party systems are more able to drive their policies through the legislature because they often have a clear majority of representatives there. Consequently, they can implement important changes quickly and without compromise.

Multiparty systems tend to produce coalition governments that have to work to balance interests and produce a consensus. Thus, the electorate is likely to accept important changes these governments make and not reverse them at the next election.

Because two-party systems tend to be less volatile, voters retain their representatives as incumbents longer. Consequently, the legislators are very experienced. This results in better and more consistent policy and more effective scrutiny of the executive branch.

Incumbency can mean complacency. The longer people hold office, the more comfortable they become and the less likely they are to take risks and make controversial decisions. They can be highly influenced by lobbyists and lose touch with the people they are supposed to represent. The freer marketplace of ideas in a multiparty system forces politicians to adapt their message and become more responsive to minority voices.

Because parliamentary majorities in multiparty systems can shift suddenly, these systems are far less stable than two-party systems. Multiparty systems are also less fair to the electorate because policies formed after an election are often the result of backroom deals that ignore campaign promises and voter wishes.

The threat of a no-confidence vote, a collapsing coalition, or the departure of a coalition partner from a governing majority force leaders to make compromises, and compromises make for policies that serve the interests of the majority of the voters. Moreover, most countries have constitutional mechanisms to ensure a relatively smooth transition to a new government.

Two-party systems better reflect mainstream, centrist views. To remain competitive, parties will tend to moderate their platforms.

Moderation is not necessarily in the public's best interest. A multiparty system helps ensure that the views of a variety of different interests are considered in policy making.

Sample Motions:

This House believes rule by a majority party is superior to coalition government.

This House believes a two-party system is superior to a multiparty system.

This House would amend nations' constitutions to increase electoral competition.

Web Links:

- Amato, Theresa. "The Two Party Ballot Suppresses Third Party Change." <http://hlrecord.org/?p=10575> Argues that a two-party system denies citizens meaningful elections.
- Op Ed News. <http://www.opednews.com/articles/opedne_chestert_080430_the_two_party_system.htm> Article on why the two-party system has failed, from a conservative writer.
- Schofield, Norman, and Itai Sened. "Multiparty Democracy. <http://sened.wustl.edu/publications/multi_democracy.pdf> Comprehensive research paper on multiparty democracy.

Further Reading:

Amato, Theresa. *Grand Illusion: The Myth of Voter Choice in a Two-Party Tyranny*. New Press, 2009.

Disch, Lisa Jane. *The Tyranny of the Two-Party System*. Columbia University Press, 2012.

Schoen, Douglas. *Declaring Independence: The Beginning of the End of the Two-Party System*. Random House, 2008.

Ware, Alan. *The Dynamics of Two-Party Politics: Power Structures and the Management of Competition*. Oxford University Press, 2009.

■ ■

VEGETARIANISM

Very few human societies have forsworn eating meat, fowl, and fish, although in some parts of the world grains constitute almost the whole of the diet, with meat, fowl, or fish rare additions. These diets often have been the result of poverty, not choice. In modern Western societies, however, voluntary vegetarianism is on the increase. Recently many have become vegetarians because of the health benefits of the diet. Many also believe it is immoral for human beings to eat other animals. Some take an even more absolute line, refusing to eat dairy products or eggs as well because of the conditions in which the animals that produce them are raised.

PROS

The main reason to be a vegetarian is to reduce animal suffering. Farm animals are sentient, living beings like humans, and, like us, they can feel pleasure and pain. Farming and killing these animals for food is wrong. The methods of farming and slaughter are often barbaric and cruel, even on "free range" farms. Also, in most countries, animal welfare laws do not cover animals farmed for food.

To suggest that farm factories are "natural" is absurd; they are unnatural and cruel. To eat meat is to perpetuate animal suffering on a huge scale, a larger, crueler, and more systematic scale than anything found in the wild. Humanity's "superiority" over other animals means humans have the reasoning power and moral instinct to stop exploiting other species. If aliens from another planet, much more intelligent and powerful than humans, farmed (and force-fed) human beings in factory farm conditions, we would think it was morally abhorrent. If this would be wrong, then is it not wrong for "superior" humans to farm "lower" species simply because of our ability to do so?

Human beings are omnivores and are rational agents with free will, thus they can choose whether to eat meat, vegetables, or both. It might be "natural" for humans to be violent toward one another but that does not mean that it is right. Some natural traits are immoral and should be restrained. In any case, our closest animal cousins, the apes, eat an all-vegetable diet.

CONS

Eating meat does not need to mean cruelty to animals. A growing number of organic and free range farms can provide meat without cruelty. We can extend animal welfare laws to protect farm animals, but that does not mean that it is wrong in principle to eat meat.

It is natural for human beings to farm, kill, and eat other species. The wild offers only a brutal struggle for existence. That humans have succeeded in that struggle by exploiting our natural advantages means that we have the right to use lower species. In fact, farming animals is much less brutal than the pain and hardship animals inflict on each other in the wild.

Human beings have evolved to eat meat. They have sharp canine teeth for tearing animal flesh and digestive systems adapted to eating meat and fish as well as vegetables. Modern squeamishness about eating animals is an affectation of a decadent society that flies in the face of our natural instincts and physiology. We were made to eat both meat and vegetables. Cutting out half of this diet will inevitably mean we lose this natural balance.

PROS

Becoming a vegetarian is an environmentally friendly thing to do. Modern farming is one of the main sources of pollution. Beef farming is one of the main causes of deforestation, and as long as people continue to buy fast food, financial incentives will be in place to continue cutting down trees to make room for cattle. Because of our desire to eat fish, our rivers and seas are being emptied and many species face extinction. Meat farmers use up far more energy resources than those growing vegetables and grains. Eating meat, fowl, and fish causes not only cruelty to animals, but also harm to the environment.

"Going veggie" offers significant health benefits. A vegetarian diet contains high quantities of fiber, vitamins, and minerals, and is low in fat. A vegan diet (which eliminates animal products) is even better because eggs and dairy products are high in cholesterol. Eating meat increases the risk of developing many forms of cancer. In 1996 the American Cancer Society recommended that red meat be excluded from the diet entirely. Eating meat also increases the risk of heart disease. A vegetarian diet reduces the risk of serious diseases and, because it is low in fat, also helps to prevent obesity. Plenty of vegetarian sources of protein, such as beans and bean curd, are available.

Going vegetarian or vegan reduces the risk of contracting food-borne diseases. The inclusion of animal brains in animal feed led to outbreaks of bovine spongiform encephalitis ("mad cow disease") and its human equivalent, Creutzfeldt-Jakob Disease. Meat and poultry transmit almost all of the potentially fatal forms of food poisoning.

CONS

All of these problems would exist without meat farming and fishing. Deforestation has occurred for centuries as human civilizations expand, but planting sustainable forests can now counteract it. Meat farmers contribute little to pollution, and many worse sources of pollution exist. Vegetable and grain farmers also pollute through use of nitrates, pesticides, and fertilizers. Finally, the energy crisis is one of global proportions in which meat farmers play a minute role. Finding alternative sources of energy, not limiting meat farming, will solve this problem.

The key to good health is a balanced diet, not a meat- and fish-free diet. Meat and fish are good sources of protein, iron, and other vitamins and minerals. Most of the health benefits of a vegetarian diet derive from its being high in fiber and low in fat and cholesterol. We can achieve these benefits by avoiding fatty and fried foods, eating only lean grilled meat and fish, and including a large amount of fruit and vegetables in our diet. A meat- and fish-free diet is unbalanced and can result in protein and iron deficiencies. Also, in the West a vegetarian diet is a more expensive option, a luxury for the middle classes. Fresh fruit and vegetables are extremely expensive compared to processed meats, bacon, burgers, sausages, etc.

Of course we should enforce the highest standards of hygiene and food safety. But this does not mean that we should stop eating meat, which, in itself, is a natural and healthy thing to do.

Sample Motions:

This House believes that if you love animals you shouldn't eat them.

This House would go veggie.

Web Links:

- Corliss, Richard. "Should We All Be Vegetarians?" <http://www.time.com/time/magazine/article/0,9171,1002888,00.html> Presents health and environmental arguments in favor of and against vegetarianism.
- Earthsave. "Factory Farm Alarm." <http http://www.earthsave.org/news/factfarm.htm> Provides information in opposition to factory farming and in support of a grain-based diet.
- People for the Ethical Treatment of Animals. <http://www.peta.org> Radical animal rights organization offers arguments in favor of vegetarianism and information on how to become a vegetarian.

Further Reading:

Francione, Gary L. *The Animal Rights Debate: Abolition or Regulation?* Columbia University Press, 2010.

Grumett, David, and Rachel Muers. *Eating and Believing: Interdisciplinary Perspectives on Vegetarianism and Theology.* Continuum International, 2011.

Keith, Lierre. *The Vegetarian Myth: Food, Justice, and Sustainability.* PM Press, 2009.

Safran Foer, Jonathan. *Eating Animals.* Back Bay Books, 2010.

■ ■

VOTER IDENTIFICATION LAWS

Voter identification laws are controversial precisely because they touch on one of the most fundamental political rights: voting. Advocates of these laws point to voter fraud as a real and serious threat to democracy and insist that voter identification laws are the most effective way of combating it. Its detractors largely believe that the laws are a Republican strategy to disenfranchise poor and minority voters who tend to vote Democratic. Several challenges to these voter identification laws have been mounted in recent years. In the Indiana case of Crawford v. Marion County Election Board *(2008), the US Supreme Court held that voter identification requirements are permissible and do not violate the US Constitution. This ruling paved the way for identification laws in other states; between 2011 and 2012, legislators in 41 states introduced over 180 bills designed to tighten up voter identification laws. Overall, 25 laws and two executive actions were passed in the run-up to the 2012 elections. With nearly all of these laws being passed by Republican-majority legislations, critics saw this as an attempt to influence the election by disenfranchising traditional Democrat voters. Amid intense controversy, many of these laws were either overturned by courts or blocked by the Department of Justice, under the 1965 Voting Rights Act. However, a June 2013 Supreme Court ruling invalidated a key part of this act, allowing nine states and numerous counties, all with a history of racially discriminatory voting laws, to change their election laws without approval from the federal government. Following this ruling, Texas announced that a voter identification law that had been blocked would now go into immediate effect. Voter identification laws are still pending in several states, and are sure to be the subject of controversy in the run-up to the next elections.*

PROS

Voter identification laws are necessary to combat the serious danger of voter fraud. There is a long history of voter impersonation throughout the US. Voter fraud not only interferes with individual elections but also undermines voter confidence in representative government generally. Identification requirements are the most direct and effective way of combating election fraud. As such, states have a compelling interest in implementing voter identification laws.

Voter identification laws are not discriminatory because they apply uniformly to all state residents. The laws require everyone to obtain valid, photo identification (ID), and therefore cannot be said to target poor and minority communities. No evidence in states that have enacted such laws reveals any discriminatory intent toward these populations. Furthermore, most of the required IDs can be obtained free of charge. The rationale

CONS

Voter impersonation fraud is a smokescreen for a growing conservative strategy of disenfranchising poor and minority voters. The extent of voter fraud has been greatly exaggerated. If voter impersonation were such a grave problem, the government would prosecute violators. Although the Department of Justice poured unprecedented resources into voter fraud prevention under the Bush administration, they did not prosecute a single offender. This tends to show that the true purpose behind these laws is to resurrect Jim Crow–era barriers to voting for poor and minority communities, who are more likely to vote Democratic.

These laws disproportionately impact poor and minority communities, who are less likely to have the money and/or documents needed to obtain photo ID. Federal passports are not cheap. Although most states do not charge to issue ID, some states do. Furthermore, poor individuals, especially the homeless, are also less likely to have the documents (such as birth certificates, Social Security cards, etc.) necessary to obtain photo IDs. Since behind these laws is to increase fairness and confidence in American democracy.

Voting is an important right, but it can be qualified by the government for an important reason. Voting rights are not made totally meaningless by voter ID laws. In most states, voters who lack identification can still cast provisional ballots that can be counted later. The ID requirement is a mere inconvenience, not a complete barrier to voting. And, again, the government's interest in preventing voter fraud greatly outweighs the minor inconvenience suffered by a small group of voters.

people of color are disproportionately poor, the law disproportionately prevents these populations from voting.

Voting is a fundamental right that should only be infringed by the government for a compelling reason. The interest in preventing voter fraud is not compelling enough to warrant disenfranchising voters. In many states, voter ID laws will completely prevent certain people from voting. It is estimated that roughly 12% of the US population has no photo ID. Although the laws allow voters to vote by provisional ballot, this measure is largely meaningless because voters are then required to travel to the county seat and submit an affidavit in order for their vote to be counted. As previously mentioned, the government's concerns about fraud are exaggerated and largely pretextual. Therefore, the fraud prevention rationale should not trump the right to vote.

Sample Motions:

This House supports overturning voter identification laws.

This House encourages more states to pass voter identification laws.

Web Links:

- Overton, Spencer. "Voter Identification." <http://www.michiganlawreview.org/assets/pdfs/105/4/overton.pdf> Argues that politicians should be cautious about implementing voter identification laws before more serious empirical research is published.
- The Supreme Court of the United States. "Crawford v. Marion County Election Board." <http://www.scotusblog.com/wp/wp-content/uploads/2008/04/07-21.pdf> Case upholding Indiana's voter identification law.
- Von Spakovsky, Hans. "Voter Identification Laws Were A Success in November." <http://online.wsj.com/article/SB123327839569631609.html> Presents data showing that voter turnout during the 2008 US presidential election was higher in states that had voter identification laws.

Further Reading:

Fund, John. *Stealing Elections: How Voter Fraud Threatens Our Democracy.* Encounter Books, 2004.

Overton, Spencer. *Stealing Democracy: The New Politics of Voter Suppression.* W. W. Norton, 2006.

..

WAR CRIMES TRIBUNALS

Always controversial and shrouded in the solemn aftermath of terrible crimes, war crimes tribunals are the international community's response to national wrongdoings. They raise serious questions about sovereignty and international law. Whether held after World War II, Rwanda, Bosnia, Congo, or Liberia, they never fail to provoke outrage from one corner and vindictiveness from the other. Would such matters be better left alone? The trial of Slobodan Milosevic in The Hague in the opening years of this century was an example of how complicated issues of international justice and power come to the fore in such tribunals.

PROS

Wrongdoing and wrongdoers must be punished. When a crime has consumed an entire nation, only a foreign trial can supply disinterested due process.

Countries can explicitly cede jurisdiction for such crimes to international tribunals. These bodies are trying to achieve justice and closure that will benefit the entire nation.

The world community must send a clear message that it will act against appalling war crimes. This must be done on an international stage through international courts.

The issue of sovereignty is increasingly less important in a globalizing world. The pooling of sovereignty occurs with increasing frequency, and any step toward an internationalization of legal systems, such as the use of international tribunals, is welcome.

We have to uphold the principle that if you commit serious crimes, you will be punished. If we do not take action against war criminals, we will encourage future crimes.

CONS

Of course wrongdoing should be punished. But the trial should be held in the country where the crime was committed. Any outside intervention in matters of sovereign states is high-handed and imperialistic.

Closure is the last thing tribunals bring. These trials alienate large portions of the nation and turn people against the new government, which is seen as collaborating with foreign imperialists. Such trials increase tension.

No one can dispute the enormity of such crimes. But these trials damage a nation by reopening old wounds. Spain, for example, did not embark on witch hunts following the bloody and repressive regime of Francisco Franco. Instead, it turned the page on those years and moved on collectively with no recrimination. Between justice and security there is always a trade-off. Where possible, peace should be secured by reconciliation rather than recrimination.

Whatever the truth about globalization and sovereignty, war crimes tribunals do not standardize justice. They are nothing more than victors' arbitrary justice. This type of justice undermines international law.

The threat of possible legal action has not stopped countless heinous crimes in the past, so why should it now? These people are not rational and have no respect for international law.

Sample Motions:

This House would have war crimes tribunals.
This House believes war crimes must be punished.

Web Links:

- American University: Research Office for War Crimes Tribunals for the Former Yugoslavia and Rwanda. <http://www.wcl.american.edu/pub/humright/wcrimes/research.html> Detailed site on actual tribunals.
- McMorran, Chris. "What International War Crimes Tribunals Are." <http://www.beyondintractability.org/essay/int_war_crime_tribunals/> Article discussing what war tribunals are and the positive/negative sides of them.
- Special International Criminal Tribunals. <http://www.globalpolicy.org/intljustice/tribindx.htm> Provides information on UN war crimes tribunals in Rwanda and the former Yugoslavia as well as efforts to establish tribunals in East Timor, Cambodia, and Sierra Leone.

Further Reading:

Futamura, Madoka. *War Crimes Tribunals and Transitional Justice: The Tokyo Trial and Nuremberg Legacy.* Routledge, 2008.
Richards, Peter. *Extraordinary Justice: Military Tribunals in Historical and International Context.* NYU Press, 2007.
Schabas, William. *Unimaginable Atrocities: Justice, Politics, and Rights at the War Crimes Tribunal.* Oxford University Press, 2012.

■■

WARRANTLESS WIRETAPPING

In December 2005, Pres. George W. Bush acknowledged that he had signed a secret order permitting the National Security Agency (NSA) to wiretap communications between American citizens and terrorists overseas. Several months later, the press revealed that the NSA had amassed the domestic call records of millions of Americans as part of its antiterrorism campaign. Critics say that such eavesdropping violated the 1978 Foreign Intelligence Surveillance Act (FISA), which makes it a crime to conduct domestic surveillance without a warrant. Asserting an expansive concept of presidential power that many experts reject, the president contended that he had the right to approve the program. In 2010, a federal district court judge ruled that the NSA's program of surveillance without warrants was a violation of FISA.

PROS

Both the Constitution (Article II) and the 2001 law authorizing the use of "all necessary and appropriate force" against those responsible for the September 11 attacks give the president the legal authority for the no-warrant surveillance. Under the Constitution, the president is commander in chief, and as such he is responsible for defending the nation and should have the right to determine how best to do so.

Communications have changed since the passage of FISA, as has the nature of our enemy. In 1978 the Soviet Union was our foe, and the NSA could easily retrieve telephone satellite communications. Today our enemy is not a super power but terrorist organizations that can move easily and change cell phones and e-mail addresses at will. To fight terror, US intelligence operatives need to act quickly, with a minimum of red tape, and must gather information in new ways. Also, most of the world's broadband communications pass through the US, making monitoring of potential enemies easy for NSA; however, distinguishing between "foreign" and "domestic" is difficult.

As proved by the attacks on September 11, terrorists can do tremendous damage. If we are to protect ourselves in the future, we may have to abridge the privacy of many individuals, however innocent they may ultimately prove to be. Simply put, you can never know who is a terrorist until after his or her privacy has been violated or an attack has occurred; in addition, why should the innocent be afraid if they have nothing to hide?

CONS

Conducting surveillance without FISA authorization is a felony. The Constitution clearly states that the president "shall take Care that the Laws be faithfully executed" and gives Congress the sole right enact or modify laws. Claiming expansive constitutional powers in an effort to justify violating laws is unacceptable—the president cannot choose which laws he will obey. Furthermore, the law that the proposition cites authorized military force against Afghanistan. It was never meant to justify domestic surveillance.

The US has faced many threats in its history and has often reacted with policies it later regrets. Consider the mass internment of Japanese Americans during World War II. We have often been tempted to abridge our liberties in times of stress, but this is precisely when we must defend them most vigorously. The United States was founded on certain values—if we ignore or reject these values, we may win the war on terrorism but lose the freedoms that define us.

The ends do not justify the means. The right to privacy is crucial in a democracy and should not be abridged, particularly as no evidence has been offered that warrantless surveillance is effective in fighting terrorism. Finally, as our own history has shown, we have no guarantee that the government will not violate privacy for its own, less-than-just ends. Look at what happened in the McCarthy era or during Watergate. To date, the government has not articulated the specific criteria it uses to determine which conversations to monitor—itself a reason for worry.

Sample Motions:

This House believes that in a democracy, the right to privacy should be valued over the need for security.

This House believes that Americans should not give up freedom for security.

Web Links:

- Godoy, Maria. "NSA Wiretapping: The Legal Debate." <http://www.npr.org/news/specials/nsawiretap/legality.html> Analysis of legal issues involved, with links to more resources.
- Williams, Carol J. "Federal Court Finds Warrantless Wiretapping of Lawyers Illegal." <http://articles.latimes.com/2010/apr/01/local/la-me-wiretap1-2010apr01> Summary of federal court's 2010 decision that the warrantless wiretapping of two lawyers at an Islamic charity was illegal.
- Yoo, John. "Why We Endorsed Warrantless Wiretaps." <http://online.wsj.com/article/SB124770304290648701.html> Former official in the US Department of Justice defends the Bush government's use of wiretapping.

Further Reading:

Ambinder, Marc, and D. B. Grady. *Deep State: Inside the Government Secrecy Industry*. Wiley, 2013.

McChesney, Robert W. *Digital Disconnect: How Capitalism Is Turning the Internet Against Democracy*. New Press, 2013.

Schulhofer, Stephen J. *More Essential Than Ever: The Fourth Amendment in the Twenty First Century*. Oxford University Press, 2012.

Swire, Peter P., and Kenesa Ahmad. *Privacy and Surveillance with New Technologies*. IDEBATE Press, 2012.

■ ■

WATER RESOURCES: A COMMODITY

With increasing population and growing water usage, water shortages have become a source of potential and ongoing conflicts. One of the main issues is the competing claims of upstream and downstream nations. As downstream nations attempt to win more water rights, upstream nations try to keep control of the water resources in their territories. While current resources are insufficient in many regions, water will become even scarcer in the future, producing tension among nations sharing rivers.

PROS

Water occurs randomly, just like oil and gas, which are treated as commodities that can be bought and sold. If countries can take advantage of their geographic location to sell oil and gas, they are justified in using water resources to support their economies. Failure to view water as a precious, marketable commodity makes it far less valued and leads to unrestricted water use by environmentally unconscious societies.

Control and management of water—the maintenance of dams, reservoirs, and irrigation systems—costs millions of dollars and is a burden on upstream states' budgets. All of these expenses, including the opportunity cost of fertile lands allocated for reservoirs and dams, should be covered by downstream states, which are the primary consumers of water. For example, that an upstream state cannot use the water flowing through it to produce electricity to offset the costs of water management is unfair.

CONS

Water is the most vital of Earth's randomly occurring resources; it is essential for survival. Consequently, water-rich countries have no moral right to profit from this resource. Every inhabitant of the planet has an equal right to water, and flowing water has no political boundaries.

It is immoral to charge for water beyond the cost of water systems' maintenance. Water is a commodity only up to a certain point. Once water exceeds a reservoir's capacity, it is not a commodity because it will flow free over the dam. Dams may also create dangerous conditions because downstream states may be flooded if a dam breaks.

PROS

Water resources are distributed unequally. Uneven distribution and wasteful consumption warrant the introduction of the "pay-for-water" approach. Is it fair to prefer to use water to irrigate infertile semi-deserts downstream rather than using water more efficiently upstream?

CONS

Faced with scarcity and drought, states may resort to force to gain control of water resources. Therefore, making water a commodity is a potential cause of many conflicts and should be avoided.

Sample Motions:

This House agrees that water flows can be an article of trade.

This House should endorse international commerce in water resources.

This House does not support legislation for trading of water resources.

Web Links:

- The Transboundary Freshwater Dispute Database. <http://www.transboundarywaters.orst.edu> Comprehensive resource on water treaties.
- Wood, Chris. "Is Water a Commodity or A Right?" <http://thetyee.ca/News/2006/03/22/WaterRight> Article presenting an overview of the issue.
- World Water Council. <www.worldwatercouncil.org> Site maintained by an international organization dedicated to improving world management of water; offers articles and resources on water issues.
- The World's Water. <www.worldwater.org> Up-to-date information on global freshwater resources.

Further Reading:

Grigg, Neil S. *Water Finance: Public Responsibilities and Private Opportunities*. Wiley, 2011.

Haugen, David M., and Susan Musser. *Will the World Run Out of Fresh Water?* Greenhaven Press, 2012.

Melosi, Martin V. *Precious Commodity*. University of Pittsburgh Press, 2011.

• •

WHALING, LIFTING THE BAN ON

Whaling became an important industry in the nineteenth century because of the increased demand for whale oil used in the lamps of the time. The industry declined in the late nineteenth century when petroleum began to replace whale oil. Nevertheless, whales were still hunted for meat and other products, and modern technology made hunters more efficient. The increasing scarcity of many whale species, together with growing recognition of the intelligence and social nature of whales, led to the creation of the International Whaling Commission (IWC), which instituted a ban on whale hunting effective in 1986. In years since, whale stocks appear to have recovered, although the extent of the recovery is a matter of debate. Some whaling continues for research purposes, mostly by Japan, which has been widely criticized for taking hundreds more whales than can be justified by the needs of scientific inquiry. In 2007 the IWC voted down Japan's bid to lift restrictions on commercial whaling. Pro-whaling countries such as Japan and Norway indicated that they would circumvent the ban by increasing the numbers of whales killed for scientific research programs.

PROS

Whales should be treated in the same way as other animals, as a resource to be used for food and other products.

CONS

Killing whales for human use is morally wrong. Many people believe that no animal should suffer and die for

PROS

Whales should not be hunted to extinction, but if their numbers are healthy, then hunting them should be permitted. Scientists have conducted studies of intelligence on dolphins, not whales; these studies, however, cannot measure intelligence in any useful way. Although people in some Western nations view whales as special and in need of protection, this view is not widely shared by other countries. To impose it upon others is a form of cultural imperialism.

Whale populations are healthy, particularly those of minke whales, which now number over a million. A resumption of hunting under regulation will not adversely affect their survival. The IWC did not impose the ban on whaling for moral reasons but to prevent extinction. Numbers have now greatly increased. The ban has served its original purpose, and it is time to lift it.

Whale hunting is an important aspect of some cultures. For some groups the hunting of a small number of whales is an important feature in the local subsistence economy, a way of reconnecting themselves with the traditions of their ancestors and affirming their group identity against the onslaught of globalization.

Economic factors argue for a resumption of whaling. In both Japan and Norway remote coastal communities depend on whaling for their livelihood. Both countries have an investment in ships, research, processing centers, etc., that would be wasted if the temporary whaling ban were extended indefinitely.

Modern whaling is humane, especially compared with the factory farming of chickens, cows, and pigs. Most whales die instantly or very quickly, and Japanese researchers have developed new, more powerful harpoons that will make kills even more certain.

CONS

the benefit of humans, but even if you do not hold such views, whales should be treated as a special case. Whales are exceptionally intelligent and social beings, able to communicate fluently with each other. The hunting and the killing of animals that appear to share many social and intellectual abilities with humans are immoral.

We should adhere to a precautionary principle. Actual whale populations are not truly known, but they appear to be nowhere near as great as pro-whalers suggest. Until the international ban several species were close to extinction. This could easily happen again if the ban were lifted, especially because regulation is difficult. Even if hunting were restricted to the more numerous species of whales, other, less common species may be killed by mistake.

Traditional hunting methods are often cruel; they involve driving whales to beach themselves and then killing them slowly with long knives, or singling out vulnerable nursing mothers with calves. Because only small numbers are taken with relatively primitive equipment, the hunters do not develop enough skill or possess the technology to achieve the clean and quick kills necessary to prevent suffering. Also, what if the whales these groups wish to hunt are from the most endangered species? Should these groups be permitted to kill them because of their "cultural heritage"? In any case, many traditional practices (e.g., slavery, female genital mutilation) have been outlawed as abhorrent in modern society.

Whale watching now generates a billion dollars a year, more income worldwide than the whaling industry brought in prior to the hunting ban. This industry and the jobs it creates in remote coastal areas would be jeopardized if whale numbers fell or if these intelligent animals became much more wary around human activity.

Whaling is inherently cruel. Before the whale is harpooned, it is usually exhausted by a long and stressful chase. Because whales are moving targets, a marksman can achieve a direct hit only with great difficulty. The explosive-tipped harpoon wounds many whales, who often survive for some time before finally being killed by rifle shots or by additional harpoons. Even when a direct hit is scored, the explosive often fails to detonate. Japanese whaling ships report that only 70% of whales are killed instantly.

PROS

Whales damage the fish stocks on which many people depend for their food and livelihood. Culling whales will reduce the decline in fish stocks.

A policy of limited hunting could prevent the potential collapse of the International Whaling Commission. The IWC ban was intended to allow numbers to recover; this temporary measure has served its purpose. If prohibition continues and the IWC becomes more concerned with moral positions than whaling management, Japan and Norway may leave the organization. Nothing in international law prevents them from resuming whaling outside the IWC. Thus, whaling will again be unregulated, with more whales dying and perhaps greater cruelty.

CONS

The decline in fish stocks is caused by overfishing, not whale predation. Many whales eat only plankton. The oceans had plenty of fish before large-scale whaling began. Indeed some whales eat the larger fish that prey on commercially important species. A whale cull might have the perverse effect of further reducing valuable fish stocks.

Any system that allows whaling will be open to cheating, given the demand for whale meat in Japan. DNA tests reveal that Japan's "scientific whaling" has resulted in scarce species being taken and consumed. Japan and Norway could leave the IWC but this would provoke an international outcry and possibly sanctions, so it is not in their best interests to do so.

Sample Motions:

This House would allow whaling to resume.

This House would harvest the bounty of the sea.

This House would save the whale.

Web Links:

- Greenpeace. <http://www.greenpeace.org/international/campaigns/oceans/whaling> Information on whaling from an environmentalist organization.
- International Fund for Animal Welfare. <http://www.stopwhaling.org/> Website dedicated to stopping whaling.
- Japan Whaling Association. <http://www.whaling.jp/english/index.html> Information from a pro-whaling group.
- Whale and Dolphin Conservation Society. <http://www.wdcs.org/> Provides information on the status of whales, dolphins, and porpoises as well as efforts to protect them.

Further Reading:

Kalland, Arne. *Unveiling the Whale: Discourses on Whales and Whaling.* Berghahn Books, 2011.

Kalland, Arne, and Brian Moeran. *Japanese Whaling? End of an Era.* Taylor and Francis, 2010.

Stoett, Peter J. *The International Politics of Whaling.* UBC Press, 2011.

■ ■

WIKIPEDIA, FORCE FOR GOOD

Wikipedia is a free online encyclopedia, produced entirely by the voluntary efforts of hundreds of thousands of people from all over the world. It was founded by Jimmy Wales and Larry Sanger in 2001, after an earlier effort to build a traditional "expert" encyclopedia online became bogged down in the slow complexities of academic review and professional editing. Instead, Wikipedia adopted wiki software, which allows groups of people to cooperate dynamically in writing and editing material online. To many people's surprise, this open-access approach was a rapid success, attracting many high-quality submissions from a wide range of contributors. This was despite (or because of) online warfare between rival volunteers who sought to edit and reedit entries. As of November 2010, the English-language Wikipedia site has over 3.4 million articles; combined with entries from versions in other languages, the total is more than 9.25 million. Wikipedia is one of the most heavily visited sites on the Internet—particularly by school and college students, to the concern of some educators. From the start, Wikipedia has had its critics, and co-founder Larry Sanger left the project early because of disputes over the direction of the site. Past and present editors of Encyclopedia Britannica *have criticized Wikipedia for inaccuracy, arguing that its democratic ethos lacks academic rigor and provides no guarantee that any entry can be relied upon. Others have criticized the agenda of the site, and the way in which its rules for contributors (including the famous "Neutral Point of View" or NPOV) are applied in practice. Despite a number of well-publicized scandals, however, the site has continued to grow, both in size and importance.*

PROS

Wikipedia's goal is to make all human knowledge freely available to everyone with an Internet connection. It already has over 2.5 million articles in English alone. This is more than 25 times those of *Encyclopedia Britannica*, its nearest printed rival. Traditional reference works were incredibly expensive, which meant that knowledge was restricted to the wealthy or those with access to well-funded public libraries. Wikipedia liberates that knowledge.

Wikipedia seeks to achieve its democratic goal by democratic means. As an open-source project, it relies on the collaboration of tens of thousands of people who constantly add, check, and edit articles. This "socialization of expertise" ensures that errors and omissions are rapidly identified and corrected, and that the site is constantly updated. No traditional encyclopedia can match this scrutiny, which has also been used successfully to develop and improve open-source software such as Firefox and Linux.

Wikipedia harnesses the best qualities of humanity—trust and cooperation in pursuit of an unselfish goal. Skeptics essentially take a negative view of society, unable to understand why people would join together to produce something so valuable without any financial incentive. Wikipedia is not naively trusting—the majority of entries are written by a close online community of a few hundred people who value their reputations. Examples of abuse have led Wikipedia to tighten up its rules, so that cyber vandals can easily be detected and editing of controversial topics restricted to the most trusted editors. But overall

CONS

Wikipedia may make articles available for nothing to those with access to the Internet (i.e., still only a minority of people in the world), but many of these articles are not worth reading. Entries are often very badly written and can be very unreliable or misleading. Even on the Internet there is no such thing as a free lunch—the high cost of a traditional encyclopedia pays for articles written, checked, and edited by experts and professionals. And Wikipedia does not simply provide a poor quality alternative. Worse, it will drive traditional, high-quality encyclopedias out of business by destroying their business model.

Knowledge created by consensus or some kind of Darwinian democracy is fatally flawed. A fact is not true simply because lots of people think so. Traditional encyclopedias are written and edited by academics and professional experts, whose reputation is put on the line by the articles they produce. Anyone can write a Wikipedia article, regardless of how much or how little knowledge they have of the subject. Worse, because contributors are effectively anonymous, it is impossible to assess the quality of an article on an unfamiliar topic by assessing the credentials of those who have produced it.

Wikipedia is not immune to the worst qualities of humanity—as is shown by a number of scandals affecting the site. Entries can be deliberately vandalized for comic effect (as happens every April Fool's Day), for commercial gain, or simply to mislead or insult. Some of these deliberate errors are picked up and corrected quickly, but others remain on the site for long periods. Notoriously, a respected journalist, John Siegenthaler, was extensively libeled in an almost solely fictitious article that was not detected for months. Recently, one very senior editor was exposed as a college dropout, rather than the distinguished professor

PROS

Wikipedia is a tremendous human success story, which should be celebrated rather than criticized.

Wikipedia emerged very well from the only systematic comparison of its quality against its leading traditional rival, the *Encyclopedia Britannica*. A survey in the leading journal *Nature* compared 42 pairs of articles on a wide range of subjects. Experts in each topic found that Wikipedia's user-contributed articles had only 30% more errors and omissions than *Britannica*, despite the latter's much vaunted pride in its expert authors and editors. And as Wikipedia is a constant work in progress, these faults were very quickly corrected, whereas a traditional publication will only revise articles at intervals of years, if not decades.

Nobody at Wikipedia has ever claimed that it is a definitive account of human knowledge or a replacement for in-depth research. But it is an excellent starting point for an inquiry, giving a quick guide to an unknown subject and pointing the inquirer to more specialist sources. It is used to good effect by students, teachers, journalists, and even judges, among many others—showing that it is a valued reference source. Experienced users can quickly assess the quality of an article by the quality of its writing and the thoroughness of its references. Nothing on the Internet should ever be accepted uncritically, but Wikipedia has earned its reputation and has never tried to oversell itself.

Patchiness of coverage has been a recognized shortcoming of Wikipedia, but it is one that the online community of Wikipedians has been debating vigorously, and is being rapidly addressed. Critics often use out-of-date examples to berate the site, failing to recognize that Wikipedia's key strength is that it constantly changes and improves through the contributions of its users. Perhaps those who note that a particular topic is unsatisfactory should sit down and write something to improve it!

It is the nature of any encyclopedia to present facts, and to emphasize these over expressions of opinion. If this is a criticism of Wikipedia, then it is a criticism of any reference work, traditional or collaborative. In any case, the main Wikipedia entry for a controversial topic is not the only material available to the user—discussion pages

CONS

of theology he had claimed to be. Such examples seem to confirm the doubts of Larry Sanger, the original project coordinator for Wikipedia. He has since left and written a number of warning articles about how open to abuse the online encyclopedia is.

The 2005 *Nature* comparison of Wikipedia and *Britannica* clearly found that the online encyclopedia was less reliable. However, the *Nature* study itself was badly skewed, and *Britannica* disputed nearly half the errors or omissions for which it was criticized. On this basis, Wikipedia is not just 30% less accurate than *Britannica*; it would be two and a half times less reliable. In addition, the *Nature* study did not take the quality of writing into account. All of *Britannica*'s entries are edited carefully to ensure they are readable, clear, and an appropriate length. Much of Wikipedia's material is cobbled together from different contributions and lacks clarity.

Wikipedia has become a standard source of reference because it is free and easy to access, not because it is good. It is frightening that some US judges are beginning to cite its articles in support of their judgments. Many of its users are students who lack the experience to determine the quality of an article. Overdependence on Wikipedia means that they will never develop proper research skills and thus come to believe that an approximately right answer is good enough. Wikipedia should be banned for student research papers and other serious uses.

One of the major problems with Wikipedia is its very patchy coverage. Traditional reference sources provide consistent coverage over the whole field of knowledge, with priority given to the most important topics in terms of space and thoroughness of treatment. By contrast, Wikipedia has very detailed coverage of topics in which its main contributors are interested, but weak material on other, much more important issues. Thus, just as much space is devoted to the imaginary language of Klingon as to Romany or Welsh—real languages.

A notable shortcoming of Wikipedia is its obsession with recording facts and difficulty in presenting rival arguments or hypotheses. For many topics this is not a major problem, but in many more the nature of truth is hotly disputed and any entry that seeks to document the issue should present both (or more) strands of opinion. Yet reveal its editing history, conflicting viewpoints, and rival authorities. These are a rich source of opinion and they complement the main articles.

attempts by contributors to express academic arguments, for example, over different historical interpretations, are often edited out as being insufficiently factual. What remains is then either unhelpfully bland or worryingly one-sided.

Wikipedia is not threatened by variants and rivals that also seek to promote freedom of knowledge. Jimmy Wales, Wikipedia's founder, has consistently said that he is not trying to drive traditional encyclopedias such as *Britannica* out of business, nor to become a monopoly provider of online information. The key principle is the freedom of information, presented as neutrally as possible. This led to the banning of Wikipedia in China, after Jimmy Wales refused to censor articles to make the site acceptable to the Chinese government.

Wikipedia can also be criticized for its inbuilt bias: its intolerance of dissenting views. Religious conservatives object to the secular liberal approach its editors consistently take and have found that their attempts to add balance to entries are swiftly rejected. This even extends to the censorship of facts that raise questions about the theory of evolution. Some conservatives are so worried about the widespread use of Wikipedia to promote a liberal agenda in education that they have set up Conservapedia as a rival source of information.

Sample Motions:

This House trusts Wikipedia.

This House believes that open-access sources such as Wikipedia are strongly beneficial.

This House believes that Wikipedia is a force for good.

Web Links:

- Johnson, Caitlin A. "The Good and the Bad of Wikipedia." <http://www.cbsnews.com/stories/2006/12/10/sunday/main2244008.shtml> Outlines some of the common arguments for and against use of Wikipedia.
- Schiff, Stacy. "Know It All: Can Wikipedia Conquer Expertise? <http://www.newyorker.com/archive/2006/07/31/060731fa_fact> Article on the history and controversy surrounding Wikipedia.
- Wikipedia Watch. <http://www.wikipedia-watch.org> Anti-Wikipedia site.

Further Reading:

Keen, Andrew. The Cult of the Amateur: How Today's Internet Is Killing Our Culture. Doubleday Business, 2007.

Lih, Andrew. *The Wikipedia Revolution: How a Bunch of Nobodies Created the World's Greatest Encyclopedia*. Hyperion, 2009.

Reagle, Joseph M. *Good Faith Collaboration: The Culture of Wikipedia*. MIT Press, 2010.

..

WOMEN IN COMBAT

In January 2013, US Secretary of Defense Leon Panetta removed the military ban on women serving in combat. Feminists had long fought for this change, considering the combat exclusion to be discriminatory against women. The wars in Iraq and Afghanistan brought the issue of women in the military to the forefront, with over 280,000 women deployed to the region since 2001. These female soldiers engaged in a wide range of duties, including flying helicopters into combat zones and treating the wounded; in Afghanistan, the Marines even set up all-female teams—designed to engage Afghan women—who were reported to have come under enemy fire. Internal army memos recommended permitting women to serve in support units in light of troop shortages that made sustaining all-male units difficult. With the ban now lifted, the armed forces have until 2016 before they must fully open all positions to women. However, the issue remains controversial, with critics arguing that standards in the military will inevitably slip and unit cohesion will be compromised.

PROS

This position upholds equality between the sexes. As long as an applicant is qualified for a position, gender should not matter. Critics often mention that women cannot meet the performance targets set for their positions. This is rank hypocrisy. The US army regularly calibrates performance targets for age and position. A 40-year-old senior noncommissioned officer faces a much easier set of targets than his 20-year-old subordinate, yet both are deployed in active combat. The 20-year-old woman will outperform her NCO in physical tests. Recruiting and deploying women who are in better shape than many men we send into combat is easy. In any case, in modern high-technology battlefields, technical expertise and decision-making skills are more valuable than simple brute strength.

Allowing a mixed-gender force keeps the military strong. The all-volunteer force is severely troubled by falling retention and recruitment rates. Widening the applicant pool for all jobs guarantees more willing recruits. Not only does it help military readiness, it forestalls the calamity of a military draft. Without the possibility of serving in combat, many patriotic women will not want to enlist because they know they will be regarded as second-class soldiers. Because combat duty is usually required for promotion to the most senior ranks, denying female personnel the possibility of such duty ensures that very few will ever reach the highest ranks and so further entrenches sexism

Some studies have shown that women can perform as well as, if not better, than men in combat. The Israelis make frequent use of women as snipers. The RAND Corporation studied increased deployment of women in all three branches of the US military throughout the 1990s. It wholeheartedly endorsed further integration, having found no ill effects from expanding the roles of women in the different services over that period.

Of the more than 20 nations that permit women in positions where they might see combat, none has reversed that decision. Regardless of whether women are as well suited to combat as men, they are clearly good enough for many countries to rely on them.

CONS

Women are equal to men in the armed forces, but they are not the same as men. While the vast proportion of jobs in the military is open to both men and women, some are just not physically suitable for women. Some women are able to meet the physical requirements for frontline combat, such as carrying a wounded soldier, throwing grenades, or digging a trench in hard terrain, but most are not. One expert estimate put the number of physically qualified female candidates at 200 a year. These could be integrated into combat units, but their small number does not make the additional logistical, regulatory, and disciplinary costs associated with integration worthwhile.

Men, especially those likely to enlist, maintain traditional gender roles. On the one hand, they will probably resent the introduction of women into a heavily masculine military subculture. (As we have seen, as more women enter the armed services, abuse incidents rise. At the three US service academies, one in seven women reports being sexually assaulted, and fully half have been sexually harassed.) On the other hand, men are likely to act foolishly to protect women in their combat units. Both attitudes create tensions and affect morale, and so weaken the military in combat situations.

Much has been made of integration's effect on morale and readiness. Having women in combat units weakens the will to fight. Combat is a team activity. Soldiers under fire must have confidence in their comrades' abilities, and women don't have the mental and physical toughness to perform combat duties. They cannot contribute equally to the team. Their presence undermines the team's effectiveness.

The threat of abuse of women prisoners is also a serious one. Male prisoners also contend with the threat of torture and rape, but misogynistic societies will be more willing to abuse woman prisoners. The threat of female prisoners of war being abused may adversely affect the way in which their captured male comrades react to interrogation. And in a media age, the use of captured

PROS	CONS
	female soldiers in propaganda broadcasts may weaken the nation's determination and commitment to the war effort.
This debate is becoming purely academic. We are now fighting in what the military calls "Low Intensity Conflicts" (LICs) in which there is no front line, so the distinction between combat and noncombat positions and units is increasingly moot. Americans have shown broad support for women serving in the armed forces—a 2005 poll revealed that more than 60% favor allowing women to participate in combat.	The fact that the character of war is changing is irrelevant. We should not purposely put women in combat situations. Moreover, the public's support for women in combat is not clear. Another poll taken during the same period as the one the proposition has cited indicates that while Americans favor having women serve in support jobs that often put them in or near combat, a majority oppose women serving as ground troops.
Women are vitally needed for Low-Intensity Conflicts. LICs require tasks to "win hearts and minds" such as intelligence gathering, medical assistance, policing, and mediation, as well as the ability to kill an opponent in close combat. Cultural differences and demographics enable women to be vastly more effective in some circumstances than men. For example, conservative populations would be outraged if male soldiers searched women; they would be more accepting of female soldiers performing this task. Allowing women to serve also doubles the talent pool for delicate and sensitive jobs that require interpersonal skills not every soldier has. Having a wider personnel base allows militaries to have the best and most diplomatic soldiers working to end conflict quickly.	Women can perform the tasks the proposition describes without going into combat. As we saw in Iraq, the army does not teach combat troops the skills needed to win hearts and minds. Obviously, we need more soldiers who can win hearts and minds, but these troops do not need combat skills. And the suggestion that conservative societies may be more willing to accept female soldiers in certain situations is absurd. Conservative Muslim societies do not believe that women should have roles beyond the home, so they are not going to be comfortable with female soldiers under any circumstances.

Sample Motions:

This House believes that women should be allowed to serve in ground combat units.

This House would allow women to serve on the front line.

This House calls for equality in the military.

This House believes female soldiers should not receive special treatment.

Web Links:

- Kirkwood, R. Cort. "What Kind of Nation Sends Women Into Combat?" <http://www.lewrockwell.com/orig3/kirkwood3.html> Article opposing women in combat written by a former member of the Presidential Commission on the Assignment of Women in the Armed Forces.
- Newsweek. "The Case Against Women In Combat." <http://www.newsweek.com/id/61568> Interview with author Kingsley Browne, who believes that women are not suited for combat.
- NPR. "Special Series: Women in Combat." <http://www.npr.org/templates/story/story.php?storyId=14964676> Five-part radio series on the expanding role of women in the military.

Further Reading:

Browne, Kingsley. Co-ed Combat: The New Evidence That Women Shouldn't Fight the Nation's Wars. Sentinel HC, 2007.

Alfonso, Kristal L. M. *Femme Fatale: An Examination of the Role of Women in Combat and the Policy Implications for Future American Military Operations.* BiblioBazaar, 2012.

Putko, Michele M., and Douglas V. Johnson II. *Women in Combat Compendium.* BiblioBazaar, 2012.

Skaine, Rosemarie. *Women in Combat: A Reference Handbook.* ABC-CLIO, 2011.

■ ■

ZERO TOLERANCE POLICING

Zero tolerance policing aims at stopping serious crime by clamping down on all types of disorder, including minor misdemeanors such as spray painting graffiti. It mandates set responses by the police to particular crimes, although the courts still maintain discretion in sentencing criminals. Adherents of this policy believe in the "broken windows" theory, which postulates that quality-of-life crimes, like littering or graffiti writing, prompt "respectable" citizens to leave communities, which then fall into decline. They also emphasize that most serious criminals begin their careers with minor crimes. By punishing minor crimes, zero tolerance policing prevents future crimes and, in the process, stops neighborhood decline.

PROS

Zero tolerance policing provides a powerful deterrent to criminals for three reasons. First, it is accompanied by a greater police presence. Research shows a direct link between the perceived chance of detection and crime rates. Second, strict and certain punishment deters criminals. Third, it provides the "short, sharp shock" that stops petty criminals from escalating their criminal behavior. It gives a clear message that crime is not tolerated.

Zero tolerance policing is extremely effective against small-scale drug pushers whose presence in a neighborhood creates an atmosphere in which crime flourishes. Drug use is a major cause of crime because addicts usually steal to support their habit.

Zero tolerance also allows for rehabilitation. A prison sentence, particularly for juveniles, takes them away from the environment that encouraged criminality. Rehabilitation is a central tenet of most penal codes. The large number of police on the streets also increases the supervision of released prisoners, preventing repeat offenses.

Zero tolerance improves the standard of policing. It reduces corruption and racist treatment because individual officers are not given the scope to decide their actions on a case-by-case basis. Their response is set. In addition, zero tolerance policing takes officers out of their cars and puts them into the community where they have contact with individuals. Chases and shootouts actually are less common under zero tolerance.

Zero tolerance is vital for rebuilding inner cities. Zero tolerance reduces the amount of dead ground used for drug dealing and so returns parks and open spaces to the community. By offering protection against petty crime,

CONS

Minor offenders, gang members, and the poor are very unlikely to be aware of the punishments for their crimes, so the threat of punishment has little effect on them. Many crimes are a result of poverty and drugs and can be reduced only by structural changes to the society, not by threatening punishment. The idea of a "short, sharp shock" is unconvincing. Labeling people criminals at an early age causes them to perceive themselves as such. This leads petty criminals to commit more serious offenses.

Arresting small-scale pushers and users targets the victims to stop the crime. As well as being unfair, it is ineffective. As long as there is a demand for drugs, there will be drug dealing. Demand can be stopped only by rehabilitation.

Prison sentences contribute to repeat offenses. Prisons should have a rehabilitative role, but they don't. Juveniles with criminal records have difficulty finding jobs, and so are likely to resort to crime. In prison they meet established criminals who both encourage the lifestyle and teach the skills needed to be a successful criminal. Prison often fosters resentment of the police. The harassment that juveniles associate with zero tolerance also creates an extremely antagonistic relationship with the police.

Zero tolerance gives the police almost limitless power in poor communities. They are able to stop and search and harass individuals constantly. Usually ethnic minorities are targeted. New York City saw a tremendous growth in complaints about police racism and harassment after zero tolerance was instituted.

Rebuilding inner city neighborhoods is one of the most powerful ways of targeting crime, and it occurs independent of zero tolerance. For every city where urban renewal and zero tolerance have together been associated

PROS	CONS
it encourages small businesses (vital for neighborhood rehabilitation) to return to an area.	with a falling crime rate (New York City), there is an area where renewal has worked on its own (Hong Kong). Most important for urban renewal is individuals taking pride in their area. This is far more likely to happen when people don't feel persecuted by the police. No police presence is sufficient to defend a business that has not cultivated good relations with the community.
We can afford zero tolerance. Protecting businesses and developing a reputation for low crime attracts both people and investment. Deterrence reduces crime and thus the cost of policing; although prisons are expensive, the reduction in recidivism should empty them in time. The most important question is whether we believe spending our tax dollars to guarantee our safety is a good use of that revenue. Most voters say yes.	The enormous expense of zero tolerance in money, manpower, and prisons limits policing. It leaves little money for addressing serious crime. So, although total crime rates may drop, serious crimes may still be a problem.

Sample Motions:

This House believes in zero tolerance policing.

This House would clamp down.

This House believes in strict punishment.

Web Links:

- PBS. "Rising Crime: Is Zero Tolerance Policing the Answer?" <http://www.frontlineonnet.com/fl1901/19011080.htm> Column in India's leading newspaper about whether zero tolerance policing would be effective in India.
- Inwood, John. "Zero Tolerance Policing." <http://news.bbc.co.uk/2/hi/programmes/politics_show/7385778.stm> Article on Boris Johnson's decision to ban drinking and how some believe this is the beginning of zero tolerance policing in London.
- Nuttall, Paul. "The Case for Zero Tolerance Policing." <http://www.ukip.org/content/features/250-the-case-for-zero-tolerance> A case for zero tolerance policing.

Further Reading:

Burke, Roger Hopkins. Hard Cop, Soft Cop: Dilemmas and Debates in Contemporary Policing. Willan Publishing, 2009.

Punch, Maurice. Zero Tolerance Policing. Policy Press, 2007.

Joyce, Peter. Policing: Development and Contemporary Practice. SAGE, 2010.

Ross, Jeffrey. Policing Issues: Challenges & Controversies. Jones and Bartlett, 2011.

■ ■

TOPICAL INDEX